Towards a postmodern
theory of narrative

POSTMODERN THEORY

Series editor:
THOMAS DOCHERTY
School of English, University of Kent at Canterbury

This series openly and vigorously confronts the central questions and issues in postmodern culture, and proposes a series of refigurations of the modern in all its forms: aesthetic and political, cultural and social, material and popular. Books in the series are all major contributions to the re-writing of the intellectual and material histories of socio-cultural life from the sixteenth century to the present day. They articulate or facilitate the exploration of those new 'post-theoretical' positions, developed both inside and outside the anglophone world – inside and outside 'western' theory – which are pertinent to a contemporary world order.

Other titles in the series include:

After Theory
Thomas Docherty

Justice Miscarried: Ethics, Aesthetics and the Law
Costas Douzinas and Ronnie Warrington

Postmodern Wetlands: Culture, History, Ecology
Rodney James Giblett

Jarring Witnesses: Modern Fiction and the Representation of History
Robert Holton

Towards a postmodern theory of narrative

ANDREW GIBSON

Edinburgh University Press

© Andrew Gibson, 1996

Edinburgh University Press
22 George Square, Edinburgh

Typeset in $9\frac{1}{2}$/12 point Melior by
Photoprint, Torquay, Devon and
printed and bound in Great Britain

A CIP record for this book is available
from the British Library

ISBN 0 7486 0841 9

The right of Andrew Gibson to be identified as
author of this work has been asserted in accordance
with the Copyright, Designs and Patent Act (1988)

Contents

Acknowledgements

Various sections of this book were first given as papers at the College of Ripon and York St John and the International Conference on Narrative at the University of Nice in 1991; at the Second International Samuel Beckett Symposium in the Hague in 1992 and at the Samuel Beckett International Foundation at Reading University in 1993; in the Literature and Politics series at the London University Centre for English Studies in 1994 and the conference on Theory and Computing Culture at the Centre for English Studies in 1995. I am grateful to Mary Bryden, Warren Chernaik, David Peirce, John Pilling and everyone else who made those presentations possible. General editor Thomas Docherty was enthusiastic to start with, patient, encouraging, helpful and resourceful later. Without his assistance, the book would have been much the poorer. Phil Baker, Steve Connor, Martin Dzelzainis, Monika Fludernik, Jonathan Hall, Robert Hampson, Tracy Hargreaves, Alison Light and Adam Roberts all read and commented on individual chapters or discussed some of the issues raised in the book with me. Laura Marcus pointed me in useful directions. Noel Heather and David Sweeney provided invaluable assistance with computers and interactive fiction. Jackie Jones worked hard for me at Edinburgh University Press, and Ann MacDougall and Ivor Normand edited my text with learning, patience and care. Véronique Laurens advised me on French, and Lisa Haskel at the ICA stepped in when all seemed lost. I am grateful to them all. Many of the ideas contained in this book first emerged out of discussions in the two-year series of seminars on

Contemporaneities at Royal Holloway. My thanks to the various members of staff and students who came to those seminars; and also to the students on the new MA in Postmodernism, Literature and Contemporary Culture, who have been an inspiration. Above all, my gratitude to the many members of the Holloway and Birkbeck English departments who offered me so much help and support while I was writing this. The book is dedicated to them.

Introduction

THE NARRATOLOGICAL IMAGINARY

In *The Psychoanalysis of Fire*, Bachelard sets out to study the psychological problem presented by our convictions about fire. He assumes that those convictions are charged with falsehoods inherited from the past. They therefore have only a superstitious force. In particular, Bachelard writes of endeavouring to study 'the efforts made by objective knowledge to explain the phenomena produced by fire, the pyromena'. This problem, he suggests,

is not really one of scientific history, for the scientific part of the problem is falsified by the importation of the values whose action we have demonstrated in the previous chapters. As a result, we really have to deal only with the history of the confusions that have been accumulated in the field of science by intuitions about fire. These intuitions are epistemological obstacles which are all the more difficult to overcome since they are psychologically clearer. (Bachelard 1987, p. 59)

For Bachelard, the 'confusions' and 'epistemological obstacles' in question are 'intuitions' that are poetic in kind. Scientific thought claims to declare and authenticate itself in the break with or opposition to poetic knowledge. In fact, says Bachelard, science constantly resorts *to* the imagination and traffics in the world of images, in a discourse that is radically other to the discourse that it tells us is its own. And not only is there always a 'continuity' or interinvolvement of 'thought and reverie'. In 'this union of thought and dreams', says Bachelard, 'it is always the thought that

1

is twisted and defeated' (ibid.). The precise purpose of his own psychoanalysis of the scientific mind is to prevent that defeat, to 'bind' the scientific mind 'to a discursive thought'. Far from continuing the reverie, this thought 'will halt it, break it down and prohibit it' (ibid. pp. 59–60).

There is, then, a specifically Bachelardian conception of the imaginary as a complex of what he calls 'unconscious values' haunting the discourse of a given *savoir*. In the case of scientific discourse, Bachelard sees those values as unhelpful and a weakness. He wants to see them disempowered and dissolved. The Bachelardian idea of the imaginary has recently been noted and developed by the French feminist philosopher Michèle le Dœuff, most explicitly in *The Philosophical Imaginary* (Le Dœuff 1989b). Le Dœuff herself includes a Bachelardian essay on Galileo in that book. The essay draws out an iconography of error in the sciences. It shows the affective twists and turns, the imaginative or metaphorical connectives in what is supposed to be empirical discourse. Elsewhere, Le Dœuff carries this method over into philosophy itself. She suggests that philosophy is never pure of the literary, the poetic, narrative and descriptive. The 'allegedly complete rationality of theoretical work' is always compromised (ibid. p. 2). Indeed, philosophy has its own distinctive and traditional literary repertoire. That repertoire constitutes the 'philosophical imaginary'. In its resorts to the repertoire, we see how far philosophy repeatedly depends, not on logical argument alone, but on persuasion, rhetoric, seduction and fantasy. The philosophical imaginary constitutes 'the shameful face of philosophy' (ibid. p. 20). But the imaginary is not 'shameful' in its essence. It only appears shameful to philosophy – at least, as the latter has thus far defined itself. In fact, a poetic dimension is indispensable to philosophical discourse as a necessary supplement to the limits of logic. Philosophical discourse is therefore always a hybrid thing, and philosophers cannot escape its hybridity. They can only become more knowing and deliberate in their relation to the latter.[1]

Bachelard and Le Dœuff clearly differ as to the most appropriate response to a given imaginary. I shall come back to that difference later. For the present, I just want to wonder whether, for all the subtleties of our various poststructuralisms, we have yet thought quite hard enough about the critical imaginary, particularly in the case of narratology. Predictably, however, the narratological imaginary has been very different to Bachelard's scientific or Le Dœuff's philosophical imaginary. Thought about narrative has traditionally concerned itself with two distinct kinds of space. The connection between them is profoundly ideological. On the one hand, there is the space of representation. This is understood as the space of the real, the homogenous space of the world. On the other hand, there is the space of the model or describable form. In this second dimension, the narratological imaginary has been haunted by something like the reverse of poetic intuition, by dreams of the geometric. Narratology is pervaded by a 'geometrics' as opposed to an 'energetics', in the sense in which Derrida uses the two terms in 'Force and Signification' (Derrida 1990). Derrida takes Rousset to task for granting 'an absolute privilege to spatial models, mathematical functions, lines and forms' (ibid. p. 16). For 'in the sphere of language and writing', Derrida goes on, quoting Leibniz's Discourse on Metaphysics, such models and forms 'are not so distinctive as is imagined, and . . . stand for something imaginary relative to our perceptions' (ibid. pp. 16–17). Narratology has turned away from the Leibnizian and Derridean caution. It has continued to grant Rousset's kind of 'absolute privilege' to geometrical description. It was precisely a geometrisation of textual space, for example, that underlay attempts to establish narrative grammars, like Todorov's grammar of the Decameron. 'The linguist', Greimas wrote, 'will not fail to take note that narrative structures present characteristics which are remarkably recurrent, and these recurrences allow for the recording of distinguishable regularities, and that they thus lead to the construction of a narrative grammar' (Greimas 1971, p. 794). Beneath this assertion and its terms – 'recurrence', 'regularity' – is a fantasy of a geometrical clarity, symmetry and proportion to narrative or the narrative text. The fantasy is also one of power.[2] If it is evident in Todorov's grammar of the Decameron, it equally emerges in narratological descriptions of plot and narrative structure. Even an ostensibly non-geometrical narratological theme like 'focalisation' can lead to a geometrisation of the text. For example, when Mieke Bal provides her account of focalisation in Arjuna's Penance (a seventh-century Indian bas relief), she takes the 'logical relation' of 'successive events' in a 'causal' narrative 'chain' as her starting point (Bal 1985, pp. 102–4). But she then supplements it with another dimension consisting of vertical 'layers', of which 'focalisation' is one. This kind of geometrisation of narrative was present in narratology from the start. Indeed, it virtually constituted one of the basic principles of narratology. According to Barthes, understanding narrative did not merely involve following 'the unfolding of the story'. The reader was also required to recognise the 'construction' of narrative 'in "storeys"' and project 'the horizontal concatenations of the narrative "thread" on to an implicitly vertical axis' (Barthes 1985, p. 87). In other words, any given narrative is a geometrically proportioned and 'storeyed' house of fiction, and the reader must reconstruct it as such. Barthes himself becomes such a reader in *S/Z* (Barthes 1970). It has sometimes been suggested, most recently by Mieke Bal, that *S/Z* constituted a radical break with Barthes's earlier accounts of narrative and questioned their neat and orderly systematisations (Bal 1992, pp. 299, 304). But as far as the geometrisation of the narrative text is concerned, *S/Z* merely offers a subtler version of the familiar procedure. This is perhaps most clearly evident in Barthes's diagrammatic account of *Sarrasine*. What purports to be a musical score is actually a grid. For Barthes, it functions as a concrete demonstration of his point that '*le texte classique est donc bien tabulaire*' (Barthes 1970, pp. 36–7). In fact, however, the 'tabulation' is the theorist's, and does no more than repeat a well-established gesture whereby the space of a given text is neatly segmented, symmetrically mapped, closed in and closed down by a geometrical system of thought or representation. This 'system' is evident everywhere in narratology: in its discussions of 'levels', 'frames', 'embedding' and 'Chinese box' narration; in Propp's conception of 'spheres of action', Iser's '*Gestalten*', Greimas's 'semiotic square' and Eco's 'intertextual frames'.[3] It is implicit in narratological approaches to thematics, and responsible even for a spatialisation of narrative time. In the work of narratologists like Seymour Chatman, character itself becomes a kind of geometrical construction, a paradigm of traits in which a 'vertical assemblage' intersects with 'the syntagmatic chain of events' (Chatman 1978, p. 127). The geometry of the text and its intelligibility become inseparable. This is hardly surprising. For narratology, geometry is a kind of universal law. The universal forms of narrative are taken to be geometric in nature. The earlier Barthes claimed that narrative is 'international, transhistorical, transcultural . . . simply there, like life itself' (Barthes 1985, p. 79). If this is the case, then the particular geometric manifestations of universal narrativity are merely instances of a larger geometry implicit in the human, narrative mind. This larger geometry is presumably what is gestured to in all the narratologists' diagrammatic representations of the narrative system as a whole, from F.K. Stanzel's typological circle to the various typological charts of the arch-geometrician of narrative, Genette (Genette 1980b, p. 248; Stanzel 1984, p. xvi). In *Palimpsestes*, Genette calls the repertoire of this larger geometry 'transtextuality', and refers to its categories, significantly, as not only general but transcendent (Genette 1982, p. 7).

But narratology had its roots in structuralism. It has largely shared the latter's strengths and weaknesses. The weaknesses include an overly geometric schematisation of texts; a drive to universalise and essentialise the structural phenomena supposedly uncovered; and a tendency to conceive of 'universal' or 'essential' forms in geometric terms. In these and other respects, however, recent narratology has not so much broken with venerable traditions of thought about narrative and the novel as fulfilled them, brought them to a kind of completion, made explicit a kind of imagining that has long been latent within them. In other words, narratology constitutes a kind of delayed paradigm. In narratology, an aspect of the critical imaginary is finally brought to conscious light. Of course, not all thought whatsoever about narrative form has resorted to implicitly geometrical assumptions. But the geometrical theme has surely been a general if irregular dominant in narrative theory. This is evident in the reception of Genette's work in England and America. English and American critics have been noticeably positive in their responses to Genette. But this comes as no surprise. Genette's work has looked like a culmination or *non plus ultra* of a narratological geometry or technology of narrative that has clearly long been present in Anglo-American criticism. Some of Genette's typological charting, for example, is anticipated by and arguably a

fulfilment of Wayne Booth's much earlier account of the distinctions between 'types of narration', or, as Booth himself puts it, his
'tabulation of the forms the author's voice can take' (Booth 1987,
p. 150). Genette's skilful geometrisation of narrative 'duration'
(Genette 1980, pp. 86–112) owes much to Gunther Müller's work
on *Erzählzeit* and *erzählte Zeit*. But it is also the culmination of a
line of work that can be traced back to Percy Lubbock's account of
the distinction between summary and scene, which Lubbock
presents as reducible to measurable structural elements (Lubbock
1921). We can go further back than Booth and Lubbock. The
geometrical theme is repeatedly evident in Henry James's theory
and criticism, the source of so much modern thinking about
narrative. The theme is perhaps most clearly enunciated in the
Preface to *Roderick Hudson*:

> Really, universally, relations stop nowhere, and the exquisite problem of the
> artist is eternally but to draw, by a geometry of his own, the circle within
> which they shall happily *appear* to do so. (James 1984, p. 1041)

James's Prefaces return repeatedly to the idea of this 'geometry'. In
particular, they return to it as a means of circumscribing or
controlling what the Preface to *The Portrait Of a Lady* calls 'the
lurking forces of expansion' in 'the fabulist's art . . . these neces-
sities of upspringing in the seed, these beautiful determinations,
on the part of the idea entertained, to grow as tall as possible, to
push into the light and the air and thickly flower there' (ibid. p.
1072). In the Preface to *Roderick Hudson*, the important geometrical figure is the circle. In the Preface to *The Awkward Age*, on the
other hand, more generally, the concern is with artistic 'measure-
ments' resulting ('after much anguish') in 'decent symmetries'
(ibid. p. 1122). In James's account of 'In the Cage', it is more a
question of setting a 'scenic system' into 'play', with its 'massing
of elements' in terms of regular recurrences and 'intervals' (ibid.
p. 1171). The geometric theme is often intertwined with either
the theme of pictorialism or that of narrative architectonics. In the
Preface to *The Portrait of a Lady*, geometrics emerge in the
concept of a 'careful and proportioned pile of bricks' that 'arches
over' the novel's basic plot of ground, 'constructionally speaking'
(ibid. p. 1080). In the Preface to *The Awkward Age*, on the other
hand, Jamesian geometrics produce the image of the text as 'small

square canvas' (ibid. p. 1121). We can even go further back than James. 'Geometrics' appear in Fielding's adherence to rules connected with the Unities and the doctrine of 'epic regularity', a doctrine which still had its weight for Scott, Dickens, Trollope, Hardy and Ford Madox Ford. Geometrics are evident in Fielding's praise of Charlotte Lennox's *The Female Quixote* as having a 'regularity' to its 'connections' that is missing in *Don Quixote* itself, with its 'loose, unconnected adventures' (Fielding 1752). Thus the order of the former's parts cannot be 'transversed' without 'injury to the whole'. For Fielding, Charlotte Lennox institutes the novel as an organised, spatial system whose elements are so interlinked that they constitute a stable geometry. Fielding's contemporaries saw Fielding himself as doing the same, praising *Tom Jones* for 'the grace and symmetry' of its plot. The words, here, are Richard Cumberland's, and Cumberland thought of Fielding as achieving a kind of eighteenth century equivalent of Jamesian geometry, curbing unruly 'excrescences', keeping 'monsters, and prodigies and every species of unnatural composition' at bay (Cumberland 1795, pp. 215–16).

Narrative theory, then, has repeatedly constructed the space of the text as a unitary, homogenous space, determined by and organised within a given set of constants.[4] Narratological space has seldom been disturbed by blurrings, troubling ambivalences or multiplications. In it, boundaries are clearly defined and categories clearly distinguished. Proportions and regularities establish and maintain certain harmonious and orderly relations. The most recent developments in narratology have hardly disturbed those relations at all. The 1980s saw the growth of what I shall call a revisionist narratology as exemplified in the work of Peter Brooks (Brooks 1984), Ross Chambers (Chambers 1984, 1991), Karl Kroeber (Kroeber 1990), James Phelan (Phelan 1989a) and others. In one way or another, such theorists both drew on and sought to move beyond the rigidities of narratological structuralism. But they also returned to and promoted concepts and concerns – plot, storytelling, theme – that narratology was seen as having sought to discredit or reduce in significance. What remain unchanged in the various revisionist models – have partly been consolidated by them – are the dimensions of narratological space. The latest developments in American narratology have

only further reconfirmed narratological geometrics. Such developments stem from modal logic, philosophy of science and artificial
intelligence, and are associated with the work of Marie-Laure
Ryan (Ryan 1991), Katherine Hayles (Hayles 1990), Paisley Livingston (Livingston 1991) et al. In Chapter Seven of her recent book
on narrative theory, for instance, Ryan not only reinstates plot as
the most general feature of narrative and sets it before us in terms
of a state-transition diagram. She also sketches a system of
automatic story generation according to the assumption that there
are basic, cognitive elements to all narratives.[5] We are back with
emphasis to the early narratologists' assumption of a unity and
homogeneity to mental and cognitive behaviour; in other words,
to the supposed purity, clarity, uniformity and universality of
narrative space.

POSTMODERN SPACES: VIRILIO, ALMEREYDA, INTERACTIVE FICTION

In fact, there are one or two signs elsewhere that narratology is
becoming more aware of the importance of questions of space
and spatialisation for narrative theory. One example would be
Florence de Chalonge's recent work on Marguerite Duras (De
Chalonge 1993, pp. 325–46; 1992, pp. 33–45). But narratology has
usually seemed very far removed from what, for a Bhabha or a
Rushdie, is constitutive of narrative itself: 'hybridity, impurity,
intermingling, the transformation that comes of new and unexpected combinations of human beings, cultures, ideas, politics,
movies, songs' (Rushdie 1990, p. 14). Nor does narratology share
Bhabha's sense of the importance of 'the theoretical recognition of
the split-space of enunciation' (Bhabha 1988, p. 22). The homogenous space of narratology is likewise radically at odds both with
an emergent postmodern aesthetics and the contemporary sense of
space. Virilio writes of a current 'crisis of "whole" dimensions . . .
in which our habitual notions of surface, of limit and separation,
have decayed, and given way to those of interface, commutation,
intermittence and interruption' (Virilio 1991b, p. 110). Whether
it is a question of new optics, infography, holography,
macrocinematography, telematics, telemetrics, informatics,
tele-topology, supersonics or quantum mechanics, for Virilio,

'geometric dimensions' are increasingly ceding to 'fractionary dimensions' and 'becoming nothing more than momentary surface effects' (ibid. p. 111). This is an inevitable feature of 'the epoch of non-separability' (ibid. p. 119). We are losing 'the dimensional mechanics spawned by ancient Greek geometry', and with them, as Mandelbrot noted, 'a certain relationship of conformity, such as entity, unity and symmetry' that came from a distant past (ibid. p. 104). Ours 'is a world of dispersed or scattering structures whose amplitude – contrary to the structuralists – we can no longer measure' (ibid. p. 72). Hence the resonance, for Virilio, Lyotard, Deleuze and others of the idea of anamorphosis (ibid. p. 67). Virilio develops an 'aesthetics of disappearance' which will register the multiple spatiality of our world, the present 'crisis of the intelligible continuum', (ibid. p. 49) and the breakdown of 'the traditional partitioning of space' (pp. 36, 52; Virilio 1991a). Equally, he argues the need for an interrogation of the structures of 'mental space' (Virilio 1991b, pp. 113–15). For Virilio, it is in such an interrogation that we may 'finally . . . close the gap between physics and metaphysics' (ibid. p. 63).

The mental space of classical kinds of thought, then, is rapidly beginning to look obsolescent. The 'dispersed or scattering' sensory spaces of postmodern culture are calling it in question. Visual culture, for instance, has long been insistently displacing the spaces, dimensions and regularities of what we think we see. There have been innumerable examples in the cinema, from Gance and Dziga Vertov to Jonas Mekas. Film can double or multiply visual spaces, constitute, dissolve and reconstitute different visual spaces or make them exist simultaneously. Michael Almereyda's PXL-generated film work or 'pixelvision' provides just one striking new form of example. 'Pixelvision' simultaneously both maintains the representational image and blurs it and causes it to disintegrate. It therefore offers us the space of the real as a multiple or radically indeterminate space. As Almereyda himself has said, 'there's no such thing as a static image in pixelvision. There's always a granular, shifting quality, so it's dreamy and poetic, no matter what. It's sort of enchanted.'[6] The space of the real and 'enchanted' space are fused, become one and the same. The effect is the more powerful for the ordinariness of Almereyda's locations (a New York apartment in *Another Girl,*

Another Planet, a video arcade in *Aliens*). It is not possible to 'read' such films in terms of a single dimension. Fascinatingly, in *Another Girl, Another Planet*, this 'doubling' of the space of the real and the space of 'enchantment' is doubled again, in that the two male characters in the film play a video of Fleischer's *Dancing on the Moon* to each new female visitor to their apartment, and sequences from Fleischer's animated film run like a refrain through Almereyda's. Some of Almereyda's fantastication of the real thus involves filming an animated film, and therefore a fantastication of what was already fantasy. Almereyda appears to be seeking to link his film up to early traditions of the cinema and to an earlier sense of cinema as magic. The link excludes the homogenous spaces of Hollywood on the one hand and realism on the other. So too in *Aliens*, where the PXL-generated images of the boys playing the video game *Alien* include sequences from the game itself. But Almereyda offers merely one instance of a kind of self-cannibalisation that is repeatedly evident in the art forms of the visual media, at the moment. Recent British video art, for example, has variously filmed the video monitor (Steve Partridge's *Monitor*), television (David Hall's *TV Fighter*), Hollywood footage (Mark Wilcox's *Calling the Shots*, George Barber's *Yes Frank, No Smoke*), video games and reproductions of classic paintings (Cerith Wyn Evans's *Degrees of Blindness*), photographs, post-cards and television again (Steve Hàwley's *A Proposition is a Picture*). Contemporary British video would appear to be fascinated by space as it is defined by other media, the way in which space dissolves or metamorphoses as it is translated from one medium into another. Such videos break up, double, relativise or reconfigure pre-constituted space. Effectively, they register the constant contemporary displacements of 'recorded space' itself.

Narratives like these, like Almereyda's, radically disrupt the kind of presumption of a singular space on which narratological thought depends. The same is true of the currently burgeoning form of computer-generated narrative, as in computer games, 'participant novels' or 'interactive fiction' (IF). IF might seem eminently reducible to the terms of classical narratology. Successful IF is said to require 'a strong model of the world and its physical laws' and 'careful attention to the issue of grammar' (Graves 1987, pp. 4–7). Its models often appear to be dependent on or equivalent to those produced by familiar narratological segmentations. In the case of plot, the creators of IF are still thinking in terms of 'plot units' and 'plot rules' (Graves 1991, pp. 10–12). The characterisation in IF assumes that 'no organism's behaviour is ever unmotivated' (Graves 1988, pp. 10–11). Furthermore, insofar as the 'writers' of 'participant novels' refer back to narrative theory, it is classical theory: Aristotle, Propp, etc. (Graves 1991; Laurel 1986). Of course, IF is still stuck at 'a rudimentary stage of development' (Graves 1991, p. 10). Nonetheless, it powerfully challenges the spatial models on which narratology has thus far depended. IF allows the reader a certain freedom of movement within the story. But it does so in producing narrative as a system of forking paths or what Graves calls 'decision trees'. There are multiple sequences of events in IF which the participant may or may not elect to pursue. 'Plot becomes a path selected through a set of "plot potentials"', and 'each character's emotional state and current goals drive the selection of a specific behaviour from a large set of possible behaviours' (Graves 1988, pp. 10–11). Some interactive narratives provide the participant with a 'picture-in-picture interface' which allows him or her to 'channel surf,' jumping from one character to another and viewing their different narratives. These narratives continue whether the participant chooses to join them or not, though the choices the participant makes may cause changes throughout the whole system of different narratives. Elements of narrative may be randomised. The sum of a multitude of different choices may even have consequences that neither the designer nor the participant foresaw.

Here, then, narrative becomes what it is in relation to other, virtual narratives. It clears a space for itself only in relation to other spaces bordering upon it. It no longer simply involves construction on the one hand or reading on the other, but what is called 'browsing around' in a given narrative environment. We can 'fill narrative in,' both visually and aurally, choosing and adding to what is seen and heard in a given narrative space. Text is both 'canned' and generated: 'the constant attributes of a location', for example, may be describable with 'fixed text', but 'not the descriptions of the objects there' (Graves 1987, pp. 4–7). Once again, there is more than one narrative space to be reckoned with. This is even more evidently the case as IF begins to depart from the 'obstructionist model' (Graves 1988, pp. 10–11). Within the latter, narrative may culminate in failure at a 'dead end' of the plot tree. When a player cannot solve a given puzzle, narrative comes to a halt. But plot trees are now ceding to plot networks, in which plot will appear as process rather than sequence or data, and 'the player may have a number of plot experiences, rather than [follow] a single path' (Graves 1991, pp. 10–12). Thus IF is increasingly producing narrative as a multiplicity of spaces. Indeed, interactive fiction may soon have effectively destroyed any identification of narrative with a unitary space.[7] The digital technologies currently disrupting the stable characteristics of older media – photography, film, video – are having something like the same effect:

One of the nice things you can do with the technology as it's advanced now, on your own desk top, is you can take a videotape or a laser disk of a film, and you can send the signal to the computer and watch the film on screen. . . . The computer gives you the power to shift everything round in the film. I can take a character from one scene, store the character in the attitude I've selected, and then I can move the character into any one of the other scenes.(Burgin 1991, p. 8)

Narrative space is now plastic and manipulable. It has become heterogenous, ambiguous, pluralised. Its inhabitants no longer appear to have an irrefutable or essential relation to any particular space. Rather, space opens up as a variable and finally indeterminate feature of any given narrative 'world'.

Serres and Narrative Space

Like all established literary criticism, classical narratology has no vocabulary adequate to such developments. It has no mental equivalent for the crisis in ' "whole" dimensions' or the 'intelligible continuum' of which Virilio writes and which Almereyda's films reflect. Contemporary theory, on the other hand, has engaged in various kinds of interrogation of the structures of 'mental space'. In particular, Michel Serres's work constitutes a powerful mode of postmodern theorising to which the thought of space is crucial. For Serres questions the validity of the spatial models on which narratology vitally depends. Serres is not only committed to a pluralised conception of space. He is also concerned to pluralise the spaces of knowledge, the mind, and, indeed, the psyche, and to relate such thinking specifically to narrative. He thus provides an excellent starting point for a deconstruction of the narratological system as a whole, and the development of a postmodern theory of narrative.

In the first instance, the model of Euclidean or geometric space is an insufficient model for thought and art. It predicates a homogenous space of knowledge, a global configuration comprising all local configurations and placing them within a uniform network, '*un réseau qu'elle jette sur les choses*' (Serres 1972, p. 12). But the space of contemporary knowledge is actually in tatters. Knowledge functions only in pockets, in a scattered number of haphazard, plural spaces. Thus rationalities and the real itself are *sporadic*. They are distributed, not in geometrically regular patterns, but as archipelagos in a turbulent, disordered sea. For the Serres of *L'Interférence*, there is no ruling science, and a pluralistic epistemology is urgently required. But it is not only epistemology that must be pluralised. Aesthetics must become polymorphic, too, an aesthetics of multiple proliferations of spaces. It must turn away from laws and regularities to exchanges and interferences, connections and disconnections between spaces. It must choose against Kant, in opting for what Kant saw as 'denaturation', a confounding of different knowledges (ibid. p. 28). It must concentrate on perturbations and turbulences, multiple forms, uneven structures and fluctuating organisations. The 'site' such an aesthetics indicates for the knower, thinker or observer is not the apparently stable site of the narratologist. It is rather Serres's own site:

Mon site, dès lors, comme penseur, comme être du monde, comme être plongé irrémédiablement dans la cité savante ou culturelle, comme épistémologue, est ce site sans site, ce point toujours décentré puisque indéfiniment mobile, ce lieu sans lieu, cet ici-ailleurs, le chemin de mon errance, le long duquel je traverse une multiplicité de réseaux. (ibid. p. 16)

Furthermore, it is in pluralising all our forms and finally ruining all dogmatisms that we will best resist the political danger of a unified and systematic knowledge (ibid.). In their subjugation of the local to the global or their distension of the former into the latter, all unitary spaces are geometries of violence, 'blind and closed in on themselves' (ibid. p. 23). This is the case with the very space of representation itself.[8] To fragment space and to break with all system and strategy is thus to declare war on the thanatocrats themselves (Serres 1977a, p. 290), to oppose *'le vainqueur singulier [qui] peint l'espace à sa couleur'* (Serres 1993, p. 77).

Geometric thinking is precisely a kind of global victory of a local phenomenon. This latter originated in ancient Greece and was spread by Western culture:

Cet espace blanc, la Grèce l'habita et fit que nous ne cessâmes de l'habiter depuis elle, comme notre propre territoire. (ibid. p. 335)

But geometry vitrifies space and freezes duration. It ensures the repetition of the identical and the rule of the same (ibid.). Thus difference cannot be thought within geometrical models. In geometry, *'un là particulier gagne et se maintient'* (ibid.). But the geometrical model is fast becoming obsolete:

Au cours du XXe siècle, nous décollâmes peu à peu de l'espace de la terre que nous habitions depuis trois millénaires, de sorte que disparaît, à nos yeux, peu à peu, celui de la lumière solaire, de l'agriculture, du sacré, de la guerre, des États, de la page d'écriture, que la géometrie exprimait, ensemble, dans sa pureté sommatrice.

Circulent, en masse désormais, des corps, des messages, de l'information, des savoirs, la lumière en sa vitesse plus qu'en sa clarté: un espace nouveau de transports neufs s'installe, sur une Terre globale, *moins pur que mêlé, moins lisse ou homogène que nué, arlequiné, tigré, zebré, en réseaux multiples et connexes.* (ibid. p. 336, italics mine)

It is in terms of this multiple space – *'nué, arlequiné, tigré, zébré'* – that we must think today.

But where does that leave narratology, whose *raison d'être* is geometrical thinking? Serres surely leaves narratology with deconstruction as an imperative: deconstruction of its classifications and categories, its 'levels' and 'frames,' its geometrics of narrative space and its freezings of narrative time, the oppositional structures according to which it elaborates its thematics.[9] As Marcel Cornis-Pope puts it, narratology must be persuaded to give up its 'fantasy' of taxonomic ordering and scientificity, 'its schematising rationality devoted to intellectual mastery' (Cornis-Pope, p. 164).[10] By a practice of deconstruction, narratology may conceivably become a multiplicity in itself. As practised by narratology, the geometry of partition makes decisions about its objects, methods and results before it registers their historicity. It is therefore profoundly ideological. Its ideal of exact, closed, definitive knowledge '*implique l'horizon indéfiniment repoussée de l'avenir*' (Serres 1977a, p. 36, italics mine).

There are clearly numerous different strategies, however, by which narratology and its ideal of exact, closed and definitive knowledge might be deconstructed. Metaphorical substitution is the first. Take for instance Serres's account of the metaphors of fire and mist in Zola, of clouds, flows, turbulences, motors and so on. The attempt to describe narrative phenomena in Zola's novels in terms of such metaphors involves a radical rethinking of the descriptive equipment appropriate to narrative. Narratives are conceptualised in terms of a reservoir of metaphors internal to them.[11] Such a practice refuses to structure narrative in terms of 'invariants' (Serres 1975, p. 11). It merely describes a certain state of the text. Secondly: if a given narrative text is not to be comprehended with reference to a system of invariants, then the metaphorical apparatus for describing it is itself open to variation. In other words, there can be a pluralisation of the narratological imaginary. Thus the Rougon-Macquart series may be variously described in terms of arborescent growth, narrative motors, chemical transformations, a circulational game involving chance, and so on. The result is a diversification of models corresponding, not only to the actual absence of textual invariants, but also to the multiplicity of resources made available by the proliferation of knowledges (Serres 1972, p. 39). The practice produces a complexification of the narrative text appropriate to what – following Bachelard – Serres calls '*complexité essentielle*' (ibid. p. 37).

Thirdly: a text may be presented in terms of a spatial model radically different to those proposed by established geometrics. Lucretius's *De Rerum Natura*, for example

est écrit en tourbillon. Il forme en tout un tourbillon. Il se boucle sans se boucler. Il meurt et renaît, mais ailleurs, en un autre temps. Muni des coefficients d'aléa. D'où la critique, en chœur, depuis sa production: il est en désordre, son auteur est furieux. Non. Lucrèce a écrit un texte exactement

expressif de la physique à dire. Son discours est rigoureusement conforme à
son contenu . . . (Serres 1977b, p. 172)

It is not just the production of an 'alternative model' for texts that
is important, here, however, nor that the model in question
derives from the physics actually developed in the text in question. The specific model is itself of particular interest. It posits the
text as flow and turbulence, of course. But it also produces the text
as a turbulent dispersal of little births or emergences:

ici et là, jadis, demain, naguère, c'est ainsi que fonctionne le *clinamen*.
L'origine, éclatée, se distribue stochastiquement, temps et lieux incertains . . .
Les relais ne se prennent pas en série, comme chez les stoïciens, mais en
explosions polymorphes. (ibid. p. 170)

The model in question is hence one of an endless repetition of
difference, a constant process of 'bifurcation' (ibid. p. 179). Sense
itself emerges out of that bifurcation, which also means that sense
always appears in the local, 'here, there, yesterday, tomorrow'
(ibid. p. 181). Like matter itself in *De Rerum Natura*, the linguistic
atoms of the text both resemble and differ from themselves as they
appear and disappear in different contexts (Serres 1977b, p. 175).
The text is both flow and eddy or backwash, pulling its elements
forwards in a single direction but also redistributing them backwards into new compounds, vortices, turbulences. This is Serres's
model of what he calls 'fluent form', and it is surely immensely
suggestive for a postmodern theory of narrative. It produces the
text as multiplicity, as plural or chronically polymorphous (ibid.
pp. 169–70). There can be no fixed and stable representation of the
text. But the latter is not pure chaos or indeterminacy either. In
this model, the same conserves itself in repetition even as it
evolves (ibid. p. 185).

So too if, with Serres, we substitute the notion of narrative
parcours (narrative as a voyage or 'course through') for that of
narrative discourse; providing we add that the *parcours* is to be
thought of precisely as a movement through multiple spaces.
Paradoxically, the invariant principle is that of transport or
transferral, '*un voyage à travers des variétés spatiales séparées*'
(Serres 1977a, p. 200). The idea of narrative *parcours* is not a
variation on the old theme of the novel as quest or journey. It

rather involves a theory of narrative that radically breaks with the
unitary space of narratology. The Oedipus myth, for example, both
establishes separations between spaces and effects 'difficult junc-
tions' between them (ibid. p. 204). The discourse of the myth is
like Oedipus's itinerary itself. It is a succession of spatial accidents, bifurcations, catastrophes, loops, crossroads between various spaces that have no common measure and no boundaries in
common. This is even more evidently the case with *The Odyssey*.
The story of Odysseus rigorously separates all the various spaces
in the story, defines them perfectly in their own right. They cannot
be reduced to any homogenous or global whole. The mythical
adventure of Odysseus is nothing more or less than the connecting
up of these incommensurable spaces, as if the main object of the
discourse were to connect '*les niches écologiques séparées,
défendues bec et ongles*' (ibid. p. 206). One figure for this activity
would be female, Penelope weaving and unweaving her infinitely
varied and nuanced web (ibid. p. 207). To turn away from
narrative as *parcours*, to fix and freeze it into hypostasised forms,
is to obscure the principle of narrative as communication, connection across divides, links formed between irreducible disparates.
It is Euclidean space that actually stands most opposed to narrative, in this respect. For it suggests that displacement is possible
without a change in state, that the *parcours* is the movement of a
self-identical being through a homogenous exteriority. Euclidean
space buries and represses a '*topologie sauvage*' which we hardly
know how to begin to find our way back to, even today. It does so
precisely in producing the universal.

Zola's work offers an exact example of 'multiple spaces' in
narrative. In the Rougon-Macquart series, narrative is actually
born of communication between different spaces, above all, perhaps, those of science and myth. These distinct knowledges
produce distinct kinds of space, and narrative is generated as the
pathway through and the link between them. So too in *Moby Dick*,
the *parcours* of the *Pequod* connects multiple spaces up together,
and also allows them to proliferate in the range of 'explicatory
grids' that the narrative produces (Serres 1975, p. 139). Jules
Verne's narratives are likewise caught up in constant displacements between spaces. There are the three spaces within which
the voyages are conducted, for instance: the literal, the space of

the ordinary voyage; the scientific, the space of the intellectual or
'encyclopaedic' itinerary; and the initiatory, religious or mythic
pilgrimage (Serres 1974b, p. 23). Thus in *Michel Strogoff*, for
example, the plausibility of scientific space may yield to mythic
or magical space, the '*scène primitive*', and vice versa (Serres
1974, p. 41). But beyond the tripartite division, a given space can
splinter or proliferate to the point where analogies with a varieties
of other 'worlds' in a range of writers from Homer and d'Urfé to
Faulkner and St John of the Cross become evident (ibid. p. 56).

It is not hard to extend Serres's case. *Don Quixote*, for example,
is clearly a *parcours* through heterogenous spaces. In the first
instance, this is quite literally true. The space inhabited by Gines
de Pasamonte and the galley slaves is simply irreconcilable with
the space of the pastoral as the latter is elaborated in Part One,
Chapters 11–14; except, of course, that the narrative does link
them, and the border between same and other is obscured. The
heterogenous spaces are literary, too: those of epic, history, legend
and fable, pastoral romance, chivalric romance, exemplary tales,
encomia, the picaresque, verisimilitude and so on. But the itinerary of *Don Quixote* lies equally through the spaces of heterogenous knowledges, from those of ancient authority and classical
aesthetics to those of contemporary Catholic doctrine, Arab schol-
arship, necromancy, contemporary exploration, Baconian scepticism, nascent empiricism and so forth. Quixote's own complexity
is surely best described as analogous to that of Oedipus, a figure
repeatedly both standing at and functioning as a *carrefours* or
crossroads, a point of intersection between separate realms. There
is hence no point to asking whether the Canon of Toledo is
'speaking for' Cervantes in Part One, Chapter 48. The question
presumes a unitary knowledge coming from a fixed position
which *Don Quixote* as a journey through multiple spaces in no
respect promotes.

Serres's work, then, produces a variety of different conceptions
of the narrative text that may serve as alternatives to the geometric
space of established narratology. He deconstructs the narratological imaginary by displacing its system of metaphors and
replacing them with others. He mixes metaphors. He devises new
spatial models for narrative texts, ones more appropriate to a
concept of the text as polymorphous. Our structural accounts of

narratives have the force only of superstitious valuations. They do not deal in the self-evident and have no essential validity. They are not descriptions of fixed and given entities. They are not 'descriptions' at all. Narratives do not require us to formulate our narratological accounts of them, or even indicate the pertinence of those accounts. Serres's terms encourage us to dream of a different kind of thought about narrative, different modes of thinking and reading, and their political significance resides in just that. Such terms engage with the horizon of the future, where geometric thought ceaselessly sets it at a distance or holds it at bay. In the end, then, we do not need to choose between a Bachelardian purification of the narratological imaginary and Le Dœuff's kind of wry acceptance of its complicities. The more appropriate strategy will involve a pluralisation of the narratological imaginary, in which the idea of the unitary space of a given knowledge and the idea of the dominant perspective from which it might all be surveyed are radically destabilised, if not destroyed.

GEOMETRICS AND THE 'FIXED POINT'

This book thus sets out to interrogate the structures of our thought about forms of narrative. It does so in terms of the kind of relativisation and diversification of mental space produced by contemporary theory. It draws both on Serres and on a range of other recent theorists – Deleuze, Braidotti, Lyotard, Kristeva, Derrida, Badiou, Rosset et al. – whose work has large implications for thought about narrative. Some of the theoretical work in question addresses narrative or narratives themselves. But I shall often be more concerned to tease out the implications of or to note the connections made possible by contemporary theory. In 'Structure, Sign and Play in the Discourse of the Human Sciences', Derrida writes of the extent to which classical conceptions of 'structure' make it inseparable from the idea of a 'centre'. They therefore limit 'what we might call the play of the structure' (Derrida 1990, pp. 278–93). According to Derrida, the idea of the centre both orients and organises the coherence of the structural system, and contains the play of the latter by permitting play only within a total form. The centre itself is thought of as escaping structurality:

This is why classical thought concerning structure could say that the centre is, paradoxically, *within* the structure and *outside* it. The centre is at the centre of the totality, and yet, since the centre does not belong to the totality (is not part of the totality), the totality *has its centre elsewhere.* (ibid. p. 279)

This concept of centred structure 'is in fact the concept of a play based on a fundamental immobility and a reassuring certitude, which itself is beyond the reach of play' (ibid.). The history of the 'linked chain' of determinations of or metaphors for the centre is also the history of Western metaphysics, and its matrix 'is the determination of Being as *presence* in all senses of this word' (ibid.).

Postmodern theory requires us to think that the centre has no natural site at all. The centre is not a fixed locus but a function. Thus 'everything' becomes 'discourse', that is, 'a system in which the central signified, the original or transcendental signified' is never absolutely present outside or within a system of differences (ibid. p. 280). If narratology has never escaped a 'geometrics' of structure, it has surely never escaped an accompanying insistence on the full presence of a 'centre', of 'the original or transcendental signified'. In this respect as in others, our thought about narrative has never escaped from metaphysics. Where Derrida emphasises the interrelationship between ideas of 'structure' and the idea of the 'centre', Serres writes of the interdependence of determinate systems and the '*point fixe*'.[12] Serres puts it thus:

Il est paradoxal et malheureux, à la fois, de constater que la seule pensée rigoureuse par schémas spatiaux et non linéaires, le *mos geometricus*, ait servi justement de modèle pour une pensée segmentée selon un ordre univoque et irréversible. (Serres 1972, p. 129)

The virtue of geometrical thought is that it releases us from merely linear models. But that virtue is compromised, because geometrical segmentations appear according to an irreversible and, above all, a univocal order. Indeed, the univocal, irreversible, geometrical scheme has become the fundamental model for our traditional conceptions of structure. If the scheme is univocal on the one hand and single, homogenous and invariant on the other, then these two facts are actually inseparable. In Serres' terms, the scheme is a 'system of reference' which cannot permit 'interference' or 'inter-reference'. It cannot recognise its own hybridity, its own necessary implication in or dependence on other systems of reference. It maintains its own purity precisely in its attachment to univocity or the 'fixed point'. The clarity and order of any given system of reference or geometrical structure will inevitably require an assumption of the unchanging singleness of the 'fixed point.' Fixed point and system of reference are therefore bound together (ibid. p. 138). On the one hand, the assignment of the 'fixed point' is only possible through a specific construction of a particular space. This epistemological operation circumscribes space in general and appears as limitation, closure, definition, interruption, arrest (ibid.). On the other hand, it is precisely the 'fixed point' – 'situation ici-maintenant et situation centrale' – in relation to which the geometry of 'spatio-temporal situations' is distributed (ibid. pp. 139–40). As Serres points out, this is the phenomenological structure *par excellence*, and one that structuralism and therefore narratology substantially inherit from phenomenology. Within such a structure, segmentarisation, a philosophy of origins and a phenomenology of the fixed object are all dependent on one another (ibid. p. 140). Geometric spatial models and ideas of origin, fixity and essence cannot be separated. In this respect, any simple geometrical system of thought like narratology produces a resistance to postmodernity, and requires reformulation in postmodern terms. For the same issue is always in question. The model is always associated with assumptions of invariance. Indeed, however indirectly, it is inevitably associated with the ideal of universal knowledge as subject to the omnipresent (i.e. God's) point of view (ibid. p. 138).

But what of the politics of spatial models? In one chapter of *Les Origines de la Géometrie*, Serres considers the transformation of Greek social practices and the emergence of the Greek city between the times of Hesiod and Anaximander. He suggests that this development involved the 'total disappearance of a hierarchy of levels' and the emergence of a new space involving a symmetry and reversibility of spatial relations. This latter space privileges the circle or sphere (Serres 1993, p. 115):

La mise en commun des affaires sur l'agora publique, place située au centre des habitats privés, suppose une désacralisation, une rationalisation de la vie politique. Le *logos* apparaît comme discours communautaire des concitoyens égaux, d'où il surgit comme raison, tout aussitôt. Arrachées au secret des propriétaires et des classes privilègiées, aux comptables et aux prêtres d'un roi, les affaires de la cité passent à la publicité du public. (ibid. p. 120)

There is thus a profound shift from a hierarchical geometry with particular theological, epistemological and political implications to a more democratic geometry:

Voici deux schémas pour les pratiques de la cité: le premier, hiérarchique, exhibe le roi au sommet, dominant la classe dominante, écrasant le peuple soumis. Égalitaire, par centre et circonférence, les relations du second se déploient dans l'identité, la symétrie et la réversibilité. (ibid. p. 121)

Serres's crucial point, however, is that the two geometries ultimately implode into one another. In fact, it was always a question of the same scheme or model. The second structure – of concentric circles – is merely the hierarchical geometry of levels displaced throught ninety degrees, what Serres calls 'ce quart de tour qui fait croire à la démocratie' (ibid. p. 126).[13] By virtue of the assumption of a centre, hierarchical geometry always remains, is virtually identified with reason itself:

En tout généralité, un système à hiérarchie reste un modèle à référence. On rend raison de tous ses lieux, points ou phénomènes, en les référant à un élément, par là privilégié; pôle, sommet, point, droite ou plan, quelle importance? Il ordonne, commande et prononce la loi. On y transfère le pouvoir et la raison. Alors, ce transport, ce rapport, c'est le logos. (ibid. p. 124)

Both the geometries in question, then, are *equally* centred or dependent on having a centre. The very assumption of a 'centre' institutes, homogenises and organises certain structures according to which difference is contained and given order and significance.[14] This is the very structure of our ways of seeing, of what – since the Greeks – we have understood as 'the scene of vision' itself.

DECONSTRUCTING NARRATOLOGY

The logic of Serres's position is therefore as follows: no deconstruction of a given geometry or system of reference can be effective without the displacement of the 'fixed point' or centre on the basis of which the geometry in question is organised. Accordingly, this book seeks to perform a double deconstruction. On the

one hand, it interrogates and displaces some of the most familiar
terms and categories by means of which narratology has geo-
metrised narrative and narrative texts. It questions the narratological conception of narrative form as intrinsically geometric. In
this respect, the book aligns itself with Lyotard's as well as
Serres's distrust of geometrics. Lyotard is critical of efforts to
construct or think in terms of *'une grammaire profonde'*, for
example (Lyotard 1985, p. 310). This is the case whether the
grammar in question is that of the individual text or the narrative
system. For Lyotard sees such Apollonianism as immediately and
decisively hierarchical. It leads the theorist into privileging certain narrative features at the expense of others (ibid. p. 310). It
repeatedly opens up what is always a particular and specifically
politicised space. As Lyotard puts it, *'nulle confiance ne peut être
faite aux règles de langage (ou de perception réaliste) qui per-
mettent de distinguer des niveaux ou des formes'* (ibid. p. 311).
We should therefore pay particular attention to what Lyotard sees
as the 'undisciplined continuity' of the play associated with the
primary process, as opposed, for example, to the hierarchised
space of narratology.

But hierarchical geometrics are also an aspect of what Deleuze
calls *'la recherche du clair et distinct'* (Deleuze 1968, pp. 208–9).
For narratology promotes the assumption of *'résolubilité'*, the
conviction that 'solution' can always be 'clapped on problem', as
Beckett once put it, 'like a snuffer on a candle' (Beckett 1983,
p. 92). Without a reversal of the terms of this assumption, writes
Deleuze, *'la fameuse révolution copernicienne n'est rien'*. We
should therefore seek to deconstruct the methodological procedure which moves from imbricated narrative text to its clear
reformulation in geometric terms. 'Moreover', Deleuze adds, 'there
is no revolution so long as we remain tied to Euclidean geometry:
we must move to a geometry of sufficient reason, a Riemannian-
type differential geometry which tends to give rise to discontinuity on the basis of continuity, or to ground solutions in the
conditions of problems' (Deleuze 1994, p. 210). This book sets out,
then, to deconstruct or interrogate certain aspects of narratological
geometry. Chapter 6, for example, is specifically devoted to
deconstructing the narratological notion of narrative levels. In
doing so, it also deconstructs the geometric relation between more

and less privileged elements of the narrative text that the concept of levels institutes. Chapter 3 is concerned with thematics. It returns to, seeks to specify, elaborate on and give a few new twists to Derrida's deconstruction of thematics (Derrida 1981b, pp. 173–286). In particular, it goes back to Derrida's project as a resistance to a particular thematic spatialisation of the text. It suggests, in Derrida's phrase, that thematisation of a text involves a 'carefully spaced-out splitting of the whole' (ibid. p. 252). Chapter 5 deconstructs the geometrics involved in the narratological spatialisation of narrative time.

But I also heed Serres's arguments and attempt to decentre the geometry in question, to displace the 'fixed point' according to which the geometry in question is repeatedly centred. 'Point,' or rather, points: for the Derrida of 'Structure, Sign and Play,' the centre may have different manifestations, as origin or 'central' or 'transcendental signified'. So, too, for Serres, the forms taken by the '*point fixe*' are multiple:

les modèles particuliers du point [fixe] vont à l'exhaustion: unité, référence métrique, site perspectif optimal, centre d'équilibre, de mouvement ou de forces, pôle céleste ou point d'arrêt astronomique, foyer optique, nœud acoustique, germe premier d'un organisme vivant, origine temporelle, historique ou autre, point final ou instant courant . . . (Serres 1972, p. 143)

Taken formally, the fixed point can equally be translated into notions of substance, subject and object, God and man, origin and telos (ibid. p. 144). The issue here is not the centre as a single, empirically definable point, but a familiar, theological system of thought to which some kind of 'fixed point' is always necessary. Some of the following chapters accordingly aim to deconstruct different kinds of 'fixed point' on which narratological geometry depends. Chapter 4 is concerned with the concept of narrative voice, for instance, as the central locus from which narrative discourse is conceived as issuing. Chapter 2 focuses on the 'world' about which that voice is deemed to speak as a fixed and homogenous 'point' precisely in that it is placed as irreducibly opposite to the voice as part of 'the Same-Other couplet' (Serres 1993, p. 153). The chapter returns yet again to the questions raised by mimetic theory, insofar as mimesis always involves the constatation or pseudo-constatation of a 'fixed point'. For, as Derrida puts it, the mimetic assumption is always inseparable from 'the *ontological*'. It takes for granted the 'possibility of a discourse about what is, the deciding and decidable *logos* of or about the *on* (being-present)' (Derrida 1981b, p. 191). To set to work on 'voice' and 'world' together is to aim precisely to deconstruct narratology's reliance on both a philosophy of origins and a phenomenology of the fixed object (Serres 1972, p. 140). Many of the terms into which Serres 'translates' the 'fixed point' will be in question in the following pages: substance, subject and object, origin and end; and, finally, 'man', too. Far from 'overcoming' humanism and the anthropological prejudice, narratology has never left them behind. It has always remained complicit with both, sustaining the notion of the centrality and unity of the essential anthropos, most evidently but by no means only in narratological accounts of narrative 'essences'. Accordingly, in my seventh and last chapter, I seek to interrogate and to displace this anthropocentrism as it has remained implicit in narratology. For there is no more crucial place at which narrative needs to be dissociated from a notional 'fixed point'. It is here precisely that narrative theory most needs to let go of retrospection and think towards the future.

The mode of deconstruction adopted in this study is specific. I interrogate various terms conventional within and intrinsic to established narratology: voice, levels, representation, form, narrative time, theme, the human subject. I try to displace them with substitute terms culled from a range of works by contemporary critical theorists: force, hymen, inauguration, event, monstrosity, laterality, writing. If I range widely through kinds of contemporary theory that often seem radically dissimilar, this is because I intend my strategy to be 'nomadic', in something like the powerful sense that Rosi Braidotti has recently given the word (Braidotti 1994). My substitute terms are intended as experimental or 'play' terms. They do not lay claim to the singular, empirical validity attributed to their more familiar, narratological counterparts. They exist partly to contest the supposedly ungainsayable 'validity' of these latter. My terms might be thought of as existing 'under erasure'. They are what Derrida calls 'unities of simulacrum, "false" verbal properties' (Derrida 1981a, p. 43). They take their existence from the inessentiality, the lack of incontrovertible truth to the more conventional terms they displace. They are important as means of destabilising a given system or interrogating its boundaries. They are also incitements to dreams of a different system or different systems, and therefore have a political significance. They are not necessarily or, at least, not merely descriptive of narrative features. If, for Baudrillard, as Jeremy Tambling has it, theory must recognise itself as simulation, the present study aims to be less empirical description than simulation model (Tambling 1990, p. 20). It adopts a postmodern practice of 'precession', serving as a map poised ambiguously between a territory to be covered or described and a territory to be anticipated or produced.[15] If I have called my terms 'substitutes', then, this does not mean that they simply efface their better known equivalents. Rather, they constitute a kind of double response to the more orthodox terms, displacing but also feeding off them, in a parasitic or hybridised relation. The intended effect is precisely the destruction or, better, the pluralisation of what Serres calls the 'ici-partout', the unitary, homogenous space commonly opened up by narratology. For Serres, the 'ici-partout' must be replaced by the 'ici-ailleurs'. We should seek to elaborate

un type de pensée dé-centrée, non référenciée, où l'essentiel n'est pas de se frayer un chemin vers un ancrage supposé, et toujours présupposé, quel qu'il soit, mais de se poser la question du chemin lui-même . . . Nous retrouvons la forme pure de l'ici-ailleurs, après l'épuisement de l'ici-partout; de l'ici-ailleurs, c'est-à-dire du transfert, dans un espace définitivement décentré . . . (Serres 1972, pp. 144–5)

If the multiplicity of the 'ici-ailleurs' is in some measure constitutive of 'the postmodern condition,' it remains for us to open up our intellectual models to an adequate reflection of it, to set it to work within them. This is what my 'substitute' terms, as 'unities of simulacrum', are intended to achieve.

Narratology, then, has always sought to reduce the plural spaces connected by the narrative parcours to geometric space, and the 'mobile site' in narrative to a 'fixed point.' This study attempts to destabilise the system of domination implicit in both reductions. But it also does the same with two analogous forms of narratological reduction. The first is the reduction of modernist and postmodernist forms of narrative to structural models derived from and determined by classical and realist narrative. In this respect, again, narratology and thought about the novel have always looked back. Thus, for example, Stanzel reads Robbe-Grillet's *Jealousy* as trying to achieve 'a complete reification of represented reality by freezing the mediator optically (for instance by reducing a character to the function of a camera eye' (Stanzel 1984, pp. 8–9)). Stanzel interprets this as Robbe-Grillet's 'extreme solution to the rendering of mediacy', a problem, he suggests, that has preoccupied narrative theory since the end of the nineteenth century (ibid. p. 9). Stanzel is clearly concerned to fit Robbe-Grillet into the terms of a discussion that stems from James's and Lubbock's engagement with nineteenth-century, classic realist texts. He can accept that works like Robbe-Grillet's require the formation of additional narratological categories. But he cannot afford to admit that Robbe-Grillet's work might simply be incommensurable with narratology as system, that it puts the narratological system itself radically into question. In fact, *Jealousy* surely frees itself from the mimetic 'constatation of the fixed point'. It refuses to allow us definitively to humanise its narrator, but is equally irreducible to the simple form of camera eye recording human drama. In effect, it resists what I will later call the terms of the anthropological dyad, and, with them, an anthropocentric mode of reading. Stanzel's narratology provides him with no vocabulary for this. But his kind of reduction of the corrosive difference of modernist or postmodernist texts – corrosive, that is, with respect to narratology itself – is characteristic of classical narratology. By contrast, the present study seeks largely to deploy modern or postmodern narratives as its prime instances. It works towards a postmodern theory of narrative precisely on the basis of texts that ask the most searching questions of narratology itself. That may mean stretching the reader's definition of narrative. But, if so, I also want to ask whether the very term 'narrative' itself is and has always been only a 'unity of simulacrum'.

The second form of narratological reduction whose terms and implicit valuations this study seeks to displace is that which privileges verbal over visual narrative. Hence the amount of attention I give to film. Narratologists have repeatedly asserted that their systems are valid for the latter as well as the former.

They have increasingly sought to apply their terms to visual narrative, film in particular. In doing so, however, they have repeatedly granted priority to modes of thought and description emerging out of work on verbal narrative. Even as he argues, for example, that cinema resists traditional language-centred notions of the narrator, Seymour Chatman seeks to reinstate the concept of narrative agency in film. Where a film theorist like David Bordwell suggests that there is no agency in film corresponding to a narrator, that to assume one is precisely to re-originate film in human being (Bordwell 1985, pp. 61–2), Chatman insists that a film gets 'sent'. A narrator thus exists in a given film, at the very least, as an organisational and sending agency. Indeed, Chatman goes on to suggest that films have implied authors, too (Chatman 1990, Ch. 8; pp. 126–31 and passim). But this kind of insistent reduction of cinema to the novelistic surely depends on a neglect or marginalisation of the phenomenon of narrative visibility itself. Narratology operates according to an established principle which maintains the identity of the visible and the legible, asserting that the relations between the elements in the world before our eyes are 'comme entre celles du discours pour pouvoir former une phrase lisible'.[16] What we need to set against the established narratological principle as I have just outlined it is the Lyotardian 'protestation': 'que le donné n'est pas un texte, qu'il y a en lui une épaisseur, ou plutôt une différence, constitutive, qui n'est pas à lire, mais à voir' (Lyotard 1985, p. 9). For the Lyotard of Discours, Figure, we do not free aesthetics from metaphysics unless we separate ourselves from a tradition which insists on reading the visible world and thus represses the 'figural' in favour of the 'discursive'. Lyotard is vitally concerned to destabilise the structure of thought which commonly privileges the linguistic over the sensory, the discursive over the visible, reading over seeing. He argues that we cannot break from metaphysics in putting language everywhere. On the contrary, it is thus that we fulfil metaphysics, in repressing the sensible and jouissance (p. 14). Hence Lyotard's interest in the figural as force transgressing the law of discourse and refusing to respect the invariant spacing and rules of substitution which define the system of langue and its derivatives. Indeed, far from the figural being reducible to the discursive, the discursive is never free of the figural:

La froide prose n'existe presque pas. . . . Un discours est épais. Il ne signifie seulement, il exprime. Et s'il exprime, c'est qu'il a lui aussi du bougé consigné en lui, du mouvement, de la force. . . . Lui aussi en appelle à l'oeil, lui aussi est énergétique. Traçons les parcours de l'oeil dans le champ du langage, saisissons le bougé-fixe . . . (Lyotard, p. 15)

I shall be returning to some of Lyotard's terms as he deploys them here in my first chapter. But it is precisely in the contemporary burgeoning of the visual arts itself that the structure of thought in question is increasingly being interrogated. In certain cinematic narratives, for instance, the discursive and the figural haunt each other, manifesting their interdependence, their actual inseparability. The discursive here is not distinct from the figural, is constantly being disturbed or set in motion by the latter. Chatman's kind of methodology, then, ignores the extent to which the visual media immediately and definitively 'thicken' narrative, adding an extra dimension to it, endowing it with an unprecedented materiality and mobility. In fact, the now dominant culture of the moving image poses the most searching challenges to all established narrative aesthetics. In particular, it calls in question the unreal, hypostasising forms and dematerialising abstractions of narratology. Narratology absolutely privileges 'discourse' over the 'figural.' But visual narrative resists that polarity and the hierarchy of values associated with it, and refuses to be reduced to 'une organisation géometrique entièrement pensable par concepts' (Lyotard 1985, p. 20). Cinema makes available to us the possibility of apprehending a given narrative 'system' as traversed by more or less continual rearrangements (ibid. p. 34). In Lyotard's words, we plunge into a world whose structures are incessantly undoing and reforming themselves (ibid.). In fact, cinema may be thought of as having the power of putting us in touch with the 'transcendental activity' as Lyotard understands it. This power is the gift not of the verbal arts, but of the arts that ask us to see, and to see *in the first instance*:

Sans doute la peinture est ce qui nous approche aussi près que possible de l'activité transcendentale, s'il est vrai que cette activité est bien force de disjoindre plutôt que de synthésizer. Ce que le tableau montre, c'est le monde en train de se faire. . . . De ce point de vue, le tableau est le plus étrange des objets quand il remplit la fonction dont le dote la peinture moderne: c'est un objet où se montre l'engendrement des objets, l'activité transcendentale même. (ibid. p. 28)

What Lyotard says of painting and modern painting, here, is true *a fortiori* of film. Its *'force de disjoindre'*, its imaging of *'le monde en train de se faire'*, of *'l'engendrement des objets'* is not to be reduced to the homogenising syntheses of classical narratology. Film rather resists and interrogates those syntheses. Accordingly, this study seeks to weave analyses of film in with its analyses of novels and verbal narratives without privileging the kind of openings made possible by the latter. My intention is to allow a sense of the figural and its trangressive work to begin to trouble the categories that have been and are still so readily established on the basis of a perception of the discursive order alone. At all events, in both cases – verbal and visual narrative – it is not the notional priority of one kind of model over another that matters. What is crucial is the deconstruction of a system that, in setting such models before us at all, continues to express a nostalgia for a unitary space. But we are ceasing to inhabit that space, and it can no longer be that of our thought.

NOTES

1. For a conception of the philosophical text as both hybrid form and phantasmagoria with regard in particular to philosophy's discourse on women, see Le Dœuff 1989a, passim.
2. This has been made particularly evident by Philippe Hamon in a recent article on the 'status and outlook' of narratology. See Hamon in Berben-Masi 1992, p. 363.
3. See Propp 1968, passim; Iser 1974, passim; Greimas 1966, p. 222 and passim; and Eco 1979, passim.
4. Michel Serres even suggests that the constants in question may be a function of 'mimetism' itself, since 'mimetism' is a form of triangulation. See Serres 1993, p. 148. He has Girard's triangular models partly in mind. See Girard, 1965.
5. Ryan has also restated the same theme in different ways in more recent work. See Berben-Masi 1992, pp. 368–87.
6. ICA documentation, 1994.
7. On some of the relationships between interactive fiction, space and the event see the appendix to this study. See also Gibson 1996.

8. For narratology as a 'geometry of violence', see Hamon on the phase of 'imperialist expansion' in which it conquered 'other fields of research' (Berben-Masi 1992, p. 364).

9. The poststructuralist assault on narratology has been under way for some time, of course. See for instance Coste 1989; Cornis-Pope 1992; and Gibson 1990.

10. A necessary process is also bound to take place. As Robert L. Sims puts it: 'it seems inevitable that the dynamics and inexhaustibility of the text would eventually produce "narratological leakages," or breaches, in the formalistic scientificity of fortress narratology'. See Sims 1992, pp. 21–60, p. 22.

11. Serres calls such practices 'auto-applications' or 'interior applications'. See Serres 1975, p. 23.

12. See in particular Serres 1972, pp. 127–59. But the theme is a recurrent one in Serres's work.

13. Serres illustrates this with a helpful diagram. See Serres 1993, p. 116.

14. Cf Deleuze's critique of Saussure and structuralism in Deleuze 1968, especially p. 264.

15. On 'precession' and 'the map that precedes the territory', see Baudrillard 1990, pp. 166–84, p. 166.

16. Claudel 1941, pp. 74–5. Quoted Lyotard 1985, p. 9. The italics are Lyotard's.

1

Narrative Force

FORM AND FORCE

My project, then, is a postmodern revaluation of the categories most crucial to classical theory of narrative. Historically, narratology was remarkable for shifting narrative theory decisively in the direction of formalism. This was true even when it claimed to be primarily concerned with ideology, as in some of Barthes's work. Narratology steered away from an old-fashioned conception of 'form' as always in some sense subordinate to 'content' to a new concern with the 'content of form', in Hjelmslev's phrase. This was part of the narratological break with what Derrida called the 'mimetologism' of an older criticism. The earlier criticism sustained an innocent faith in the logic of mimetic thought; or rather, it failed to perceive the historicity or cultural specificity of that thought, the latter's character *as* a particular logic. But there were losses as well as gains in the shift from a mimetologically oriented theory and criticism to a more formalist one. The losses included a vocabulary of affect. An anti-mimetological formalism seemed to have little or no place for that vocabulary. For it saw as formal constructions precisely those features of narrative – characters, plots, themes etc. – around which the vocabulary of affect had so richly accrued. This was one of the various factors that allowed narratological geometrics to consolidate itself as *merely* a geometrics. For a sense of the affective or the *pulsive* in narrative art seemed inextricably tied to an outworn aesthetics, and so irrelevant to the proper concerns of narrative theory. Yet, at the same time, this left the wind howling through the clear, methodical, symmetrical but

32

desolate architecture of the new narratology. Critics of narratology heard the sound of that wind and called it 'inhuman'.

But at the same time, almost before narratology had constituted itself as a field, significant and relevant questions were being raised about the structuralist methodology in which narratology has its roots. In particular, they were questions about the extent to which that methodology excluded the pulsive, the passional, the mobile – *energeia* – from its objects of inquiry. This was notably the case in Derrida's essay 'Force and Signification'. In Derrida's terms, in structuralism, 'geometrics' triumphed at the expense of 'energetics'. In *Forme et Signification*, said Derrida, Rousset 'grants an absolute privilege to spatial models, mathematical functions, lines and forms'. But that 'privileging' also means 'ignoring force' (Derrida 1990, p. 16). Classical narratology has operated according to the same system of priorities. As Derrida says of Rousset on *Le Cid*, narratology is determined to subject 'beauty, which is value and force' to 'regulation and schematisation' (Derrida 1990, p. 18). In narratology as in Rousset, '[e]verything that defies a geometrical-mechanical framework' is 'reduced to the appearance of the inessential' for the sake of an 'essentialism or teleological structuralism' (ibid. pp. 20–1). This is true not only of force and quality, which are meaning itself, but also duration, 'that which is pure qualitative heterogeneity within movement'. Narratology is therefore captive to what Derrida calls 'the metaphysics implicit in all structuralism'. In particular, narratology presupposes and appeals to 'the theological simultaneity of the book'. If the 'natural tendency of the book' is to reveal itself 'only in successive fragments' (ibid.), narratology seeks to transform the book 'into a simultaneous network of reciprocal relationships', thus neutralising 'the surprises of non-simultaneity' (ibid. p. 24). But if a narrative text 'is beautiful, it is so by virtue of that within it which surpasses schemes and understanding'. There is thus a need to think force. Force is 'a certain pure and infinite equivocality which gives signified meaning no respite, no rest, but engages it in its own *economy* so that it always signifies again and differs' (ibid. p. 25). Indeed the 'force of the work', writes Derrida, 'is precisely that which resists geometrical metaphorisation and is the proper object of literary criticism' (ibid. p. 20).

It is difficult, however, to think of the (narrative) work in terms of pure force or the play of forces without lapsing back either into mimetologism or into a psychologism which traces the text back to a disposition of intentions and drives within the author as subject. The difficulties in question are more clearly focussed if we refer to a line of thought which goes back as far as Nietzsche and from which Derrida's terms undoubtedly partly derive. The second book of *The Will to Power* develops a 'critique of the highest values hitherto'. In Book Three, Nietzsche embarks on a statement of his 'principles of a new evaluation'. Much of Book Three is actually taken up with familiar Nietzschean concerns: fact as interpretation, truth as value, the 'real world' as fable, the 'artificial arrangements' on which we insist 'for the purposes of intelligibility' (Nietzsche 1968, p. 264). 'There exists neither "spirit," nor reason, nor thinking', Nietzsche writes, 'nor consciousness, nor soul, nor will, not truth: all are fictions' (ibid. p. 266). In *The Will to Power*, substance, attribute, unity, knowledge, causality, object, subject, space, time are all laid open to the same sceptical interrogation as aspects of 'our metaphysical-logical dogmatism' (ibid. p. 282). Yet, at the same time, all these are presented as 'errors' without which 'a certain species of life could not live' (ibid. p. 272). They are the product of 'the inventive force' that has 'laboured in the service of our needs', and their 'value for life is decisive' (ibid. pp. 277, 272). It is will to power or force that lies behind and expresses itself within them. Force wills error. This, then, is the anti-metaphysical conception of the relationship between being and becoming, forces and forms elaborated in *The Will to Power*. It has two consequences that seem particularly relevant, here. The first is the suggestion that 'the body and physiology' must be 'the starting point' for thought, that it is 'essential . . . to start from the *body* and employ it as guide' (ibid. pp. 271, 289); the body, that is, not as unity or whole, still less as the instrument of a subjectivity, but as what Nietzsche calls 'idioplasm', as a nexus or play of forces. The second point is that, in *The Will to Power*, art and the artist take on a crucial importance. For the Nietzsche of this book, it is the artist, above all, who values 'the seductive flash of gold on the belly of the serpent *vita*' (ibid. p. 310), who reckons with becoming rather than being, force rather than form. He thus prefers error and invention to the 'truth' as which they otherwise masquerade.

Hence the emergence, in Book Three, Part Four – 'The Will to Power as Art' – of Nietzsche's 'physiological aesthetics'.[1] *The Will to Power* suggests that 'metaphysics, religion, morality, science' are 'all of them only products of the will to art', but that they mask their own foundation as and in art (ibid. p. 452). Art itself occupies a privileged place as a site where the founding character of the will to power can be grasped in itself, bringing something into being that does not simultaneously lose itself as force in identifying itself with Being. Art is better than truth. 'Art is *worth more* than truth' (ibid. p. 453):

truth does not count as the supreme value, even less as the supreme power. The will to appearance, to illusion, to deception, to becoming and change here counts as more profound, primeval, 'metaphysical' than the will to truth, to reality . . . (ibid. p. 453)

The artist is haughtily indifferent to 'eternal values' and essentially serious in 'play'. He is wholly given over to a 'desire for becoming' which is 'the expression' of his 'overfull power pregnant with the future' (ibid. p. 432, 446). It is because this 'power' appears as itself in art that, for Nietzsche, art can serve as the basis of his 'new evaluation'. This is where 'physiology' comes in. The condition of art and the artist is 'an *explosive* condition', writes Nietzsche. Artists themselves are 'full of surplus energy, powerful animals, sensual' (ibid. p. 421). The corollary of that is that art itself is close to 'states of animal vigour'. On one level, at least, Nietzsche sees the work of art as effectively communicating the aesthetic state of the creator – his plenitude, his energy, his 'superabundance' – to the receiver of the work. 'The effect of works of art', he writes, 'is to *excite the state that creates art* – intoxication' (ibid. p. 434). The aesthetic experience for both creator and receiver is thus one of an 'extraordinary expansion' of the 'feeling of power, riches, necessary overflowing of all limits' (ibid. p. 422). And this experience is in origin physical, since 'all art exercises the power of suggestion over the muscles and senses, which in the artistic temperament are originally active' (ibid. p. 427). Art is thus the site of force conceived of and experienced as something prior to truth and reality. In the end, that site is prior to questions of subjectivity, too, of creator and receiver, subject and object. For force is what traverses them all, impartially.[2] Art 'appears in man like a force of nature', writes Nietzsche, 'and disposes of him whether he will or no' (ibid. p. 420). Only an 'aesthetics of force' can be commensurate with such a radical reformulation of the nature of art or radical 'transvaluation' of its value.

But there are difficulties with the Nietzschean conception of force. In particular, it has been rethought by Heidegger, along with the concept of a 'physiological aesthetics' and Nietzsche's alleged biologism. For Heidegger, the trouble with Nietzsche's idea of force as developed in *The Will to Power* is that it never really escapes the Cartesian tradition, that it lapses back into the very metaphysics it seeks to escape. For Heidegger, this is the case, above all, in that Nietzsche's nihilistic negation of reason actually finally reinstates it by placing it in the service of force. More precisely, *The Will to Power* ultimately posits force, the will to power itself as finding its fulfilment in command, mastery, a calculative thought that is the very apotheosis of reason as Nietzsche had originally sought to negate it.[3] Heidegger rightly grants a crucial importance to the question of aesthetics in *The Will to Power*. He actually begins his massive account of Nietzsche with precisely that question, recognising the central significance the Nietzschean scheme of things finally gave to art. He recognises, too, that, for the later Nietzsche, it is in art that 'Being lights up for us most immediately and brightly'. It is therefore in art that we glimpse 'will to power' or force as 'the basic character of beings' (Heidegger 1991, p. 69). For Nietzsche, Platonism, Christianity and philosophy since Plato have all argued for a supersensuous world. They have understood the world of the senses as a world of appearances. But Nietzsche's intervention is decisive: after Nietzsche, truth as 'supersensuousness' becomes an error. The sensuous world is the true world, and, since 'the sensuous, the sense-semblant, is the very element of art' (ibid. p. 72), art becomes the sovereign form of thought. Art reinstates force where the idea of the 'supersensuous' only drains and weakens it. But what does Nietzsche really see as the relationship between art and force? As *Nietzsche contra Wagner* makes clear, says Heidegger, force does not manifest itself for Nietzsche as 'sheer upsurgence of the Dionysian upon which one might ride' (Heidegger 1991, p. 88). In fact, Nietzsche always thinks of art as *leashing* force and giving it form. For Nietzsche, form in art – *morphē* – is 'the enclosing limit or boundary, what brings and stations a being into that which it is'. It 'defines and demarcates for the first time the realm in which the state of waxing force and plenitude of being comes to fulfilment' (ibid. p. 119). It has the sense of 'lawfulness' that is granted it by common and familiar understanding. This is precisely a 'logical', 'arithmetical' *and 'geometrical'* lawfulness (ibid. p. 120, italics mine). In fact, in Nietzsche, 'estimates of aesthetic value' always have as their 'ground floor' feelings that relate to this lawfulness. Such feelings involve delight 'in the ordered, the surveyable, the bounded' (ibid. p. 120). Thus in *The Will to Power*, according to Heidegger, force in art is seen as ultimately converting itself into its opposite in order to *contain* force. Nietzsche's aesthetics is finally one of control and mastery. But it is also an aesthetics in which force is self-mastering, dividing itself from itself in order to subdue itself. Thus Nietzsche is not principally concerned with the banality of an aesthetics which sees chaos as shaped by form, but rather with one designating a 'mastery' which 'enables the primal wilderness of chaos and the primordiality of law to advance under the same yoke, invariably bound to one another with equal necessity' (Heidegger 1991, p. 128). So the physiological rapture which, according to Heidegger, is for Nietzsche the basic aesthetic state is 'no mere turbulence and ebullition' (ibid. p. 113). In fact, it is all to do with order, 'the most measured determinateness' (ibid.). Rapture is itself always drawn 'to major features, that is, to a series of traits, to an articulation' which is what 'we call "form"' (ibid. p. 118). Equally, the physiological in art is both a condition of the creative process, and that which in 'the created thing' is 'to be restrained, overcome and surpassed' (ibid. p. 129). Nietzsche's 'physiology' of art itself reflects this final privileging of the very reason Nietzsche thought he was negating. His 'physiological aesthetics' is in the last analysis a resort to the methods of natural science and thus a surrender to his opposition. It merely relegates aesthetics to 'the science of facts', a knowledge as *technē* establishing a mastery over art as *physis*.

But it is Vattimo, more than anyone else, who has made the question of Nietzsche's aesthetics, of force and form, a question for postmodernity. Effectively, Vattimo seeks to go back before Heidegger's critique to Nietzsche himself, at the same time re-reading Nietzsche on art in *The Will to Power* in a way that twists him free of Heidegger's clutches. Vattimo specifically identifies Heidegger's critique of Nietzsche with his (Heidegger's) well-known critique of technicist rationalism in general, and the 'forgetting of Being' endemic to the final accomplishment of the total technological organisation of the world.[4] Vattimo also notes the political implications of Heidegger's critique. It is founded on the familiar Heideggerian fear of the possibility of a world 'in which there is no longer anything "unforeseen" or historically new, nor anything that escapes the programmed concatenation of causes and effects' (Vattimo 1993, pp. 85–6). For Vattimo, Heidegger's critique of Nietzsche is of a piece with that fear. But Vattimo thinks that the Heideggerian critique rests on a misunderstanding of the aesthetic model which in reality underlies the will to power. This model is not to be identified '*tout court* with the will to a total technocratic organisation of the world' (ibid. p. 88). Indeed, Vattimo partly suggests the reverse: Nietzsche's emphases are much closer to Heidegger's than Heidegger himself is prepared to admit. Thus Vattimo argues, for instance, that from *Human, All too Human* through to *The Will to Power*, Nietzsche was concerned with art as 'pre-eminently the "place" where, in the history of Western culture, there persists a dionysiac residuum, a form of liberty of the spirit'. It was this liberty – a 'liberty' from the Western *ratio* and from metaphysics – that Nietzsche ended up calling the will to power. The Nietzschean view of art casts it as the exemplary form of excess. Nietzsche's later 'discovery' is that 'alleged "values" and metaphysical structures are just a play of forces' (Vattimo 1993, p. 93). This discovery 'is the revelation of the will to power as that which dislocates and subverts prevailing hierarchical relations' by 'unveiling them as relations of force rather than orders corresponding to "values"' (ibid. pp. 93–4). Art for Nietzsche is the primary locus of this 'destructuring activity' (ibid. p. 96). Thus, if Heidegger's sense of form as the expression of the victory of force is one motif in *The Will to Power*, another is force, intoxication, superabundance as the Dionysiac negation of form. In fact, Nietzsche's case slips away from him:

On [the] one hand the power achieved by art seems to be related to its representation of the triumph of unitary organization over centrifugal thrust, multiplicity and the disorder of impulses. On the other hand, it seems that the more Nietzsche strives to analyse the meaning of this victory of force in art, the more he realizes that the idea of the organic, *of geometrical simplicity, of* ✦ *structural rigour* crumbles in his hands. Art comes to look more and more like an activation of impulses recalcitrant to unification and coordination, forces so highly refined as to be almost pathological. (ibid. p. 99, italics mine)

Thus Nietzsche's 'physiological aesthetic' actually involves an appeal in despite of 'values' to 'a subtle flexibility of the body' (Nietzsche 1968, p. 427). That aesthetic construes art as 'a pulsive mechanism with a destructuring effect' insofar as it physically triggers 'the subject's impulses and so breaks up the subject's established hierarchies' (Vattimo 1993, pp. 99–100). Thus force does not resolve itself into the imposition of form. The force in art rather imparts mobility to the body. Form is 'for ever being exploded by a play of forces, of particular forces, namely the body's instincts, sensuality and animal vitality' (ibid. p. 105).[5] Art in Nietzsche becomes what it must also be for postmodernity, the place

where the subject to whom technique has given the capacity to exploit the world, actually exploits, dislocates and destructures itself as subjected subject, as the last incarnation of the structures of domination. The Heideggerian hope of a new epoch of Being must probably pass . . . through this operation of radically disorganising the subject, which for Nietzsche is accomplished first and foremost in the will to power as art. (ibid. p. 107)

But there is in fact an extent to which Vattimo does not counter Heidegger's interpretation of Nietzsche. What Vattimo produces, in the end, is an account of *The Will to Power* that isolates what is important for postmodern aesthetics in it, rather than getting the measure of its paradoxes or contradictions. For *The Will to Power* surely understands force in art as both finding an apotheosis in form and as exceeding or 'destructuring' form. Hence the fact that, for Nietzsche, while 'Euclidean space is a conditional "truth" . . . a mere idiosyncrasy of a certain kind of animal' (Nietzsche 1968,

p. 278) and the term 'geometry' applies only 'to fictitious entities that we have created' (ibid. p. 280), the 'grand style' which he prefers to all others has a 'logical and geometrical simplification' which betokens an 'enhancement of strength' (ibid. p. 420). Yet 'perfection' in art is also a 'necessary overflowing of all limits . . . an excess and overflow of blooming physicality into the world of images and desires' (ibid. p. 422).[6] There is even a sense in which, for Nietzsche, force is better thought of in terms of this paradox than it could possibly be if somehow 'taken in isolation'. 'Fascination of the opposing point of view', writes Nietzsche, 'refusal to be deprived of the enigmatic' (ibid. p. 262). Furthermore, the Nietzschean paradox, here, is one that Heidegger eventually expresses in his own terms, and he does so by making his own account of *The Will to Power* more paradoxical than I have so far credited it with being. It is true, says Heidegger, on the one hand, that, in art, Nietzsche sees 'the sensuous' as 'directed toward overview and order, toward what can be mastered and fixed' (Heidegger 1991, p. 212). But it is equally true that for Nietzsche there is really no such thing as 'overview and order', since 'all being is in itself perspectival, perceptual, and that means . . . "sensuous"' (ibid. p. 213). Thus the sensuous or force resolves itself into form only to reveal itself again for what it is, the sensuous. Something else is thus always perceptible within form as larger than form. It is that which 'genuinely radiates' within form, bringing form 'to show itself'. Here, Heidegger moves beyond an account of the Nietzschean conception of form as simply opposed to Wagnerian Dionysianism. For Nietzsche, he says, in the end, art 'as "forming and shaping" . . . coheres most intimately with perspectival shining and letting shine', with 'bringing waxing life itself to power'. So, too, for Vattimo, force must be thought through form rather than in the abeyance of form. For if force is what 'operates against form inasmuch as it reveals and throws into crisis the violence of form', form is '*for ever* being exploded' in this activity (Vattimo 1993, p. 105, italics mine). Derrida has likewise been well aware of the problems involved in seeking to 'turn literary criticism over' to the consideration of force as object:

Our intention here is not, through the simple motions of balancing, equilibration or overturning, to oppose duration to space, quality to quantity, force to form, the depth of meaning or value to the surface of figures. Quite to the contrary. To counter this simple alternative, to counter the simple choice of one of the terms or one of the series against the other, we maintain that it is necessary to seek new concepts and new models, an economy escaping this system of metaphysical oppositions. This economy would not be an energetics of pure, shapeless force. The differences examined simultaneously would be differences of site and differences of force. (Derrida 1990, pp. 19–20)

Force is not to be thought without form. The need is for a new economy which will permit us to think form and force together, as an endless self-difference within the (narrative) text.

Some Versions of Force

I want to consider three contrasting examples of ways in which contemporary theory and criticism describe the relationship between force and form in narrative texts. The first is Peter Brooks's influential *Reading for the Plot*. Brooks shares many of my misgivings about the fixity of structuralist and narratological models of the text. One of his starting points, indeed, is precisely Derrida's 'Force and Signification'. Brooks also sees Derrida's essay as pleading for a recognition of 'the existence of textual force'. Force, he says, is a concept which may 'help us move beyond the static models of much formalism' (Brooks 1984, p. 47). Accordingly, his own concern is rather 'with the dynamic aspect of narrative' (ibid. p. xiii), especially 'the temporal dynamics that shape narratives in our reading of them, the play of desire in time' (ibid. p. xi). It is exactly force, says Brooks, that we need to find ways to describe. This argument leads him to psychoanalysis, particularly Freud. According to Brooks, Freud 'presents a dynamic model of psychic processes' and thus may offer 'the promise of a model' pertinent to textual dynamics and to an elaboration of textual force (ibid. p. xiv).[7] Freud sees unconscious life as 'investments, movements and discharges of energies . . . the place of drives or instincts in conflict, a basic dualism whence comes its permanent driving force' (ibid. p. 42). The driving force in question is desire, and desire is 'the motor of narrative' (ibid. p. 52). Insofar as that desire is Eros, for example, narrative desire, desire in narrative, desire as generated by narrative seeks, as Brooks has it in the recent *Psychoanalysis and Storytelling*, to bind 'all living substance together' (Brooks 1994, p. 109); or, in Freud's phrase, 'to combine organic substances into ever greater unities'.[8] But Brooks does not conflate desire in narrative with erotic desire alone. Since desire is also 'desire *for* the end', for instance, it may also be appetency, ambition, quest, a desire for quiescence, for non-narratability or death (ibid. pp. 52, 107). What is important is that we recognise in the workings of narrative desire the character of the narrative text as a field of force. It is thus that Brooks aspires to produce a psychoanalytical model of the text that is neither a study of its psychogenesis nor of the dynamics of literary response nor of the hidden motivations of the characters, but rather 'the superimposition of the model of the functioning of the psychic apparatus on the functioning of the text' (ibid. p. 112).

There are problems, however, with this psychological model, particularly as an account of textual force. Consider what Brooks has to say about the power of repetition in narrative. For Brooks, repetition contains or rather constrains 'the instinctual excitation reaching the primary process' in the interests of 'the creation of an energetic constant-state situation which will permit *the emergence of mastery*' (ibid. p. 101, italics mine). In other words, it makes for

a binding of textual energies that allows them to be mastered *by putting them into serviceable form*, usable 'bundles,' within the energetic economy of narrative. Serviceable form must . . . mean perceptible form: repetition, repeat, recall, *symmetry*, all these journeys back in the text, returns to and returns of, that allow us to bind one textual moment to another *in terms of similarity* or *substitution rather than mere contiguity*. Textual energy, all that is aroused into expectancy and possibility in a text can become usable by plot *only when it has been bound or formalized*. (ibid., italics mine)

It is thus, too, that, in *Psychoanalysis and Storytelling*, Brooks suggests that psychoanalytic theory 'can go beyond formalism only by becoming more formalistic' (Brooks 1994, p. 26). The point, here, is not just the extent of Brooks's reliance for his Freudian model on *Beyond the Pleasure Principle*, so easily available to interpretation as identifying the principle of organic life as a conservative principle.[9] Nor is it that Brooks's way of thinking force and form together always privileges form in making it the 'ultimate product' of force. Nor is it even that Brooks's emphasis on 'formalisation' seems strikingly close to the formalism he is ostensibly rejecting. It is rather that, for Brooks, in general, force produces plot as 'ordered' and 'significant form' (Brooks 1994, p. xi). Narrative dynamics are shaping and 'organising' dynamics (ibid. p. 7). Hence Brooks's repeated emphasis on 'the textual middle' as a 'highly charged field of force', but also as a kind of interim or parenthesis, 'held in' by the determinations of beginnings and ends (ibid. p. xiii). Whatever the play of forces within narrative, narrative always 'demarcates, encloses, establishes limits, orders', makes 'figures of design' (ibid. p. 4). Even those localised discharges of narrative energy which Brooks admits to finding in novels – Proustian or Joycean epiphanies, for example – are always 'reincorporated' back into plot (ibid. p. 124). The energy displayed in narrative always resolves itself into logic, always produces sense, is always teleological. Again and again, desire in narrative reveals itself to be 'inherently totalising' (ibid. p. 39), a desire for completion, closure (ibid. p. 94). Force 'enchains' itself in the service of a good that is greater than itself (ibid.). The result is a geometry of the text that is not essentially different to that of established narratology. This geometry projects from a horizontal axis, for instance, ('mere contiguity'), on to a vertical one ('similarity or substitution'). Plot must be understood as 'diagramming that which was previously undifferentiated' (ibid. p. 12), the diagram being 'a precipitation of shape and meaning, some simulacrum of understanding of how meaning can be construed over and through time' (ibid. p. 35). For, in the terms of *Psychoanalysis and Storytelling*, form is our very situation, 'our siting, within the symbolic order, the order within which we constitute meaning and ourselves as endowed with meaning' (Brooks 1994, p. 34).

We are a long way, here, from Vattimo's conception of force as continually exploding form and throwing its violence into crisis. We may seem closer to that technological resumption of force into form of which Heidegger accuses Nietzsche. But actually we are just back with a familiar Anglo-American humanism which projects our lives as 'ceaselessly intertwined with narrative' (ibid. p. 3), sees plot as 'the syntax of a certain way of speaking our understanding of the world' (ibid. p. 7), and turns the poststructuralist enterprise into an endeavour 'to reconnect literary criticism to human concern' (ibid. p. 14). For Brooks, the structure of narrative is in some sense the structure of mind *tout court*, 'mind' apparently being thinkable only in terms of 'a process of structuration' (ibid. pp. 24–5). Like other 'revisionist narratologists', Brooks gives himself out as post-structuralist and even post-deconstructionist, post-Derridean. The move forwards, however, is finally retrogressive, a circling back to critical values dominant in the Anglo-American tradition before structuralism. Brooks manages his 'move beyond' only in refusing to ask or answer the questions put most forcefully by theory, in refusing to put certain cherished 'foundational truths' at risk.[10] Thus he 'shields [an] essential order from any radical destruction or reordering'.[11]

In the context of narratology in the eighties, then, Brooks's brilliant and widely admired book served powerfully to protect narratology against the incursions of post-structuralism, precisely by giving itself out as an advance guard of a new post-structuralism. In fact, revisionist narratology has no more adequate an account of narrative force to offer than classical narratology or theory of the novel. But where else is there to look? The answer has to be outside narratology *per se* and within critical theory and the latter's dealings with narrative. Serres's work on narrative – on Zola, for instance, and Verne – might actually seem to offer a reversal of the structure into which Brooks casts his terms. Serres develops the metaphor of fire among others, for example, as he picks it up from Verne's works, as a way of characterising certain aspects of Verne's narratives and staying faithful precisely to their force. In the process, he also seeks to repudiate the kind of value placed upon mastery by a critic like Brooks. To think in terms of 'mastering fire', writes Serres, is to think only in terms of problems and solutions, programmes and responses:

Le problème est de maîtriser le lieu de nos maîtrises . . . de trancher les vieilles adhérences, de transférer le feu, de transporter l'énergie, de traduire, de transcrire la puissance, oui, de transvaluer le savoir, sur et dans un espace non structuré par la relation d'ordre . . . (Serres 1974b, p. 278)

It is geometrical space that must be abandoned if we are to 'translate' or 'transcribe' textual force. Hence the extent of Serres' reliance, in the studies both of Zola and Verne, on systems of metaphorical description of the text that are radically unlike those supplied by a more familiar textual technology. Hence too Serres's effort to read Verne, for example, in terms of the accumulation and expenditure of forces or 'energies': the law of Verne's narrative is one of condensation and displacement, accumulation and discharge, filling and explosion (ibid. p. 157). There is a 'language of energy' in it. Verne's texts do not 'contain' or 'represent' energy, however. We must read narrative in Verne in terms of its vectors, rather than trying to reduce it to a static system. Serres repeatedly substitutes metaphorical systems deriving for example from thermodynamics for the geometrical metaphors of an established formalism. Yet geometry – regulation – is not simply abolished in the substitution. Serres argues the need to take the text back into '*le feu même de sa naissance*' (ibid. p. 282). Confusingly, however, he also tells us that the text is a 'network of figures':

Parmi ce réseau, parmi ces figures, dans cette constellation, dans ce complexe, le feu. Gelé comme un mot parmi les autres. Il n'y a de réseau, de constellation et de texte que si le feu est gelé. (ibid.)

If textual force is always 'frozen' in place, has it not lost its character as force? Doesn't form 'master' force, after all? In his work on Zola, Serres rejects the very idea of 'explication' of the text, and with it, the spatialisation of narrative texts in terms of relations between a surface and 'depths'. He also rejects the idea of the Zola text as 'closed laboratory', according to which all diagrams are complete and finite, and the subject remains outside them, as supervisor and master (Serres 1975, p. 39). The corollary of these rejections would appear to be a determination to think force:

Il n'y va plus . . . de la vérité, mais du mouvement, mais de la force, mais de la puissance, mais de la production . . . mais de la vie, conçue comme énergie. (ibid. p. 26)

Yet Serres also insistently resorts, here, to images of closed or limited, organised or regulated space. Thus the '*impulsion impétueuse des pulsions et des appétits*' across the narrative of *Le Docteur Pascal*, for instance, is also clearly contained or held in equilibrium:

Le rapport des forces est posé, les vecteurs, leur intensité, leurs directions, leur sens, dans un espace qualifié en hauteur et bassesse. (ibid. p. 42)

Nonetheless, Serres's account of force is clearly very different to Brooks's. The difference lies in Serres's assertion that his study of Zola deals not in texts themselves but in states of the text (as physical substances have states (ibid. p. 23)). Form is not to be gainsaid. But it is always relational, a function of the relation between text and reader, text and context etc. This is to think form in its most particular historicity, its radical contingency. Not surprisingly, Serres supplements his metaphors from thermodynamics with others taken – for instance – from electrostatics. We must think the stasis and the mobility of the narrative text *together*, as a paradox we cannot get beyond. That paradox itself reflects the extent to which narrative texts are always available to and in excess of our 'fixing' descriptions of them. But there are different ways of thinking force and form at once. Serres's is arguably never quite sufficiently refined or strenuous. He is at least partly ambiguous about whether force can really be thought as working within as well as through forms. He tends to conceive of movement as something that happens between stases. Movement is not something immanent to apparently static forms. It does not trouble or displace them or render them equivocal. Serres provides an image of the text as a '*réseau mouvant*', and this is undoubtedly a refinement on the fixity of structuralist models. But all the same, is it sufficiently distinct from structuralist spatialisations of the text? Is it really adequate to the radical contingency of form on which Serres elsewhere insists? Is it adequate to the self-difference of the narrative text?

Foucault provides a very different conception of the relationship between force and narrative form to that offered by both Brooks and Serres, especially in his book on Roussel. For Foucault, as Deleuze points out, every form is a compound of forces (Deleuze 1988b, p. 124). But forms never bind, 'match' or neutralise forces:

The diagram, as the fixed form of a set of relations between forces, never exhausts force, which can enter into other relations and compositions. The diagram stems from the outside, but the outside does not merge with any diagram . . . (ibid. p. 89)

Forces combine with others to compose forms, but also exceed any given composition. In exceeding it, they move on to other combinations with other forces and other compositions. This, says Deleuze, is precisely what modern literature evokes, for Foucault. Firstly, in the work of Joyce, Mallarmé, Péguy, Artaud, cummings, Burroughs and Roussel, we find 'a finite number of components' yielding 'a practically unlimited diversity of combinations'. The image here is of a play of forces and forms in its 'unlimited finity' (ibid. pp. 130–1). Secondly, the same literature emphasises a 'strange language within language' that is itself a play of forces and enters into or produces new compositions. The literary work becomes a composition *with* rather than a composition *of* forces. Thirdly, in *Finnegans Wake*, Mallarmé, Burroughs and so on, force manifests itself above all in the importance of chance. For chance, says Deleuze, 'the relation of force with force, is also the essence of force' (Deleuze 1983, p. 40).

All three conceptions of the relationship between force and narrative are there in Foucault's reading of Roussel. In the first instance, in the narrative 'process' in Roussel, according to Foucault, we have Deleuze's 'unlimited finity', a surface game 'of continually changing repetitions' traversed by force (Foucault 1987, p. 25). In the second instance, there is the force of 'the eruption of language', the constant emergence of the text from 'the depths of language' as a reserve (ibid. pp. 39, 51). Roussel's texts compel our attention to language itself as a play of forces out of which his narratives appear but with which they are not of course to be identified. Roussel is not concerned with any supposed duplication 'of the reality of another world', but with new compositions with the forces of language which will '*discover* an unexpected space, and *cover* it with things never said before' (ibid. p. 16). Thirdly, to open a Roussel text 'in all its force' is to recognise in the narrative a 'succession of disruptive and explosive lights' which constitute a constant play or radiance of possible meanings, given and withdrawn (ibid.). Here precisely 'chance' is acknowledged as 'triumphing' in the forms that constantly 'rise' to the 'surface' of the narrative (ibid. p. 38).

For all his concern with the 'dynamic', Brooks's version of the relation between force and form asserts the primacy and centrality of reason, the cogito, the ego, the human subject – the human subject, above all, again, as *master*. More Nietzscheanly, Foucault and Deleuze affirm force itself, in its materiality, as – in Deleuze's terms – an *outside*, never graspable in itself but always visible within forms as what produces and inhabits them. Serres, Foucault and Deleuze all share a sense of the double aspect of narrative as both commensurate with and resistant to description in terms of either forces or forms. But Serres produces no model that is altogether adequate to the intimacy of the twin aspects, their constant reversals into one another. The Foucauldian approach works very well for postmodern or, at least, post-Joycean modes of narrative, but is not easily transferable to other modes. How, then, might we start to produce a narrative energetics whilst keeping the force/form paradox in mind? Deleuze and Lyotard suggest some useful responses.

DELEUZEAN ENERGETICS

Deleuze can provide us with a textual that is also in large measure a narrative energetics. This latter is linked to the principle of multiplicity.[12] For Deleuze and Guattari, everything is composed of multiplicities. A text is 'made of variously formed matters, and very different dates and speeds' (Deleuze and Guattari 1988, p. 3). As multiplicity, everything 'is permeated by unformed, unstable matters, by flows in all directions, by free intensities or nomadic singularities' (ibid. p. 33). The 'metrical principle' of these multiplicities is to be found 'in forces at work within them' (ibid. p. 31). It is not a geometrical principle or a principle of regularity. Structural models composed of 'points and positions' are therefore not appropriate, for they establish 'resemblances in a series', 'internal homologies', the 'structuration of differences', the 'identification of terms with an equality of relations', all in the name of 'symbolic understanding' (ibid. p. 236). Thus structuralism has no way of attending to becoming, which it can only see as diachrony and 'degradation' (ibid. p. 237). The models employed by structuralism must deal in invariants, when the problem is always one of how to conceptualise continual variation. Like the narratology it produced, structuralism can never move beyond the thought of 'characteristics'. The text must be reduced to certain privileged, recurrent features. These are presumed to be a kind of distillation of the whole where others are not, a kind of miniaturisation of the whole which, at the same time, weirdly, is somehow larger than the whole, since it contains the latter. Deleuze and Guattari, however, are 'not interested in characteristics' but in 'modes of expansion, propagation, occupation, contagion, peopling', the 'legion', force or forces at work (ibid. p. 239). However, the more familiar conceptions of structure cannot simply be 'thought away'. Rather, the familiar structures must be conceived of as tools for which new purposes must be invented (ibid. pp. 188–9). Their proportions must be revised, their grasp on what they purport to describe loosened. If invariant structures cannot attend to becoming, for example, equally, becoming is not to be thought in isolation from invariant structures. It must rather be conceived as carrying along components of those structures with it even as it escapes them, components which then form 'passages or perceptible landmarks for the imperceptible processes' of becoming itself (ibid. p. 303). We are back, here, to a conception of form which places it as partial and epiphenomenal in relation to forces. This is also the case as Deleuze and Guattari develop their concept of the 'armature' rather than the structure of a literary (narrative) text (ibid. pp. 329–30). This 'rhizomic' concept is also specifically literary. (They relate it, for instance, to James's conception of proceeding by 'blocks of wrought matter' and Woolf's idea of 'saturating every atom'). Its analogy would be certain kinds of architecture in which reinforced concrete is used in its nature as 'a heterogenous matter whose degree of consistency varies according to the elements in the mix'. This makes for an architectural system of 'different sections and variable intervals' depending on 'the intensity and direction of the force to be tapped'. In general, form now becomes, not something imposed on matter, but an elaboration of 'an increasingly rich . . . material, the better to tap into increasingly intense forces' (ibid. p. 329). It holds heterogeneous forces together without them ceasing to be heterogenous. It also spells the end of the compartmentalising, centralising, hierarchising thought endemic to the classical idea of form, most forcefully in the case of cinema.

For Deleuze, cinema, above all, requires the postmodern thought of form and force together. It is cinema *par excellence* in which narrative force is to be apprehended. For the cinema is an art of the 'movement-image'. But Deleuze does not simply equate this with the idea of the art of the *moving* image. The Deleuzean thought of becoming is in large measure Bergsonian. Deleuze enlists Bergson in the cause of his own radical empiricism and in support of an ontology which connects forms to 'intensive forces'. For Deleuze, says Boundas, Bergson

creates the possibilities for an investigation of the 'nonhuman' or 'superhuman' originary world wherein images move and collide in a state of universal variation. . . . This is a world with no axes, no centres, no ups or downs (Deleuze 1991, p. 5).

In the material universe, movement surpasses all closed systems. It insistently establishes itself between the parts of a system and one system and another, traversing them all as a play of forces, stirring them all up together and preventing them from being absolutely closed. Furthermore, in *Matter and Memory*, Bergson understood that movement, as physical reality in the external world, and the image, as psychic reality in consciousness, could no longer be opposed. This was the Bergsonian discovery of the movement-image. Phenomenology, for example, turns away from the 'acentred state of things' that is universal variation, according to Deleuze, in a dream of a 'natural state' of 'centred perception'. But cinema can 'go back up towards' the 'acentred state' (Deleuze 1986, p. 58). For it is 'acentred' itself: it can get us up close to things or take us away from them, revolve around them. It can thus suppress both the anchoring of the subject and the horizon of the world:

IMAGE = MOVEMENT . . . There is nothing moved which is distinct from the received movement. Every thing, that is to say every image, is indistinguishable from its actions and reactions. This is universal variation. (ibid. p. 58)

Cinema and matter may thus be identical – molecular, dispersed, multiple and always active and reactive. It is cinema, above all, which can take us beyond the secondary procedures which organise our 'worlds' as 'outlines or solids or rigid and geometric bodies'. These procedures introduce the intervals according to which 'outlines of axes appear in an acentred universe, a left and a right, a high and a low' (ibid. p. 63). But in the case of cinema the mobility of its centres and the variability of its framings lead it to restore vast acentred and deframed zones. It thus tends to return to the first regime of the movement-image, universal variation, total, objective and diffuse perception. (ibid. p. 64)

Of course, Bergson himself did not believe this to be true of cinema. He saw cinema as giving us only false movement – not the movement intrinsic to matter and duration, to universal variation or force, but movement as constructed mechanically out of pre-existent, immobile sections, a movement behind and within which there always lurks a geometrics. Deleuze argues, however, that, whilst cinema certainly proceeds with immobile sections – twenty-four images per second – it does not actually *give* us those images, but an intermediate one. Movement is not appended or added to this intermediate image, but is endemic to it as an immediate given, as force. Images in cinema are always points of transmission, inseparable from their own modification. This means that familiar conceptions of form are simply not applicable to film. In antiquity, movement refers to intelligible elements, Forms or Ideas which are themselves eternal or immobile. Of course, these forms will be grasped as close as possible to their actualisation in a matter-flux. But movement is only ever a secondary phenomenon, the regulated transition from one form to another, 'an order of *poses* or privileged instants' (ibid. p. 4). The modern scientific revolution, however, has above all consisted 'in relating movement not to privileged instants, but to any-instant-whatever'. Movement is thus '*no longer recomposed from formal transcendental elements*' but '*from immanent material elements*' (ibid.). We understand movement in itself, as force or the play of forces. Cinema is the art form commensurate with and expressive of that conception of movement. In cartoons, for example, the drawing

no longer constitutes a pose or a completed figure, but the description of a figure which is always in the process of being formed or dissolving through the movement of lines and points taken at any-instant-whatever of their course . . . It does not give us a figure described in a unique moment, but the continuity of the movement which describes the figures. (ibid.)

Paradoxically, forms are what we see and yet never quite see. Force is what we cannot see in itself and yet can be apprehended everywhere as preventing cinema from ever coming to rest in or hardening into mere forms. Force in cinema is thus that 'power of transformation, the Dionysian power' which for Nietzsche, says Deleuze, 'is the primary definition of activity' (Deleuze 1983, p. 42).

Deleuze himself provides a rich array of analyses of relevant films in his two volumes on cinema. It might therefore be more useful to ask how his account of cinema can also be applied to other kinds of narrative. What for example of the novel? In fact, Deleuze and Guattari say that the novel's true element, too, is 'the perpetual living present', Bergsonian duration (Deleuze and Guattari 1988, p. 192). The Anglo-American novel in particular – Lawrence, Melville, Henry Miller – constantly appeals against invariant structures. Like Kafka, such novelists 'tie' their writing 'to real and unheard-of becomings' (ibid. p. 243). In considering their work, we must thus resort to a model 'that is perpetually in construction or collapsing' (ibid. p. 20), that will operate in terms not of centred forms but of a form that is continually transformed, as material constantly acted upon by forces. Form thus becomes a minimal principle or principle of the surface. Deleuze and Guattari's readings of *The Crack-Up* and, above all, James's 'In the Cage' in *A Thousand Plateaus* are effective examples of how this kind of thought might operate with respect to narrative. The analysis of 'In the Cage' – elaborated and to some extent adapted here – proceeds on the basis of a distinction between 'segmentarity' and 'lines of force' in narrative texts. Segmentarity is geometric and totalising. It overcodes everything, 'assures the dominion of the great signifying break everywhere' (ibid. p. 200). To see 'lines of force', on the other hand, is to see a whole micro-segmentarity, details, possibilities, tiny movements that cannot be overcoded at all. The second runs under the first: rigid and large segmentations are crosscut underneath by small, intense, varied, subtle, molecular movements of force. In fact, the relations between 'lines of force' and segmentarity is the relation between becoming and all determinations:

What is real is the becoming itself, not the supposedly fixed terms through which that which becomes passes. Becoming has no term, no subject distinct from itself . . . It runs its own line 'between' the terms in play and beneath assignable relations. (ibid. p. 238)

To think segmentarity is to produce 'a homogenous and isotopic space', to constitute 'fixed or ideal essences', to collude in the 'damage' done by 'geometrical justice' (ibid. pp. 202, 210, 212). To think segmentarity and 'lines of force' together, on the other hand, is to refuse to find a logical order in a world of transformations and symbioses. It is to produce altogether more supple 'morphological formations' as registering force and form at once. This is precisely what Deleuze and Guattari do with 'In the Cage'. They see the dividing principle of segmentarity and 'lines of force' as constantly interfering with each other. The telegrapher heroine leads a clear-cut, calculated life 'in framed and wired confinement', doling out 'stamps and postal orders', 'fenced out or fenced in, according to the side of the narrow counter on which the human lot was cast' (James 1936, p. 367). Her fiancé Mudge is constantly plotting out their lives with his 'famous "plans"' (ibid. p. 456). 'Here', write Deleuze and Guattari, 'there is a line of rigid segmentarity' on which everything – all identities – seem calculable and foreseen (Deleuze and Guattari 1988, p. 195). It appears likewise in the clear and firm economic and class divisions between characters of which the story makes so much. The heroine's pride in her own powers of interpretation is part of this principle of segmentarity. But there is also a quite different aspect to her make-up at odds with that principle: her 'flickers of antipathy and sympathy . . . fitful needs to notice and to "care," odd caprices of curiosity', the 'flashes' of thought and feeling, 'the quick revivals, absolute accidents all' (James 1936, pp. 371, 373); and so on. Then the rich couple intrude into the heroine's world and reveal the existe·ce of another life, of 'coded multiple telegrams signed with pseudonyms'. Instead of a 'rigid line of well-determined segments', telegraphy itself now forms 'a supple flow' (Deleuze and Guattari 1988, p. 195) or what James calls a 'world of whiffs and glimpses' (James 1936, p. 386). This world is marked by a play of forces 'that are like so many little segmentations-in-progress grasped at the moment of their birth' (Deleuze and Guattari 1988, p. 195). Eventually, the young woman develops a 'strange passionate complicity' with Everard (ibid. p. 196), experiencing 'impulses of various kinds . . . which were determined by the smallest accidents' (James 1936, p. 388). Thus a very different type of relation enters the story – not a segmented one, as in the case of the young woman and her fiancé, but an altogether less localised, more fluctuating one. This new relation is characterised by '*a line of molecular or supple segmentation*' (Deleuze and Guattari 1988, p. 196), as exemplified in the heroine's deepening sense of being virtually merged with Everard:

She was literally afraid of the alternate self who might be waiting outside. *He* might be waiting; it was he who was her alternate self, and of him she was afraid. (James 1936, p. 469)

The principle of segmentarity and the line of molecular force constantly break in and act and react upon each other (as the first intrudes on the second again with the return to the world of Mudge in Chapter XVIII). The divisions of a fixed segmentarity are constantly run through and swept up by force operating as '*micromovements*', fine differences distributed in an entirely different way, 'unfindable particles of an anonymous matter, tiny cracks and postures operating by different agencies' (Deleuze and Guattari 1988, pp. 196–7). Finally, however, the telegraphist and the telegraph sender are 'propelled toward a rigid segmentarity', he marrying Lady Bradeen, she marrying her fiancé. Nonetheless, says Deleuze, everything has changed. The two colliding principles have produced a new line, a 'line of flight' which no longer tolerates segments and explodes both principles together. The telegrapher ends up losing all faith in interpretation, in clarity, in the self, and becomes like everyone else: 'but this, precisely, is a becoming only for one who knows how to be nobody, no longer be anybody' (ibid. p. 197). Thus 'In the Cage' is constructed 'from fragment to fragment' as 'a living experiment', one in which, in the end, 'there is no longer perception or knowledge, secret or divination' (Deleuze and Parnet 1987, pp. 48–9).

Yet, in fact, Deleuze and Guattari's account of 'In the Cage' proceeds only within certain fixed horizons. It partly relies on the very 'characterising' procedures presented elsewhere as effecting a kind of rigid closure of the text. The problem seems to be connected with the very opposition Deleuze and Guattari establish between 'segmentarity' and 'lines of force'. But it has even more to do with the use of that distinction in conjunction with an unproblematically and homogeneously representational reading of James's story. For the distinction between 'segmentarity' and 'lines of force' is largely identified with a distinction between characters, relationships between characters, even themes. The metaphysics Deleuze and Guattari seek to escape in their reading of James's story insidiously reappears in their reliance on an established hermeneutics. This latter still works in terms of clear divisions between subjectivities, substances, essences. We might briefly attempt a rather different application of Deleuze and Guattari's terms, then, with reference to a different text: Lawrence's *Women in Love*.

Lawrence, of course, was abundantly clear about his interest in 'that which is physic – non-human, in humanity', in 'the inhuman will' and the 'physiology of matter', in people as 'phenomena' rather than in their feelings 'according to the human conception' (Lawrence 1967, pp. 17–18). 'Morality and the Novel' argues that it is specifically the interinvolvement, the 'subtle inter-relatedness' of man and the 'circumambient universe' at 'the living moment' that the novel should attend to. The proper concern of the novel is the 'trembling instability of the *balance*' of that relation (ibid. p. 108). But this concern also involves a fidelity to the principle of constant variation. Other discourses, says Lawrence – philosophical, religious – always nail that principle down to a stability, to 'thought-forms that have no sensual reality' (ibid. p. 162). The novel's virtue is that it does not nail anything down. The novel, then, remains true to force, resistant to form – or rather, resistant to form as final description. Hence Lawrence's plea for more 'looseness' and 'apparent formlessness', his asser-tion that definite form is mechanical (ibid. p. 289). For the novel must above all remain close to man's existence as a 'passional phenomenon' (ibid. p. 284). It must also stay true, however, to the fact that man is never really a chooser or decider, never really master. Man is always mastered by something else, by what Deleuze would call an outside that is also an inside, by physics, matter in all its interminable variations – by the endless play of force.

It is not hard to show that *Women in Love* presents the idea of mastery as a snare and an illusion, as with the ironies attendant on Gudrun's attitude to Gerald's mastery. The novel clearly grants the more fortunate fate to those more willing to be mastered (Birkin and Ursula), to accept the sway of forces both within and without that they cannot control. People in the novel are offered to us in terms of such forces, either immediately and directly, as when Birkin refers to the Japanese as possessed of 'a curious sort of fluid force' (Lawrence 1970, p. 303); or by means of metaphor (as when Gerald is referred to as having 'the power of lightning in his nerves' (ibid. p. 272)) or through dramatic situation (Gerald's tussle with the rabbit, for example, is defined as one of force with force). So too with all the various attempts to connect characters up to animals, communicating a suggestion of weird, inhuman, physiological or animal energy. But force also manifests itself in a very different way, too, as for example in the case of Ursula's state of mind at the beginning of Chapter 19, 'Moony', after Birkin has gone to France:

> There was nothing for it now, but contemptuous, resistant indifference. All the world was lapsing into a grey wish-wash of nothingness, she had no contact and no connexion anywhere. She despised and detested the whole show. . . . She could be very pleasant and flattering, almost subservient, to people she met. But no one was taken in. Instinctively each felt her contemptuous mockery of the human being in himself, or herself. She had a profound grudge against the human being. That which the word 'human' stood for was despicable and repugnant to her. (ibid. p. 275)

Moments like this are common in Lawrence's work. There is a marked disparity between the grandiosity and apparent finality of the character's thoughts and their tenuous purchase, their actual transiency. In Lawrence, the power, even the dogmatism with which a given concept is asserted will be directly proportional to its eventual lack of weight and conviction in the novel as a whole. Ursula will very soon think very differently. Ideas or attitudes are grasped as sheer violence of feeling. Yet Lawrence does not treat this as material for irony. Rather, in Lyotard's terms, thought is itself understood as libidinal. What counts is its intensity (Lyotard 1974, p. 37). By the same token, character is grasped as a succession of 'allotropic states' (Lawrence 1967, p. 18), as caught up in a play of forces. Character is always not just influenced by but in composition with its surroundings – always protean, but also always hybrid, always becoming, in the sense in which Deleuze and Guattari write of 'becomings-animal', for instance

(Deleuze and Guattari 1988, p. 236). Hence all those images of interpenetration of which *Women in Love* is full, and which are almost never literal or sexual.

Lawrence, then, can clearly be aligned with Deleuzean theory insofar as he refuses to think of characters in terms of characteristics. In this respect, *Women in Love* is an act of determined resistance to 'completeness' and 'finality' as they are so often anathematised by its author. It would be tempting to say, in Deleuze and Guattari's terms, that here precisely 'an energetic materiality' overspills prepared moulds, 'and a qualitative deformation or transformation overspills . . . form' (Deleuze and Guattari 1988, p. 114). But I have hardly shown that. Yet Lawrence does in fact construct scenes, chapters, narrative itself on principles that are very much the same as those we just saw governing the construction of Ursula's responses at the beginning of Chapter 19. They are principles of conscious incompletion, in which different forces are always in play. Thus we sense force both as an element in Ursula's self-expression and something, at the same time, that is drawing her on beyond the self expressed there, with all of Lawrence's urgent, Deleuzean drive towards the new rather than the old, the future rather than the past. In the separate chapters or scenes in *Women in Love*, this 'subtle inter-relatedness' of forces is present precisely as movement and counter-movement. On the one hand, there *is* a kind of segmentarity to it: the novel is composed of clear, episodic sections focussing on specific set scenes given over to a particular concern or mood. At the same time, the apparent homogeneity of those scenes is continually being disrupted, thrown 'out of true' by elements which run counter to it, lines of force that pull in a different direction. In the climax to Chapter 23, 'Excurse', Lawrence appears to provide us with the apotheosis of Birkin and Ursula's love for each other. Yet, even here, he adds that 'something was tight and unfree in [Birkin]. He did not like . . . this radiance – not altogether' (Lawrence 1970, p. 353). Such cross-currents appear again and again in *Women in Love*. Within the neatly segmented, set scene there is always a measure of instability. We glimpse the limits, above, of any attempt to read *Women in Love* or its separate chapters in what Deleuze and Guattari criticise as 'hylomorphic terms', terms which see form as fixed or fixing and matter as homogeneous, and assert the controlling primacy of the former over the latter. According to Deleuze and Guattari, such terms must be supplemented 'by an entire energetic materiality in movement' (Deleuze and Guattari 1988, p. 408). It is possible to suggest that, in *Women in Love*, 'molecular particles' – textual, thematic, emotional – are continually moving off or migrating in new directions. Thus for example in Chapter 24, 'Death and Love', where Gerald and Gudrun spend the night together. Gudrun responds intensely to Gerald's 'extreme beauty and mystic attractiveness', also experiences 'overwhelming tenderness' for him and 'jealous hatred' for him in his sleep. At the same time, she worries about the dirty footprints he may have left on the carpet. She, we, the scene are pulled in a number of different directions, a fact reflected in abrupt shifts between different styles. There are forces pulling us back into the past of Gudrun and Gerald's relationship, for instance, and forces pulling us forwards towards its future, particles 'migrating' both ways. Indeed, there is a constant 'migration of particles' throughout the novel, witness in particular the extent to which there are allusions to earlier scenes in later ones. Thus for example in Chapter 20, 'Gladiatorial', when we are told that Gerald's eyes 'flashed with a sort of terror like the eyes of a stallion, that are bloodshot and overwrought, turned glancing backwards in a stiff terror' (Lawrence 1970, p. 302), there is of course a reference back to Gerald's struggle with the terrified horse in Chapter 9, 'Coal-Dust'. A host of such connections are established, if fleetingly, in the novel. But to interpret them as a kind of structural grid (as in the idea of 'image patterns') is precisely to mistake their power. What happens with such 'allusions' is that a given complex of emotions or what Deleuze would call 'intensities' migrates from one area of the novel to another, colouring or adding to the second, entering into some kind of link or composition with it, supplementing its play of forces. As it does so, lines of force transpose textual elements, traverse the divisions established by segmentarity, and make them indefinite. Form – again – becomes merely a provisional container to be exploded repeatedly by force. Force is made most perceptible precisely in its deformations of form.

Lyotardian Energetics

It is Lyotard more than anyone else who has given us the most fully elaborated sense of the place of force in postmodern aesthetics as – in Vattimo's terms – a 'destructuring' and 'de-forming' power. In particular, in *Discours, Figure, Des Dispositifs Pulsionnels* and *Économie Libidinale*, Lyotard developed a powerful critique of structuralism, still applicable in many respects to current narratology, in the name of the pulsive, of energy, libidinal economy, and of the Nietzschean valuation of intensity. For Lyotard, the liberation of forces is both an aesthetic and a political project:

> Le temps vient de ne pas s'en tenir à noter la capture et l'effacement des flux libidinaux dans un ordre dont la représentation et ses cloisons jointives-disjonctives sont, seraient le dernier mot, car cette capture et cet effacement sont le capitalisme, mais le temps vient de servir et d'encourager leur divagation errant sur toutes les surfaces . . . (Lyotard 1980, pp. 9–10)

Yet the issue is not reducible to a simple either/or, either form or force. For Lyotard, structuralism crucially neglects the coexistence of 'mobilisation' and 'immobilisation', force and form in art, in texts, as contrasted to thought (Lyotard 1991, pp. 169–80). Structuralism (and narratology) deal in the clear and distinct, therefore the opposable (Lyotard 1974, pp. 288–9). They stabilise intensities into configurations in the name of understanding (ibid. p. 37):

> Le désir de toute 'science', y compris la linguistique ou la sémiotique, a pour *objet* la régulation des déplacements, la loi: donc l'exclusion des intensités libidinales dans son objet, et donc aussi, dans son discours. (Lyotard 1980, p. 131)

But Lyotard calls in question that most fundamental principle of the structuralist project, the desire to penetrate the secret identity of the object: 'understanding', he writes, 'being intelligent', is not his predominant passion. He asks rather to be set in motion ('*mis en mouvement*' (Lyotard 1974, p. 66)). Deconstruction, however, will no more help us to possess intensities than structuralism does. For it is only the negative of a negative, and therefore remains in the same space (ibid. p. 305). The point is not so much to deconstruct established geometries as to recognise the workings within and across them of what they alternately seek to represent and to hold at bay. This means noting a mobility which structuralism omits, and which transgresses geometrical spacings (Lyotard 1971, p. 53). Force is one name for this repressed other of geometry.

In marked contrast to Brooks, as Geoffrey Bennington points out, Lyotard stresses the distinction in Freud's work between two kinds of force or desire: desire-wish, Brooks's sole concern, which implies a teleology, a goal, a dynamics with an end; and desire-libido, desire-process, primary process (Bennington 1988, p. 15). On one level, the limitation to Freud's conception of force (and to Brooks's) is its confusion of 'dispositifs libidinaux' with structural formations (Lyotard 1974, p. 36). But on another level, for Freud, desire is both a principle of unification and a principle of dispersion (Lyotard 1980, p. 75). It both struggles with form and accounts for its constitution. Form is a particular dispositif among others, a particular modification of the primary process. There can never simply be an art of the primary process and its pure displacement of energy. Art is always and irremediably situated in the secondary sphere. Equally, we will never be able simply to think intensities, will always be inclined to flee them for system and its binarism (Lyotard 1974, p. 42). In any case, to conceive of libidinal economy as constituting a kind of free territory outside and in opposition to systems would only be to open it up as a fresh domain for exploration and conquest. But it is nonetheless possible to discover the effects of the primary process on the secondary sphere in at least certain kinds of art (Bennington 1988, p. 23). One such effect is constituted in the eruption of the figural into the discursive. For Lyotard, the figural is what is repressed by the order of language, of discourse, and by the metaphysics that is accomplished as discourse spreads everywhere. The figural is the visible in its density as the sensible, as jouissance, force (Lyotard 1971, p. 14). It is what energetics realises as expression and affect, as contrasted with rationality, signification and all forms of 'geometric organisation' (ibid. p. 20). Its manifestations are various. One of Lyotard's most important examples is Cézanne's immobility for hours in front of le Mont Sainte-Victoire. That immobility involves a suspension of known or familiar forms (Lyotard 1980, pp. 82–3). Its eventual consequence is that not only

colours and values but the very homogeneity of space itself begins
to shift (Lyotard 1971, p. 159). The 'Euclidean prejudice' gives
way (ibid.). In Cézanne's paintings, such an awareness manifests
itself in a suspension or loss of unity:

le peintre, au lieu de répondre à la question: à quelle loi unitaire obéit la
production de l'objet pictural? parait hésiter et maintenir en suspens sa
réponse. De fait le tableau répond: *il n'y a pas* de telle loi unitaire; la question
de l'unité sensible reste ouverte, ou cette unité est manquée. (Lyotard 1980, p.
74)

This shifting of space and loss of visible unity are events that
phenomenological description can only jettison in its constructions of coherent form. Such events take place as the irruption of
the figural as force into the structures and oppositional organisations of form. So, too, in poetic language, when a sentence breaks
rules but does not thereby become senseless, an energy is effectively disrupting a formal system and cannot be accounted for by
any scientific mode of description of the system, e.g. structuralism. Indeed, structuralism can only repress such force. Lyotard
(rather feebly) cites as an example a phrase from a poem by
Pichette, '*je te musique*'. This, he says, constitutes a '*figure*'. It
produces the effect of a discharge which comes from another
order to that of language itself. The figure gives itself out as a kind
of wandering trace which defies reading and can only be grasped
in the terms of an energetics (Lyotard 1971, pp. 144–6). So too
with Mallarmé's 'displacement' of prose punctuation. Here, again,
the figural is at work, not least in its restoration of pure visibility
into the domain of the legible (ibid. pp. 215–17). In the case of
Mallarmé, for instance, or concrete poetry, the figural obliges
thought to abandon its own element, the world of language as a
galaxy of signifiers, as signification. We experience again the
actual opacity of the thing seen (ibid. p. 218). The figural, then, is
an energetic and trangressive force which violates the rules of
discourse, refuses to respect the laws of its invariants and its
spacings, and cannot be accommodated within any account of
pure forms. It is the Dionysian activity which disrupts the
negative totality of Apollonian 'good form', '*en tant qu'énergétique indifférente à l'unité de l'ensemble*' (Lyotard 1971, p. 277). It

works against any poetics of reconciliation, harmony and balance. It traverses form without destroying the latter, acts as the threatening movement of desire which denounces what is taken to be form, and opens form to its other. Above all, it defies the aesthetician as geometrist, the person who, 'anguished by difference', has discovered how to bring order into the domain of sensibility by establishing constant intervals that are seemingly capable of reducing opacities, distortions, variations, '*surimpressions*', '*arythmies*' (ibid. p. 222). Into the 'luminous organisation' of the discursive, the figural infiltrates the most 'redoubtable disorder' (ibid. p. 223). The result has what Lyotard calls the critical and ironical force of a deformation (ibid. p. 225).

In *Des Dispositifs Pulsionnels*, Lyotard does actually write of narrative discourse as intimately inhabited by the figural. Narrative discourse itself, he announces, is a '*dispositif libidinal*' or '*figure-dispositif*' (Lyotard 1980, p. 134). The assertion briefly involves him in a difference with Genette. Lyotard takes issue with Genette's hierarchical structuring of the relation between *discours* and *récit*, which leaves *discours* looking natural and universal, and turns *récit* into a particular mode of *discours*. From the point of view of a libidinal economy, says Lyotard, no such distinction is possible (ibid. p. 135). *Discours* is as marked as *récit* by specific affects. In other ways, however, this particular essay of Lyotard's is rather disappointing. Force, here, is imagined as captured, conserved, even pacified in and by discourse (ibid. p. 132). The '*dispositifs*' identified by Lyotardian energetics are merely thought of as '*l'organisation de branchement, canalisant, régulant l'arrivée et la dépense d'énergie*' (ibid. p. 133). Lyotard scarcely mentions narrative as a place in which the figural can manifest itself as a transgressive force. Unlike Deleuze's energetics, too, Lyotard's leaves little or no place for force as operating at the level of representation. For the figural is partly to be thought of as the intrusion of the visible or sensible in its actual thickness into an art or a discourse that purports to represent the sensible. This might seem to suggest that the emergence of the figural into narrative is easily identified but infrequent. The typographical play in *Tristram Shandy* and *Ulysses* immediately springs to mind. But where else is there to look, beyond such obvious examples?

To begin with, for Lyotard, the traces of the figural in writing are not chiefly represented in a self-reflexive attentiveness to the materiality of the text or the visibility of the signifier. Lyotard's point about the Pichette that he quotes is that there is a kind of 'denaturation' of the discursive system itself and its formal structure of oppositions. The system is not maintained in place as a virtuality behind the strange usage, conveying the sense of '*je te berce*' or '*je te charme*' latent in the phrase '*je te musique*'. The linguistic 'aberration' does not stand in a vertical relation to a set of alternatives. It does not belong to the system itself and is not subject to the rules of the system. It is not 'coded' at all. Therefore its presence '*témoigne qu'il y a en sous-sol, non pas un système, mais des forces, une énergétique qui bouscule l'ordonnancement du système*' (Lyotard 1971, p. 145). Once we are aware of this aspect of Lyotard's conception of the figural, it is surely not hard to find other instances of the latter in narrative discourse. Henry Green's novels, for instance, are marked by something like an obsession with figural transgressions of the discursive order.[13] The capitalised sounds in *Living* ('OOEEE', 'Da da DID DEE') are obvious examples (Green 1978, pp. 224–5). So too are the (irregular) uses of numbers for notations of time ('It wants a $\frac{1}{4}$ to 4, Bert' (ibid. p. 212)). Similarly, the irregular paragraphing so often evident in *Living* draws our attention to material space as part of the text. The irregular spacing of the relations between narrative and dialogue makes us aware of and transgresses conventions of 'lay out' as part of a discursive system. The spacing therefore also recalls us to the sensible aspect both of the text and of our own physical relation to it. The intermittent dropping of grammatically necessary words, however – as with 'said' in 'Mr Gates asked Mr Craigan if he had ever taken rhubarb wine and that it was very strong' (ibid. p. 218) – is a more striking and complex case. It too alerts us to space – but a space that is no more there in the text than is the word that has been 'omitted'. Such a space exists only in the abstract geometry of the linguistic system and not in the text as concrete fact, and is therefore a space that is violated, here, by the textual figure.

But the transgressive force of the figural in *Living* is still more remarkable in the irregular omissions of definite and indefinite articles and personal pronouns. The very irregularity of this feature of the discourse leaves it unavailable to any consistent recuperation (as sociolectal, as stylistic 'constant', etc.). It cannot be thought of as part of or in relation to any system of the text's. It emerges as a kind of discursive turbulence whose recurrences are unpredictable and whose opacity asks only to be noticed, perceived. What we have here, precisely, is deconstruction in the specific and more positive sense given to it by the Lyotard of *Discours, Figure* – deconstruction of the discursive by the figural – at work within a narrative text:

Le lisible n'est jamais répudié. Paradoxale du figural venant se faire héberger par le texte sans le détruire. Nous disons qu'il le déconstruit. (Lyotard 1971, p. 307)

Similar recurrent if irregular aberrations run through *Living*. But there are other aberrations that are even less rule-bound. The more we examine Green's novel, in fact, the more likely we are to recognise a deconstructive practice that is not only pervasive but various and complex. Take for instance the description of Lily Gates's and Jim Dale's kiss:

Boys at school had been singing outside schoolroom on screen, had been singing at stars, and these two heard them and kissed in boskage deep low in this lane and band played softly, women in audience crooning. (Green 1978, pp. 216)

The word 'boskage' partly functions like the word '*musique*' in Pichette's poem. But it is not only a deviation from discursive norms. It also transgresses the modes of the irregular play with discursive norms in Green's novel as we have just noted it. This further introduces what Lyotard calls an 'illegal mobility' into the discursive order (Lyotard 1971, p. 290). It testifies to the deconstructive activity of figure in this instance as '*la continuité indisciplinée des jeux*' associated with the primary process in relation to '*l'espace discontinu et hiérarchisé du discours*' (ibid. p. 311). It reminds us that discourse is not simply generated by or in response to an exterior space, but is also the product of an unconscious matrix whose effects cannot be coded. Like other, similar features in *Living*, such a transgression cannot be placed as part of the novel's dominant modes of aberration. It is an aberration from them. It therefore refuses to allow us to systematise the aberrations themselves and thus establish a kind of collusion between discourse and figure. It sustains and emphasises the gap between the two, maintains the trangressive and irreducible opacity of the figure against all attempts to 'illuminate' the latter. The discursive features of *Living* are thus distributed arhythmically. It is possible to identify recurrences, but not any patterns into which such features fall. As Lyotard says of Gerard Manley Hopkins's 'Pied Beauty', the displacements act as though discursive space were not constructed as a system of invariants and gaps at all (Lyotard 1971, p. 316). They vary continually in their intensity. Those features of the text which continue to ensure its readability also ensure a certain form and order. But that form and order is constantly being traversed by forces which we know as such precisely because they cannot be given shape or construed as something else. The corollary of this is that, in *Living*, to adapt a fine phrase of Lyotard's, form takes on the guise of '*[une] combinaison fortuite parmi d'autres possibles*' (ibid. p. 70).

Perhaps the greatest power of Lyotardian energetics, in this context, is that it helps us to attempt to think force in narrative in terms of the sensible. As we saw earlier, Heidegger suggests that, with Nietzsche, truth as supersensuousness becomes falsehood, and art becomes crucial because the sensuous is the very stuff of art. It may be that the very element of art is the unresolved or (in Lawrence's terms) the incomplete. It may equally be that art is where we go to see ideas break down and lose their grip on the world, as with Ursula's misanthropy in 'Moony'. Yet neither point is the same as identifying art with the sensuous principle, and it is hard to see how Nietzsche's assertion can really be sustained. If it has much weight at all, it is surely through Lyotard's concept of the force of the figural and its workings within discourse and representation. Lyotard's aesthetics of force, then, is perhaps the closest we can really come to a Nietzschean physiological aesthetics which truly takes the material and corporeal as its starting point.

But Nietzsche also conceived of the aesthetic experience as an overflowing of limits, and the idea of the figural bears some relation to this. For in Lyotard's terms, the irruption of figure into discourse takes place precisely as such an 'overflowing'. The irruption of figure manifests itself as excess – specifically, an excess of force within form. It appears as a peculiarly vivid instance of those 'surprises of non-simultaneity' that, according to Derrida, any text holds in wait for us. In general, the thought of force and form together is always a thought of the non-simultaneity of the text. To think of narrative and its movement in terms of force, then, is to conceive of it as a constant folding into and unfolding out of form. Above all, to think form and force together is to begin to work free from an aesthetics that, in privileging form in the way it did, also continually reaffirmed a metaphysics and a transcendental principle, and insistently gave priority to the thought of being over that of becoming. Here, at last, in a turn towards more subtle and supple morphological formations, we also start to move towards a thought of the work as composed of immanent material elements. In doing so – and in recognising how far a given form may be described in differential or heterogeneous terms – we conceive of narrative as activating those impulses 'recalcitrant to unification and coordination' of which Nietzsche and Vattimo speak. It is here that postmodernity may find a place where, as Vattimo suggests, the pulsive mechanisms of art destabilise the subject as constructed by certain modes and strategies of power. It is here precisely that the thought of force becomes a radical hermeneutics.

NOTES

1. To emphasise Nietzsche's notion of 'physiology' in a postmodern context is itself a relatively new departure. See Koelb 1990, pp. 1–18, p. 14.

2. This of course is very much the Deleuzean view of Nietzsche and textuality. See Deleuze 1977.

3. David Farrell Krell suggests that Heidegger's critique of Nietzsche in these respects has to be understood in the context of his growing opposition to German National Socialism in the years in which he was producing his lectures on Nietzsche, 1936–40. See his introduction to Heidegger 1991, p. xx.

4. For a corroborative account of Heidegger's view of Nietzsche's philosophy in general as crucially prefiguring 'the rise of what [Heidegger] calls the modern "technological" experience of the world', see Havas 1992, pp. 231–46, esp. pp. 237–40. Heidegger's view was shared by Kenneth Burke. See Burke 1954, p. 46.

5. 'Force' for Nietzsche is never a unified or homogenous entity, always '*play* of forces'. Claudia Crawford has put the point well with regard to

Nietzsche's model of physiology. See her 'Nietzsche's Physiology of Ideological Criticism', in Koelb 1990, pp. 161–86.

6. Cathryn Vasseleu equates the *vita femina* with the metaphor of the sea in Nietzsche's work, arguing that Nietzsche's masculine 'affirmative being' is dependent on and carried by both, though Nietzsche 'ultimately' strives to forget it. See her 'Not Drowning, Sailing: Women and the Artist's Craft in Nietzsche', in Patton 1993, pp. 71–87; p. 85. The problem for me lies with Vasseleu's 'ultimately'. As the metaphor of 'overflowing' in the passage from which I quote suggests, Nietzsche saw masculine 'affirmative being' as both defining itself against the *vita femina* and as overwhelmed by or included within the latter. The paradoxical relationship between form and force established in *The Will to Power* is also one between masculine and feminine principles. Frances Oppel gets closer to the paradox I am stressing. See '"Speaking of Immemorial Waters": Irigaray with Nietzsche', in Patton 1993, pp. 88–109, pp. 106–7.

7. Brooks is well aware of and writes interestingly about the conception of force in Freud, referring us to the latter's 'physicalist-energetic' ideas and – with the help of Ernest Jones – the influence of Ernst Brücke on Freud. See Brooks 1984, pp. 41–2. See also Jones 1953, Vol. 1, p. 41.

8. Brooks is quoting from *Beyond the Pleasure Principle*. See Freud 1953–74, Vol. 18, p. 50.

9. There are of course more challenging readings of *Beyond the Pleasure Principle* that are much more inclined to problematise Freud's text than Brooks's is. See for instance Derrida's 'To Speculate – On "Freud"', in Derrida 1987c, pp. 259–409; and Connor 1992, pp. 61–71.

10. The manoeuvre described here has actually been peculiarly widespread in English criticism. Obvious examples of 'the revisionist reflex' are David Lodge's work in the late seventies and the eighties (*Working with Structuralism, The Modes of Modern Writing*) and Frank Kermode's most important work, from *The Sense of an Ending* to *Essays in Fiction 1971–82*. A particularly recent example would be Cunningham 1994. For Terry Eagleton, too, theory has always been something to negotiate with along the way and then 'bring back round' to some sort of relation to foundational truths. The truths may be Marxist, but the refusal to risk them – and the assurance and power made possible by that refusal – are those of the English moralist. See for instance Eagleton 1990. Christopher Norris's virulent polemics against postmodernism would be another case in point. See for example Norris 1992b. It has taken a different generation to start thinking within the terms of theory and to shake off a reflex – *sauter pour mieux reculer* – that has been so depressingly common in English intellectual life over the past few decades.

11. The phrase is Michael Hardt's, and applied to Kant. See Hardt 1993, p. 116.

12. For a clear sense of exactly what is meant by 'multiplicity', here, and for some of the sources of the idea, see Deleuze and Guattari, 1988.
13. The distinctiveness of the narrative idioms in Green's novels – and the extent to which they rely on linguistic 'deformations' – are evident enough. For one account of both features, see Gibson 1990, pp. 118–39.

$$=== \quad 2 \quad ===$$

Deconstructing Representation: Narrative as Inauguration

THE MIMETIC FIX

The single most important achievement of narratology over the past two decades has been the change wrought in our views of narration as representation. The progress of narratology was inseparable from a developing critique of representational theory and practice in literature and criticism. With roots in Russian formalism, Saussurean linguistics, structuralism and semiotics, narratology was well equipped to insist on the gap between narrative and world. What mattered was to break with the referential illusion, to analyse narratives as sets of signifying practices, to explore and describe them in terms of the codes by which they operated. The notion of verisimilitude appeared to be mere acquiescence, in Culler's terms, in a 'naturalisation' of contingent and conventional modes of discourse (Culler 1975, pp. 134–60). Barthes's sceptical and irreverent account of the 'classic realist text' – and his consequent valuation of modernism and self-reflexivity in the avant-garde – were enormously influential (Barthes 1975). Even the more distinguished defenders of realism, like Raymond Williams, seemed trapped in circular arguments, or unwilling to rid themselves of a naive fidelity to unexamined premises. Realism thus became at best a generic description or 'period concept' (Martin 1986, p. 57). Representationalism seemed wedded either to an empiricism that refused to interrogate its own bases, or to an essentialism opened up to question, not only by structuralism but by prior and subsequent thought (Heidegger, Sartre, deconstruction). It is therefore hardly surprising to find

69

Raymond Tallis arguing that the view that 'realism is outmoded and the realistic novel or form has had its day' is a 'critical commonplace' that is widespread at various different levels of contemporary culture (Tallis 1988, p. 1).

Yet Tallis's worries actually seem premature (or passé, or both). The situation is far more complicated and confusing than he suggests. There has been no critical demise of the classic realist text. Representationalism has had its occasional defenders in the past decade, like Tallis and A.D. Nuttall (Nuttall 1983). But it has hardly needed them. Representational assumptions have continued more or less subtly to pervade most work in the fields of literary and cultural studies. It is worth recalling the familiar terms of Barthes's derogation of realism:

What evaluation finds is precisely this value: what can be written (rewritten) today: the *writerly*. Why is the writerly our value? Because the goal of literary work (of literature as work) is to make the reader no longer a consumer, but a producer of the text . . . Opposite the writerly text, then, is its countervalue, its negative, reactive value: what can be read, but not written: the readerly. We call any *readerly* text a classic text. (Barthes 1975, p. 4)

The writerly text was '*ourselves writing*', before 'the infinite play of the world' was stopped by some 'singular system' (ibid. p. 5). By contrast, readerly texts – the 'enormous mass' of our narratives – were 'products (and not productions)' (ibid.). Barthes not only gave value to the *scriptible* as opposed to the *lisible*. He clearly saw the latter as no longer producible. The *lisible* was simply 'obsolescent' (ibid. p. 95). Correspondingly, in Barthes, there glimmered the dream of a utopia of the *scriptible*, in which 'the wall of utterance, the wall of origin, the wall of ownership' were all decisively 'breached' (ibid. p. 45). But what Barthes called 'the kerygmatic civilisation' (ibid. p. 76) did not founder. The hold of the *lisible* proved to be tenacious. There has in fact been, if not a devaluation of the *scriptible*, at least a displacement of its centrality within postmodern projects and descriptions of postmodern culture, as in Thomas Pavel's new 'referential theory of fiction' (Pavel 1986, p. 10), or feminist and postcolonial valuations of representation. Steven Connor notes that Ihab Hassan's and Brian McHale's association of postmodernism with self-reflexivity is ceding to Linda Hutcheon's view of 'the most characteristic form

of postmodernist literature' as 'historiographic metafiction', with
all the gains for a representational aesthetic that that might
involve (Connor 1990, p. 127).[1] Frederic Jameson, too, has shifted
theory of the *nouveau roman* in a similar direction, away from
Robbe-Grillet, Ricardou and 'textualist' ideology to Claude Simon,
with his 'new equipment for registering the raw material of
everyday life', his comparative 'realism' (Jameson 1991, pp. 140,
145, 153). Like others, Jameson has also stressed pastiche,
Lefebvre's 'increasing primacy of the "neo"', as the most distinctive mode of postmodern culture.[2] Representation thus reappears
in a double figure, in the imitation of imitation, the simulation of
imitative form. Since the seventies, then, postmodern culture has
grown less wary of representationalism. If 'the real is no longer
what it used to be', as Baudrillard suggests, nostalgia has also
come into play:

> There is a proliferation of myths of origin and signs of reality; of second-hand
> truth, objectivity and authenticity. There is an escalation of the true, of the
> lived experience; a resurrection of the figurative where the object and
> substance have disappeared. And there is a panic-stricken production of the
> real and the referential . . . This is how simulation appears in the phase that
> concerns us: a strategy of the real, neo-real and hyperreal . . . (Baudrillard
> 1990, pp. 166–85)

This 'resurrection of the figurative' has emerged as a dominant
feature of immediately contemporary culture. In Vattimo's terms,
here as elsewhere, postmodernity demonstrates its scepticism
with regard to *Überwindung* or critical overcoming, its refusal to
believe in its own capacity to progress definitively beyond post-
Cartesian modernity (Vattimo 1988, pp. 164, 171). Representation,
mimesis, the *lisible* are not simply to be overcome. Rather, they
are now being reworked, as Vattimo would have it, again, in
weakened form.

Postmodern culture, then, remains deeply wedded to representation, even as it seeks to question and disentangle itself from
representation. Representation and scepticism about representation continually reverse back into each other, reveal themselves as
inseparable. The most straightforwardly representational, popular
film like *Robocop*, *Wayne's World* or *Reservoir Dogs* now contains
its arch, Godardian self-reflexivities. On the other hand, even an

extremely sophisticated theoretical text that is rigorously opposed to totalising thought may nonetheless depend on representation in a manner that runs counter to its theoretical impetus. Defenders of representation lapse involuntarily into scepticism, or turn sceptical arguments to their own advantage, only to have the positions they have borrowed subvert their own defensive project. Sceptics or opponents of representation interrogate representational assumptions on one level, only to reintroduce them or equivalents of them on another. Kathryn Hume can both argue for the 'manifest inadequacy' of 'the idea of representing reality' whilst also maintaining that very idea, at least, in the assertion that 'fiction consists of that simulation that Aristotle called mimesis' (Hume 1984, p. xi, 15). Barthes himself 'de-originates the utterance' only to 're-originate' it, most conspicuously in the banal, collective wisdom of the cultural code (Barthes 1975, p. 21). Or take the questioning of representationalism within film theory, as exemplified in the work of Teresa de Lauretis and Stephen Heath. De Lauretis wishes, for instance, to go beyond the formalist prioritisation of *mise-en-scène* over questions of realism to be found at its best in the work of David Bordwell and Kristin Thompson (Bordwell and Thompson 1990, pp. 44, 128, 138, 152–3, 167). She argues that it is necessary 'to reclaim iconicity, the visual component of meaning' in cinema 'for the ideological', dissociating it from 'the domain of the natural' and 'an immediacy of referential reality' (De Lauretis 1984, p. 45). But the concept of ideology in play, here, immediately reinstates the reality principle it had seemingly just disposed of. It assumes representability all over again and, with it, what Thomas Docherty calls 'the identity of the subject *vis-à-vis* a particular historical situation' (Docherty 1990, p. 211). Representability and the reality principle are actually intrinsic to 'demystification'. What ideological critic does not tell us that representation is ideological only to reassume the reality principle in ideology itself?

So if we are all given up to hermeneutics, now, we have also hardly learnt as yet to free ourselves from an established epistemology. We are caught in an irreducible doubleness: on the one hand, Vattimo's 'oscillation, plurality and, ultimately . . . erosion' of the very 'principle of reality' (Vattimo 1992, p. 7), and, on the other, Baudrillard's 'hysteria of production and reproduction of the real' (Baudrillard 1990, p. 180). The two are interdependent, of course, nowhere more so than in literary studies, where the industries continue to pour out versions of their special objects, whilst the latter grow less and less stable and accessible – less and less real – by virtue of that very fact. *Die Wüste wächst*. Post-modernity, then, seems trapped in insolubly contradictory thought about representation. This has been strikingly the case with recent philosophy concerned with realism (in the philosophical sense of the word).[3] It has been ambiguous and looked uneasy. There have also been some curious attempts to unify incongruous positions. No consensus has emerged as to the existence of a describable reality, let alone the terms in which it might be described. At one end of the spectrum, there is David Papineau's 'naturalised realism', within which there is always the possibility of the 'one true belief' which gets reality right (Papineau 1987, p. 7). In fact, any argument for classical representationalism now has to proceed like Papineau's. For Papineau begins in dogma or by fiat: the simple, unquestioned assertion, for instance, that '[h]uman beings are *normal* inhabitants of the *natural* world' (ibid. p. ix). Papineau's case for representation is actually circular. He gives himself the 'one true belief' even before he sets out to argue for it. At the other end of the spectrum, Feyerabend's scepticism may be more challenging, but is equally fraught with difficulty. For instance: Feyerabend refuses to accept that we know more about the world than Aristotle. But he sustains this view by means of an implicit certainty that Aristotle knew more on specific points than modern scholars or scientists (Feyerabend 1987, p. 160). Here as repeatedly, Feyerabend thus falls back surreptitiously on representationalist certainties at a key point in his radically sceptical and anti-representational arguments.

In the middle ground between extremes, the ironies only proliferate. As part of his case against postmodernism, for example, Christopher Norris opposes both what he takes to be post-modernist 'relativism' and realisms that trade too willingly 'upon notions of inward certainty, privileged access, authentic revelation' (Norris 1992a, p. 303). But Norris's defence of 'realist ontology' has an 'inward certainty' of its own (Norris 1992b, p. 13). For Norris is quite assured as to the modes of thought or inquiry (logic, reason, argument, 'reflexive autocritique', all of them singular) that will provide access to the real, and the intellectual criteria ('consistency, external reference, evidence'), that will guarantee accounts of 'true' reality (Norris 1992a, p. 291). But the assurance is only that of a familiar, masculine, Western and, in large measure, simply English logic, asserted imperially, as valid for all. Roger Trigg argues for a metaphysical realism beyond all questions of knowledge, claiming his case is anti-authoritarian and anti-totalitarian: realism means knowing you're fallible (Trigg 1989, pp. xviii, xxx). But he also has a Piercean faith in ultimate consensus and argues that realists 'should not tolerate the prospect of unending divergence of views of reality' (ibid. p. xix), which presumably means that some group of realists will eventually emerge who are not fallible at all. Putnam tries to escape metaphysical realism whilst preserving commonsense realism, and to defend us against Rorty, Feyerabend, cultural relativism and 'relativism à la française' whilst recognising 'the concept of conceptual relativity' (Putnam 1987, p. 15). The result is a notion of 'internal realism' within which logical fundamentals like object and existence have no determinate meaning. There is no absolute reality of which there can be accurate representations. Reality is never independent of our choice of concepts. However, according to Putnam, once we have made clear our version of reality, the answers to questions about 'objects' and 'existence' are not at all a matter of 'convention' or 'cultural relativism' (ibid. p. 16). But there seems to be little reason why not, save that, for Putnam, to believe it would be disastrous (ibid. pp. 70–3).

Current philosophical arguments about realism, then, seem either to prove what they have assumed from the beginning, or to find themselves trapped in inconsistency or paradox. Rorty's *Philosophy and the Mirror of Nature*, however, is rather different. Rorty wishes to resist the old, established picture of 'epistemology-and-metaphysics' as the 'centre of philosophy' (Rorty 1980, p. 133). He thus both develops a critique of epistemology and seeks to move beyond the assumption that there can be any understanding of the foundations of knowledge. Crucially, this is also a movement beyond a conception of the mind, discourse, philosophy itself as faithful 'mirrors of nature'. Rorty wants us to abandon the notion of knowledge as accurate representation. Yet if truth is only 'what it is better for us to believe' (ibid. p. 10), this does not mean an end to representation. No description of the world has a privileged ('mirroring') relation to reality. But that simply means that the horizons of such descriptions are now determined pragmatically – by social practice, 'the context of general agreement' (ibid. p. 309). Viable representations are those which nobody has been led to question or which a given community is satisfied with. If there is no 'canonical notation' which is wholly adequate to the true and ultimate structure of reality, if correspondence has no ontological preferences, we should still not cancel out reference (ibid. pp. 299–300). 'Objective truth' merely becomes 'no more and no less than the best idea we currently have about how to explain what's going on' (ibid. p. 385). There may be no transcendental standpoint from which we can inspect the relations between our present representations and their objects. But that does not mean that we should push any further with our scepticism about representation. Rather, we should be pragmatically aware of but also settle for the present-ness of our own representations in themselves.

It is therefore not surprising to find Rorty conceding that he conducts his critique of epistemology only by telling stories about history, i.e. by a kind of 'mirroring' that he himself questions. In the end, Rorty's argument is just a more knowing and sophisticated example of the kind of paradox I have described. The state of current philosophy, in this respect, is strikingly relevant to the whole issue of postmodernity, representation and reality. As I have sought to illustrate from one angle, postmodern culture is caught in a double bind. For the present, there seems to be no possibility of 'purity' on either side, representationalist or sceptic, no avoiding contamination or supplementation by the other. This is surely equally the case with literary criticism and narratology. It is worth recalling that, in its most important and interesting manifestations, and before it became institutionalised, narratology – like the structuralism that fed it – was a relativising, critical project. It sought to dissolve any connection between narrative and the representation of 'nature', to make us see narratives as forms of cultural production. The determinations of narrative were conceived of as internal to the system of narrative itself, rather than external to it, in the world it represented. Yet, precisely in its elaboration of a 'system of narrative', narratology relapsed into the very essentialism, representationalism and meta-physics it had sought to resist. This was always evident enough in Propp, Lévi-Strauss, Todorov, Bremond, Greimas and – later – Chatman and Prince, and their attempts to define a 'grammar' or universal model of narrative.[4] But it was equally evident in Barthes's descriptions of the codes underlying the 'classic realist text'. That description cannot finally escape Baudrillardian indict-ment as implying 'a theology of truth and secrecy' to which 'the notion of ideology' still belongs (Baudrillard 1990, p. 170). Narra-tology invariably worked in terms of essences that could be or were representable: the universal essence of human narrativity (Lévi-Strauss), the characteristic nature of bourgeois, narrative mechanism (Barthes). In fact, then, the narratological project never lost a certain complicity with the very kinds of thought it seemed to be opposing. Hence its rapid institutionalisation. Fur-thermore, even whilst it 'emptied out' the narrated world, narra-tology reproduced that world in its fullness, in insisting that narrative systems always structured something. As Culler puts it:

the narratological analysis of a text requires one to treat a discourse as a representation of events which are conceived of independently of any partic-ular narrative perspective or presentation, which are thought of as having the properties of real events. (Culler 1981, p. 170)

This is evident enough in Gérard Genette's work. In *Narrative Discourse*, for example, it is always clear that Genette conceives of the narrative system of Proust's *Recherche* as *supervening* upon a certain material that is taken to have some kind of prior existence, as in orthodox mimetic theory. The narrative 'cuts' fall in a material that could have been 'cut' otherwise and constitutes a 'world' beyond the narrative system itself. For Genette, there are clearly 'events recounted by the narrative in the *Recherche du temps perdu*' (Genette 1980, p. 28). These 'events' might be 'recounted' otherwise. It is not surprising, then, to find Genette, in his recent musings on his earlier work, saying, precisely as Hume does, that 'fiction consists of that simulation that Aristotle called mimesis' (Genette 1988, p. 18). For his narratological undertaking has always been implicitly neo-Aristotelean, even whilst seeming to claim a decisive break with representationalism.

Marxist theory of the novel, too, has been equally caught in the toils of metaphysics, both in its own theoretical elaborations and in its collaborations with critical narratology. For the Marxist critique of representation is itself dependent on representation for its critical momentum. Even more importantly, Marxist theory of the novel – Fischer, Lukács, Goldmann et al – historicises and de-essentialises narrative representation only on the basis of accounts of history or historical narratives that are deeply complicit with metaphysical forms of thought. As Baudrillard has brilliantly shown us, Marxist theory hypostasises and universalises the concepts crucial to it – historical materialism, dialectics, modes of production, labour power – with 'a "critical" imperialism' as ferocious as that it opposes (Baudrillard 1975, p. 127). Marxism's assumption that its concepts are not merely interpretative hypotheses but translations of universal movement depends on pure metaphysics. The assumption evades 'the explosive, mortal, present form of critical concepts' and constitutes them as essences. As so constituted, from Engels to Althusser, the concepts in question cease to be analytical and become canonical, an expression of an 'objective reality', and part of a Marxist version of 'the religion of meaning' (ibid. p. 127). In particular, instead of recognising the historicity of the concept of history itself, Marxism transhistoricises history and universalises it. This is strikingly evident in Marxist theory of the novel. Narrative is still conceived of as bearing a very precise relation to a set of abstract universals it supposedly embodies or reflects, notably in Lukács's work. Lukács knows that narrative representation itself has no essence at all, that 1848, for example, can transform the narrative possibilities available to the French novelist. But he also thinks of great narrative as an embodiment or representation of essences. Thus Stendhal and Balzac, for instance, 'by conscientiously uncovering the true driving forces of the social process', strive 'to present to the reader the most typical and essential traits in every social phenomenon' (Lukács 1964, p. 70). There is as it were an eschatological divide in Lukács's thought, a separation out of the elect (Stendhal, Balzac, Tolstoy, Mann for instance) who are empowered to pierce the veil and grasp and represent the metaphysical truth of history, and the damned (Flaubert, Zola, Kafka, Joyce) who are doomed to wander outside, in a phantom world of 'trivial' appearances. In the end, this dualism merely reflects the contradictions endemic to Lukács's thought: he historicises, but he also remains deeply embroiled in Aristotelean and Hegelian methods of thinking, on the one hand, and affection for 'the great heritage of *bourgeois* humanism' on the other (ibid. p. 63). Hence, for Lukács, Zola's representational art is 'placed' historically as founded in dogma rather than realism (ibid. pp. 92–5), whilst Balzac's can simply be exalted for its mimetic adequacy. But Lukács's paradoxes are not merely eccentric. They are paradigmatic of the paradoxes that beset Marxist theories of representation. For the Marxist theorist shares the classical belief in a deep ontological furniture to the universe. He or she may refuse to naturalise capitalist constructions as eternal and necessary forms. But s/he nonetheless continues to prefer a dream of deep structures to a rigorous practice that opens up surfaces.

This is not to argue that there is a disabling 'special flaw' in Marxist aesthetics; merely that, like structuralist narratology, Marxist narrative theory offers us no privileged basis for a critical 'overcoming' of representationalism. The problem lies rather with the project of 'overcoming' itself. Postmodernism advises us to abandon the grandiose: Beckett, Warhol, the *nouveau roman*, the $L = A = N = G = U = A = G = E$ poets, Rorty on epistemology, Derrida on metaphysics, Vattimo on Heidegger's *Verwindung* and *An-denken*,[5] Lyotard on grand narratives, totalising systems and the differend: there is a persistent call for a withdrawal of faith from certain kinds of ambitious cognitive enterprise, Enlightenment and other; for a repudiation of the heroic or romantic illusion of the kinds of conquest available to intellect. This can be glossed in a phrase of Heidegger's that Derrida is fond of quoting: 'All cannot be thought in one go'.[6] In Vattimo's terms, postmodernism summons us to a 'weakening' of thought, of the strong categories of Being, truth, logic, totality etc. That weakening also involves a scepticism with regard to *critique*, and the structures of opposition according to which it functions. For if, as Nietzsche suggested, there is no Platonic *ontos on*, no absolute foundation for thought, nothing that will establish what Derrida calls a 'pure cut' between truth and error (Derrida 1987b, pp. 85–119), then critical overcoming must cede to something like deconstruction.

This is arguably the moment, then, for narratology to abandon its own project of 'overcoming', whether as total description or critique. Such an abandonment is particularly appropriate in the case of representation. Narratology as critique has repeatedly sought to 'overcome' representation. But it has done so only to find representation reasserting its hold in the very practice of critique itself. Rather than seeking to transcend such contradictions, it may be better to inhabit them, pursue, explore and even expand them. This would not mean an end to critique. Critique itself is no more to be left behind than the paradoxes in which it is ceaselessly caught. Part of the effort, indeed, would rather be to deepen, multiply and vary the forms of the narratological critique of representational thought. It is striking, for example, that recent anti-mimetic theory in narratology has drawn so heavily on Saussure. Other, adventurous forms of narratological critique are possible that would resort to Wittgenstein, for example, or Heidegger, Feyerabend or Quine. To reconcile ourselves to contradiction, however, is also to recognise that any critique of representation will continually fall back into the positions from which it seeks to free itself. In this respect, a postmodern theory of narrative might hope, not only to be more resigned to the limitations of critique, but to grow more playful in its approach to them.

We might hope to grow wiser, then, about the ironic interdependence of the mimetic and the anti-mimetic, both in theory, and in narrative itself. Film comes into question, here, in precisely the terms of my introduction: in its challenge to the privilege classically afforded to the linguistic over the sensory, the discursive over the visible, reading over seeing. Increasingly, the modes of narrative dominant in our culture have what Teresa de Lauretis sees as the 'greater perceptual richness', the immediate visibility of cinematic narrative (De Lauretis 1984, p. 43). Narrative and mimesis take on a new density, sensuousness and mobility. In a sense, mimesis now seems incontestable. Yet film, too, can be thought of in terms of the contemporary paradoxes surrounding representation. In some of Robbe-Grillet's cinematic work, for instance, there is a kind of exhilarated, joyful revelling in violations of the codes of verisimilitude. Take the humour, for example, with which, in *L'Homme qui Ment*, Robbe-Grillet plays off a

Trintignant in very obviously postwar dress against a wartime setting. Like the appearance of the car in Greenaway's period setting in *The Draughtsman's Contract*, the moment effects a kind of explosion of representational horizons. The film both allows and radically disallows the possibility of mimesis. Something of the same might be said of a film like Resnais's *Providence*, and, in a different way, of more famously postmodern films like *Blade Runner*, *Terminator* and *Total Recall*, where there is an ironic play with the film's own excesses, a wilful straining at a plausibility that was only ironically established, to start with.[7] The standard theoretical reflex is to read Robbe-Grillet's anti-representationalism 'oppositionally', as a quarrel with a powerfully representational tradition. But a work like *L'Homme qui Ment* can actually encourage us to approach representational texts themselves in a different manner. We may thus be better equipped to 'demystify' the representational text or 'unmask' its 'conventions'. But Robbe-Grillet's hilarious deployment of representational absurdity and paradox – the simultaneity of the mimetic and anti-mimetic in his work – can also alert us to a similar and repeated coexistence of the two in many orthodox, mimetic texts. At the end of Hitchcock's *Marnie*, for instance, after Marnie has relived her trauma and been purged, as she and Rutland leave her mother's house, there is an extraordinary, eerie, brief cut to a group of very obviously and almost surrealistically 'posed' children playing awkwardly in the street. The paradoxical quality of this image overflows, too, into the closing shot of the street and harbour which – again – looks all too evidently pictorial or scenic. The mimetic narrative draws to its end in a sequence in which the mimetic illusion briefly founders, and is even made to look absurd. It would not be hard to read back and out from this brief sequence into the rest of *Marnie* (which it does indeed invite us to re-view) and others of Hitchcock's films, *The Birds*, for example, or *Vertigo*, where, as Teresa de Lauretis notes, the image of the stairwell is 'entirely made-up, constructed, filmic, illusionistic, non-referential' (De Lauretis 1989, p. 110). Intermittently, at least, Hitchcock's films inhabit a kind of threshold of representation. The representational relation is both confirmed and contradicted. So too, for instance, in films that include sequences in which, in Branigan and Heath's terms, the camera occupies 'impossible places' (the dead man's point of view from the coffin in Dreyer's *Vampyr*); or films which admit camera movement as a kind of autonomous figure (*Taxi Driver, Touch of Evil*) (Heath 1981, pp. 50–1). So too in the work of a variety of novelists usually largely read in mimetic terms, from Gogol and Dickens to Céline. Here, we might want to explore the fissures and breaks in the continuity of the mimetic relation in such work, its mimetic failures; the extent, in fact, to which it is haunted in advance by the presence of the postmodern text. Equally, with cinema, Heath argues that it is too readily assumed

that the operation – the determination, the effect, the pleasure – of classical cinema lies in the attempt at an invisibility of process, the intended transparency of a kind of absolute 'realism' from which all signs of production have been effaced. The actual case is much more complex and subtle, and much more telling. Classical cinema does not efface the signs of production, it contains them . . . (Heath 1981, p. 51)

If so, it remains for postmodern modes of (mis)reading to disrupt those modes of containment, to expose, foreground and exploit the non-mimetic within the mimetic itself.

REPRESENTATION, SURFACES AND DEPTHS

But there are other ways of deconstructing representational thought, too. The rest of this chapter concentrates on one of them. An established, critical narratology has tended to pursue the structuralist preoccupation with language in a structuralist way. This has shaken but not radically destabilised the cultural prestige of representation. There are thus good reasons for turning away and looking in a different direction. Classical theory develops two accounts of narrative representation. One considers representation to be a matter of surfaces. The other theorises it in terms of depths. 'Surface representation' is a realism of particulars. Its view of language is innocent. It conceives of language as unproblematically adequate to what it represents. It thinks of representation as a rendering of individual phenomena, as documentation, description or 'evocation', a movement over or an experience of surfaces. Henry James called this the 'solidity of specification' of realism (James 1972, pp. 27–44). 'Surface representation' is apparently founded in the visual. Of course, this is only a 'visibility' by convention or contract, and is not to be confused with cinematic visibility. But in the terms of the old contract, 'surface representation' emerges in the first instance as an 'optical realism' (Feyerabend 1987, p. 151). Strictly speaking, it is not confined to the 'visible', but equally includes what is heard, felt and so on, the world as apprehended by the senses. Nevertheless, 'surface representation' does give primacy to the visible. Here vision stands as paradigmatic of the representational relation as a whole. Thus James himself glosses 'solidity of specification' as meaning that the author competes 'with his brother the painter in *his* attempt to render the look of things, the colour, the relief, the expression, the substance of the human spectacle' (James 1972, p. 36). On this account, representation always means looking before describing. 'Representation of depths', on the other hand, means *penetrating* the visible. In James's terms, it 'guess[es] the unseen from the seen' (ibid. p. 35). This is the representation of essences, general features, types which thus depends on and expresses ontological conviction. It pierces through the veil of the visible to what the visible supposedly secretes or embodies, capturing that distilled essence and saturating language in it. This metaphysical conception of representation is that of Western mimetic theory from Aristotle to Lukács and beyond. It is rooted in a faith in the existence of universals and in the natural aptness of sign-systems as a mirror for them. 'Deep representation' is even prior to 'surface' or empirical representation. For the very terms of the latter are partly underwritten by the former's knowledge-claims.

Yet both kinds of representation are radically open to question. 'Surface representation' puts itself forward as a realism of self-evidence. Both depending on and promoting what Sellars calls 'the myth of the given', of entities given us to know in immediate experience, it insists on truth as correspondence (*homoiosis*). Surface representation has its own equivalent of the Newtonian *hypotheses non fingo* – a categorical assumption that the bases of representation are not arbitrarily invented. As such, it is immediately open to sceptical challenge. Quine shows, for example, that objects are always objects relative to certain theories (Quine

1969, p. 50). For us and our systems of representation, any given object is available only as an object-profile. Even that simplifies, since it implies that stasis is intrinsic to the object. If representation, like thought itself, is always a kind of cutting process, how to 'slice' things representationally can never be finally determined. For there is in the end no 'fact of the matter' beyond language, as Quine shows in relating the 'cuts' established by Japanese classifiers to those produced in English (ibid. pp. 35–6). But the terms of another system of 'slicing' are never wholly apprehensible as such, either, precisely because, in converting them to ours, we adapt an alien pattern to our own, and thus efface its alienness (ibid. pp. 1–25). There is always what Quine calls an 'impossibility of radical translation' and an 'inscrutability of reference' (ibid. pp. 35–41). There is no stable or enduring matrix for any description, and therefore no sense in which a representation of a given surface can have any final validity at all. All reference is 'nonsense' save relative to a co-ordinate system (ibid. p. 46). It can prevail only insofar as we refuse to notice that words and concepts are what produce distinguishable particulars. Or, in the case of cinema, only insofar as we forget the frame, for example. As Heath reminds us, it is precisely within the frame that film narrative 'contains the mobility that could threaten the clarity of vision in a constant renewal of perspective' (Heath 1981, p. 36). Heidegger suggests that it is likely that we constantly confuse the structure of propositions with the structure of the world (Heidegger 1971, pp. 15–89). If the statement has an object, then it is a discursive object which is particular to the statement and not isomorphic with the visible object (Deleuze 1988, p. 61). Surface representation tells us about things only within certain norms of justification that determine what things are from the outset.

Surfaces, then, can never be said to be represented in narrative discourse at all. In Heidegger's terms, surface representation always has a prior 'blueprint of nature', and it is only 'within the framework of this blueprint that a natural event becomes visible as such' (Spanos 1979, pp. 1–15). But surface representation also privileges a certain mode of vision. It hypostasises clarity and distinctness, for example. It privileges the adult scheme of the visible over the child's or the 'primitive's.' In cinema, it privileges 'life in its truth as scene' (Heath 1981, p. 37). It is always a language game: simply one that has usually been rather successful at effacing the traces of its own decisions – choice of aspect of the object, choice of materials and so on (Feyerabend 1987, pp. 129–30). Surface representation depends on the assumption of a 'neutral observation language'. But as philosophers from Kuhn to Feyerabend have shown, observation must always be theory-laden. Surface representation purports to describe, but is actually just a particular manner of picking out entities, one which obliterates the strangeness or obscurity which first solicited the process. It cannot recognise that there is no Archimedean point inherent in the world which absolutely guarantees the reality of the objects represented. Committed to its own version of the scientific principle of 'saving the phenomena,' it thus also becomes merely what Quine calls a 'provincial physics' (Quine 1969, p. 20).

In the case of cinema, nothing has better demonstrated this than Deleuze's work. Deleuze suggests, for instance, that there is a kind of cinema – the cinema of the time-image and its 'crystalline regime' – that is not representational at all. It does not assume the independence of its object, as other forms of cinema do, where 'the setting described is presented as independent of the description which the camera gives of it, and makes for a supposedly pre-existing reality' (Deleuze 1989, p. 126). 'Crystalline description' rather stands for its object, replaces it, both creates and erases it. Descriptions constantly give way to others which contradict, displace or modify preceding ones. In other forms of cinema, the movement of the image is not at all opposed to the idea of truth in representation. For movement is still presented in terms of invariants. But in 'crystalline description' a cinematographic mutation occurs. Aberrations of movement 'take on their independence', and moving bodies and movements themselves 'lose their invariants' (ibid. p. 143). In some sense, representation presupposes a single world, not least with regard to temporality. But in the cinema of the time-image – *Muriel, L'Homme qui Ment, L'Année Dernière à Marienbad,* even *Citizen Kane* – the concatenations of the 'single world' are absent, or break up. In this cinema, says Deleuze, from Italian neo-realism to Cassavetes, it is 'the description itself which constitutes the sole decomposed and multiplied object' (ibid.). The real is no longer recognisable by its 'legal, causal and logical connections', the imaginary by its caprice and discontinuity (ibid. p. 127). Rather, real and imaginary constantly exchange roles and become indiscernible from one another. In Fellini, Antonioni, Bresson, Varda, Wenders, 'description stops presupposing a reality and narration stops referring to a form of the true at one and the same time' (ibid. p. 135). This cinema puts the representation of truth into crisis. In Deleuze's phrase, the cinema of the time-image testifies 'to the power of the false as principle of production of images' (ibid. p. 131).

Deleuze's conception of 'the power of the false' is Nietzschean, of course. The time-image insists that the representation of surfaces is perspectival, a mode of valuation, creativity, emergence itself. But surface representation is less curious a phenomenon than 'representation of depths.' The latter insists on the validity of foundations and essential intuitions at the expense of linguistic habits, social conventions and ideological constructs, and this insistence may be as understandable as any other optional superstition. But it is also quite as arbitrary. It would seem important, as Quine again suggests, to recognise the contingency of 'our culture's ontological point of view' (Quine 1969, pp. 3, 15). There is no permanent, neutral matrix for all inquiry guaranteeing the doctrines of 'deep representation'. There is not and never will be a transcendental standpoint outside representations – a Platonic *focus imaginarius* – from which the relations between representations and their objects can be inspected. Epistemic shifts continually change the meaning of terms. There are therefore no representations that can claim incontestably to have captured deep, hidden, metaphysically significant natures, once and for all. To think otherwise is to lapse back into the belief in a 'common ground' dear to epistemology, to privilege ideas of being over the reality of becoming. This, says Deleuze, is what essentialism and metaphysics have always done: they double things with a world of ideas which have a density, unity and agelessness that things themselves lack. Thus 'deep representation' refuses to find life at the level of life itself, as surface, flux, proximity (Buydens 1990, p. 26). It must have wholes. But no whole is ever surveyable. In Habermas's terms, there is always *Unübersichtlichkeit*. We can never have a privileged set of descriptions that will ensure any universal commensuration of representations. There is no

special ingredient in any narrative that makes possible a knowledge of general truths. As far as cinema is concerned, there is no
'reality of space' existing beyond all challenge of the kind to
which Bazin gave priority in his realist theory of film (Bazin 1967,
Vol. 1, p. 108).

The actual primitivism of a belief in 'deep representation' thus
becomes apparent, and other unexamined assumptions begin to
break up, too. Why imagine that certainty must always be implicit
in representation?[8] Isn't it simply bizarre to suppose – as in all
thought of types or universals – that the larger can be reduced to
the smaller without loss? As Nietzsche and Heidegger thought,
perhaps the belief in truth as representable, permanent essence is
fearful, a flight from the sensuous multiplicity of the world and its
unbearable proliferations. Above all, it is clear that both conceptions of representation give primacy to seeing. For 'deep representation' is itself a version of what Rorty calls the Platonic and
Aristotelean 'spectator theory of knowledge', the analogy the
Greeks drew between perceiving and knowing (Rorty 1980, p. 41).
It turns the narrating mind into an eye contemplating universal
truths. As Heath puts it with regard to cinema, it is the view of a
'detached, untroubled eye . . . an eye free from the body, outside
process, purely looking' (Heath 1981, p. 32). In fact, both forms of
representation make knowledge a matter of seeing, on the assumption that seeing itself is unproblematic. This in turn is reflected in
the privileging of certain terms in narratology and novel criticism:
'point of view', 'focalisation', 'way of seeing', 'scene', 'panorama',
'vision', 'world view'. The primary relation to the world is
conceived of as one involving a view, rather than agency or
eroticism, sensibility, communion, discursive exchange, *Mitsein*
and so on.

In Heidegger's terms, thus, 'the existent as a whole is now so
understood that it is existent when and only when and in the
degree to which it is held at bay by the person who represents and
establishes it' (Spanos 1979, p. 10). Thus in representation there is
always detachment or severance; severance, above all, of gaze
from what is gazed at, subject and object. But the subject/object
distinction is already a choice. It is not value-free, and excludes
other distinctions. The 'object' produced in representation must
be understood as merely a certain position available for the

existent. Representation is a practice of forcing the existent back into a relation with oneself. The practice 'determines' the existent as present, before and near but also apart from oneself as subject. Only thus can the existent receive the seal of being within representation. Heidegger suggests that this is in fact the very essence of humanism and anthropology (ibid. pp. 9–13): the production of the *Vorstellung*, man's act of setting something before himself. This 'achievement' is in fact a misfortune. For it merely reflects our intransigent self-assertion, forcing the world under human dominion and annihilating the existent in robbing it of its depth, obscurity and suggestiveness. So, too, for Levinas, objectification involves loss. It suspends alterity, because it is always effected according to the subject's measure and scale (Levinas 1985, p. 59). Objectification therefore constitutes a failure of relation to the Other, a turning away from the primary relation, which is of course the ethical relation. Not surprisingly, Levinas raises questions, above all, about the attitude involved in scrutiny. Deleuze, Foucault, Lyotard and others[9] have likewise recently sought to question the destructiveness of objectivity, of the '*distance objectivante-maîtrisante*' that representation inserts between man and world (Buydens 1990, p. 71). On all sides, postmodern aesthetics would seem to be interrogating the structure and meaning of the relationship between subject and object. Yet the thought of that relationship is crucial to our conception of narrative, to 'surface representation' and 'deep representation' alike.

'INAUGURATION' FROM HEIDEGGER TO VATTIMO

A particular set of structures, then – subject and object, observer and observed, narrative text and pre-existent, narrated world – has dominated thought about narrative representation. These structures are metaphors to which we are so profoundly accustomed that we can hardly keep their metaphorical status in sight. They inhabit all thought about narrative. It may nonetheless be important to destabilise them, at least, in experimenting with different metaphors and terms. One such term (as elaborated by Heidegger, Derrida and Vattimo) designates art, not as imitation, but as *inauguration*. For Heidegger, the awareness made available by art

is qualitatively different from those proposed to us by the established forms of knowledge (especially scientific knowledge). As
his discussion of the Hyginus fable in *Being and Time* makes clear
(Heidegger 1990, pp. 241–2), for Heidegger, literature makes a
deposition 'prior' to scientific knowledge. In poetry, there is a
disclosure of existence before the latter is operated on by the kind
of activity that holds it at bay in order to understand it. To
structure either world or text in terms of subject and object, then,
is to engage in a secondary activity in relation to the work of art
itself. To think of the work in terms of mimetic truth or adequation
is to assimilate one's conception of it to scientific truth, a truth
already given and determined. The 'truth' of art, on the other
hand, is a truth that 'arises out of nothing', 'becomes' and
'happens' only in the work (Heidegger 1971, p. 71). It is a clearing
or *Geworfenheit*. Hence the fact that, in art, everything is, not a
mirror of the usual, but other than usual. The ordinary becomes
uncanny, and that uncanniness is determining and constitutive.
Poetry can be thought of as a retrieval of ontological beginnings,
but only if we conceive of it, not as returning us to any absolute
origin, but to a sense of origin as occasion, beginning 'in the
midst'. Art is thus not *homoiosis* but disclosure, a happening of
truth that is in the 'work-being' and belongs 'uniquely within the
realm that is opened up' by the work itself (ibid. p. 42). The artwork might be said to hold open the openness of the world, rather
than conserving or casting a gaze backwards at a pre-existent
object or reality. It is therefore important to recall that 'invention
gives being to what did not exist' (Deleuze 1988, p. 15). The work
and its world were not required or determined by a larger world.
They might never have happened at all.
   The concept of 'inauguration' is radically opposed to any
thought of the work as reflection. In Derrida's words, it resists all
thought of the work in terms of either 'empirical origin' or
'essential provenance' (Derrida 1987c, p. 31). For Derrida, what
appears in the work 'does not . . . take place in an elsewhere
which the work of art could illustrate by referring to it. It takes
place properly (and only) in the work' (ibid. p. 295). Texts are not
governed by a transcendental referent or signified which regulates
their movement (Derrida 1981b, p. 44). For the source of the work,
writes Derrida, is really always a void, an absence, nothing. It is

not a reflection of the world, but always, immediately, an addition to it. Contrary to our apparently unshakeable allegiance to what Derrida calls 'economimesis',[10] emptiness is always the situation of literature. Writing always breaks with the domain of empirical history to inaugurate something (Derrida 1978, pp. 3–30).

In two essays, 'The Shattering of the Poetic Word' and 'Art and Oscillation' (Vattimo 1988, pp. 65–78; 1992, pp. 45–61), Vattimo likewise proposes the 'truth' of art as more 'fundamental' than that of science insofar as it is not a stable, metaphysical structure at all, but an emergence, always new and different; a truth the more important for never being rendered as a 'fully unfolded luminosity', but only in a 'faint light' (Vattimo 1988, p. 75). Truth in art thus comes to us 'stripped of its authoritarian traits of metaphysical evidence' (ibid. p. 76). Art's is that 'weak ontology' which, for Vattimo, is now all that is left us (ibid. p. 85). Art does not represent but inaugurates or founds a world, in that it presents itself as a new historical event or 'opening' of Being. This 'inaugurality' might 'be understood above all as the originality or as the irreducibility of the work to whatever has already been' (ibid. p. 67). It is thinkable in Heideggerian terms as a mode of showing not reducible to representation, *Zeigen* as *Erscheinen lassen* (ibid. p. 68). Here, '[t]he long struggle of the aesthetics and poetics of modernity against the Aristotelean definition of art as imitation' attains 'its full meaning' (ibid. p. 97).

This theory of art might seem to coincide with Thomas Pavel's account of fiction in terms of 'possible worlds' theory. In Pavel, fictional discourse – allowing as it does 'for any imaginable kind of confabulation without constraint' (Pavel 1986, p. 2) – may be thought of as inaugurating 'possible worlds'. Possible worlds 'can be understood as abstract collections of states of affairs' (ibid. p. 50). They may or may not be 'accessible from the actual world' (ibid. p. 51), identifiable with metaphysically possible worlds, violations of the laws of logic. All the same, what Pavel chooses to call 'the really real world' enjoys a definite ontological priority over the world of 'make-believe' and serves as 'the *foundation* upon which the latter is built' (ibid. p. 57, italics mine). The relationship is one of salience. Thus in Borges's 'The Library of Babel', for instance, if the 'library' in question is not to be understood as belonging to the class of objects called 'libraries' in the primary universe, our grasp of its significance requires a knowledge of what libraries in that universe actually are. But for Vattimo, on the other hand, art establishes a nexus between founding and unfounding. Like Heidegger, he dwells on the work of art as an experience and communication of 'utter gratuitousness' (Vattimo 1992, p. 50). Hence that *Unheimlichkeit* of art that Heidegger also stresses. The work of art stimulates 'a preoccupied wonder at the fact . . . that the world is there' (ibid. p. 51). Aesthetic experience is thus an experience of estrangement, but also one *'directed towards keeping the disorientation alive'* (ibid. p. 51). This constitutes the distinctiveness of the theory of art proposed by Heidegger (and Benjamin) as opposed to that of Aristotle, Kant and Hegel. The former theory presents the 'state of disorientation' in art as 'constitutive and not provisional' (ibid. p. 52). It repudiates a more commonplace description of aesthetic experience in terms of an ultimate *Geborgenheit*, harmony, reconciliation, 'security, "orientation" or "reorientation"' (ibid.). It emphasises the shock of the work – Heidegger's *Stoss* – its 'disorientating effect with regard to any world whatsoever' (ibid. p. 54). The work of art, thus, is seen as inaugurating something that is never stable as a represented object might be thought of as stable. It produces and sustains a certain relation to the precarious structure of existence in general. It carries with it the traces of the obscure and thematically inexhaustible depths from which it emerges, and which bring forth interminable forms and meanings. In 'The Origin of the Work of Art', Heidegger had suggested that the truth of art finally lay in its elaboration of the primal conflict or *Urstreit* between clearing and concealing, clarity and confusion, approach and withdrawal, presence and absence. Vattimo reformulates this in his conception of art as a founding and unfounding together. Art therefore offers a model of the experience of freedom in a pluralistic, postmodern culture as 'a continual oscillation between belonging and disorientation' (Vattimo 1992, p. 10).

To conceive of art accordingly would be to respond to Quine's injunction that we dispense with the assumption that there is 'no entity without identity', and move beyond an 'object-oriented conceptual scheme' towards thinking in terms of 'twilight half-entities' (Quine 1969, pp. 23–4). The art-form most resistant to

DECONSTRUCTING REPRESENTATION

such thinking, however, is arguably narrative. For narrative characteristically appears to efface the traces of its own 'inaugurality'. The narrative contract seems to insist neither on founding nor unfounding, but on a relation to the already founded. Far from making itself available to us as disclosure or the happening of truth, narrative appears to put itself forward as a reflection of what preceded it, of the already given. And if this is not after all 'the nature of narrative,' narratology and theory of the novel have customarily worked to conceal the fact. Even when asking radical questions, they have held other kinds of question at bay, and defended narrative against them. According to Deleuze, what is involved in Proust's 'literary machine' is 'no longer an extra-literary experience which the man-of-letters reports or profits by, but an artistic experimentation produced by literature, a literary effect' (Deleuze 1973, p. 135). Proust turns from subject and object alike to production, rather than observation or imagination (ibid. p. 137). In adding to nature in this manner, his art presents itself as free rather than determined. Clinging as it has to modes of investigation that have been so doggedly (pseudo-)scientific, narratology has never been able to develop the kind of terms Deleuze constructs for Proust. But the possible modes of insertion of such counter-terms are not self-evident. 'Inauguration' cannot simply be 'substituted for' the concept of mimesis, and all proceed accordingly. In Heidegger's phrase, we live in an epoch dedicated to 'the conquest of the world as picture' (Heidegger 1979, p. 13). Representational assumptions cannot simply be shed or transcended at once. Any attempts at such immediate transcendence merely return us to our starting point in another guise. As Heidegger remarks in 'The Thing', for instance, the need for a shift away from representational thought is counterbalanced by the impossibility of its being achieved through 'a shift of attitude, since all attitudes, including the ways in which they shift, remain committed to the precincts of representational thinking' (Heidegger 1971, pp. 163–87). If, on the one hand, as Quine suggests, 'we have had the wit to posit an ontology massive enough to crumble under its own weight', it is also an ontology that seems practically inescapable (Quine 1969, p. 17). 'We talk so inveterately' in representational terms that to grow more critical and say that we know we talk thus 'seems almost to say nothing at all; for how else is there to talk?', Quine asks (ibid. p. 1). For the present, it may be more useful to experiment both with the concept of representation and with the reach and effectiveness of counter-terms, of which 'inauguration' is one.

Rosset and Godard

How might we describe narrative in terms of inauguration? By distinguishing 'disclosive' narratives from others which – in Derridean terms – disguise the nothing that is their origin (Derrida 1978, p. 8)? We might put Balzac at the latter end of the spectrum, with his determination, as expressed in the preface to *La Comédie Humaine*, to sustain a conception of narrative as a recording device subservient to a reality understood as already given and complete. At the other end, there is Flaubert's dream – in Derrida's words – of 'the "book about nothing" ... the total Book that haunted other imaginations' (Derrida 1978, p. 8). We might place much of Robbe-Grillet's work at this pole, too.

But this may seem merely to have restated the opposition between *scriptible* and *lisible* in different terms. Narrative as inauguration is not simply or even chiefly to be identified with self-reflexive narrative or narrative of 'multiple variants'. Some of Godard's work provides a different example, particularly as it has been described by Clément Rosset. Rosset is fond of quoting Ernst Mach's description of the real as '*un être unilatéral dont le complément en miroir n'est pas ou, du moins, ne nous est pas connu*' (Rosset 1977, p. 43). This is very much what Rosset himself means by the *idiocy* of the real. The real is 'idiotic' in a sense partly given in the etymological root of the word (the Greek *idios*, meaning private, own, peculiar). Any given thing is 'idiotic' precisely in its simplicity, its '*émergence insolite dans le champ de l'existence*':

Idiôtès, idiot, signifie simple, particulier, unique; puis, par une extension sémantique dont la signification philosophique est de grand portée, personne dénuée d'intelligence, être dépourvu de raison. Toute chose, toute personne sont ainsi idiotes des lors qu'elles n'existent qu'en elles-mêmes, c'est-à-dire sont incapables d'apparaître autrement que là où elles sont et telles qu'elles sont: incapables donc, et en premier lieu, de se refléter, d'apparaître dans le double de miroir. (ibid. p.41)

The real is idiotic in that, if it is random, its randomness is also determined in the invariable singularity of its emergence. For the aleatory must always appear, if not as this rather than that, then at least as something, *'un quelconque ceci ou ici'* (Rosset 1979, p. 28). In fact, *'toute indétermination cesse au seuil de l'existence'* (Rosset 1977, p. 12). The real is not stable, fixed or 'clearly constituted'. But this also means that the real cannot be modified, at least in its inaugural character (ibid. p. 21). The real gives out only a single, monotonous tone or message. Paradoxically, that message is that it (the real) is ungrounded, changes in unforeseeable ways and necessarily always has a random sense. Inauguration *is* determination. Any representation of the real that seeks to go beyond that fact merely deals in *'une valeur ajoutée'*, a value added to the real (ibid. p. 35). So art cannot duplicate the real. Yet it can nonetheless strip away false duplications. It can resist the *'escamotage du réel'* that is evident everywhere, not least in collective representations (ibid. p. 98). Finally, art can also put us back in contact with the inaugural character, the ontological frailty of the real on which Rosset, like Heidegger, insists (Rosset 1976, p. 83), its unforeseeable, ineluctable, necessary uniqueness (ibid. pp. 46–7).

For Rosset, too, narrative can perform such functions, as in the work of Lowry, Beckett, Faulkner, Flaherty, Siegel and Godard, either through its own inaugural power, or through a rendition of the experience of the idiocy of the real. Robbe-Grillet's work is an example of the first, Godard's of the second. The only adequate representation of the real is that which gives it to us as unrepresentable (Rosset 1979, p. 15). Godard achieves this, but not primarily, as Robbe-Grillet does, through self-reflexivity, self-reflexive as his films may sometimes be. Godard gestures towards the unrepresentability of the real, not so much in drawing our attention to representation as production as in the element of gratuitousness captured in the famous phrase from *Vent d'Est*, *'Ce n'est pas une image juste, c'est juste une image'* (ibid. p. 56). Godard's films represent or, better, dramatise the real only insofar as the real can be 'shown' at all, as inapt to conform to the contours of any double. They do not suggest an ungraspable, hidden set of significations gesturing towards some distant, mysterious sense. On the contrary, they offer 'an immediate, flat, mute

signification' which promises no echo or reflection and 'evapo-
rates as soon as it is disclosed' (Rosset 1977, p. 20). In effect, what
we find in Godard is what Rosset also finds in Homer but is
subsequently massively effaced by mimetic aesthetics:[11] a latent
challenge to the credibility of any given reality, a challenge
founded in a sense that the advent of that reality takes place only
as other possibilities are eliminated (Rosset 1979, pp. 11–12).
Godard refuses to allow a represented world to take form as a
display of identities. Rather, his films preserve the non-
assimilable quality of different things existing in different
moments, the gaps intrinsic to the real in an inaugural conception
of it (ibid. p. 19). Godard gives us the real in its character of
having no assignable character, as always 'solitaire et seul de son
espèce' (ibid. p. 22). Pierrot le Fou, for example, is a narrative folly
or piece of folly, or, rather, of narrative idiocy. As opposed to
realist cinema, which is always a cinema of preformed ideas,
presupposed significations, the clichés of representation, Pierrot
le Fou produces images only in and as themselves. Hence the real
appears in its brute, inaugural, non-signifying form. The film is
distinguished by what Rosset calls allégresse, that gift of the rare
work that can produce an experience of the real without recourse
to a metaphysical Other (Rosset 1979, p. 95).

In fact, it is precisely the nexus of founding and unfounding, the
Heideggerian Urstreit that we find in Godard, particularly the
earlier films. Godard does not seek to expunge all reference. His
films self-evidently allude to given historical realities. Les Carabiniers and even Weekend might be thought of as containing and
intermittently recycling elements of a bleak, Rossellini-like realism. The desolate panoramas in both films, for example, seem to
belong specifically with similar visual features in Paisa. However,
unlike Rossellini, Godard refuses to allow realism and reference to
have any kind of founding or final status within a given work. He
grants them no privilege over other narrative elements. They are
rather caught up themselves within a play of appearance and
disappearance, and thus resituated, transformed, 'reinaugurated'.
This is appropriate enough, in 'un film égaré dans le cosmos', to
quote the subtitle of Weekend. Les Carabiniers, for instance,
splices documentary footage from the second World War together
with what Weekend will later call 'faux-tographie': non-realistic

battle sequences in a non-realistic portrayal of a war. Godard insistently punches holes in reference, inserting spaces between segments of referential narrative, as Ferdinand's diary in *Pierrot le Fou* has large spaces between words or phrases. This partly reflects an impulse expressed in the book about Velasquez that Ferdinand is reading at the beginning of *Pierrot le Fou*, an impulse, not to describe lives or a world, but – as later rearticulated by Ferdinand himself – to evoke the space that surrounds lives and out of which they emerge. Hence the theme and practice of simultaneous continuity and separation in *Pierrot le Fou*. Hence, too, that play with sound and silence in various of Godard's films from *Une Femme est Une Femme* to *Deux ou Trois Choses que Je Sais d'Elle*. The visual sequence remains unbroken, but the sound comes and goes. It is as though reference itself were being switched on and off, as though what is being reproduced were not the real but narrative's inaugural power to bring the real forth. This is likewise the case when two narratives 'cross' in some of Godard's films, as when the two detectives looking for terrorists enter Émile and Angela's apartment in *Une Femme est une Femme*.

Godard's films tend to have a similar effect on *other* narratives, too. Fragments of other narratives are picked up, cited, put in circulation, then dropped, as with *Guignol's Band* in *Pierrot le Fou*, or the use of Boetticher's *Westbound* in *A Bout de Souffle*, where a section of Boetticher's soundtrack becomes a section of Godard's, too. In a remarkable sequence in *Une Femme est Une Femme*, Angela (Karina) arrives at the Zodiac, the club where she works. The sequence keeps on cutting away from Angela and then back to her. The camera alternately follows her, and rapidly turns, pans, scans the club, registers various figures in it. An accompanist's organ music bursts on to the soundtrack, then stops, abruptly, then bursts back, in a manner that bears no realistic relation to the visual level of the film. The most revealing item in the sequence is a magic screen through which a girl walks, and from which an Indian promptly appears, on the other side. A few minutes later, the film reproduces the theatrical trick in (more effective) cinematic terms, by having Karina herself enter the screen wearing one set of clothes, and promptly emerge wearing another. As a whole, the 'Zodiac sequence' works in a similar way:

it intermittently follows a continuous narrative thread both through a multiplicity of sounds and images, and through various different manifestations of its verbal forms. It thus repeatedly insists on the determined randomness of its own narrative emergence.[12]

Godard emphasises that randomness in other ways, too. His films repeatedly tell us that what they represent may be determined by elements internal to the film rather than external to it. Thus a station called *Gland* in *Le Petit Soldat* seemingly really exists, but appears partly because of Bruno Forestier's current sexual interests, and partly because a woman on the train has just read out the title *Le Gland et la Citrouille: Poésies de Jean de la Fontaine*. When Ferdinand decides to count to 137 before following Marianne at the end of *Pierrot le Fou*, the ensuing sequence lasts precisely as long as the counting. Sound in Godard can 'inaugurate' image (as a blare of trumpets 'brings on' a glare of neon in *Une Femme est une Femme*). But images can also 'inaugurate' sounds: a snatch of Chinese music in *Une Femme est une Femme* is called up by Karina's wearing a pan shaped like a Chinese straw hat on her head. By the time of *Deux ou Trois Choses que Je Sais d'Elle*, Godard was making an art of narrative inauguration serve more immediately political ends, successfully amalgamating a postmodern aesthetic practice and a radical political project, before he cast his politics into a more limiting Marxist-Leninist mould and his aesthetics into a more Brechtian one. As the narrator reiterates, the film is partly concerned with change and transformation: the formulation of 'the hope for a genuine new city' and the creation of 'a new world where man and things exist in harmony'. The narrative does not shirk contemporary reality. On the contrary: it continually returns to a world of tower blocks, building sites and arterial roads. At the same time, contradictorily, it blatantly alters historical reality and tampers with plausibility. We are told, for example, that Lyndon Johnson bombed Peking. Bare, familiar images of a concrete, specific social and historical reality – suburban Paris, 1966 – are made to look simultaneously both real and fictional. Thus *cinéma vérité* reverses into something like its opposite. The possible invades the actual, as the narrator insists that thought both meshes with reality and calls it in question, as Juliette Janson simultaneously both identifies with her everyday life and is set apart from it by what she is allowed to articulate as her consciousness. It is therefore not surprising that the most frequent images in the film should be of building sites. As a whole, the film itself works by reinaugurating the real, redistributing and reusing blocks of the real in order to open up a space in which the creation of the new may be possible again.[13]

INAUGURATION AND MIMESIS

But can we also read classic narrative texts in terms of inauguration rather than mimesis? After all, such narratives self-evidently emerge out of a historical culture with a more confident faith in mimesis than our own. A mimetic text can surely not be simply converted into an inaugural one. Yet, at the same time, many narratives are marked by inaugural modes of thought and imagination which may enter into complex relations with mimetic modes of thought and put the latter in question or tend to deconstruct them. Here, precisely, it is possible to start destabilising the opposition between mimesis and anti-mimesis, in exploring the multiplicity of anti-mimetic elements in narrative, recognising how far they go beyond mere self-reflexivity and the productive generativity of the *texte scriptible*. Rosset makes much of *Under the Volcano*, and Lowry's Consul in particular. In Rosset's reading of Firmin, we may start to see how certain narratives may catch the reader up in an oscillation between the mimetic and the inaugural. In particular, Rosset emphasises what he sees as the Consul's extraordinary '*hébétude*'. The Consul is no ordinary drunk, says Rosset, in that he has no returns to lucidity. For Geoffrey Firmin, there are simply no fixed co-ordinates. (If 'right through hell there is a path' for the Consul, he knows that he 'may not take it' (Lowry 1981, p. 42)). Instead, he finds himself surrounded by a hopeless infinity of possible paths. Everything is a possible path. He is thus doomed repeatedly to experience the pitiless coexistence of necessity and *alea*, the identity of determination and indeterminacy, the emergence of the real as '*un quelconque ceci ou ici*'. Hence, one might add, the fact that Firmin's book – on the question of the existence of an 'ultimate reality' (ibid. p. 44) – does not get written.

The Consul thus inhabits the site of *insignifiance*, '*lieu où se confondent tous les chemins*' (Rosset 1977, p. 20). This is the site of the real as simultaneously founded and ungrounded. The Consul sees things as utterly simple, that is, he grasps them in their 'stupefying singularity', their 'astonishing emergence into existence' (ibid. p. 41). Thus he is capable of harbouring the most extraordinary doubts about his world ('Was he in the bathroom now or half an hour ago?' (Lowry 1981, p. 145)). Hence, too, his reproach to the non-drunk world: 'how, unless you drink as I do, can you hope to understand the beauty of an old woman from Tarasco who plays dominoes at seven o'clock in the morning?' (ibid. p. 55). Hence his response when Yvonne tells him that he is not sober:

As if, as if, he were not sober now! Yet there was some elusive subtlety in the impeachment that escaped him. For he was not sober. No, he was not, not at this very moment he wasn't! But what had that to do with a minute before, or half an hour ago? (ibid. p. 89)

But if the Consul's reality is idiotic, '*sans ailleurs*' (Rosset 1977, p. 43), the novel's can hardly be described in the same way. It is itself a duplication of the real, mimetic and therefore metaphysical in its intent. In the terms of *Le Réel et Son Double*, it refuses the immediate, rejects the primary for the secondary (Rosset 1976, p. 59). But not entirely: in *Under the Volcano*, the 'Consular' or inaugural principle contaminates without substantially displacing the mimetic principle. Thus the very first paragraph emphasises the emergence of the narrative's own particular focus – 'the town of Quauhnahuac' – as merely one amidst a range of possibilities on a single latitude: 'the Revillagigedo Islands to the west in the Pacific, or very much farther west, the southernmost tip of Hawaii', and so on (Lowry 1981, p. 9). The first half of the paragraph is concerned with the reality that will be that of the book, the second with what that reality excludes. Furthermore, having 'inaugurated' its own landscape in this way, Lowry's narrative subsequently goes on to internalise the inaugural principle *within* the landscape. 'How continually, how startlingly, the landscape changed!' thinks M. Laruelle to himself:

another planet, he reflected again, a strange planet where, if you looked a little further, beyond the Tres Marías, you would find every sort of landscape at once, the Cotswolds, Windermere, New Hampshire, the meadows of the Eure-et-Loire, even the grey dunes of Cheshire, even the Sahara, a planet upon which, in a twinkling of an eye, you could change climates, and, if you cared to think so, in the crossing of a highway, three civilizations . . . (ibid. pp. 15–16)

Like the world of *Under the Volcano* itself, this world is irreducible, non-assimilable. To represent such non-assimilability lies largely beyond the scope of Lowry's mimetic narrative. Yet irreducibility will nonetheless continue to haunt the story with the awkward, problematic, destructive vigour of the Consul himself. The Consul, of course, is ultimately prepared to surrender his own reality:

What did it matter? Let it go! . . . There was a kind of fierce delight in that final acceptance. Let everything go! Everything particularly that provided means of ingress or egress, went bond for, gave meaning or character, or purpose or identity to that frightful bloody nightmare he was forced to carry around with him everywhere upon his back, that went by the name of Geoffrey Firmin. (ibid. p. 226)

Under the Volcano does not go to the same lengths, in narrative terms. When the Consul's world speeds up and spins 'madly round', for instance, then 'gradually' slows down, (ibid. p. 226), there is no equivalent for or materialisation of the process in the narrative itself. If Firmin is capable of arriving at a conception of time as 'moving at different speeds' (ibid. p. 248), there is no narrative embodiment of this time. The novel nonetheless deconstructs its own representational dimension, if only intermittently. It soberly identifies as an error of the Consul's a 'quixotic' lack of contact with the real as established truth (ibid. p. 39). But it is also capable of quixotically destabilising its own more sober versions of reality. Indeed, a quixotic if fearful sense of ontological insecurity – of the the extent to which the 'Consular principle' can enter and trouble their world – is common to various other characters in the book, too. As *Under the Volcano* draws to its close, the Consul is ever more inclined to descend into a world in which 'matter' can be 'disjunct' (ibid. p. 316), a world of 'drifting mists' and 'elusive subtleties of ribboned light', the 'phantom dance of souls' (ibid. p. 288). The novel does not descend there with him. Rather, it allows for a certain 'invasion of dissolution' (ibid. p. 253) which disturbs and unsettles the apparently solidly founded certainties of the mimetic narrative. Lowry's novel hardly moves us beyond object-oriented vision or thought to the twilight world that Quine posits as an alternative. But that second world glimmers behind or opens crevices in the mimetic world, as the Consul himself knows

> that the earth was a ship, lashed by the Horn's tail, doomed never to make her Valparaiso. Or that it was like a golf ball, launched at Hercules's Butterfly, wildly hooked by a giant out of an asylum window in hell. Or that it was a bus, making its erratic journey to Tomalín and nothing. Or that it was like − whatever it would be shortly, after the next mescal. (ibid. p. 289)

If, then, like most mimetic narratives, *Under the Volcano* blurs the traces of its own inaugurality, it also allows a 'disclosive' or inaugural conception of the real to emerge in other ways that disturb or raise awkward questions about the stable, metaphysical foundations of the mimetic narrative itself.

The same is the case in Kerouac's *On the Road*. The point, here, is not so much that Kerouac permits a principle of ontological instability to haunt his mimetic narrative, as that that narrative is actually about a certain kind of instability, from the start. Kerouac's world is one without finalities. Characters go on in the knowledge that the 'last thing is what you can't get . . . Nobody can get to the last thing' (Kerouac 1972, p. 48). Thus the relevant question − for America as well as individual characters − becomes the repeated 'Whither goest thou?' (ibid. p. 114). For Kerouac, it is a more important question than where one has been, or what one can refer back to. Living and narrating become indefinitely prolonged movements 'all the way down the line' (ibid. p. 59). Both are modes of 'adventuring in the crazy American night' (ibid. p. 96). Being 'on the road' becomes both a subject in and a metaphor for the narrative as a whole. 'I had a book with me', says Sal Paradise, '*Le Grand Meaulnes* by Alain-Fournier, but I preferred reading the American landscape as we went along. Every bump, rise and stretch in it mystified my longing' (Kerouac 1972, p. 99). American landscapes − America itself − unfold themselves as ongoing narratives, available if not intelligible to willing readers. Thus Sal and friends can happen upon 'a manuscript' of a particular 'night' that they find themselves unable to 'read' (ibid.

p. 149). A state like Nebraska can 'unroll' before Sal's eyes like a
script, and Iowa can 'unreel' like a film (ibid. pp. 216, 220). The
landscapes are also profuse, multiple, various, caught up in 'the
incredibly complicated sweetness zigzagging every side' (ibid. p.
115). They are thus beyond being narrated, not only in Alain-
Fournier's kind of narrative but in Sal Paradise's and Kerouac's,
too. In other words, *On the Road* is a mimetic narrative about a
reality that it also declares is not narratable in mimetic terms, a
reality that has instead its own unpredictable, irreducible, disclosive narrative to offer, its 'unforeseen events' waiting 'lurking
to surprise you' (ibid. p. 128). It is as though America itself is
proposed as having the instantaneous multiplicity of a narrative
by Joyce or Dos Passos; whereas *On the Road* does not have or
describe such a multiplicity. Kerouac's novel rather allows multiplicity to seep through into and leave certain marks on its own
determined form. In this respect, it resembles the jazz Kerouac
and the beats so adore – George Shearing, for instance, is referred
to as producing 'great rich showers' of chords which he nevertheless just manages to get into some sort of 'line' (ibid. p. 122). In
On the Road, the result may turn out to be zany, offbeat narration,
as in this segment:

Had to get rid of my joint clothes and sneaked the neatest theft of a shirt and
pants from a gas station outside Flagstaff, arriving LA two days later clad as gas
attendant and walked to the first station I saw and got myself a room and
changed name (Lee Buliay) and spent an exciting year in LA, including a
whole gang of new friends and some really great girls . . . (Kerouac 1972, p.
218)

The casual shifts in the passage – in identity, perspective, time –
convey a sense of the aleatory, improvisatory, disclosive character
of beat life. This is the dimension of the novel in which, as Sal
Paradise says, at one point, 'it's an anywhere road for anybody
anyhow' (ibid. p. 237). This side of the narrative is opposed to
'smooth, well-ordered, stabilised-within-the-photo' realism (ibid.
p. 239). But beat improvisation is not strictly typical of Kerouac's
narrative. Instead, in an undecidable oscillation, improvisation
and inauguration are both contained by and disruptive of the
narrative's mimetic logic. On one level, this reflects the fact that

the characters do not finally and unequivocally commit them-selves to life on the road. On another level, it leaves Kerouac's narrative in something like the situation Sal fantastically imagines Denver in before Dean gets there: an unresolved state of struggling to 'widen the gutters' and 'foreshorten certain laws' at 'the imminent arrival of Gargantua' (ibid. p. 244).

Even as narrative purports to represent, in *On the Road*, Kerouac also insists that the representation of stable and settled presences is not at issue. There is nothing to say about the stable and settled. Rather, driving becomes a metaphor for narration and representation. It is not surprising to find Stan 'swinging into' his life story as he swings the car out of Colorado Springs and they shoot 'across the dark' (ibid. p. 253); or to find Sal and Dean pounding 'plot after plot of books we'd read' into Stan 'all the way from Amarillo to Childress' (ibid. p. 254). For Kerouac, the story is linear, a road along which things constantly appear and disappear and the real is constantly inaugurated, as a city appears on the horizon, comes close and recedes again, 'breaking up in the air and dissolving to . . . sight' (ibid. p. 252). No underlying essences ensure concatenation between one disclosure and the next, between what the beats leave behind and the subsequent 'new and unknown phase of things' (ibid. p. 260). But the characters know this more than the narrative shows it. The experience of reality as disclosure is largely a private affair. In *On the Road*, narration itself does not produce an effect of the inaugural. Kerouac provides us with a narrative in which there are many of the regulatory unities and consistencies that we associate with mimetic orthodoxy. The alternative conception of the real – the inaugural conception – emerges in play with or as it is offset against a mimetic practice that remains dominant throughout.

In Rosset's terms, then, Kerouac remains tied to the metaphysics intrinsic to all efforts to duplicate reality, whilst paradoxically refusing to entertain any teleology that would neutralise the gratuitousness of the real. Or to put it differently: in the end, *On the Road* produces a mimetic 'content' that actually questions the adequacy of the mimetic relation that the novel otherwise implic-itly insists on. What interests me here is how far other mimetic narratives might be read in such terms. Contrary to the dreams of theorists in the sixties and seventies, mimesis is not simply to be 'overcome'. We are not about to leave it behind as an anachronism a more sophisticated intellectual culture can afford to dispense with. The signs are that something like the reverse is taking place: postmodern culture is working through a fully developed scepticism about mimesis only gleefully if knowingly to return to it. It may be precisely this coexistence of mimetic practice and scepticism about mimesis, and the various forms of thought and art the two generate together, that are currently most in need of proper understanding and accurate description. On the one hand, there can be no 'adequation'. Mimesis can never be 'adequate' to anything at all. We cannot even have any certain knowledge of what it might be adequate to. But we may never be finished with mimesis, either. We may simply be starting to register how far we are straitly enclosed within a mimetic culture, as in some strange, fateful double-bind. Narrative theory has hardly begun to think in such terms. Yet they might even lead it to re-imagine the history of narrative. Certainly, we have so far hardly begun to explore the extent to which some of our most classic mimetic narratives might harbour their own particular intimations of postmodernity. The richly varied strains of anti-mimetic thought may be present in a host of more traditional narratives. It may even be that the mimetic project was bound to breed them, as inevitable by-products of the determination with which it pursued its own ends. At all events, it is time for postmodernity to to think mimesis and anti-mimesis together, as intertwined parts of a puzzle that we shall possibly never solve.

NOTES

1. See Hassan 1982; McHale 1987; and Hutcheon 1988.
2. The phrase quoted here is actually Jameson's. See Jameson 1991, p. 18. For Jameson on pastiche, see Jameson 1991, pp. 16–19, 21–5, 133–53.
3. I am aware, of course, here, that philosophers and literary theorists do not mean the same thing by 'realism'. Terry Lovell argues, for example, that the connection between epistemological realism and realism in art is at best tenuous. See Lovell 1980, p. 64. But from Plato and Aristotle to Feyerabend, the two debates have always tended to overlap. For a recent example of this, see Christopher Norris 1991b, pp. 97–107.
4. See Propp 1968; Bremond 1973; Greimas 1970, 1983; Todorov 1969; Prince 1973; and Chatman 1978.

5.   See for instance Vattimo 1988, pp. 164–82.
6.   See for instance Derrida 1976, p. 23.
7.   Cf. De Lauretis on the shift towards a cinema where 'reality is hyper-reality', especially her remarks on Nicholas Roeg's *The Man who Fell to Earth*, De Lauretis 1984, pp. 44–5.
8.   On 'certainty of representation', see Heidegger in Spanos 1979, especially pp. 9–10.
9.   Cf. also Putnam 1987, pp. 26–7 and passim.
10. See for instance Norris 1992a, p. 118.
11. Perhaps the most obvious and relevant example of the aesthetics in question here is Auerbach's *Mimesis*, which begins with Homer. See Auerbach 1973, p. 13.
12. Cf. some of Seijun Suzuki's films. In *Tokyo Drifter*, for example, especially in the 'drifting' sequence, the mixture of self-consciously artificial settings (clearly showing as they do the influence of Japanese cartoons and comic books); an anti-realistic use of colour; shifts between incongruous tones; abrupt jump cuts and other sudden disruptions of narrative logic, concatenation, order and sequence, are all features that subject the film itself to a kind of 'drift'. The world of the film 'stutters' unpredictably into being. It is interesting to note how far, in *Tokyo Drifter* in particular, Suzuki seems to have been reacting against the conventions (and the dictates) of the Nikkatsu studio, with whom he spent twelve years as a contract director. His company orders specifically required him to 'play it straight' on the film. Not surprisingly, Nikkatsu fired him in 1967.
13. A more ample account of Godard's narrative art in this context might draw on McCabe's illuminating reading of Godard's disruptions of the institutionalised fixity of relations between sound and image, relating it to Foucault's account of the 'questioning of the document' as a distinctively contemporary activity. See McCabe 1980, p. 18; and Foucault 1991b, p. 8.

3

Interrogation of Thematics:
Narrative and the Hymen

THE LIMITS OF THEMATICS

In Christa Wolf's *Cassandra*, the Trojan heroine comes to a consciousness of the strangeness or otherness of the Greeks:

For the Greeks there is no alternative but either truth or lies, right or wrong, victory or defeat, friend or enemy, life or death. They think differently than we do ... It is the other alternative that they crush between their clear-cut distinctions, the third alternative which in their view does not exist, the smiling vital force that is able to generate itself from itself over and over: the undivided, spirit in life, life in spirit. (Wolf 1991, pp. 106–7)

What sets Cassandra apart from the Greeks is her sense of 'depths' to her self where division no longer holds sway and where she is able, for instance, to experience the whole of 'Hector's fight, his wounding, his tenacious resistance, and his death' as Hector himself (ibid. p. 112). This is precisely Cassandra's 'primitive' mode of sensing and feeling – a mode which does not exclude culture, intellect or sophistication – and it is placed as prior to all structures of self and other, interiority and exteriority, all cuts made into the phenomenal continuity of the world. For Cassandra, Greek thought is that 'evil' whose name eventually becomes war (ibid. p. 104). Wolf's novel partly charts the slow slide of Troy into Greek structures of thought and feeling. Only the Trojan women can finally escape and resist these structures. For their relative powerlessness and their absence from the battlefield means that they are not drawn into that resemblance-in-

105

opposition that characterises the Trojan (and Greek) men. Hence Cassandra must differ from Penthesilea, must utter a 'we' that includes even Achilles, though 'it is so much easier to say "Achilles the brute"', like Penthesilea, 'than to say this "we"' (ibid. p. 119). This difference is a triumph for the Trojan spirit, the spirit of 'the undifferentiated age' (ibid. p. 294) and the feminine and 'the undivided'.

The essays Wolf appends to *Cassandra* also supply a theoretical account both of narrative and of *Cassandra* itself that is cognate with my account of her novel. *Cassandra* positions what Wolf calls 'the unfruitful antinomy of the pair of opposites' as intrinsic to Greek structures of valuation, to what Irigaray calls the 'new logical order' of (Greek) patriarchy which censured women's speech (Irigaray 1993, p. 17). *Cassandra* also seeks to interrogate that 'antinomy' (Wolf 1991, p. 241). The latter is understood as part of 'the hierarchical male reality principle', (ibid. p. 257), one of those 'prevailing delusional systems' into which women so often seek to 'integrate themselves', wearing themselves out in the process (ibid. p. 259). But at the same time, Wolf also sees her novel as trying to move beyond such 'delusional systems' insofar as they inhabit narrative itself. Hence her commitment rather 'to the fragmentary structure from which (for me) [*Cassandra*] is actually composed' than to 'the closed form' which it might also be thought of as having (ibid. p. 266)." Hence, too, her critique of Aristotelean aesthetics, particularly as represented in a single sentence from the *Poetics*: 'The mimetic artist depicts human beings in action. These people are either good or bad' (Wolf 1991, p. 278). Aristotle becomes an Achilles of thought, slicing, dividing, opposing. For Wolf, in relation to a prehistory seen guttering and fading with the fall of Troy, the rise of Apollo is one 'mythological reflex of the patriarchal revaluation of values'. But the same is also true of the *Iliad* in the arts and 'Aristotle's *Poetics* in the realm of art legislation' (Wolf 1991, p. 282). Historically, all are part of the same radical transformation:

This whole earthy-fruitful hodgepodge, this undisciplined tendency to merge and change into each other, this thing which it was hard to put a name to, this throng of women, mothers, and goddesses which it was hard to classify and to count, was brought under control, along with the right of male inheritance and private property . . . (ibid. p. 282)

Wolf connects this process with the emergence of the Aristotelean mode of differentiation – or, better, the Aristotelean thematisation of difference:

Aristotle: 'For example, character is good when a man has courage; but in general it is not appropriate for a woman to be brave and manly or even alarming.' (ibid.)

Here is that 'one-track-minded route . . . followed by Western thought: the route of segregation, of the renunciation of the manifoldness of phenomena . . . in favour of closed systems and pictures of life' (ibid. p. 287). For Wolf, narrative itself is possibly such a 'route.' For it is narrative too that, with 'the advent of property, hierarchy, and patriarchy extracts a blood-red thread from the fabric of human life' (ibid. p. 296). By contrast, in the older 'choral song of the priestesses', the hymn, 'there is no narration' (ibid.). Narrative itself, then – epic – is intimately allied from the start, '*by its structure*', with patriarchy and the struggle and victory or defeat of heroes. It is equally allied with a classical narrative aesthetics which acts as a system of 'categorisation and control' and 'does not so much enable us to get closer to reality' as ward it off (ibid. p. 300). The system achieves such effects by its fetishisation of clarity, its obsession with oppositions, with 'definite forms' (ibid. p. 301), chiefly, 'definite forms' as they take the shape of themes.

The narrative aesthetics of which Christa Wolf is so suspicious has substantially been ours at least since Aristotle. Thematisation has been an almost indispensable part of our thought about narrative. Criticism that seeks to 'go beyond' thematics repeatedly lapses back into it, or reinstates its systems in different terms. Nothing, for instance, could have more resembled the thematisation of narrative texts than the post-Proppian structuralist and narratological attempt to see character in narrative as reducible to proper names or predicates. Indeed, the initial operation from which much structuralist and narratological analysis proceeds is arguably of a thematising kind. To give a classic example: the deep structures that Lévi-Strauss sought to describe under the diverse surface structures of mythic narrative were precisely structures of thematic opposition: life versus death, heaven versus earth, and so on (Lévi-Strauss 1977, pp. 202–28). In effect, therefore, in Lévi-Straussian narratology, the unconscious is thematic in its essence, and has always already mirrored the structures of the theorist's or analyst's thought before he or she has applied them to the text. There is no easy escape from thematics. Christa Wolf's critique of Greece in the name of Troy might itself be thought of as working with the kind of 'unfruitful antinomy' she characterises as Greek and therefore negative. Part of the difficulty, here, is the attitude involved in critique itself. For thematisation is intrinsic to critique. By virtue of that very fact, however, it is also implicated in the current epistemological problematisation of critique itself.

James Phelan has recently given a new twist to thematics, taking issue in the process with Robert Scholes's more classical defence of it in *Textual Power*. As Phelan points out, thematisation is perhaps the most widely practised contemporary interpretative manoeuvre in the study of narrative. So well-established a critical practice has hardly stood in need of theorists to plead its cause. But there have also been some cogent challenges to thematics.[1] Scholes's defence is therefore not without point.[2] Scholes asserts that 'interpretation proper' is 'the thematising of a text' (Scholes 1985, p. 29). Hermeneutics equals thematics, *tout court*. Thematisation is 'the practice of generalising from textual particulars to cultural codes' and thereby uncovering 'the grail of contemporary criticism – the ideology of the text' (ibid.). Scholes actually appears to conceive of *Textual Power* as a post-structuralist project. But his own terms of reference largely oscillate between those of classical humanism and the structuralism that first engaged him in the seventies (Scholes 1974, 1982). For all its references to 'cultural codes' and 'ideology', *Textual Power* relies on a thoroughly traditional, Aristotelean kind of thought. Indeed, it precisely demonstrates the extent of the possible complicity between Aristoteleanism and semiotics. The two principal operations involved in thematisation, for Scholes, are characteristically Aristotelean: the construction of 'the binary oppositions that interpretation seeks to reveal as the axes of value in a text' (Scholes 1985, p. 53); and the expression of the connection between the particular and the general. 'The first things to look for' in interpretation, writes Scholes, 'are repetitions or oppositions that emerge at the manifest level of the text' (ibid. p. 32). But the analyst will then want to connect 'the singular oppositions of the text' to 'the generalised oppositions that structure our cultural system of values', the latter being 'the master code that the literary text both depends upon and modifies' (ibid. p. 33). The theorist will also seek to understand 'the unique quality of the particular version of the larger instance'. This latter procedure will enable him or her to move 'from noting the cultural codes invoked to understanding the attitude taken towards these codes by the maker of the text' (ibid. p. 34). Ideology is less in question, here, than a traditional conception of the most significant level of meaning in a text as authorial and moral. Thus thematics not only works to assure the continuing ideological dominance of the binary principle and philosophical essentialism. It also confirms the assumption of an authorial intention as central to narrative texts, and moralises that intention accordingly. Scholes's study makes peculiarly clear the ideological convergence in thematics of dualism, essentialism, a foundational ethics and an ideology of the author in narrative as unified, coherent and purposive subject. Here precisely we glimpse how far metaphysics is at stake (and at risk) in thematics as it has been classically conceived.

By contrast, Phelan's approach to thematics might seem postmodern, not least in its rejection of the grandiosity of Scholes's project. Phelan's notion of the role and scope of thematics is deliberately limited and modest. Thematics is not a totalising mode of thought. Narrative texts are not amenable to thematisation as totalities. Not surprisingly, then, thematics is only one strand in Phelan's *Reading People, Reading Plots* (Phelan 1989). The principal focus is on character. Phelan is concerned to 'draw a circle around the thematic functions of character', to be able to say 'not only "these are the appropriate generalisations, and these are not", but also "just so much generalising and no more"' (ibid. p. 61). He identifies three components in narrative texts and their characters: mimetic, thematic and synthetic ('artificial' or self-consciously literary). The three components are of varying importance and occupy different relations to each other in different narrative texts. None of the three can subsume or be subsumed by the others. The relationship between them is not hierarchical. Unlike Scholes, then, Phelan grants only a relative importance to thematic assertions, seeing them as arising in the midst of other elements of the text. One corollary of this is his rejection of the static nature of structuralist models. He puts a great deal of emphasis on narrative temporality or progression. For Phelan, themes are not to be grasped and described once and for all. They must rather be understood as emerging gradually through a given narrative, and as themselves affected by their own linear emergence. Phelan is wary of 'the kind of binary reasoning underlying much thematic criticism' (ibid. p. 217). But what really matters to him is what he takes to be the connection between binarism and totalising abstraction. For Phelan, for instance, in putting such crucial weight on binary opposites, Scholes's thematics produces abstract schemes of a structuralist kind which take him too far away from the text's 'forest of particulars', the dynamics of the text as 'temporal process' (ibid. p. 75).[3] But the real problem with such thematics is the claim it makes for the centrality of a given theme, the extent to which binarism is globalised, turned into *the* logic of the text, rather than understood as merely one logic amongst others. What matters above all is the sacrifice of the particular to the general in binarism, the determination of the function of every element of a narrative text according to the structure of a single matrix. In other words, Phelan recognises that the binarism of the thematists is always double itself, that it always has a vertical as well as a horizontal dimension, that its principle of organisation is actually the symmetrical geometrics of the box. On the one hand, there is the structure of the thematic opposition, on the other, the opposition of particular and general or instance and model that founds and guarantees the thematic opposition as one between static quantities.

But the logic whose insufficiencies Phelan so clearly sees is also the logic he is bound by. For Phelan's understanding of theme depends on a distinction between the thematic dimensions of character, or what he calls *attributes*, and the same character's thematic *functions*. Attributes can apparently be identified and described in isolation from the work itself. Functions are particular applications of the 'attributes' and evanescent, textual phenomena. Attributes are virtual, and may or may not be actualised as functions. Functions change with the progression of the narrative in which they are located. But perhaps the key word, for Phelan, is 'representative'. The relation between function and attribute is a representative relation. Functions 'reveal ideas' (Phelan 1989, p. 18). Indeed, 'the importance of thematising' precisely derives 'from the assumption that a narrative achieves its significance from the ideational generalisations it leads one to' (ibid. p. 27). In other words, behind the dynamic lies the static, the already formulated, just as in Scholes's thematics or in structuralist narratology. Yet again, meaning and 'depicted world' turn out to be to language and text as soul is supposed to be to body: pre-existent and free-floating wholes. We are thus at once returned to a model that is both binary and idealist. We go back to what Phelan has seemingly objected to in orthodox thematics: the theological assumption that themes somehow exist as wholes, outside and independent of their momentaneous and successive textual manifestations.

Such an assumption, however, immediately prioritises themat- ics all over again. For it effectively provides character with a foundation in abstract essence, irrespective of any forest of textual particulars. Phelan may argue that reading and interpreting narrat- ive involve a passage or 'progression' through the 'instabilities' of the text. But in fact, such 'instabilities' are always variants on or 'twists' to a theme that has actually been decided from the start. Phelan's idealism means that the structure of any given thematic resolution is always fore-ordained: and fore-ordained, too, as dualistic. His accounts of texts repeatedly resort to the very binary structures of which he is otherwise so wary. Even his two major categories – the mimetic and the thematic – become another form of dualism. Textual 'instabilities' and the play of thematic ele- ments are ultimately sorted out, again, into a structure of opposi- tions.

SERRES, CRITIQUE AND THE 'EXCLUDED THIRD'

So far from elaborating a thematics which finally has done with dualism, Phelan merely confirms the inescapability of dualism itself, and its seemingly inevitable implication in thematics. For all his poststructuralist sophistication, Phelan sidesteps what, for any postmodern approach to thematics, is arguably the most crucial concern of all: the phenomenological structure of the critical act itself. For critique and thematisation have always been intimately involved with one another. In the first instance, critique and its 'attitude' to the text – observation, scrutiny – can hardly proceed without that abstraction from the particular, on the one hand, and that separation out of opposed abstractions, on the other, which is characteristic of thematics. Equally, thematics feeds off the olympian structure which is intrinsic to critique. This structure not only categorically separates off observer from observed, but also places the first 'above' the second. Hence the close connection between thematics and moralism. If thematics implies categorical decision, it also implies decision leading to judgment or valuation. Decision and judgment, writes Michel Serres, are the primary senses of the 'acte critique' (Serres 1987, p. 61). Serres interrogates the positions and operations involved in critique in L'Hermaphrodite, his book on Balzac's Sarrasine. For Serres, with Kant, philosophy entered its phase as critique, 'c'est-à-dire au tribunal'. Kant inaugurated that sombre period 'où tout se décidait au-devant d'une dernière instance, préalablement choisie' (ibid. p. 64). As we emerge from that period, we find ourselves called on to abandon, not just the negativity of separation involved in critique, but also the dividing operation of critique as a judicial procedure that opposes observer to observed as dominator to dominated or power to its disempowered object. Serres confirms that the dualism of critique always has a vertical dimension. The incompatibility or inter-exclusivity of the opposites in question in critique (and in thematics) is determined from a 'superior' position that is also one of power (ibid. p. 79). In Éclaircissements, Serres describes this as the 'august position' endemic to critique as a theological practice, 'cette place auguste' in which one is always in the right, the most knowledgeable and strongest (Serres 1992, p. 195). But, at the end of the 'parenthesis' that has seen the rise of critique, the tone and rhetoric of this position must sound increasingly hollow and anachronistic (ibid. p. 186). So, too, the spatial model which has made the 'august position' tenable is presently crumbling.

For Serres, the rule of critique is phallic law (ibid.). Critique seeks to climb its way back to and categorically to identify what it conceives of as 'la décision du tribunal' (ibid. p. 149). It hates mixtures, impurities, indistinctness, originary chaos, interimplication. It can therefore accomplish its work through the practice of thematisation, because thematisation produces and insists on clarity, purity and distinction. *L'Hermaphrodite* clearly responds to Barthes's account of *Sarrasine* in *S/Z*. More specifically, it is a critique that repudiates or eschews critique as Barthes himself produces it. Serres's is actually involved in what Lyotard would call a differend with Barthes, since Serres deliberately claims no 'higher ground' or more absolute foundation for his case. He is well aware, too, of the extent to which Barthes's critique depends on a thematisation of the text. This is particularly true in the case of Barthes's 'symbolic code', the code which allegedly structures *Sarrasine* in terms of antitheses and stimulates the reader to extrapolate to themes. For Serres, the antitheses in question are clearly Barthes's, not Balzac's. The antithetical, thematic structures supposedly present in *Sarrasine* are actually the mirror-image or reflection of critique itself and its Socratic, segmenting methods. Barthes fails to see, for instance, that, at the beginning of *Sarrasine*, Balzac is actually making fun of the kind of philosophical curiosity, endemic to the human sciences, that can only regularly ask a certain kind of question of the text. Equally, Barthes fails to note that the story begins, not so much with antithesis as with the image of a hesitating, anxious body caught between two states, '*préposé aux régions critiques*' (Serres 1987, p. 62). The narrator in *Sarrasine* is a point of intersection or mixture, '*un sympathique*'. He understands all and rejects nothing. He brings together the diverse. That is his function (ibid. pp. 153–4). He is a point at which opposites are reconciled – as they are in Sarrasine himself and in la Zambinella – rather than one from which opposites are specified and defined. It would thus be more appropriate to think of the beginning of *Sarrasine* in terms of orientation than thematisation. In general, the narrator finds bearings or constructs a succession of positions for himself in what is otherwise a multiple, precritical space (ibid. pp. 73–6). Originary chaos haunts the work – a point Balzac makes explicit in *The Unknown Masterpiece*. Balzac is not really interested in criteria for judgment, but in the conditions which make production possible, the resources of the multiple that the artist plumbs. *Sarrasine* is therefore better conceived of in the figure of the hermaphrodite than the figures produced by thematics. For the figure of the hermaphrodite corresponds to Balzac's *Sarrasine* as

'*éblouissant montage*', a 'complex multiple' of associated connections, 'hybrid like chimerae' (ibid. p. 95). This is the very figure of
the narrative text itself.

But Serres is not simply opposed to the kind of polarising
distinctions that make thematics possible. Rather, he insists that
such distinctions advance us little if we do not grasp the site of
their union or what he repeatedly calls the 'link' (*le lien* (Serres
1992, p. 226)). The figure of the hesitating narrator at the beginning of *Sarrasine* is precisely that of the threshold or frontier
between states, the connection or point of contact between
extremes. So too the hybrid figure of the hermaphrodite is the
figure of the middle ground, the mediator, the excluded third.
Such a figure serves precisely to situate us beyond '*la pathologie
sotte de division*' (Serres 1991a, p. 21), in what has for so long
been the blindspot of philosophy: the point of junction (Serres
1992, p. 237). In *Rome: The Book of Foundations* Serres identifies
the principle of thesis and antithesis, of disputes of any kind –
'polemical, dialectical or apologetical' – with the principle of war
(Serres 1991b, p. 146). It is here precisely, he suggests, that
philosophy has been 'the reprisal of barbarism in and by culture'
(ibid. p. 147). What matters for Serres, however, is not primarily
any crude equation to be drawn between different kinds of
violence, but rather questions of time and – particularly – space.
Dispute, dialectic, war, all work by the establishment of borders, a
peculiarly precise tracing of space (ibid. p. 148). Theirs is the
rigour, 'the hard logic of boxes' which operates according to a
space which is never deformable (ibid. p. 178). The thought of
thesis and antithesis is therefore always an imperial thought,
seemingly in movement but actually always static (ibid. p. 158). In
fact, however, there is always a 'double law' which is liable to
convert opposites into or make them resemble one another. This
subtler element or 'principle of incertitude' is the primitive itself,
and continually 'makes the partition porous, makes the boundaries waver, blurs definition' (Serres 1982, pp. 141–3). This again
is the 'excluded third', and its exclusion is at the foundation of
our logic, as the scapegoat is at the foundation of our anthropology
(ibid. p. 149). The logic of the excluded third thus becomes 'the
logic or the strategy of the joker' (ibid. p. 160), its image the joker's

motley.[4] For to think the third is not only to think a middle point but to think the point from which systems radiate, and therefore to think the mélange or multiplicity.

The thought of the third thus invites us to 'apprehend the reasonable in the nonrigorous', in 'the soft, the extensible, the textile and the fluid' (ibid. p. 178). For Serres, thematics or what he refers to as 'the whole fabric of interpretation' is part of 'the great classical rationality' and shares the latter's limitations (Serres 1991b, p. 227). Thematics cannot recognise the inter-involvement of the elements it isolates and codifies into structures. It is blind to narrative as weave or *parcours* among multiple spaces. Effectively, it needs to be replaced by a '*tierce critique*' on the model of what Serres calls '*la tierce philosophie*' or '*la tierce instruction*' (Serres 1991a, pp. 27, 77). This is one manifestation of what Vattimo calls 'weak thought'.[5] '*Voici venu l'âge des lueurs*', writes Serres, '*l'age des éclats et des occultations locales, l'âge du scintillement*' (ibid. p. 77). A postmodern philosophy of the third relinquishes dreams of the unity of knowledge or the prospect of whole illumination. In that respect, at least, it might be said to move 'beyond' Plato and the Greeks, classical science, the Enlightenment, the monotheistic thought of the one God. It abandons the '*cruels partages*' of truth and error, science and reverie, progress and obscurantism. It offers itself, instead, as a 'harlequined' or chromatic form of knowledge, a knowledge whose inescapable condition is always chiaroscuro, the '*clair-obscur*' (ibid. p. 94). It works between 'conscious and clear organisation' and what, in *The Parasite*, Serres calls its 'obscure opposite . . . lapping behind everyone's back, the dark side of the system' (Serres 1982, p. 12). The thought of the third is the equivalent in the human sciences of the mathematicians' 'fuzzy set'. It is where the geometrical mode of thought finally makes its peace with finesse (ibid. p. 60). If 'fluctuation, disorder, opacity and noise are no longer affronts to the rational', are even needed by it (ibid. pp. 13, 79), the philosophy of the third places itself between such features and the rationality they sporadically confound. The philosophy of the third 'speaks in a logic considered irrational up to now' and at the same time ushers in 'a new epistemology and a new theory of equilibrium' (ibid. p. 36), a new spacing for knowledge, one that is 'conditional' rather than 'systematic' (ibid. p. 70). In fact, knowledge itself has always been such a space, a space of transformations, which only lack of knowledge has been able to obscure with systems. In Serres's terms, 'there are only *metabalas*' (ibid. p. 72). There is only the third.

DERRIDA, DECONSTRUCTION AND THEMATICS

But what would a narrative theory that 'thinks the third' look like? How would a '*tiers critique*' work? In *Le Tiers-Instruit*, Serres gives us some sense of this, largely in his various accounts of texts he himself describes as 'textes tiers-instruites' (Serres 1991a, p. 112): texts by Leibniz, Diderot and Goethe, Pascal's *Pensées*, Zola's works, Musil's *A Man Without Qualities* and Mérimée's *Carmen*. With its networks of bifurcations, writes Serres;

> [*Carmen*] enseigne excellement le tiers-instruit . . . à un moment et même à tout instant, puisque les fourches abondent, l'aventure reste en tiers, en équilibre, en une origine courante, entre les jugements, l'amour et la mort, la science et la littérature, l'érudition et le racontar . . . (ibid. pp. 107–8)

But it is Derrida who has 'thought the third' most effectively in connection with literature, specifically in his conception of the hymen. The idea of the hymen, too, is precisely linked to an interrogation of thematics, specifically as instanced in Jean-Pierre Richard's account of Mallarmé.[6] Richard understands there to be an 'active system' in Mallarmé's work in which 'themes . . . tend to organise themselves as in any living structure' (Richard 1961). These themes combine 'into flexible groupings' in a search for 'the best possible equilibrium' (Ibid). In particular, says Richard, themes 'arrange themselves into antithetical pairs', or, 'in a more complex manner, into multiple compensating systems', but systems where the 'pair' is the basic unit (ibid.). In Richard, then, we are inexorably returned to thematics as a dualism. Effectively, too, thematics has a vertical dimension again. The point is clearly implicit in Derrida's description of the dialecticity of Richard's model of the Mallarméan text, particularly in that the model presents the dialectic in question as oriented towards a final, felicitous 'synthesis', 'resolution' or – precisely – *Aufhebung*. But if Scholes's and Phelan's work reveals how far a given geometry of textual dimensions associates thematics with moralism, Derrida suggests that Richard's terms of reference belong to a critical psychologism (Derrida 1981b, p. 248).

Like New Criticism from Richards to Tate and beyond, Richard conceives of the text, not just as a dualistic 'play of forces very precisely pitted against each other', but as a 'total balance' of forces which 'amounts to the euphoria of a "suspension"' (ibid. p. 247). To the horizontal level on which the 'antithetical pairs' arrange themselves is added a 'higher' vantage or pivotal point which allows 'tension' to be 'eased into new synthetic notions or into concrete forms that realise a satisfactory equilibrium' (ibid.). This, then, is the 'ideal architecture' that constitutes 'the internal reality of a poem' by Mallarmé, for instance (ibid.). If the idea of equilibrium is crucial here, then so too is the idea of dimensions, of the work as an architecture in which 'the mind or spirit' becomes the 'keystone' whereby 'everything communicates, balances out and is neutralized' (ibid.). Here precisely, in a given geometrical figure, is a theological formulation of the text as constructed along a spirit/matter axis, with spirit serving – Godlike – to pacify the oppositions generated by the thematic divide.

Derrida attempts to think the text differently, with theme no longer available in 'an imaginary, intentional or lived domain beyond all textual instances' (ibid. p. 251). He deconstructs Richard's geometry of textual dimensions in the service of an account of what he (Derrida) calls textual laterality (ibid. p. 251). The idea of the hymen emerges precisely here. As Derrida formulates it, the hymen bridges a gap, seals a bond, connects, fuses, confuses or confounds opposites, 'unites *and* differentiates' (ibid. p. 252, italics mine). It is a figure for the principle of interdependence or interinvolvement, of inseparability. It is a practice, but it is also a conception of the very element of the text, 'the medium, the pure medium, of fiction' (ibid. p. 211); 'medium in the sense of middle, neither/nor, what is between extremes, and medium in the sense of element, ether, matrix, means' (ibid.). The hymen is 'the element of the *same* (to be distinguished from the identical)' in which all 'oppositional concepts' are 'announced' (ibid. p. 9). Difference is not obliterated in the hymen. But, as medium, the hymen denies that difference can be cast in the hard moulds supplied by thematics. Difference now emerges only in a ceaseless movement of appearance and disappearance. Every discursive 'step' is understood as implying 'a *fort/da*', rather than as a movement over or across a set of stable bases (Derrida 1987c, p. 357). Derrida writes of 'the confusion and continuity of the hymen' in which 'difference inscribes itself' but 'without any decidable poles, without any independent, irreversible terms' (Derrida 1981a, p. 210). If polarity yields to undecidability, then here precisely we move, not towards the end of thematics (which can hardly be conceived) but a postmodern relaxation of its imperious constraints, an abandonment of its too ambitious project, an undoing of what Derrida himself understands as its 'assurance' of 'mastery' (ibid. p. 210). Derrida connects the hymen with 'the very progression' of the text which produces but also abolishes difference, thus thwarting 'an overall meaning system or even a structural semantics' (ibid. p. 245). Indeed, for the geometric image of the text as pyramid or box, or the architectonic image of the text as storeyed house of fiction, Derrida substitutes the image of the text as fan, ceaselessly deployed then retracted, opened then closed. As fan, the text institutes theme, not as presence established and guaranteed by antithetical pairing, but as a play of 'meaning-' or 'theme-effects', with writing constantly 'setting them up in relations of difference and resemblance' (ibid. p. 251). Here precisely the grandiose fantasy of an established thematics begins to crumble, ceding to a more modest project.

Derrida has repeatedly provided examples of how deconstruction works as an interrogation of thematics and a displacement of the latter's geometry. Thus for instance with the theme of reason and instinct in Condillac. In Condillac,

reason *is* instinct. As there is between reason and instinct only a difference in degree, the two concepts . . . do not oppose each other. And yet reason *is not* instinct. The difference of degree . . . produces and destroys the *is* of every predication, supports and deports at once each ontological statement. And already every metaphysical determination or delimitation. (Derrida 1987a, p. 98)

What 'simultaneously constructs and *ruins*' the '*discursive edifice*' in Condillac is the existence of the hymen, the tie, that reciprocity, complicity or mutuality that endlessly haunts divisions (ibid., italics mine). To read Condillac in terms of the hymen is to refuse to 'stabilise' the undecidability of his discourse, to avoid any 'annulment and equalization' of the discourse 'in the mode of *pro* and *contra*' (Derrida 1979, p. 63). For in Condillac as in Nietzsche the 'graphic of the hymen' cannot be reduced. It 'describes a margin where the control over meaning or code is without recourse, poses the limit to the relevance of the hermeneutic or systematic question' (ibid. p. 99). In fact, the thought of the hymen plunges us into '*le vertige d'une non-maîtrise*' (ibid. p. 100), that actual non-masterability of the text – finally, always, for good – from which our thematics, like our hermeneutics, has so powerfully and consistently sought to protect us. It pays the cryptic and the undecipherable their due, acknowledges the extent to which any text will slip away, be forgotten, even in the act of reading. The thought of the hymen outwits ontology itself which, with its 'inspection, appropriation, identification and verification of identity' conceals undecidability even as it presupposes it (ibid. p. 103). The hymen reinstitutes play – or, rather, reinstitutes 'the play of the world' in narrative, narrative *as* the play of the world. Thematics on the other hand makes play into an activity, the activity of a subject manipulating objects, one dominated by meaning and its finality as what surpasses and orients play. To think in terms of the hymen is to resist this procedure and to begin to engage in 'the "diacritical" work of difference *in* the constitution of sense and signs', rather than making difference 'derivative', as the metaphysics of presence does (Derrida 1973, p. 101).

FEMINIST THEORY AND THE PROBLEM OF THE 'VERSUS'

To think of narrative in terms of the hymen, however, is to engage in a problematic relationship with what has been the most interesting development in the study of narrative in the past few years, feminist narratology. As recently as 1989, Robyn Warhol was expressing concern at the absence of a feminist narratology. Narratology had been gender-blind, was still sunk in what Elaine Showalter had described as an 'androgynist poetics' which had

long since been outstripped by feminist critique, female aesthetics, gynocritics, gynesis and gender theory.[7] As Warhol asserts,
'*all* variables of context' have largely remained outside the realm
of classical narratology (Warhol 1989, p. 4). The emergence of a
feminist narratology has thus seemed to represent an important,
new resistance to narratological structuralism. But its effect has
also been double. Feminist narratology has constituted a necessary and crucial intervention in a narrative technology whose
models and methods have been almost exclusively masculine in
their sources and orientation, and whose ideology has been
profoundly patriarchal. But even as it has appeared to resist
narratological tradition and displace some of its emphases, the
feminist critique has also given a powerful new boost to narratological geometrics and thematics. It has therefore been reimpli-
cated in the very metaphysics that, on another level, it has
successfully called in question. This is precisely the effect of the
feminist insistence on rethinking relations between the 'central'
and the 'marginal' or what Molly Hite calls 'recentring the value
structure of narrative' (Hite 1989, p. 2). Hite's own primary
concern, for example, is with 'experimental', postmodern, feminist narratives. For Hite, such narratives constitute 'the other side
of the story' and therefore require an appropriate narratology. Hite
envisages her postmodern narratives as consisting of suppressed
stories '*of the Other*' (ibid. p. 4). To think of them thus is to think
'the enabling conditions for the writing and reading of feminist
narrative' (ibid.). Since stories 'entail a point of view, take sides'
(ibid. p. 5), one 'enabling condition' would clearly be opposition.
Feminist criticism has shown how female novelists from Austen
through Eliot and on have repeatedly given us the other side of a
culturally mandated narrative. For Hite, this is a narratological
issue, since 'the other side of the story' repeatedly discloses the
extent to which heroines are constrained by narrative givens not
of their own making. Hite's kind of narratology is concerned both
with a critique of those 'narrative givens' and with narrative as it
is radically other to the narratives constructed by masculine
discourse. Yet even as such an approach asserts its field of inquiry
as the 'other' discourse, it also positions that discourse in a
relation of thematic opposition to the pre-existing one. Hite then
reads the same opposition back into the texts with which she is

concerned. She thus presents Jean Rhys, for example, as continually placing 'a marginal character at the centre of her fiction', thereby decentring an inherited narrative structure and undermining 'the values informing this structure' (ibid. p. 25). But as Hite admits, this is to 'decentre' narrative only promptly to 'recentre' it again. The 'structure' in question is precisely both dislodged *and* maintained. The Rhys narrative may reverse in its very structure the economic and social dependency visited on the victim-figure. But this 'marginal character' is nonetheless completed in her meaning and value only in her thematic relation to a pre-existent, opposing value both inside and outside the text.

In this manner, Hite actually reconfirms the old, deep-rooted connections between thematics, mimetologism and moralism. For all its importance, it is clear from Hite's work that there is no immediate 'floating free' of the terms of patriarchy in narratology. It is precisely at moments of what seems like escape from or peculiarly powerful resistance to those terms that the theorist may be most in danger of lapsing back into them. In other words, I wonder about the durability and power of a feminist narratology that does not sustain the 'deconstructive turn' so brilliantly elaborated, for instance, in Alice Jardine's *Gynesis* and recently – in a rather different context – in the work of Drucilla Cornell.[8] To an uncomfortable extent, the much-needed feminist critique in narrative theory may still be deriving its terms from patriarchy. As Eagleton remarks, deconstruction may continue to be of use to feminism precisely as a means of negotiating this contradiction, since, 'though historically speaking the conflict between men and women could not have been more real, the ideology of this anatagonism involved a metaphysical illusion' (Eagleton 1983, pp. 149–50). Jardine likewise emphasises the importance of combining feminist goals with deconstructive strategies, precisely as a way of working with the fact of women's oppression on the one hand and the masculinism inherent in classical methodologies on the other (Jardine 1985). By contrast, Robyn Warhol and Susan Lanser[9] – both leading feminist narratologists – have more or less explicitly posited a move beyond Jardine's kind of feminism as a move back before her appropriation of deconstruction – in Warhol's words, a move back to the 'systematic study' of discursive conventions. According to Warhol

What makes narratology so useful is that it can take gender studies a step further into a tangible, arguable position on particular texts: instead of simply talking in generalities about 'women's styles', it can genuinely point to the features that constitute those styles in narrative. (Warhol 1989, p. 14)

But this, again, is to institute a thematics of gender as determining and structuring difference, both in the relations between different kinds of text and internally, within specific texts themselves. Warhol is not an essentialist. She and Lanser agree that

strategies of narrative perspective change over time, varying according to literary period and according to the ideology that informs each text. At any given historical moment, certain techniques may be associated with male writing, while others are associated with female texts. (ibid. p. 17)

The consequence of this line of argument, however, is that Warhol maintains the thematic division even whilst knowing that, in the end, it offers only an empty structure of non-pertinent categories. This is not to assert, as a consequence, that, for narratology, gender distinctions are insignificant. That would be absurd. Yet even as Warhol historicises in distinguishing between 'engaging interventions' (female) and 'distancing interventions' (male) in the Victorian novel, she also perpetuates a binary mode of thought as though it were somehow outside history and had not itself been at the very least inflected by gender relations. Equally, that mode of thought is also read inside the text in question. It is scarcely surprising, then, to find Warhol asserting the binding power of the classic structuralist conception of 'models', and citing largely male theorists (Barthes, Lévi-Strauss, Briaudel) as sources for them. Actually, Warhol produces her own version of the geometric diagram as it is familiar everywhere in classical narratology, repeatedly structuring texts according to the familiar pairs of terms (author/text, narratee/reader, male/female and so on). These are precisely the kinds of terms necessary to a strongly thematic reading. In fact, in Warhol's narratology, thematics and even didacticism are powerfully reinstituted as narratological concerns to a degree that the more formalist narratology preceding her had been largely unwilling to countenance.

Similarly, if Warhol refers us to Barthes and Lévi-Strauss, Lanser draws at key points on Genette's work on narrative levels and Stanzel's distinction between 'authorial' and 'figural' modes (Lanser 1992, pp. 15, 18 and passim). Much the same kind of point can be made of the essays in the section on 'Gender, Difference and Narration' in Fehn, Hoesterey and Tatar's *Never-ending Stories* (Fehn et al 1992, pp. 161–234). Thus Gail Finney, writing on 'GDR fictions of sexual metamorphosis', not only relies for her methods on Stanzel's work, but specifically accepts Stanzel's description of 'person' in narrative as 'the "*most obvious opposition*" present among the *structurally significant pairs of elements* constituting the narrative situation' (ibid. p. 163, italics mine). Susan Rubin Suleiman's account of Carrington's *The Hearing Trumpet* draws on Barthes and the Genettian geometrics of 'framing' and the '*mise-en-abîme*' to further a view of Carrington's text as a disputatious, oppositional engagement both with a masculine 'sacred text' and with male avant-garde artistic practice (ibid. pp. 179–98). The feminist narratologist repeatedly adopts models from a science that has never ceased to be masculine in all its predispositions. None of the theorists cited here raises the problem of the 'versus', as the word appears in Tatar's 'Telling Differences: Parents versus Children in "The Juniper Tree"' (ibid. pp. 199–212). For Tatar herself, a gendered reading has to be a thematised reading. So, too, for Lanser as for Hite, a gendered reading is a reading that thematises the central and the marginal, as in the case of Marie-Jeanne Riccoboni's *Lettres de Milady Juliette Catesby à Henriette Campley, Son Amie*, where 'Juliette Catesby's "free" voice opposes the conventional plot in which a heroine moves . . . "toward her inevitable end, death or marriage, along lines her body generates"' (Lanser 1992, p. 27). Gail Finney writes of a 'central antithesis' between male and female principles in the stories she considers (Fehn 1992, p. 164). For Suleiman, *The Hearing Trumpet* is always underpinned by 'the primary structure of the feminist revision' (ibid.), the argument with patriarchy. Thematics repeatedly dictates the terms in which it is possible for the feminist narratologist to conceive of the narrative text. Indeed, nowhere could the connection between thematics and the structuralist methods of classical narratology be more apparent. Here precisely we have what Jardine calls 'the essential virility of metaphysics, even when practised by women' (Jardine 1985, p. 188).

What gets repeatedly missed, then, in such feminist thematisations of the narrative text is Wolf's concept of the 'undivided', Serres's excluded third, Derrida's hymen. The thought of the hymen continues to ask radical questions of current feminist narratology in the name of a 'feminisation' of thought. Yet in return, of course, feminist theory has recently been asking the most searching questions of poststructuralist and Derridean theory and, above all, their deployment of the 'feminine'. Alice Jardine understands the 'feminine' in Derrida as an alternative logic (alternative, that is, to the logic of metaphysics, (Jardine 1985, p. 188)). Within this Derridean logic, says Jardine, the hymen functions as 'the father-less, always feminine paradigm of undecidability' (ibid. p. 191). But there are grounds for suspicion:

> Is this merely a question of a new ruse of reason, a kind of 'seducing' of feminist discourse, an attempt to render feminist discourse seductive (to men)? Might there not be a new kind of desire on the part of modern Man to occupy all positions at once (among women, among texts)? Are we here only brushing up against a new version of an old male fantasy: that of escaping the laws of the fathers through the independent and at the same time dependent female? Are men projecting their own 'divisions' onto their primordial interlocutors – women? (ibid. p. 207)

The danger is of a male construction of the feminine in the name of the feminine which 'occupies' and thus obscures the place of the feminine. This 'new ruse of reason' works as a new form of domination of the other through identification with and strategic assertion of a common cause with the other. Thus for Teresa de Lauretis, if woman as 'womb waiting to be fecundated by words, a void ready to be filled with meanings . . . is a notorious cliché, of Western literary writing', then 'the hymen, the figure of deconstruction and Derrida's model of the textual operation' is simply the 'most recent version' of the cliché (De Lauretis 1989, p. 75). The idea of the hymen constitutes nothing less than the appropriation and disallowal of the female in a textual figure of femininity. Part of de Lauretis's own concern, then, has actually been with narratology as 'feminist critique', with the interrogation of such 'textual figures of femininity' in postmodern narrative (Calvino, *The Name of the Rose*, *Juliet of the Spirits* and so on).

The point for de Lauretis would seem to be precisely not to respond to such texts with theoretical 'figures of femininity', but to unmask the figures as they appear both in theory and in narrative practice.

The most compelling and ambitious philosophical version of this 'unmasking', however, is Rosi Braidotti's. Braidotti sees the idea of the feminine as crucial to some of the most pressing concerns in contemporary theory: the critique of rationality, of unified subjectivity, of the relations of power to knowledge, and so on. But she argues that Foucault, Lyotard, Derrida and Deleuze all produce an abstraction of femininity which is separated off from real women and the ineradicable materiality of 'sexuation'. In other words, they refuse all emphasis on the sexual specificity of gender. The theorists repeatedly shift questions of gender on to a decentred or deconstructed, 'feminised' but non-female subject. In other words, they deal ceaselessly with woman as metaphor. Derrida's ' "becoming-woman" of philosophy' may be an aspect of his attempt at a 'de-phallicisation of philosophical thought'. But it is also part of the metaphorisation of the feminine evident everywhere in current male theory (Braidotti 1991, pp. 9, 98). For Derrida, 'woman' is 'that which evades and is in excess of the phallogocentric structure of subjectivity' (ibid. p. 100). But the feminine thus becomes 'indeterminacy, oscillation, play of veils and simulacra, is given as a no-where, the creative void at the heart of the will-to-know' (ibid. p. 102). Woman becomes precisely 'that which will not be pinned down by truth' (Derrida 1979, p. 55). The feminine is thereby valorised 'as difference or counterstrategy', as 'bearer' of 'relational values' within 'a discourse . . . that privileges relationship rather than opposition, gift rather than challenge, the offer of love rather than the declaration of war' (Braidotti 1991, p. 104). In all this apparent glorification of woman, Derrida is actually using the feminine 'to avoid confronting the problem of the reality of women and their relation to truth' (ibid. p. 103). He is too much the Heideggerian to surrender his conviction that ontological difference is not the same as sexual difference. As a result, he de-sexualises and disembodies women.

Braidotti's brilliance, however, might also seem to raise some awkward questions for feminist narrative theory. She suggests that the constant danger for feminist theory 'is that of homologation, and hence of disappearing into the other's text, the master's voice, in established conceptual frameworks' (ibid. p. 14). If that is so, feminist narratology would seem to offer a good illustration of the kind of 'disappearance' Braidotti mentions. As part of a new, proleptic feminist thought, Braidotti argues, not just for 'new, woman-based modalities of ... communication of knowledge', but for a constantly renewed effort to trace 'theoretical itineraries which differ from traditional reflection – and deviate from our established mental habits' (ibid. pp. 12–13). Has feminist narratology really been tracing such an 'itinerary'? What current narratology may arguably most need is a radical feminist transformation of its models and modes of thought, a woman-dominated repudiation of its masculine geometrics. But is such a transformation actually taking place? There are certainly enough examples of the kinds of models it might deploy. Irigaray's conception of a 'placental economy', for example, is precisely of a 'mediating space' which 'cannot be reduced either to a relation of fusion or one of aggression' and regulates exchanges (Irigaray 1993, p. 39). It has 'an almost ethical character', says Irigaray, and ignorance of it has a profound effect on 'the male cultural imaginary' (ibid. pp. 41–2). How might the concept help to transform our narratological models? Might Hélène Cixous's concept of *écriture féminine* also help? After all, as Braidotti herself asserts, *écriture féminine* subverts the binary structures that are intrinsic to a 'feminophobic' culture (Braidotti 1991, p. 240). It involves a new 'notion of positionality' (ibid.). Morag Shiach suggests that, for Cixous, 'feminine writing' happens 'in the "between", in that space which is uncertain'. It is 'dangerous' in 'its refusal to ally itself with one side of an opposition. Stepping outside, negotiating the between, feminine writing is to carve out a new space of representation that will not fit into old grids' (Shiach 1991, p. 22).

What would a new, feminist narratology look like if it not only took account of *écriture féminine* but also sought to be a version of it? Might it not create a space for thought that differed radically to that of the dominant narratological tradition? Most of all, perhaps, there is Braidotti's own 'new nomadism', and its attempt to raise the 'non-coincidence' of her own ideas and concerns 'to the status of a new style of thought'. This devises 'flying paths through the multiple points of intersection that make up the discontinuous line' of her project, and produces 'patterns of dissonance, a polyphonic play, a game of multiplicities' (Braidotti 1991, p. 14). But as 'a precarious conceptual geometry of the non-Euclidean type', in Braidotti's phrase, doesn't such thought presently seem remote from feminist narratology?

On the one hand, then, a feminist narratology which consolidates a classical (and, historically, primarily a masculine) thematics; on the other, a postmodern 'feminisation' of philosophy and theory barely concealing a male agenda. There cannot even be any guarantee that a new, more radical version of feminist narratology would not find itself caught in paradoxes very like those haunting it at present. In this context and at the present moment, the thought of the hymen at least contains or takes for granted such slippages and ambiguities. For it consciously seeks to avoid the purity of absolute separation, of clear polarity. Until feminist theory radicalises our models, then, as far as narrative theory is concerned, the thought of the hymen has a contingent and strategic usefulness. For it is a 'third term' of a kind that feminist narrative theory may have still to invent. Furthermore, if the thought of the hymen 'metaphorises' the feminine, some feminist theory, at least, might seem to legitimise such metaphorisation. Michèle le Dœuff, for example, has written of the actual 'incapacity of philosophical speculation, the fragility of all metaphysical constructions, the lack, the anguish, the torment' that haunt every 'world system', every theoretical system whatsoever (Le Dœuff 1988, pp. 189–209). Theory has actually projected this powerlessness elsewhere, especially on to women. But it is now time for theory to acknowledge that powerlessness, to grasp it as part of itself. The thought of the hymen surely recognises such powerlessness, not least with regard to the 'system' that is thematics. In Le Dœuff's terms, to think the hymen is at least to refuse to assume or identify with the position within metaphysics which founds 'the duality of masculine rationality and feminine disorder' (ibid. p. 198). The thought of the hymen is also the thought of the other within the same and the same within the other, for example, as recently elaborated by Kristeva in *Étrangers à Nous-Mêmes*. It is bound up with new modes of thinking alterity where '*le citoyen-individu cesse de se considérer comme uni et glorieux, mais découvre ses incohérences et ses abîmes, ses "étrangetés"'* (Kristeva 1988, p. 11). It thinks the interchange-ability of the features of what one knows as self and 'foreign'. According to Kristeva, such thought continues to challenge our particularising, intransigent, bourgeois individualism. Thematics, whether classical or feminist, is bound to sustain that indi-vidualism. For it requires precisely the 'definitive structures' that Kristeva wishes to escape in thinking alterity:

Ne pas chercher à fixer, à chosifier l'étrangeté de l'étranger. Juste le toucher, l'effleurer, sans lui donner de structure définitive . . . *Toccatas et Fugues*: les pièces de Bach évoquent à mes oreilles le sens que je voudrais moderne de l'étrangeté reconnue et poignante, *parce que* soulevée, soulagée, disséminée, inscrite dans un jeu neuf en formation, sans but, sans borne, sans fin . . . (ibid.)

This thought – for Kristeva, a thought of polyphony, of difference always in play, in movement, always linked, never annulled – is another version of the hymen.

READING AND THE NARRATIVE HYMEN

If the thought of the hymen is still to offer a useful resistance to thematics, however, it must be freed from the totalising preten-sions Derrida attaches to it. It needs to undergo a kind of postmodern reduction which rids it of traces of grandiosity, recognises the charge of appropriation, emphasises the abstract nature of the term and does not present it as a definitive alternative to thematisation. In the context of narrative theory, too, it must anticipate its own demise at the hands of feminist thought. Its value is precisely and only its mortality. Within current narrative theory, the thought of the hymen is clearly appropriate to narrative texts that either escape the discourse of thematics or make its inadequacies look self-evident. One obvious example is narrative in Nathalie Sarraute. Sarraute's concern with 'tropisms' is a concern with psychological and textual 'flow' rather than plot or intrigue, a Dostoevskean 'deep psychological anonymity' rather than 'identity' and 'character', an autonomous rather than a 'personalised' narrative discourse (Sarraute 1963, p. 8).[10] As *'mouvements indéfinissables'*, tropisms 'are located in the realm of sub-personal automatism' and 'neither originated nor assumed by a self'. They are the products of 'inter-human psychological *"matière anonyme comme le sang . . . un magma sans nom, sans contours"'* (McLure 1987, pp. 25–6).[11] 'Self' becomes nothing more than the result of a process that seeks to rise above or go beyond that 'anonymous matter'. Hence a curious reversal: tropistic psychology and tropistic narrative do not deal in 'states' or 'structures'. The latter are rather the consequence of a second-order activity, and are produced as such by and within the narrative.[12] This includes thematic structures. In Sarraute's narratives, theme becomes a narrative epiphenomenon. It is merely part of the old-fashioned realist narrative practice more or less diffidently adopted by certain 'characters'. It is caught up in and contained by something larger and more inclusive: on one level, tropistic 'movement' (Sarraute continually refers to her narratives in terms of movement); and, on another level, what she calls a narrative 'travelling' whereby the narrative keeps the pace of tropistic movement itself, its 'rapid, abundant flow' and 'restless shimmer' (Sarraute 1963, p. 108).[13] Sarraute deploys the image of the cartographer, specifically in a discussion of Proust:

these countless, tiny movements . . . are for Proust . . . what waves and eddies on a body of water are for a cartographer who is studying a region from the air; he only sees and reproduces the broad, motionless lines that these movements compose, the points at which the lines join, cross or separate; he recognizes among them those that have already been explored, and designates them by their known names: jealousy, snobbishness, fear, modesty, etc. . . .; he describes, classifies and names those he has discovered . . . (ibid. p. 115)

To the geometrics of Proust the cartographer, Sarraute contrasts her own 'dream' of 'a technique that might succeed in plunging the reader into the stream' of 'subterranean dramas' (ibid. p. 117). In *The Planetarium*, for instance, this technique implicitly repudiates the 'designations' and 'classifications' of thematics. In Sarraute, an observing subject does not exist independently of its object. 'It's all alike, outside, inside', says Alain (Sarraute 1965, p. 25). Equally, the boundaries between entities – and identities – constantly blur. 'I don't know any more where I finish and you begin', says Alain to Gisèle (ibid. p. 73), as the narrative itself refuses to mark off the flow of consciousness from dialogue,

Alain's thoughts and words from Gisèle's, and so on. The narrative mode of *The Planetarium* catches up all the 'characters' impartially within itself and its distinctive mannerisms – strings of dots, free associations, fragmentations etc. – allowing only for momentary, fleeting or incomplete differentiations. It is 'the furious little waves of the characters' looks, of their thoughts' and of their utterances that are given priority (ibid. p. 36):

> She's a little afraid . . . she hesitates . . . 'It starts from almost nothing . . . The slightest pretext will do . . . It's about that *bergère* . . .' She has the impression that he draws back a little, is on his guard: 'The *bergère*? – Yes, you know, the one we want to buy . . .' Something inside him closes; a glaze, a hard varnish veils his eyes: 'Well, what about it?' (ibid. p. 51)

The pronouns '*il*' and '*elle*', too, are largely interchangeable, gender difference being scarcely perceptible. Thus narrative in Sarraute is clearly and deliberately made subject to the law of the hymen. Alan Clayton suggests that Sarraute's narrative methods make a principle of incompletion and indeterminacy. In doing so, as Clayton says, they resist '*la sclérose de l'achevé*' (Clayton 1989, p. 24). But they also resist an aspect of the masculine narrative tradition as embodied in the work of 'Flaubert the precursor'. For in *Salammbô*, for example, writes Sarraute, '*[l]a phrase rigide, sans flottement, fige l'objet et lui donne des contours sans tremblement ni bavure*' (Sarraute 1986, p. 70). In Sarraute's own narratives, however, a narrative 'trembling' or undecidability is crucial. It refuses to establish polarities, produces the 'excluded third'. Clayton writes of a 'trembling' of narrative discourse, in Sarraute, and of the line of the phrase, the latter advancing by successive gropings, punctuated by hesitations and gaps, hollowed out by 'obscure spaces' and points of suspension (Clayton 1989, p. 26).[14] Sarraute's, he asserts, is a mode of narrative set against '*la clarté mortelle*' and the classical aesthetic of mastery alike (ibid. pp. 26–7). In Michèle le Dœuff's terms, Sarraute's narratives declare their powerlessness. (Clayton writes of her art as that of the '*pataugeur*', the flounderer, rather than the *maître* (ibid. p. 43).) But it is powerlessness as a form of resistance. In narrative, it is the 'powerlessness' of the hymen as resistance to any form of domination of the narrative text through or by thematics.

Sarraute's narratives are thus not aberrations from the main-
stream of Western narrative tradition. Indeed, they are arguably
exemplary. For they expose strata underneath the structures that
thematisation produces both within narratives themselves and in
our discourses about them. Reading Sarraute teaches us a new
way of reading Balzac. It might also make us think again about
film narrative, characterised as it self-evidently is by movement.
Indeed, in their recent book on Derrida and film theory, Peter
Brunette and David Wills suggest that, because film language is a
'language of movement', the thought of the hymen is needed 'to
supplement or redefine a critique of cinematic representation'
(Brunette and Wills 1989, p. 97). For Brunette and Wills, the
hymen is the thought of 'the site of the transfer of meaning' which
sets cinematic language 'back in movement instead of leaving it in
the stasis of controlled assignation of meaning' (ibid.). In the
hymen, there is a 'breaking down of the separation . . . between
the traditionally conceived content of a text and the formal
practice which that text engages' (ibid. p. 83). At the same time,
the term allows us to displace a hierarchy in which film as 'pure
medium' is regularly subordinated to thematics. There is nothing
interesting to be gleaned, for instance, from a thematic consideration of Jarmusch's *Down By Law*, save a few clichés (Europe versus
America, alienation versus domesticity, and so on). The film itself
seems literally to resist the mode of clarification implicit in such a
procedure, often keeping its figures in half-light or shadow,
holding them at a distance which obscures features, rather than –
say – shooting them in close-up. The film lacks complete clarity or
visibility. That lack is matched elsewhere by lacunae or disruptions of different kinds. The sound track, for example, switches
backwards and forwards between jazz, blues, pop, a kind of
heightened realism (the constant echoing sounds in the background during the prison sequences, for example) and so forth.
There are likewise occasional, radical breaks in the homogeneity
of the narrative discourse which also effectively function as
blocks to comprehensibility. Roberto's long soliloquy in Italian
goes untranslated, for instance. Jarmusch maintains certain discursive regularities or dominants in the film. But he also quite
unpredictably varies or interrupts them. The startling travelling
shot upriver before we first see the three men in their boat is a case

in point. *Down by Law* is thus a film that often appears to verge on a resolution that it never quite produces (witness, on one level, the end of the film). It never quite has or provides the clear definition necessary to the construction of theme. The very irregularities underline the extent to which the film joins, sutures, moves on, does not rest. Not surprisingly, it ends with an image of forking roads. In Derrida's phrase, *Down by Law* 'sets up and dismantles, breaks up and patches together' (Derrida 1987c, p. 235). It is never reducible to a static, thematic structure of fixed entities as separate units.

Again, the apparently stable structures of thematisation in film narrative are revealed as narrative epiphenomena. It is possible, in fact, to distinguish between kinds of film in terms of their fidelity to the mobility of the medium itself. Thus – to contrast two well-known Vietnam films – from the very beginning, when we watch a series of heads being regularly shaved, Kubrick's *Full Metal Jacket* is 'subject to the law of the hymen' (Derrida 1981a, p. 242). It institutes, not a system of thematic oppositions, but a rhythm which joins itself to the military music, the chanting and drumming repeatedly heard on the soundtrack, runs on through the young marines running in formation, marching, training, exercising, follows them through and over the assault course, and concludes in the final explosion of violence at the end of the first half of the film. This first half focuses quite obsessively on geometrical structures (the bleak geometry of the army camp and its buildings, the geometrical figure of the organised squad, the geometrical arrangement of the obstacles that form the assault course, etc.). But it resolutely refuses to internalise that geometry, to organise itself in the geometrical terms of thematics as instilled into the cadets (Hartman lectures them, for instance, on how the free world will conquer communism with the help of God and the marines). Kubrick's film refuses all collusion in the structuring of identity conferred by such a geometry ('I love working for Uncle Sam', chant the marines in formation, 'Lets me know just who I am'). *Full Metal Jacket* introduces a 'hymeneal' principle of movement, of rhythmic oscillation, of non-meaning into a situation in which the female is sternly denied. ('I don't want no teenage queen', chant the cadets, obediently, 'I just want my M14'.)

The second half of the film, however, does not consistently sustain the rhythms of the first half. It rather lets them emerge irregularly (in the military response to the Tet offensive, in the run-halt-take-cover routines of the platoon on the attack, etc.). It thus avoids positing any clear, polar, structural relationship between the two halves, any determined symmetry, save for a second, concluding explosion of violence (the killing of the Viet Cong girl). The film produces, not oppositions, but a difference in degree. In other words, *Full Metal Jacket* avoids becoming precisely the kind of thematised story that, as a military correspondent, Joker is instructed to write (stories about American charity to the Vietnamese, says his commanding officer, or stories about successful expeditions). It is not surprising, then, that Joker wears a peace badge on his lapel but has 'Born to Kill' on his helmet. This is less an evidently anti-war film than a repudiation of confrontational structures and clear divisions. By contrast, Oliver Stone's *Platoon*, though it ostensibly deplores American excesses in the Vietnam war, also precisely reinstitutes the structures of thought which made them possible. From the image it offers us early on of Willem Dafoe carrying a gun across his shoulders and looking like a crucified Christ, it plunges us into an eschatologically determined world in which good sergeant Elias confronts bad sergeant Barnes in a war for the soul of young soldier Taylor. This ramifies out into an array of other oppositions transiently expressed in the film. Even the rhythms of the film are organised in polarising terms. (Various sequences intercut Barnes and Elias or Barnes and Taylor running from opposite directions, etc.) It is evil Barnes who represents the collapse of all distinctions. ('There ain't no need or time for a courtroom out here', he says.) But the judicial thought of the courtroom is precisely what *Platoon* seeks to maintain. For all its manifest abhorrence of the war, therefore, the film nonetheless reproduces the principle of bellicosity within itself, is haunted by and cannot dispense with that principle. It would of course be easy to show that, like any film, *Platoon* 'exceeds' thematic geometry. Stone's film is caught up in rhythms as *Full Metal Jacket* is, constantly on the move with the platoon itself. At the same time, however, it is also given over to the geometry of thematics. That geometry is in fact a product of the film as movement, and yet, at the same time, an attempt to resist, limit and contain movement. In *Platoon*, in other words, thematic geometry is an epiphenomenon which, by strident insistence, gives itself out as the reverse, as the 'significant truth' of the whole film.

But how might the thought of the hymen lead us to read certain texts 'against the grain'? What happens when we try to displace thematics from the hermeneutically dominant position that it has always occupied in relation to texts? What about texts that undeniably appear to privilege theme? One answer to these questions lies in what Thomas Docherty has called 'criminal' reading (Docherty 1990, p. 58). Docherty argues that, traditionally, hermeneutics has been tragic in condition and orientation:

It depends on the notion that texts are obscure, with secret topoi in the dark tropics of their discourse, demanding epistemological sleuths for their illumination or demystification . . . . The hermeneutic train all the way from Thebes to Frankfurt has implied the presence of a reality or ground which lies behind, alongside or in front of texts. (ibid. p. 37)

But the postmodern erosion of that 'reality or ground' makes for a hermeneutic condition which 'will tend toward illegitimacy rather than verifiability', and will 'produce secrecy' rather than leading to 'demystification' or enlightenment (ibid. pp. 38–9). Hence Docherty urges upon us, not the 'tragic trajectory' of traditional hermeneutics 'based upon a topical knowledge and a truth of identity', but interpretation as 'an archetypal "comedy of errors", in which there is no truth of identity (nor of anything else)' (ibid. p. 50). To understand interpretation in this manner is to turn away from the mode of violence that is truth as illumination and 'to release the dark tropics of discourse into their full obscurity' (ibid. p. 58). It makes secrecy a condition of understanding. This erratic mode of interpretation is thus 'outside the law', both 'illegible' and a means of 'spawning illegitimate versions' (ibid.):

This postmodern hermeneutic, then . . . proposes that the interpreter actually constructs a secrecy in some sense, providing not an allegorical revelation of the 'true' story behind the text's dark and veiling words, but rather a satirical version of that text. It reveals the text precisely as it is not, thereby construing an interpretation whose founding impetus is that of parody, and whose orientation is *proleptic*. (ibid. p. 59)

The proleptic orientation of Docherty's 'postmodern hermeneutic' is inseparable from its operations, not only as an 'active forgetting' but as a 'heliotropic *transformation* of the the past and its "objects"' (ibid. p. 60). It is thus 'transgressive of a law . . . able to forge a future through the interpretive parodying of historical narrative, document, text' (ibid.).

The thought of the narrative hymen is nothing if not tran- gressive of a law. I shall illustrate the point with a reading of Genesis. For Derrida, Richard's thematics organises the 'poly- semia' of the text within 'a unitary resumption of meaning'. A 'totalising dialectics' thus annuls 'the open and productive dis- placement of the textual chain' (Derrida 1981b, p. 5). To read Genesis in terms of an 'open and productive displacement' of meaning rather than a 'totalising dialectics' is to accomplish something of Docherty's 'interpretive parodying'. Genesis is about the origin of difference itself, or, rather, it seeks to give an origin to difference in God and the Creation. The first chapter is precisely concerned with a world created and determined as a structure of oppositions: heaven/earth, light/darkness (Gen. 1,4) etc. But the 'opposition' apparently most clearly thematised is that between God and man. A classical hermeneutics must therefore either assume or produce a knowledge of what God is in the book and what man is, a totalising account of the oppositional structure of their relationship. This will certainly be true of the relationship between God and man after the Fall, since the opposition must then be absolute. But are such accounts possible? The Fall is clearly the deciding factor, the 'pure cut' which might seem to sever two opposites cleanly from each other. But in fact there is confusion. God says man has become more godlike through the Fall – 'the man is become as one of us, to know good and evil' (ibid. 3,22) – so the absolute difference must be that man knows good and evil but is capable of freely choosing evil. That depends, however, on good and evil being eternal and changeless truths, vouchsafed to man once and for all time, truths unaffected by history, the onward march of narrative and the insistent connec- tion of the narrative hymen. Such truths are not indicated in Genesis. Cain, for instance, does not appear to know that it is evil to offer fruit 'unto the Lord' (ibid. 4,3). God has to give him a moral lesson, punishing him at the same time ('If thou doest well, shalt thou not be accepted? And if thou doest not well, sin lieth at the door' (ibid. 4,7)). So the knowledge granted to man is not absolute and timeless. But surely the 'pure cut' that comes with the Fall is death? Man is made mortal. Man dies. God does not die. We must certainly assume as a given that God is eternal whilst man's life is timebound and deathbound. But the eternity and immortality of God can only remain assumptions. For the God of Genesis to remain properly opposed to man in this respect he would have to remain outside of and immune to time and history, and he does not. When he inundates the earth, for instance, he decides no longer to 'strive with man' (ibid. 6,3) because 'every imagination of the thoughts of his heart was only evil continually' (ibid. 6,5). Yet the God who has inflicted the flood but saved the good (in the figure of Noah) then contradictorily resigns himself to the fact that 'the imagination of man's heart is evil from his youth' (ibid. 8, 21). He changes his strategy, too. 'Neither will I again smite any more every thing living, as I have done,' he says (ibid.). So this is a God who takes account of history, is modified by it, and grows more like man in the process. The supposedly eternal and immutable cannot withstand the timebound pressures of narrative and the hymen. Difference inscribes itself 'without any decidable poles, without any independent, irreversible terms' (Derrida 1981a, p. 210).

So is it wisdom that absolutely separates God from man? 'Do not interpretations belong to God?' says Joseph (ibid. 40, 8). Alas, no. Thus Abraham, for example, in that marvellous bit of bartering that goes on in Genesis 18 over the fate of Sodom and Gomorrah, actually disputes God's judgment and causes him to change it. God is not infallibly omniscient, either, hearing about the state of Sodom and Gomorrah only from 'the cry of it,' (ibid. 18, 21), and having to 'go down' to see for himself. Once again, God enters and is influenced by the human world. It is not absolute power that absolutely distinguishes him, either. He can control the motions of Rachel's womb, but not the evil in men's hearts, even though he arranges the flood and leaves Noah, that 'just man and perfect in his generations' (ibid. 6,9). Nor is there any absolute quality of righteousness to God's justice either, as in his treatment of non-believers. He helps Laban the Syrian by appearing to him in a dream (ibid. 31, 24), and Potiphar is allowed to sense the God in

Joseph (ibid. 39, 3) and gets his house 'blessed' by God. But in Chapter 12 Pharaoh finds that he and his house are afflicted 'with great plagues' after he takes Abraham's wife, although Abraham has lied to him in the first place in telling him that she was his sister (ibid. 12, 17). Or take the treatment of 'subtilty'. Two creatures in Genesis are described as 'subtil': the serpent, who of course is punished for it (ibid. 3,1), but also Jacob, who cheats Esau out of his birthright and his father's blessing and is duly favoured by God (ibid. 27, 35). Abraham can dispute with and even intervene to direct God's justice. For it is a conditional and relative justice which varies according to the varied situations thrown up along the narrative chain.

Of themselves, then, writing and narrative in Genesis inexorably dismantle any absolute structural opposition in the relationship between God and man. Within narrative, both are subject to 'the law of the hymen' (Derrida 1981a, p. 242). God must differ from himself, as must man, and they must differ from each other too, but according to a gap that opens and closes, like Derrida's fan. What Derrida says of reason and instinct in Condillac is true of God and man in Genesis: between them, there is 'only a difference of degree' which 'produces and destroys the is of every predication' (Derrida 1987a, p. 98). The hymen being at work, the real figure for Genesis is that of the link, the middle ground: Jacob's ladder; the angels, halfway between man and God, who sometimes speak as if they themselves were God, as at Gen. 31, 13; and the covenant. God refers to 'my covenant' (ibid. 17, 14) and, to Noah, he speaks of 'the covenant which I have established between me and all flesh that *is* upon earth' (ibid. 9, 17). But actually he covenants repeatedly and differently, with Noah, with Abraham, with Isaac. Partly because circumstances change, the covenant has to be re-established in different forms. God no longer needs to covenant with Abraham over retribution by flood, for instance. The relations between God and individual men differ and change, however much God seeks to speak in absolute terms. History holds God in its insidious grip. The covenant is a renegotiable bond, and that is appropriate to narrative, the form par excellence of flux, flow, change, movement in and through time. God intervenes in changing human affairs *et mutatur in illos.* As subject of his own actions he is contaminated by the object of his interest.

In Genesis, then, there is a constant play of difference within the same, of the same within difference. One would expect no less of a narrative made by man about God making man in God's image. Genesis will not tell us what God is, what man is, what the difference between the two is. It is, then, a Jekyll-and Hyde text in which, suddenly, and with no warning, God may look like man or man like God. *The Strange Case of Dr Jekyll and Mr Hyde* would appear to be as available to interpretation in terms of fixed oppositions as Genesis. The very title seems to invite a structural-ist account of polarities: Jekyll/Hyde, good/evil, reason/animality, conscious/unconscious etc. It is not hard to construct Stevenson's text in terms of supposed 'patterns' of imagery that corroborate that sort of thematisation: references to devils, animals and the like. Equally, it is easy enough to reverse the hierarchy implied in such a structure and suggest that the tacit theme of the story produces Jekyll as a monster of reason – his after all is the more monstrous name – and Hyde (with the more ordinary British name) as an instance of vitality warped into brutality by conceal-ment and repression. To think Stevenson's text in terms of the hymen, however, is rather to concentrate on the 'and'.[15] The 'and' of a title has differing implications. It may suggest a relationship between the first term as supposed`essence or origin and the second term as supposed accident or subsequent development: *Dombey and Son*, *Sapphira and the Slave Girl*, *Indiana Jones and the Temple of Doom*, *Stanley and the Women*. But in other cases it merely functions temporally or connectively: *Crime and Punish-ment*, *War and Peace*. The title of Stevenson's story has both these implications. Hyde appears inseparable from Jekyll and apart from or subsequent to him. Any conception of an absolute opposition between the two is an illusion. They are one person. But that single person separates into two and yet is never two together. Jekyll and Hyde can never appear at once. But we can never be certain quite how distinct they really are, and the gap is not constant or measurable. Of course, it is only late in the book that any one else – including the narrators – connects Jekyll and Hyde, which enhances the impression of clear opposition. Enfield makes the point right at the start: it is apparently impossible that

the 'really damnable man' has anything 'to do with' the person
who 'is the very pink of the proprieties' (Stevenson 1979, p. 33).
Hyde is recurrently stigmatised as the abhorrent and unacceptable
other: 'hardly human', says Utterson, 'troglodytic' (ibid. p. 40);
'ape-like', says the maidservant who witnesses the Carew murder
(ibid. p. 47); merely 'animal', says a narrator (ibid. p. 69). All these
figures need a clarity of opposition between the respectable Jekyll
and the brutish Hyde. Jekyll himself shares it too ('the moment I
choose, I can be rid of Mr Hyde,' (ibid. p. 44)). But Hyde never
appears as simply the other, not from the start, from the appearance of the figure who, in Jekyll's tones, says 'No gentleman but
wishes to avoid a scene' (ibid. p. 32). Intermittently, then, Hyde in
Hyde's form will seem to be Jekyll – as when, to Utterson's
astonishment, he neglects to destroy the will that disinherits him
(p. 72). Jekyll in Jekyll's form may seem to be Hyde. The
relationship between the two is not constant, the text constituting
and deconstituting it as one thing and another. There is always the
hymen.

But Jekyll and Hyde are not held in equilibrium. They
may appear almost as much as each other, but the book itself
is dominated by Jekyll-consciousness rather than Hyde-
consciousness, by Utterson, Enfield, Lanyon and Guest as by
Jekyll himself. We get Jekyll's statement of the case, not Hyde's.
Hyde rather exists as apparition or trace, haunting the narrative,
and in more ways than one: games with his name, for instance, are
frequent in the text, Jekyll referring to Lanyon as 'hide-bound', for
example (ibid. p. 43). Hyde hides, is hidden away in the text, only
to show, if briefly, again and again. Jekyll and Hyde do not have
equal power in the text. What has power, everywhere, freezing
Utterson's blood 'in his veins' (ibid. p. 55), inflicting 'horror' on
both Utterson and Enfield (ibid. p. 61), 'submerging' Lanyon's
mind in the most abject 'terror' (ibid. p. 80), is the apprehension of
the link, the connection, the hymen; the fact that the Jekyll the
others know singly is also Hyde, and that the Hyde they know
separately is also Jekyll. The terror is not so much of the other as
of the connection with the other. The shock for Utterson and
Lanyon is that Jekyll and Hyde are neither distinct nor the same.

But the work of the hymen is most clearly seen in the astonishing conclusion to the story. It ends, of course, not with the

confrontation with and the death of Hyde, but with Jekyll's account of affairs prior to the final *débacle*. It is called 'Henry Jekyll's Full Statement of the Case', and it is indeed full, but its 'fullness' is that of disintegration. It begins as expected: as a clinical case history, delivered by a knowledgeable, scientific voice. But at once, in the various references to doubleness – 'dual', 'duplicity', 'double-dealer', 'divide' (ibid. p. 81) – there are traces of what will come to torment that voice. On the second page of the statement, the voice of science starts to theorise duality itself – ('man is not truly one but truly two', (ibid. p. 82)) – thus seeking to protect itself as detached from duality, unpolluted by it. But as the 'Statement' progresses that voice starts to lose control. Jekyll begins to speak as Hyde/Hyde begins to speak in Jekyll: 'With a transport of glee, I mauled the unresisting body' (ibid. p. 90). It is Jekyll who is suicidal but Hyde who repeatedly commits 'temporary suicide' (ibid. p. 96), Hyde who has the 'hatreds' that are 'raging energies of life' but Jekyll whose hatred of Hyde comes to have the passionate quality of a 'vital instinct' (ibid. p. 95). This is the final vertigo in which the narrative ends. It is compounded by a third voice which begins to speak of both Jekyll and Hyde in the third person. Strikingly, this is the voice of a third person narrator in a first person narrative. The story began with a third person narrator who faded out later. Now a third person narrator reappears, but as an aspect of a first person narrative. Another opposition has broken down: that between narrator and narrated, 'I' and 'he'. The 'third voice' in the 'Statement' might partly be thought of as another stage in Jekyll's disorder. He is moving towards an existence as 'a mere polity of multifarious, incongruous and independent denizens' which is what he predicts human beings 'will be ultimately known' as (ibid. p. 82). But that new phase is also a return to the theological voice of the third person narrator with its observing detachment. So the end of the story gestures towards the relativity, the provisionality of that classic voice, of the discursive logic of the third person narrator which has largely sustained the narrative itself. But also, finally, a monstrous, Hydean thought haunts the narrative: that that voice, with its knowledge and detachment, a scientific, very British, very masculine voice, can be presented as merely a certain phase in an process of increasing derangement.

In Derridean terms, then, classical thematics practises an 'annulment' of discourse which would 'stabilise its undecidable' in 'the mode of *pro and contra*' (Derrida 1979, p. 63). To think the narrative hymen is to resist that false stabilisation and, we might add, spatialisation of narrative. In *The Ear of the Other*, Derrida recalls the cryptic last words of Nietzsche's *Ecce Homo*: 'Have I been understood? *Dionysus versus the Crucified*'. Nietzsche, says Derrida, 'Ecce Homo, Christ but not Christ, nor even Dionysus, but rather the name of the versus . . . the combat called between two names' (Derrida 1985, p. 10). Ecce homo, the name of the versus. To think the hymen is to think the versus. For the present, the strategy remains useful as a way of resisting, seeking to move beyond, 'criminally' sabotaging a thematics that otherwise ceaselessly confirms an established metaphysics. In Derrida's words, again, it is a way of 'ruining' the 'discursive edifice' that is the theoretical house of fiction, of bringing a geometry to an end, in the hope that new models for thought will begin to appear, chiefly feminist ones. There is not just a hermeneutics or an epistemology at stake at this. The issue is an ethical one, too.

NOTES

1. See for instance Levin 1979.
2. For another defence of this kind, see Gerald Graff, 'Literature as Assertions', in Konigsberg 1981.
3. Similarly, Phelan's account of Jane Austen criticism notes how easily, in attempting to thematise the Austen novels, critics' efforts to escape dualism merely fall back into it. This comes across specifically in his account of Susan Morgan's response to Alastair Duckworth's work. See Phelan 1989, p. 44. See also Duckworth 1971; and Morgan 1980, p. 80.
4. The importance for Serres of the joker and Harlequin is made particularly clear at the beginning of Serres 1991, pp. 10–14.
5. For Vattimo on 'weak thought', see for instance 'The Crisis of Humanism' in Vattimo 1988, pp. 31–47.
6. But cf. also Derrida's discussion of the 'stricture' and 'interlacings' in Derrida 1987c, pp. 255–382, p. 340 and passim.
7. Elaine Showalter, 'A Criticism of Our Own: Autonomy and Assimilation in Afro-American and Feminist Literary Theory', ts. presented at the School of Criticism and Theory, Dartmouth College, Hanover, N.H., June 1986.
8. See for instance Cornell 1991, 1992.

9. For Lanser's theory of a feminist narratology, see Lanser 1991.
10. By 'personalised' narration I mean narration attributable to a narrator. See McLure 1987, p. 23.
11. McLure is quoting from *L'Ère du Soupçon* (Sarraute 1956), pp. 8, 91.
12. Alan J. Clayton would appear to see this as part of Sarraute's steadfast determination to preserve the 'virtual character' of the unformed. See Clayton 1989, p. 5.
13. Sarraute says that the term 'travelling' comes from the cinema, and denotes a process in which 'the camera is moving at the same speed as the object the operator wants to photograph'. See Sarraute 1961, pp. 428–9, p. 428.
14. Clayton is quoting from *L'Usage de la Parole*. For his and Sarraute's accounts of the 'points of suspension', see Clayton 1989, p. 26.
15. It is to practise an 'enactment of the copula', in Irigaray's phrase. See Irigaray 1985. p. 158.

4

Narrative, Voices, Writing

THE QUESTION OF SPEAKABILITY

One of the most curious features of classical narratology has been the interdependence within it of mutually opposed terms or discordant systems of reference. As we have seen, narratology worked to establish geometries of the narrative text or narrative system. In that respect, it manifested itself as a kind of advanced technology which moved decisively beyond the looser thought and spongier categories of a humanist critical tradition. At the same time, however, it unreflectingly maintained and even promoted certain terms deriving from that tradition, or developed its own versions of them. In other words, narratology entered into collusion with the very thought it seemed to react so powerfully against.

Nowhere has this been more evident than in the narratological emphasis on voice. At its most basic, the idea of narrative voice is of an indeterminate, non-codifiable, even unruly entity very much at odds with the systematising procedures of narratological thought. Equally, the concept of narrative voice seems inseparable from the sense of a subjectivity intimately inhabiting the text, a communicative human presence as source and origin which, in the shape of the author, narratology was precisely concerned to reduce or avoid. Narratology insistently suggested that it was concerned with an objective and systematic description of the modes of voice as 'the generating instance of narrative discourse' (Genette 1980b, p. 213). But the presumption and delimitation of the object to be categorised clearly ran counter to other aspects of the narratologists' (demystifying) project. The narratological double-bind, here, has recently been analysed by Marc Blanchard, specifically with reference to Genette. On the one hand, says Blanchard, Genette seeks decisively to separate narratology from hermeneutics. A claim for the scientific purity of narratological method is implicit in that separation. But there is in fact a covert hermeneutics within Genette's work. For if narrative can only be understood as and when it is fitted into a typology, for Genette, this is also constitutive of the modes of interpreting narratives. It is itself a means of giving them a voice (Blanchard 1992, p. 62). Genette argues that 'every narrative resonates with voice', and the concept of voice is actually indispensable to Genettian narratology (ibid. p. 65). Genette never problematises the idea of voice. Whilst the manifestations of narrative voice can be classified, voice itself simply exists as an essence. Genette simply ignores the extent to which voice is always overcoded. Such a blindspot may not be accidental, since narratology itself is in general so reluctant to admit its own contingency and historicity. For that very reason, we should insist that a narratology based on voice itself belongs to a particular cultural and ideological universe (ibid. p. 63). Other conceptions of narrative are possible.

The assertion that Genette's is a narratology of voice may startle. Surely Genette grants voice only a modest amount of attention? But in practice, many of Genette's distinctions actually turn out to be partly reducible to questions of voice. 'Data of narrative temporality', for instance, may easily resolve themselves into 'data of voice' (Genette 1980b, p. 70). Genette's reworking of the question of 'showing' versus 'telling' depends on the assertion of a difference between kinds of 'saying' (ibid. p. 166). But for Genette, what matters most is the idea of voice as the 'final instance' governing narrative (ibid. p. 157). In Genettian narratology, voice is actually the ultimate 'fixed point' to which other aspects of narrative can be referred. In the terms Genette takes over from Benveniste, discourse is in some sense both prior to and more fundamental than story. Hence part of the Genettian project is the clarification of voice, its isolation, in the sense in which a substance is 'isolated' in a chemical process. The instance of 'speaking' must be separated from 'the instance of "writing"', the narrator from the author, the recipient of narrative from the reader of the work (ibid. p. 213). Questions of voice – 'who speaks?' – must also be kept apart from questions of 'point of view' – who sees?' (ibid. pp. 185–9). Narration must always be distinguished from 'focalisation' (ibid. pp. 189–94). Of course, Genette knows that the 'narrating instance' does not 'remain identical and invariable in the course of a single narrative work' (ibid. p. 214). He knows how far novelists like Dostoevsky, Mann and Malraux refuse to grant any given narrator an ideological monopoly within their texts (ibid. pp. 257–8). He is conscious of the extent to which relations between narrating instance and narrated event can problematise identity. But he is also concerned to make of voice itself an invariant constantly in evidence through all such shifts and changes, within the play of narrative appearances and disappearances. Hence for example his criticism of the terms 'first person' and 'third person' narrative as seeking to stress a non-existent variation 'in the element of the narrative situation' (ibid. p. 243). Genette insists that 'every narrating is, by definition, to all intents and purposes presented in the first person' (ibid. p. 244). The argument massively if somewhat abstractly consolidates the idea of person as a unifying, homogenising, singular presence within a narrative text. Genette's case reverts to a theological conception of the text in which all separate narrative instances, including instances of voice, are governed by a single, authoritative, 'higher' voice. He accepts that certain modes of narrative pose awkward questions for this conception of the narrative text. 'The Borgesian fantastic', for example, 'in this respect emblematic of a whole modern literature, does not accept person' (ibid. p. 247). But such literature is understood, not so much as a radical challenge to the assumptions underlying Genette's categories as the aberration that confirms them in their dominance and general validity. In the end, for Genette, voice is partly metalinguistic, even metanarrative, establishing 'articulations, connections, inter-relationships' in narrative, 'in short, its internal organisation' (ibid. p. 255). Voice is the secure foundation that assures the coherence of narrative geometry itself.

What is true of Genette has been substantially true of narratology as a whole. Again and again, in Derrida's terms, voice serves as the 'centre' whose function is to 'orient, balance and organize' the structure of narrative (Derrida 1990, p. 278). Narrative can hardly be thought apart from voice.[1] Hence the fact that Ann Banfield's work has so scandalised and engrossed narratologists. For Banfield's *Unspeakable Sentences* put in question the very assumption that voice was an appropriate term in the analysis of narrative. Banfield attempted to open up a rift between narrative and speech or the voice. She asserted that, 'in the language of narrative fiction', literature departs 'from ordinary discourse and from those of its functions which narrative reveals as separable from language itself' (Banfield 1982, p. 10). She refused to identify speech with language: speech, she suggested, is not language but a particular linguistic performance. In any actual linguistic performance, there is always much that must escape any transcription into systems of writing. In other words, 'orthography represents some level more abstract than pronounciation' (ibid. p. 244). This is crucial for narrative theory. For what it means is that, in general, writing – including narrative – is transparent, accentless, even classless as speech never can be. Where speakers always have accents, writing can only gain an accent by violating conventional orthography. Such violations are merely the exceptions that prove the rule. The language of narrative is always and definitively 'separated from the person of its author and the subjective coloration even the most objective statement might have in the mouth of a flesh-and-blood speaker' (ibid. p. 250). Indeed, any features of an authorial or narratorial vocabulary and style actually lose their 'markedness' in narrative, and cannot be thought of as creating a 'voice' or 'personality'. In fact, 'the only place for representation of the speaking voice within a narrative is really in some sense outside it', in quotation marks (ibid.).

So we do not actually encounter a narrative voice in narrative. We encounter an equivalent of voice that we have created for ourselves as a simulacrum and insisted on identifying with voice. Narrative voice is a theoretical construction, used, not only to give narrative a secure and unitary foundation, but to protect us against the disturbing recognition of what Banfield calls the 'abstract' nature of the language of narrative as it is 'made possible by writing' (ibid. p. 253). It is precisely to render this 'abstraction' of written narrative that Banfield gives her account of her chief concern, *style indirecte libre* or what she calls 'represented speech and thought' in narrative.

Represented speech and thought actually exist in a strange hinterland in which 'subjectivity or the expressive function of language . . . confronts its other in the form of a sentence empty of all subjectivity' (ibid. p. 10). As such, it is also characteristic of that 'idealised construct' which is narrative fiction itself (ibid. p. 270). For narrative

is the site on which the subject, face to face with its opposite, the purely objective sentence of narration, no longer defined as speaking and yet defined by language, is revealed. (ibid. p. 18)

In narrative, then, we have expression without voice or person. There are two kinds of narrative sentences: those of narration per se (Benveniste's *histoire*) – 'the realisation of pure objectivity, linguistically speaking' – and the sentences which represent consciousness, 'representing and therefore foregrounding subjectivity' (ibid. p. 17). The relationship between these is what constitutes narration. It also makes it quite distinct as a category of discourse (Violi 1986, pp. 361–78). The conviction that the language of narrative is not a means of communication is thus a very important part of Banfield's theory. It has been generally assumed, says Banfield, 'that subjectivity in language is properly located within a theory of the communicative act and intention' (Banfield 1982, p. 7). But in narrative 'subjectivity or the expressive function of narrative emerges free of communication' (ibid. p. 10).

This is clear enough if we compare direct speech on the one hand, and indirect speech (or free indirect discourse or so-called narrative 'speech') on the other. The direct and the indirect are distinct from one another. Equally, there is no transformational relationship whereby one becomes the other. There are constructions characteristic of direct discourse that are entirely missing in indirect discourse. The categories of 'expressive elements' and constructions in direct and indirect or narrative discourse are not the same. The expressive elements in narrative discourse mean that it cannot be conceived of in terms of a speaker communicating to an addressee. In particular, the third person pronoun in represented speech and thought can apparently play the role usually reserved to the 'I' of ordinary sentences as subjective source of expressive elements. Thus in narrative 'the notion of point of view or subjectivity is not by definition tied to the speaker' (ibid. p. 93). Indeed, represented expressions 'cannot be simultaneously attributed to a covert or "effaced" narrator'. No-one speaks in represented expressions, 'although in them speech may be represented' (ibid. p. 97). In general, this is even more self-evidently the case with film, where we readily conceive of a non-human narrator at work, precisely in the fact, for instance, that film can reveal the appearance of things when no-one is actually present. Film can give us *sensibilia*, objects that have the same status as sense-data without necessarily being data to any mind.[2] No-one speaks in narrative, then, nor addresses anyone. But it is precisely this that – lodged in our stubborn anthropomorphic prejudices, insisting on the identity of the oral and the literary, of spoken and written narrative – we have been unable to recognise and dare not think.

From the early articles in which she began to develop it, Banfield's theory provoked debate.[3] Her rejection of the communication model appeared to strike at the very foundations of narratology. The most comprehensive and subtle response to Banfield, here, has been Monika Fludernik's. Fludernik both criticises Banfield's model and seeks to refine and even radicalise it. Her principal and most powerful objections are to Banfield's (Chomskyan) linguistic model. In the first instance, it has been made to look obsolete by subsequent developments in linguistics, not only the move towards pragmatics but Chomsky's own 'repeated modifications' of his theory (Fludernik 1993, p. 364). Thus Fludernik shows, for instance, that Banfield's specific paradigm fails, among other reasons, because root tranformations do occur in indirect discourse. Indirect discourse can accommodate expressive elements. In fact, then, Banfield's model has only a specific and restricted applicability. It clearly does not work for the kinds of narrative dominant in the eighteenth and nineteenth century, for instance. Fludernik's refinement of Banfield's theory is thus partly a question of supplementing Banfield with recent pragmatic methodology. If, for Fludernik, Banfield does not establish a general separation between narrative and voice, she does at least provide us with an effective means of understanding what is going on in certain kinds of narrative. Banfield is almost wholly correct, for instance, about 'reflectoral narrative' (ibid. p. 450).

There are clearly narratives – *What Maisie Knew, Gravity's Rainbow* – which make the concept of fictional 'voice' elusive. In such narratives, certain words and phrases, at least, are difficult to attribute either to a narrator or a 'centre of consciousness'. The reader's inferences therefore 'frequently flounder' in 'deliberate textual contradiction' (ibid. p. 364).

For Fludernik, then, Banfield partly points us in a typological direction. But, for all the skill and effectiveness of her linguistic critique, Fludernik's refinements of Banfield's theory continue to beg certain theoretical questions. Take Fludernik's account, for example, of Banfield's concept of an 'empty deictic centre'. Fludernik sees its value, demonstrating for instance that the interludes in *The Waves* seem to evoke a 'centre of subjectivity' when in fact no character or speaker is 'on stage' (ibid. p. 387). There is thus a radical 'impersonalisation' of 'fictional presentation' in Woolf's novel. But Fludernik nonetheless insists that the impersonal subjectivity in question is always eventually resoluble into or 're-emerges' as a 'speaker function' (ibid. p. 393). It is hard, however, to see what 'speaking' means, here. The concept of a voice emerging – as Fludernik has it – 'from the figural impersonal subconscious of language' in *Jacob's Room* (ibid.) seems little more than a conventionalisation of what Banfield means by writing. For all Fludernik's commitment to empirical method, what she means by voice seems unempirical, a kind of ontological stopgap. When Fludernik describes the language of *Jacob's Room* as 'a mere evocation of subjectivity without ontological anchoring' (ibid.), the concept of voice has surely become strategically important as a means of keeping the text from receding into the dizzying infinity of Derridean play. When narrative voice no longer has anything resembling an empirical reality, the concept is exposed in its ideological function as an index or unifying 'source' of what is deemed to be the text's meaningfulness and coherence. The idea of narrative voice has become inseparable from and cannot exist without a hermeneutic procedure.

Indeed, Fludernik intermittently resorts to disguised hermeneutic manoeuvres. She tells us, for example, that Banfield's theory cannot deal with textual irony. In irony, says Fludernik, we always hear the voice. But do we really hear a voice from within the text? Fludernik gives as examples the 'Nausicaa' and

'Eumaeus' chapters in Joyce's *Ulysses*. In neither case, however, is an ironic reading the only one available. Irony is not an ahistorical, universally self-evident given in either chapter. 'It is our moral convictions', writes Fludernik, 'as well as the stylistic conventions and the interpretative norms which one constructs for the text as a whole that determine the ironical reading' (ibid. p. 351). But who is the 'we' deemed to share a set of 'moral convictions?' Fludernik is treating specific hermeneutic decisions as objectively valid universals. It is thus not clear, for example, that, as Fludernik suggests, 'the unspeakable sentence theory quite clearly breaks down with authorial narrative', where there is 'a clear speaker function' (ibid. p. 381). For Fludernik means something different by voice, in this context, to what Banfield means, and something less literal, something that has to do with a mode of constructing the text and establishing a presence within it. Fludernik means something evoked 'supra-sententially' (ibid. p. 438). Banfield would presumably deny such a 'supra-sentential' dimension altogether. In general, Fludernik and other critics of Banfield's work have been able to sustain their critique only by a theoretical return to the assumption of certain unities and presences within narrative that Banfield refuses to acknowledge. For Banfield, they are not in question in the text in the first instance.

It is clearly necessary, then, to maintain a distinction as Fludernik does between the philosophical and post-structuralist foundation on which Banfield's theory is grounded, and Banfield's linguistic and transformationalist methodology (ibid. p. 362). But in doing so, we may also separate out the more and the less useful aspects of Fludernik's critique of Banfield. Fludernik's dazzling case against Banfield's linguistic methodology is not accompanied by a similar critique of the philosophical bases of her thought. Indeed, Fludernik is inclined to resort to unproblematised conceptions of an 'intuitive knowledge' of narrative. She sees Banfield as going against 'the intuitive perception of discourse in general', according to which readers 'do in fact construct a narrator's (or author's) voice' if only as 'a default value' (ibid. p. 350). Once again Fludernik's certainty about what readers do or should do seems problematic. What is clear from her work, however, is the extent to which the concept of voice relies on and is inseparable from a philosophical essentialism. Fludernik's commitment is to a reinstatement of various entities produced by classical narrative theory, where Banfield had deconstructed them. If we must admit the force of Fludernik's empirical critique, we should also put her metaphysics in question. This sends us back to Banfield's theoretical position, but without the securities of empirical validation that Banfield seems to have wanted to give herself. On one level, of course, there is self-evidently no literal voice in any narrative text. The very assumption of a voice itself constitutes a mode of reading. As Fludernik's example of Joycean 'irony' demonstrates, like its final truth or essential meaning, the 'voice' in a narrative text disappears in the process of inter-pretation and reinterpretation. For Hugh Kenner, *A Portrait of the Artist as a Young Man* was a masterpiece of consistent irony. For William Empson this reading was just 'the Kenner Smear' (Emp-son 1984, pp. 204–5). The ironic voice simply wasn't there. In this respect, Barthes was right: in the narrative text, it is only the reader who speaks (*'seul parle le lecteur'* (Barthes 1970, p. 157)). Yet Fludernik is right, too: it is not as easy to 'think beyond' the concept of voice as Barthes would have us believe. The idea of voice needs to be further problematised, its resistance further weakened. But it is not to be written off. We might begin by returning to some of the questions raised by recent theory about the singleness of narrative voice.

A Difference with Dialogics

Neither Banfield's nor Fludernik's book substantially engages with the growing body of contemporary theory that radically pluralises the voice in literary texts. Paradoxically, however, it is arguably precisely by continuing recent efforts to pluralise narrative 'voice' that we shall be able most usefully to return to the more significant aspects of Banfield's case. For pluralisation inevitably breaks up residual certainties about the fixity, unity or homo-geneity of the narrative voice and reduces the illusion of the latter's singular power. Bakhtin and post-Bakhtinian theory, of course, have apparently been particularly successful in pluralis-ing voice. As is well known, Bakhtin saw discourses as 'double-directed ... incorporating a relationship to someone else's utterance as an essential element' (Bakhtin 1984, p. 180). But the concept of dialogue is not a dualism: at its most developed, it is a theory of the multiplicity of the narrative text as 'a genuine polyphony of fully valid voices' (ibid. p. 5). For Bakhtin, the novel is multi-styled, multi-accented. Dostoevsky, for instance, 'could hear two contending voices' in every voice, 'in every expression a crack, and the readiness to go over immediately to another contradictory expression' (ibid. p. 30). The recessions of dialogue – the splintering fissures within Dostoevskean narrative – would seem on this account to be potentially infinite. This for Bakhtin is one way of expressing the novel's general spirit of indeterminacy, process, inconclusiveness, *unfinalisability*, to use one of his key terms (Bakhtin 1981, p. 7).

For Bakhtin, it is through dialogue as a diverse or multiple phenomenon that Dostoevsky works against any monistic principle which would affirm the unity of existence, consciousness or voice. One obvious example would be Bakhtin's account of *Notes from Underground* in *Problems of Dostoevsky's Poetics* (Bakhtin 1984) as 'a complex interaction of accents, counteraccents and countercounteraccents'.[4] In this novel, says Bakhtin, the '"depicting" authorial language' lies on the same plane as the '"depicted" language' of the hero, 'and may enter into dialogic relations and hybrid combinations with it' (Bakhtin 1981, p. 28). Dostoevsky is engaged in a 'dialogic activity' with his creatures, as they are with each other (Bakhtin 1984, p. 63). But Bakhtin also understands consciousness as a dialogue of voices. Styles contain internal polemics, too. The novel as form is always citational, constantly and plurally in dialogue with other novels, other writings. Dialogue is even present in the contradictions between separate elements in the development of the plot (ibid. p. 40). Dialogue, then, is a multiple and complex phenomenon.[5] In the case of plot, for example, the idea of voice in dialogics can seem very close to dissolving into the idea of writing, to becoming practically indistinguishable from and even – strangely – a metaphor for writing.

Bakhtinian theory might thus seem to be an obvious instrument to use in deconstructing the metaphysics of voice in narratology. But there are problems with this view. For dialogism always conceives of the plurality of the text in certain fixed ways and

within certain limits. The concept of dialogue always involves a
kind of hooking together or '*concordance*' of 'unmerged twos or
multiples' (Morson and Emerson 1990, p. 256). In fact, the idea of
dialogue always implies a common site; not, that is, a single
ground or foundation to which all the discourses at play within a
given text can be referred; but a common site on which the
separate utterances (or elements of text) in dialogue at any given
moment can meet. Certainly, dialogism 'militates against monad-
ism' (Holquist 1990, p. 90). But if it assumes non-coincidence and
knows no sublation of difference, it also assumes and requires
commensurability. As Morson and Emerson put it, if 'divergent
perspectives are fundamentally "incommensurable," then the
possibility of genuine dialogue' actually becomes 'illusory' (Morson and Emerson 1990, p. 233). This has to be the case, for
Bakhtin, because communication is a fundamental principle. All
utterances are bound by the conditions of 'addressivity' and
'answerability'. No utterance falls outside the 'structure of addressivity', and the latter posits a place shared by both the elements in
dialogue with one another. Bakhtin calls it a 'place of contact' and
defines it as the place of 'truth'. Furthermore, the site of truth is
also a site of struggle. As Holquist says, dialogism is based on the
assumption 'that all meaning is achieved through struggle' (ibid.
p. 39). For Bakhtin, dialogism may be quite distinct from dialectics.[6] But the dialogical model is nonetheless a conflictual one.
Whether it takes place between individuals or as an aspect of
experience or thought, for Bakhtin, dialogue is 'adorned with
polemic' (Bakhtin 1984, p. 32). The 'place of contact' in dialogue
is hence an 'arena of battle' in which clashing elements constantly
compete for hegemony.

Thus dialogics actually always offers an agonistic and even a
heavily masculine model of the text in which textual features fight
their battle out in the space of the narrative arena.[7] The dialogic
'place of contact' denies what Lyotard calls 'the differend'. Dialogism assumes the fact of communication between phrases and what
Lyotard calls 'phrase regimens'. It radically reduces both the
heterogeneity of 'phrase regimens' and the aleatory and unpredictable quality of possible crossings between them. For Lyotard, 'to
link is necessary; how to link is contingent' (Lyotard 1988, p. 29).
For Bakhtin, on the other hand, if linking is necessary, it is always

according to certain principles of commensuration. It is surely Lyotard, here, who more insistently eliminates the thought of uniform foundations or controlling totalities as present within discourse. Furthermore, in Bakhtinian theory, dialogue takes place as the encounter of unities or abstract entities existing prior to it. Bakhtin continually falls back on a conception of dialogue as generated in the connection between 'relatively stable types' of utterance (Bakhtin 1986, p. 60). They may be the types of literary genre, genres being 'the drive belts from the history of society to the history of language and literature' (ibid. p. 278). They may be the types of (primary or secondary) speech genres.[8] But the most important 'types' are the languages that go to make up hetero-glossia. As Marxist, and what Stam calls 'left', readings of Bakhtin are particularly concerned to emphasise,[9] for Bakhtin, the modes of dialogue in narrative as in life are all merely instances of a larger dialogue of social and discursive forces operating through and as languages. All such 'languages' as used by professions, generations, classes, geographical communities, ethnic groups and so on are 'specific points of view on the world, forms for conceptualising the world in words, specific world views, each characterised by its own objects, meanings and values' (Bakhtin 1981, pp. 291–2). If, then, as Holquist suggests, heteroglossia comes as close as possible to the concept of a *locus* for dialogue (Holquist 1990, p. 69), the idea of heteroglossia also traces the forces at work in dialogue back to entities conceived as having the static positionality of *loci*. In Stam's phrase, dialogue thus becomes more than just a 'conflictual relation'. It is a struggle between 'distinct socioideological positionings' or 'bounded verbal-ideological belief systems' (Stam 1989, pp. 37, 50).[10] For all his emphasis on the unalterably processual quality of discourse, its temporal dynamism, Bakhtin also argues the need to look beneath the superficial hustle and bustle of literary process to 'homogenous features that, if only relatively static and constant, can be treated as such for the purposes of analysis' (Bakhtin 1981, pp. 7–8). In that respect, Bakhtin's theoretical reflexes do not seem so very remote from Lukács's or even Aristotle's.

When Eagleton argues, then, that a grasp of heteroglossia as a political theory is vital in defending Bakhtin against 'poststructur-alist denigrations' (Eagleton 1988, p. 116) he merely confirms the complicity between Bakhtin and the metaphysical modes of thought that poststructuralism is concerned to resist. Dialogics is a theory of conflict between positions on a given site which they 'hold in common'. In that respect, the space opened up by dialogics is not radically at odds with with that made available by established forms of narrative theory.[11] Furthermore, for Bakhtin, dialogue would often appear to be very precisely contained. In 'The Problem of Content, Material and Form in Verbal Art' (1924), Bakhtin developed a critique of the formalists' 'material aesthetics'. He argues that there is no possibility of achieving a 'total empiricisation of the aesthetic object'. Attempts at such an empiricisation stem merely from fear that beyond the empirical reality of the object 'lie only metaphysical and mystical essences' (Bakhtin 1990, p. 310). We should rather seek to understand the 'distinctiveness' both of the aesthetic object and 'the purely aesthetic interconnection of its constituents, that is, its architectonics' (ibid.). There are two kinds of form in art (which formalism confuses): compositional form, a question of technique, and architectonic form, a question of content, of 'the unification of cognitive and ethical values' (ibid. p. 303).

Architectonics is a word Bakhtin gets from Kant. Architectonic form grasps content as part of the 'irreversibly occurring event of being' (ibid. p. 306). But it must detach the event from its future, 'isolate' it from 'the unity of nature' (ibid. p. 307). Narrative fiction is precisely a 'positive expression' of such an 'isolation' (ibid.). The act of isolation pacifies dialogue. It 'calms and consummates' content. Without aesthetic form, 'artistic contemplation ceases and is supplanted by purely ethical co-experiencing or by cognitive reasoning, by theoretical agreement or disagreement, by practical approval or disapproval' (ibid. p. 305). In other words, dialogue breaks forth again. Dialogue, then, must be 'held in' by the architectonic, form-making, ordering activity as 'an activity of a purely spiritual generation and selection of meanings, connections, axiological relations' (ibid. pp. 314–15). For all Bakhtin's claim not to be endowing the aesthetic object with 'some sort of mystical or metaphysical essence' (ibid. p. 300), his theory of 'architectonic form' finally turns form into a transcendent or 'spiritual' entity. The essay in question is of course an early production. But the conception of form apparent in it arguably reappears in other guises in his later work. Thus the later Bakhtin will argue that 'the absence of internal conclusiveness and exhaustiveness' that is implicit in the dialogic nature of the novel also creates a sharp demand for an external and formal completedness and exhaustiveness (Bakhtin 1981, p. 31). Equally, the conception of the 'chronotope' as Bakhtin develops it in his later work is in fact a theory of the architectonics or 'intrinsic connectedness' of the 'temporal and spatial relationships . . . artistically expressed in literature' (ibid. pp. 291–2). Bakhtin's idea of the 'matrix', too, in the work of Rabelais and others, is surely another version of 'architectonic form'.[12] Equally, in *Problems of Dostoevsky's Poetics*, Bakhtin argues for a final unity to polyphonic novels which is not produced by monologic finalisation but is a unity of several potential unities. He even flirts – if briefly – with comparing such unity to 'the church as a communion of unmerged souls' (Bakhtin 1984, p. 254). Again and again, the emphasis is on a structure within which the dialogical activity occurs, and which is thought of as more encompassing or 'fundamental' than the dialogical activity itself.

FEMINIST THEORY AND THE PLURALISATION OF VOICE

For all its pluralising effects, then, Bakhtinian dialogics works in terms of a 'hard' model of the text in which lines are clearly drawn, boundaries are clearly demarcated and entities clearly identified. Dialogics imagines or distributes its theoretical space only within certain definite limits. If the voices in the text are no longer homogeneous, for dialogics, they nonetheless emerge from and meet in homogenous spaces. To adapt Lyotard, Bakhtinian theory does not think the 'incompossibility' of voices (Lyotard 1988a, p. 83). It believes they can always be subjected 'to a single law' (ibid. p. 128). It therefore always platonically prefers 'dialogue to differend', for Lyotard a dangerous error (ibid. p. 84). Feminist theory might seem to be a more promising place to turn in search of a less rigid, more fluid conception of the plurality of voice in narrative. But feminist narratology seems rather to have returned to a more familiar, classical conception of voice. There are good reasons for this, not least the vigorous calls for a new valuation of voice within postmodern culture.[13] Feminist thought itself has increasingly privileged speaking and hearing as opposed to the patriarchal valuation of specularity, vision, the objectifying gaze. In keeping with this, Susan Lanser's powerful elaboration of a feminist narratology has been much concerned with women finding a voice, and with women's as 'other voices', notably in her *Fictions of Authority*. Lanser finds post-structuralist interrogations of voice 'compelling'. But she nonetheless insists that 'for the collectively and personally silenced the term has become a trope of identity and power' (Lanser 1992, p. 3). Hence her specific interest is in voice in relation to the female quest for discursive authority. The idea of narrative voice is thus crucially linked to a challenge to old, patriarchal forms of authority, and an expression of a different and frequently hard-won authority of women's own.

Whilst narrative in the Western novel has always been 'individualistic and androcentric', says Lanser, the novel has also offered women abundant opportunities 'for creating voices on the margins of fiction and history' (ibid. pp. 22, 15). At the same time, any given narrative mode of voice, in women's fiction, is 'a particular nexus of powers, dangers, prohibitions and possibilities' (ibid. p. 15). Lanser provides three major categories of narrative voice. In the first, 'authorial voice', the narrative situations are 'heterodiegetic, public and potentially self-referential'. Lanser thinks of Austen, Eliot, Woolf and Morrison, here, as constructing 'authorial voice within and against the narrative and social conventions' of their 'time and place' (ibid. p. 18). These novelists' productions of an authorial voice are decisive bids for a narrative hegemony, as for example in *Northanger Abbey*. In the second category, 'personal voice', narrators self-consciously tell their own histories. Here the narrative mode is less formidable for women, since there is no call for the broad powers of knowledge and judgement associated with authorial voice. On the other hand, 'personal voice' offers no gender-neutral mask, and therefore risks generating a critical or resistant reader. According to Lanser, though, 'personal voice' in women's fiction is nonetheless crucial in the production of female subjectivities and women-centred points of view. In *Jane Eyre*, for instance, Lanser emphasises precisely the power and forcefulness, the 'sharp singularity' of the narrative voice. The 'originality' and 'self-sufficiency' of Jane's voice are what matter most, as challenges to certain 'limits' conventionally placed 'on female authority' (ibid. pp. 177, 182).

Lanser seems to leave us with an insoluble contradiction. On the one hand, she sees the vital importance of showing how far her women writers more or less radically challenge patriarchal traditions in the novel, patriarchal valuations of their work and, above all, patriarchal conceptions of the narrative voice. On the other hand, she does so precisely by reinstating or maintaining terms of reference – authority, subjectivity, narratorial hegemony, originality, totalisation, the monologic voice – that have developed within and are surely fundamental to patriarchal ideology. Lanser is no Braidotti or Irigaray. She celebrates her women writers as equalling men independently but on men's terms. She even praises Jane Eyre for the 'aggression' with which she 'suppresses points of view that differ from her own' (ibid. p. 185). The contradiction in question is not to be simply resolved. On what possible grounds could one ever seek to deny the singular authority of a previously marginalised or silenced voice? On the other hand, can we happily consent to the reinstitution within narrative theory of monologic utterance and the narrator as whole and totalising presence? At the very least, we need a second mode of theorising voice which will continue to raise questions about Lanser's kind of project, for all the latter's power and importance. The assumption of any unity to the voice must surely be insistently problematised. For it is inseparable from the assumption that the narrative world is one of whole dimensions, can be 'spoken whole' and is available as a whole.

In any case, the thought of the actual multiplicity of voice is by no means alien to feminist theory. The most radical departure in Lanser's own book comes in the section devoted to her third category, 'communal voice' in women's fiction. Here, certainly, Lanser thinks of narrators as 'constructing' themselves 'as a plurality' (ibid. p. 257). Problematically, however, the concept of 'communal voice' still ultimately reduces voice to an originary 'single point', the 'sense of purpose and identity' shared by a 'narrating community' or expressed by its representative or representatives (ibid. p. 255). Michèle le Dœuff's 'Philosophy and the Larynx' thinks the question of voice through in rather different terms. Le Dœuff emphasises the importance of voice as against

writing, noting how often the latter has been placed on the side of
sterility and the law, the former on that of frenzy, lawless love,
women and the young. But she also demonstrates how often the
singing voice has been stigmatised as 'commensurable, made of
calculable intervals', promising 'an ordered and reassuring world'
(le Dœuff 1989b, pp. 129–30). The speaking voice, on the other
hand, has been made into 'a place of pure multiplicity, incommensurability, deficit' (ibid. p. 135). Plato himself suggested this,
insofar as he asserted that there was an 'infinite diversity' to the
human voice quite beyond the determinations of music (ibid.).
But he also saw the tragedians' voice as a threat that could
endanger the city precisely in being entirely unrelated to the
meaning, content or truth-value of a given discourse. Far from
speaking with authority or speaking a whole truth, the voice as
Plato fears it is characterised by an 'absence of figure and measure'
and equally 'prevents the realisation of a definite quantity' (ibid.).
But Le Dœuff inverts Plato, valuing the voice as the very principle
of fluency, as the 'genus of the indefinite' itself, continually
escaping any thought of essences (ibid. p. 135).

One useful model for narrative voice conceived of as this
'indefinite' phenomenon is arguably produced by a re-reading of
Kristeva's semiotic *chora*. The *chora* is the endless flow of
pulsions that precedes and underlies the symbolic order and its
structures. It is 'an essentially mobile and extremely provisional
articulation constituted by movements and their ephemeral stases'
(Kristeva 1984, p. 25). Kristeva calls it an articulation as distinct
from a disposition. For Kristeva, any text is the effect of an
interplay between semiotic articulation and symbolic disposition,
a genotext woven within the semiotic and a phenotext issuing
from societal, cultural, syntactical and other constraints. A disposition 'already depends on representation, lends itself to phenomenological, spatial intuition and *gives rise to a geometry*'
(ibid. pp. 25–6, italics mine). But the *chora* itself 'has no thesis
and position', is a drive economy underlying all dispositions
whether of resemblances or oppositions, and is perceptible at least
as a pressure on dispositions or within them. For Kristeva,
linguistics has always tended to 'eliminate from its field of inquiry
everything that cannot be systematised, structured or logicised
into a formal entity' (Kristeva et al. 1975, p. 230).[14] In that respect,

it is 'the kind of activity encouraged and privileged by (capitalist) society' which 'represses the process pervading the body and the subject' (Kristeva 1984, p. 13). But what is true of linguistics is also true of narratology. Neither can think the *chora*.

So there are 'dimensions (instinctual drives) and operations (displacement, condensation, vocalic and intonational differentiation)' that formalistic theory excludes from its consideration of the text (ibid. p. 22). Linguistics (and narratology) need to restore these dimensions to their description of formal relations. The reference to 'vocalic and intonational differentiation' is important, here. For Kristeva, the organisation of the *chora* is partly 'vocal' (ibid. p. 26). It is to be thought of less in terms of visibility or legibility than audibility. But it is also 'a place of permanent scission' where the drives are disunited and contradictory and there are 'waves of attack' against all stases (ibid. pp. 27–9). Thus the *chora* is 'no more than the place where the subject is generated and negated, the place where his unity succumbs before the process of changes and stases' (ibid.). Hence there are always discontinuities in the vocal organisation of the *chora*. It might in fact be conceived of as a multiple and diffuse murmur or susurration of disparate and disconnected voices. Their only certain, common site is that of the process itself, of which the voice of the 'transcendental ego' is merely 'the liminal moment' (ibid. p. 30).

The concept of the *chora*, then, offers ways of hearing texts quite different to that imposed on them by the iron categories of a logical order. But there is a problem, here. For Kristeva suggests that there are different modes of articulation of the semiotic and the symbolic in narrative, metalanguage, theory, poetry and so on. Furthermore, narrative emerges as the Oedipal mode of discourse *par excellence*. In narrative, the phenotext dominates pulsions and process. The diversity of the 'flow of drives' is 'poured into the rigid moulds' of a 'nondisjunctive' or 'dichotomous' structure (ibid. p. 90). The 'matrix of enunciation' in narrative tends to centre on 'an axial position'. Psychoanalytically viewed, this position is a projection of the paternal role in the family, the voice of the father and of law. Hence the 'subjectal structure' of narrative at best emerges as a series of entities whose very appearance as such nonetheless leaves them open to subjection and manipulation within the networks of the symbolic order. Thus language in narrative may easily function without ever 'reintroducing within the sign the instinctual nucleus that would have disarticulated it, pluralized it, and imbued it with non-sense' (ibid.).

In its own way, then, the Kristevan view of narrative might ultimately seem to reduce it to a system of homogenous spaces. Kristeva appears to make exception only of certain avant-garde texts (Joyce, Lautréamont etc.). Such texts allow the *chora* to breach and modify linguistic structures. Here 'signifying practice has inscribed within the phenotext the plural, heterogeneous, and contradictory process' of the semiotic itself, 'encompassing the flow of drives, material discontinuity . . . and the pulverisation of language' (ibid. p. 88). In *Maldoror*, the semiotic disrupts the symbolic, the subject is put on trial and thrown radically into process, and a whole 'vocal register' is also 'dismantled' (ibid. pp. 155, 219, 221). The intrusion of the semiotic into the symbolic is therefore marked by a dispersal of voice, as with Joyce's Anna Livia Plurabelle. So, too, according to *Powers of Horror*, Céline's 'narratives of abjection' take us beyond the horizons of Bakhtinian theory in shattering the very linearity of narrative (Kristeva 1982, p. 140). Narrative now proceeds 'by flashes, enigmas, short cuts, incompletion, tangles' (ibid. p. 141). This partly coincides with the 'incandescent states' of abjection itself as a 'boundary-subjectivity'. Céline's narrative method is inseparable from the way in which abjection 'cries out' in his narratives (ibid. p. 141). 'Crying out' is a multiple phenomenon, appearing for instance as slang and spoken language punctuate, interrupt and blur narrative 'utterance' (ibid. p. 191); in those constructions in Céline's narratives that are close to constructions in children's first sentences 'during syntax learning' (ibid. p. 195); and in Céline's practice of 'sentence segmentation', which allows sentences with more than one 'centre' to develop and even brings French sentences syntactically closer to sentences in other languages (ibid. p. 192). In all this, we have 'a resurrection of the emotional, maternal abyss' appearing within and through syntactical structures (ibid. p. 196). We hear 'intonation' producing 'the language system before the latter can be made explicit as such', in a series of 'successive surges', as a kind of pluralised voicing (ibid. pp. 194–5).

So, too, in 'The Novel as Polylogue', Kristeva thinks of the voice in Sollers's *H* as fragmented by increasing breaks (Kristeva 1989, p. 165). *H* is 'a polylogical "discourse" of a multiplied, stratified and heteronomous subject of enunciation' (ibid. p. 173). The sentence sequences are defined in reading by breathing motions. Each breathing movement coincides with an attitude of the speaking subject and a sphere of denotation or reference. A new movement ushers in a new attitude and a new sphere of reference, thus indicating 'the subject of enunciation's motility – his chances for resurgence and metamorphosis' (ibid. p. 169). The juxtaposition of utterances registers the plurality of the genotext, bears witness to a collision of semiotic and symbolic operations. The result is a new materialism of the voice. The voice disintegrates into the material and historical process – into the body itself as material and historical process – and must then reconstitute itself only to disintegrate again. Thus in *H* as in Joyce or Lautréamont, 'the entire history of the Western subject and his relationship to his enunciation has come to an end' (ibid. p. 178).

Joyce, Lautréamont and Sollers display the productive activity that is always at the foundation 'of subjective and ideological signifying formulas and ideological signifying formations' (Kristeva 1984, p. 16). Primitive societies called that foundation 'sacred'. Modernity rejects it as 'schizophrenia' (ibid.). The avant-garde text attests to what other forms of discourse repress, 'the process that exceeds the subject and his communicative structures' (ibid. p. 16). Read as a theory of narrative, however, Kristeva's case might finally seem limited by the (revolutionary) eschatological division she establishes between kinds of narrative text. Yet in *Revolution in Poetic Language*, Kristeva partly sees literature itself as a privileged mode of discourse whose 'essential element' is the interplay of semiotic articulation and symbolic disposition. Kristeva suggests that this is what separates it off from 'socially useful' discourse. For the latter cannot afford either to reflect back on the processes which generate its dispositions, or to make those processes perceptible (ibid. p. 16). Thus literary practice as a whole becomes an activity 'that liberates the subject from a number of linguistic, psychic and social networks, as a dynamism that breaks up the inertia of language habits' (Kristeva 1969, pp. 178–9).[15]

In part, then, Kristeva herself produces a theory of the relationship between semiotic articulations and symbolic dispositions in
literature which goes beyond and helps to obscure the clarity of
her own distinction between avant-garde and other forms of
narrative. This theory suggests that there may be a number of
different ways of conceptualising the relation between phenotext
and genotext – and therefore the play and dispersal of voice – in a
variety of different kinds of narrative. Is the genotext really wholly
buried – lost to us – in forms of narrative other than those
produced by the avant-garde? If not, then how does the genotext
manifest itself elsewhere? What residual traces does it leave? How
might we read other kinds of narrative 'against the grain', in ways
that might allow us to bring the genotext into play, too?

Rhys's *Wide Sargasso Sea* lies somewhere in between classic
realist and modernist narrative. It can help us to think differently
about narrative voice without either lapsing into an established
frame of reference or reverting yet again to a celebration of the
avant-garde. The instances of voice in Antoinette's narrative
discourse are various and shifting. The vocabulary conventionally
adopted for describing voice – first and third person, heterodiegetic and homodiegetic, extradiegetic and intradiegetic – is
hardly adequate to that variety. In the first page and a half of *Wide
Sargasso Sea*, for example, there is only a limited amount of direct
speech. But there are seventeen verbs denoting speaking relating
to a total of seven sources, singular and plural. From the start,
Antoinette's voice is plural, a conduit or point of transmission,
not so much for 'discourses' as for utterances in all their singularity, whether given directly, quoted, paraphrased or incorporated
into the flow of Antoinette's prose. *Pace* Lanser, Antoinette's
narrative voice is never really wholly hers and, as the narrator's, it
can never be. In this respect, it mirrors the politics of Antoinette's
predicament. But the politics in question is not that of possible
self-authorisation. It has to do with a rich multiplicity to Antoinette at odds with the relatively impoverished terms (of clear
identity) in which almost everyone around her thinks, and which
are peculiarly dear (the novel says) to Rochester, England and
English masculinity. Antoinette's multiplicity constitutes her
receptivity, her openness to affect. It is also reflected in the
multiplicity of her narrative – in the very fact that she is a

narrator. If we start to think of voice as instance in Antoinette's narrative, rather than as source, origin or full presence, then we may notice how varied its modes of emergence are. On the one hand, it can 'speak the narrative' (narrating, describing, commenting etc.). On the other hand, it can efface itself (unmediated speech). It may introduce or 'present' speech, report speech or report unspoken thought as speech. It may also report silence, the failure or refusal to speak. It may include speech within a narrative sentence:

What was the use of telling her that I'd been awake before and heard my mother screaming 'Qui est là? Qui est là?' (Rhys 1993, p. 39)

It may blend with another voice or voices (Banfield's and Fludernik's *style indirecte libre*), changing other voices, and simultaneously being changed by them. It may divide in dialogue with itself. There are even aporias of voice, what Barthes called 'holes' in discourse when he found them in *Sarrasine* (Barthes 1970, p. 49), moments when we cannot be sure who speaks:

I never looked at any strange negro. They hated us. They called us white cockroaches. Let sleeping dogs lie (Rhys 1993, P. 20).

Who speaks that last phrase? What is its real source? Can we know? Once we dispense with the idea of the single narrative voice – itself predicated on the assumption that a narrator is a character present in a mystifying singleness throughout her or his discourse – then we begin to see the relation between voice and text as an irremediably variable distance. In other words, the voices in Rhys's narrative constantly fade in and out.[16] Those voices are sometimes subject to interference, blurred or placed within or behind other voices. There is no regularity to this process, and there are no discernible laws to it. It is not reducible to 'codes'. In fact, it is the very play of narrative itself. Narrative utterance manifests itself as multiple cathexes, a flow of manifold and different impulses towards the world. In other words, it manifests itself as genotext. But the genotext does not so much disrupt as it works beneath and through the phenotext. Fascinatingly, Antoinette's is a plural voice, too, in that it intermittently seems to belong to different times. Or rather, the narrative continually modifies or opens and closes the gap between the time (or age) of the narrating and the narrated 'self':

> That was how it was, light and dark, sun and shadow, Heaven and Hell, for one of the nuns knew all about Hell and who does not? (ibid. p. 48)

Those last four words radically shift, 'age' and 'deepen' the narrative voice. Dark gulfs of this kind repeatedly open up in Antoinette's 'narrative of abjection'. Voice again becomes a matter of irregular pulsions, establishing and then breaking down distances; a play of emotion which disrupts, if not the symbolic, then the discursive order. So too, for example, when past tense briefly cedes to present in the narration. It does not help, then, to conceive either of voice or the 'character speaking' as a single entity. There is rather a fluency of voice which establishes itself at a varying and sometimes indeterminate distance from its subject. This, again, makes voice a multiple flow which is constantly being arrested by but also moving beyond stases. In other words, it makes voice conceivable in terms of the *chora*.

Of course, Rochester's narrative cannot be thought of in exactly the same way. A more detailed analysis would surely show that Antoinette's discourse is the repressed other in, as well as of, Rochester's discourse. Rochester hopelessly seeks to exclude Antoinette's kind of multiplicity in himself and from his narrative. In smothering it in her, he smothers it in himself. In the process, he smothers narrative, too. For what Rochester wishes to extirpate in himself is precisely the principle of narrative itself and what drives him into narration. The principle of narrative voice – in *Wide Sargasso Sea*, at least – is perhaps the principle of the Creole, not one thing nor the other, displaced, modified by context, caught between identities, always suspended somewhere between absent origin and alien context. But a white, masculine, European hermeneutics assured of its place – hermeneutics as practised by Rochester, imperious in its demand for sense, finality, determinacy, clarity, identity, judgment, discrimination – cannot acknowledge this.

DETHRONING THE *PHŌNĒ*

Voice in *Wide Sargasso Sea* would therefore seem to correspond
to what Le Dœuff has to say about the speaking voice as 'a place of
pure multiplicity, incommensurability, deficit'. The trouble is that
that is not what Le Dœuff ends up saying about voice. Towards the
conclusion of her essay, Le Dœuff abandons and deconstructs the
binary oppositions that I described above – voice versus writing,
speech versus song – suggesting that such oppositions tell us less
about the terms in question than about thought. For Le Dœuff, the
oppositions are 'mere blazons and armorial bearings – drafts of
specular objects in which the scriptor thinks himself and his
relation to the Other' (Le Dœuff 1989b, p. 135). In particular,
paradoxes immediately beset all valuations or fetishisations of
voice in writing. For they are projections of an alterity in voice
that is invested with value relative to the writer's project or the
reader's activity. According to Le Dœuff, the concept of voice in
writing or as promoted by writing always involves a certain
idealisation of 'vocal power' and risks retreating into a 'complacent daydream' (ibid. p. 137). The argument seems odd: if writing
idealises its Other, is it not modestly if implicitly proclaiming its
own limits, rather than being 'complacent?' Le Dœuff thinks not,
in that she identifies such 'modesty' with the 'suspect plaint' of
the philosopher who says that 'it is vocal capacity which decides
in the final instance – and not what is just, or what is said' (ibid.
pp. 136–7). Thought thus defeatistly submits to being worsted by
the world, common sense, 'immediacy', and declares its ineptit-
ude, its lack of purchase on the real. Voice becomes writing's alibi,
its justification for any failure, not least political failure; its
defence against the need for critique, too, since it (writing) was
always a second-order activity.

In the end, then, however challenging and effective certain
reconceptualisations of voice in narrative may be, the concept of
narrative voice needs to be deconstructed, not only in itself, but
insofar as it serves to disempower writing or ward off the dangers
of writing. Fludernik suggests that narratology has been far too
exclusively concerned with writing and argues for increased
attention to oral or 'naturally occurring' narrative (Fludernik
1993, p. xi).[17] But in one sense – with rare exceptions, like

Banfield – narratology has never really concerned itself with writing at all. For it has always provided itself with voice and person as alibi, source and origin, as first cause. Narratology thinks of voice as 'coming before' writing, even when it (voice) is pluralised. But the voice thus placed only comes to us through writing. The reality of voice is instantaneous, evanescent and irreducible. Yet can we even begin to imagine reading a narrative text without the assumption of a voice or voices speaking within it? Both narrative voice and narrative as writing persuade us that they are prior to each other, but in different ways. We return to the double-bind in which Fludernik's revision of Banfield left us: it seems impossible both to think and not to think narrative as writing. Even a conception of narrative voice as plural and dispersed must be thought together with the writing that makes voice possible.

This links up with a certain strain in Derrida's deconstruction of voice. Indeed, it is precisely through Derrida's work that we can return to Banfield's thesis. Derrida of course has consistently questioned 'the privilege of the *phōnē*' as it is 'implied by the whole history of metaphysics' (Derrida 1973, p. 16). For Derrida, the privilege historically accorded to speech is inseparable from a particular valuation of reason, the conscious will, the self-identity of consciousness itself. On the one hand, voice guarantees the certitude and unity of 'inner existence'. It guarantees our self-presence, too, for the uttering self is deemed to be immediately present to itself as living consciousness (ibid. p. 43). Speech at once expresses a whole meaning that comes from within and is intimately tied to thought. Equally, speech has classically been understood as 'mastery of objective being' (ibid. p. 75), as guaranteeing the presence of the object 'aimed at' by the speaker. The voice, in fact, is endowed with three kinds of seemingly unlimited power: the power to express an inward and intended sense; the power to grasp the external object; and a power over the signifier itself. This supposed power predetermines communication as a site of passage for univocal meaning (Derrida 1982, p. 309). Our trust in the power of voice thus holds the spectres of difference and non-presence at bay and maintains subject and object, language and meaning in a space untroubled by either spectre. The 'strange prerogative of the vocal medium' is denied to writing

(Derrida 1973, p. 70). Writing is the antithesis of speech: inexpressive, external, unsure, slippery, tending to 'remove every possible *security* and *ground*' from discourse (ibid. p. 62). It disturbs the assumption of self-presence and meaning as full presence. In Rousseau's words, we manage and contain the disruptive force of writing only by casting it as 'the simple "supplement" to the spoken word' (Derrida 1976, p. 7). Writing becomes both a kind of 'recording' of speech, a 'doubling' of the signifier (ibid. p. 29) and an extension of the communicative space of the voice. Such a concept of writing is implicit in the concept of phonetic writing itself, in the very assumption that the work says something, that it has a *vouloir-dire* that can be interrogated (Derrida 1987c, p. 22). It is thus that Hegel, Heidegger and the whole tradition they reproduce insistently subordinate the arts to speech and 'the said' (ibid. p. 23).

The 'privilege of the *phōnē*' surely finds one of its most powerful confirmations today in discourse about narrative. That confirmation has an ideological function. The paradox with which I began this chapter is no accident: by confirming 'the privilege of the *phōnē*', narratology firmly grounds a technology of the text – with all the apparently disturbing potential of an advanced or new technology – on a reassuringly familiar onto-theological foundation. It is rather like having fundamentalist Christianity broadcast to us by satellite television. What Banfield, Kristeva and Derridean deconstruction all remind us, on the other hand, is that the concept of narrative voice is always a form of idealism. Derrida suggests that the Husserlian conception of voice is not concerned with the real, physical voice but with 'the voice phenomenologically taken', a *geistige Leiblichkeit*, a spiritual flesh (Derrida 1973, p. 16). The same is also true of narratology and novel theory. Narratology powerfully reaffirms voice as 'pure spiritual intention', the soul within the text as body. As opposed to voice, writing is disturbingly material. It brings back all that is excluded in the narratological conception of voice: space, the outside, the world, the body, the sensible. It is therefore deemed to be an accidental, derivative or at any rate a secondary manifestation of language.

For Derrida, 'the history of the *phōnē* . . . is inseparable from the history of idealisation, that is, from the "history of mind"' (ibid.

p. 75). The history of narratology in the largest sense is implicated with both those 'histories'. For narratology, narrative voice is always a transcendent or ideal entity from the start. Voice as represented by narratology is actually always a metaphor for intention, meaning and totality. Voice in narrative is *Geist*. Thus, as this chapter has repeatedly suggested, when narrative theory has referred to the voice in narrative, it has never really meant voice at all. Derrida deconstructs the transcendence of voice partly by interrogating its relation to the value of presence ('presence of the object, presence of meaning to consciousness, self-presence in so-called living speech and in self-consciousness') (Derrida 1981b, p. 5). There is no essential proximity of voice and being as presence. Voice itself is always divided and adulterated. For the speaker 'is two – by definition', voice and ear (Derrida 1982, p. 288). The speaker is also a hearer, and changes as a speaker by hearing what s/he has just spoken. What we hear and respond to is not in any case our voice. We do not know its timbre and are unfamiliar with what is most spontaneous in it. Voice is never self-contained or wholly present to itself, wholly 'pure and free' in its spontaneity (Derrida 1981a, p. 22). In fact, it always takes a force 'from the world' – not least from language – and depends on that force for its emergence (ibid.). 'Discontinuity, delay, heterogeneity, and alterity' are always 'working upon the voice, producing it from its first breath as a system of differential traces, that is as writing before the letter' (Derrida 1982, p. 291). In fact, far from writing being a 'phenomenon of exterior representation' (Derrida 1981a, p. 24), a mere supplement to voice, it might be thought of as in some sense interior to or traversing voice, dislocating the latter and alienating it from itself (Derrida 1976, p. 46). Writing in fact becomes the differential principle, introducing an inexorable play of appearance and disappearance into the supposed self-presence of the voice.

But does not Kristevan pluralisation itself introduce the differential principle into voice? Derrida himself does not suggest that we should simply invert the classical hierarchy of speech and writing. Rather, he suggests that we consider every process of signification as a play of differences which 'supposes, in effect, syntheses and referrals which forbid at any moment, or in any sense, that a simple element be *present* in and of itself' (Derrida 1981b, p. 26). Doesn't the pluralisation of narrative voice mean thinking of voice as such a 'play?' But to pluralise voice is still to remain unequivocally attached to voice as metaphor. The spirit breathed into the flesh of the text is now diffuse and multiple, irreducible to the one, to source and origin. But writing and its materiality are nonetheless cancelled out. We thus ignore what Derrida thinks of as the irremediable '*anonymity*' of the written voice, the strangeness or '*impropriety*' of the voice that says 'I am writing' or 'I am speaking in writing'. To naturalise that voice is to overlook the fact that it is distinct from any subject, without a real referent, effectively equivalent to a *dead* voice.[18] There is always an 'original absence of the subject' in narrative. It is therefore necessary to think writing and voice together in narrative, to think of writing as constituting and deconstituting narrative voice. We must think 'discourse' as 'mode' along with the 'punctuality of positions' established in the pluralisation of voice (Derrida 1990, p. 194). Writing is 'an operation within voice', and voice itself is subject to a kind of 'suspension' in narrative (Derrida 1981, p. 333).

Thus in Mallarmé's *Mimique* and Sollers's *Nombres*, Derrida discovers 'the decease of a certain voice . . . that would be there only for the purpose of re-presenting the subject in his inner thoughts, so as to designate, state, express the truth – or presence – of a signified'. Narrative voice is 'authorless', here, 'a phonetic tracing . . . a power of inscription that is no longer verbal but phonic' (Derrida 1981a, pp. 331–2). These are texts, then, which make voice perceptible as writing, writing perceptible within voice. But it is harder to claim anything like the same of less avant-garde texts. In *Northanger Abbey*, for instance, surely we hear a voice that is sufficiently distinctive to have been canonised as such by a whole culture? But however clearly this might seem to be the case, the voice in question is not the compacted, self-authorising voice of Lanser's account of the novel. In certain respects, the voice in Austen's novel is not a homogenous entity at all. If we look at the appearance of a narrator who calls herself 'I' in the last two pages of the book, for instance, we notice some striking disparities:

The marriage of Eleanor Tilney, her removal from all the evils of such a home as Northanger had been made by Henry's banishment, to the home of her choice and the man of her choice, is an event which I expect to give general satisfaction among all her acquaintance. My joy on the occasion is very sincere. I know no one more entitled by unpretending merit, or better prepared by habitual suffering, to receive and enjoy felicity.

Any further definition of his merits must be unnecessary: the most charming young man in the world is instantly before the imagination of us all. Concerning the one in question, therefore, I have only to add (aware that the rules of composition forbid the introduction of a character not connected with my fable) that this was the very gentleman whose negligent servant left behind him that collection of washing-bills, resulting from a long visit at Northanger, by which my heroine was involved in one of her most alarming adventures.

I leave it to be settled by whomsoever it may concern, whether the tendency of this work be altogether to recommend paternal tyranny or reward filial obedience (Austen 1953, pp. 190–1).

The voice in the first passage in that of a narrator-character who is part of the Tilneys' world. The voice in the second is the voice of a self-conscious narrator, constrained by the limits of genre. The third voice is that of an omnipotent author who could 'settle' matters herself, but decides to leave it to others. Other examples of the intrusions of a narrating 'I' in *Northanger Abbey* would merely add to the impression of diversity, here. In Derrida's phrase, the meaning of this narrating 'I' is 'not essentially realised in the immediate idea' of a 'personality'. It is rather an 'occasional expression' (Derrida 1973, pp. 94–5). But if narrative voice is plural, here, that plurality actually indicates a 'voice' only to reduce it and the I-function to specific instances or tactics of the text as writing. If the text can effectively inform us that it both is and is not the 'speech' of a 'living subject' who is part of the Tilneys' world, for example, then it cannot be thought of as simply referring us away to a stable presence behind itself. We may wish to make sense of the divisions in the narrative voice by sorting them out into a structure of conflicts or 'tensions' (sympathy versus irony, opposed attitudes to the conventions of the genre, etc.). We might then proceed to consider that structure as intrinsic to Austen's project or her artistic personality. But that is to construct a geometry or at least a pattern where the intrusions of the narrating 'I' in the linear unfolding of the narrative are irregular. On one level, at least, the narrative voice has no uniform properties. Each narrating instance has at least a certain impropriety, in Derrida's (multiple) sense. The heterogeneity of the voice from this aspect must at least trouble the homogeneity we grant it from others. The narrative produces a presence in the text only as a spectral form that is stripped of its identity even as that identity is established. Thus author and narrator are always being constituted and deconstituted by writing as a principle of self-difference within the voice. Each separate instance of the 'I' declares its partial incompatibility with other instances. In doing so, it also declares not only its literariness but its writtenness. From instance to instance, voice emerges as if it were written 'by someone unknown' (ibid. p. 97).

JOYCE'S WRITING VOICES

Finally, however, it is to Joyce that we may turn for a paradigm. In Joyce, voice is never *Geist*. It is Joyce above all who produces a kind of narrative in which, again and again, we 'hear voices' only to register the writing that produces them. Alternatively, we find writing and difference only to recognise that we are finding them in a voice. No writer has had an ear so receptive to speech, on the one hand, coupled on the other with so keen an awareness of styles of writing. The famous styles in *Ulysses* constantly enter into composition with speech, yield to, transform and are transformed by speech, declare their own emergence from speech. Equally, voices are constantly traversed by writing and modified by their presentation in writing. If Joyce's art is monumental, in more senses than one, the relationship it establishes between voices and writing is a function of that monumentality. For Joyce insistently writes an awareness of the work as monument into the 'vividness' of what he memorialises. Joyce surely did not want the reader to recreate his Dublin without a precise and immediate sense of the absolute, particular historicity of the world in question. Joyce's is not a nostalgic and backward-looking aesthetics of presence which aims to celebrate a bygone culture by definitively 'preserving' it. It is exactly this which separates him from lesser memorialists of communities, from Fenimore Cooper and Willa Cather to Anthony Powell. The principle at stake is political as well as aesthetic. Joyce not only remembers that '[t]he masters of the Mediterranean are fellaheen today' (Joyce *Ulysses*, 7.911), but anticipates a future when a similar reversal will befall Ireland's two 'imperial masters'. The future and its difference must therefore be thought inside the past, as the 'presence' of the figures in *Ulysses* must simultaneously be conjured up and dissipated, as voices must also always be shown as writing.

In the later parts of *Ulysses* and in *Finnegans Wake*, Joyce produces a brawling, demotic cacophony of voices whilst simultaneously conferring an almost hieroglyphic inscrutability upon the discourse in which he does so. Pound rightly greeted Joyce's democratisation of the voices in narrative with enthusiasm. He argued that part of Joyce's achievement in *Ulysses* lay precisely in his having fused the discourse of the genteel and the ungenteel, 'small boys' and 'street preachers . . . bowsers and undertakers, Gertie McDowell and Mr Deasey [sic]' and so on (Read 1987, p. 196). We should nonetheless recognise how far cacophony in Joyce is always likely to be caught up in and inseparable from a writing. One particularly striking example of this comes in the closing section of Chapter 14 of *Ulysses* ('The Oxen of the Sun', 14.1440–1591):

All off for a buster, armstrong, hollering down the street. Bonafides. Where you slep las nigh? Timothy of the battered naggin. Like ole Billyo. Any brollies or gumboots in the fambly? Where the Henry Nevil's sawbones and ole clo? Sorra one o' me knows. Hurrah there, Dix! Forward to the ribbon counter. Where's Punch? All serene. Jay, look at the drunken minister coming out of the maternity hospal! *Benedicat vos omnipotens Deus, Pater et Filius.* A make, mister. The Denzille Lane boys. Hell, blast ye! Scoot. Righto, Isaacs, shove em out of the bleeding limelight. Yous join uz, dear sir? No hentrusion in life. Lou heap good man. Allee samee dis bunch. *En avant, mes enfants!* Fire away number one on the gun. Burke's! Burke's! Thence they advanced five parasangs. Slattery's mounted foot. Where's that bleeding awfur? Parson Steve, apostates' creed! No, no, Mulligan! Abaft there! Shove ahead. Keep a watch on the clock. Chuckingout time. Mullee! What's on you? *Ma mère m'a mariée.* British beatitudes! *Retamplatan digidi boumboum.* Ayes have it. To be printed and bound at the Druiddrum press by two designing females. Calf covers of pissedon green. Last word in art shades. Most beautiful book come out of Ireland in my time. *Silentium!* Get a spurt on. Tention. Proceed to nearest canteen and there annex liquor stores. March! Tramp, tramp, tramp, the boys are (atitudes!) parching. Beer, beef, business, bibles, bulldogs, battleships, buggery and bishops. Whether on the scaffold high. Beer, beef, trample the bibles. When for Irelandear. Trample the trampellers. Thunderation! Keep the durned millingtary step. We fall. Bishops boosebox. Halt! Heave to. Rugger. Scrum in. No touch kicking. Wow, my tootsies! You hurt? Most amazingly sorry! (ibid. 14.1440–64)

The section is often thought of as written up in a certain 'style', as the rest of the chapter has been given over to what are usually called parodies of a range of styles of writing.[19] Joyce himself encouraged this reading, asserting that the chapter moves from 'a Sallustian-Tacitean prelude' to Anglo-Saxon through the styles of Mandeville and Malory's *Morte d'Arthur*, the 'Elizabethan "chronicle style"', Milton, Taylor and Hooker, 'Burton-Browne', 'Bunyanesque', 'Pepys-Evelyn', 'Defoe-Swift', 'Steele-Addison-Sterne' and 'Landor-Pater-Newman' to a final 'frightful jumble of Pidgin English, Nigger English, Cockney, Irish, Bowery slang and broken doggerel' (Joyce 1957, Vol. I, p. 159). The implication would seem to be that there is a 'style' to the last section of the chapter that is on a par with all its other styles. The sheer variety of the languages that have been discovered in the section appear to confirm this. In addition to the elements that Joyce lists in the 'jumble', for instance, J.S. Atherton notes the presence of 'French, Scottish, Yiddish, German, sixteenth-century English canting, pugilists' and motor-racing slang, together with scraps of Latin, Gaelic, mock Welsh-English' and even '"Parlyaree", the strolling players' jargon mainly derived from Italian' (Hart and Hayman 1974, p. 334). However modernistic such a mixture, the passage could hardly seem more obviously 'written'. Yet some critics have not thought of it in terms of a style at all. Parrinder calls it a 'chaotic hubbub of conversation', for example, remarking that 'it is as if Joyce's tour of the stylistic museum had ended with a rejection of style' (Parrinder 1984, p. 175). Hugh Kenner has written of the passage as dominated by 'the speech of 1904 . . . spoken by a dozen voices simultaneously and picked up as if by an unseeing microphone'. If style 'had previously been an irritant', says Kenner, 'we should be grateful for some now' (Kenner 1980, p. 110).

In the passage quoted, a narrator is clearly present in the first sentence. So the section begins by announcing itself as a kind of writing. The second sentence would seem to be (though is not necessarily) an ironically toned comment of the narrator's. It is apparently the narrator who refers to the group as advancing 'five parasangs', and so on. There are other ways, too, in which the section draws attention to its writtenness: the use of italics for foreign languages, the deliberate insistence on visibility rather than sonority, on the materiality of what is on the page ('H_2O' for water, '2 night' for tonight (Joyce *Ulysses*, 14,1511, 1540)). There is a bravura flaunting of style in the very inventiveness of the passage, the consistency with which it maintains its principle of 'frightful jumble'. Yet it can also be read in reverse fashion, along the lines suggested by Parrinder and Kenner. Reading from this angle, we can repeatedly identify speakers and place discourses: the Scots accent, for instance, is that of Crotthers ('from Alba Longa' (ibid. 14.191)). The black accents, the Yiddish and pidgin are obviously partly adopted as a way of teasing Bloom about his racial extraction (ibid. 14.1448, 1526, 1557). The canting is Stephen's (ibid. 14.1495–6; cf. 3.378–84). We hear Lenehan admiring Molly's physique ('Prime pair of mincepies, no kid' (ibid. 14.1478)) and repeating one of his jokes ('Rose of Castile. Rows of cast' (ibid. 14. 1510–11; cf. 7.591)). We hear Mulligan quoting Yeats (ibid. 14. 1456–7; cf. 9.1164). We hear Dixon recounting the story of Bloom's bee-sting which he, Dixon, treated (ibid. 14.1473). We hear Bannon identifying Bloom as 'Photo's papli' (ibid. 14.1536), Lynch half-denying being seen with Kitty on the Malahide road (ibid. 14.1496), and so on. We can identify situations and events around which vocal exchanges take place. In the passage quoted, for example, a group of onlookers clearly notice (and mistake) Stephen in black ('Jay, look at the drunken minister coming out of the maternity hospal!'). Stephen promptly blesses them in Latin, but someone else in the company finds them more irritating ('The Denzille Lane boys. Hell, blast ye! Scoot') and encourages (uses?) Bloom to make a way through them ('Righto, Isaacs, shove em out of the bleeding limelight').

Yet at other moments the passage appears deliberately to prevent any such clarification. It is impossible to know who says 'Ginger cordial' at 14.1468, for example. Is this the voice of Bloom choosing his drink, or one of the younger men who is mocking his choice? Such indeterminacies obscure that very specificity of voice as source which is quite evident elsewhere in the passage. In doing so, they return us to a given phrase as writing, with no certain origin save the text itself. Furthermore, any given indication of a voice may remind us of another that we do not hear. 'Pardon?' says someone at 14.1553. 'Seen him today at a runefal?' (ibid. 14.1554). The words are clearly a response to something Bloom has said about the Man in the Mackintosh. But we are not given Bloom's words. However 'cacophonous' the passage seems, it also insistently reminds us that it is not and cannot be cacophonous enough, that we are hearing only voices selected and arranged, *rendered*. It makes us aware that, in that sense, it is always and only a stylisation. Indeed, in the end, paradoxically, the more the passage aspires to a mimetic simultaneity in the representation of a jabber of voices, the more it calls our attention to the fact that it must always fall entirely short of its purpose. With one or two exceptions (as in the bracketed 'atitudes!' in the passage quoted) no voice actually breaks in upon another. Rather, Joyce produces a written simultaneity of voices as a steady, linear unfolding that is highly conscious of being always and only writing.

In that respect, then, as has often been said of him in other contexts, Joyce pushes a mimetic project to an extreme point at which it overbalances and goes into reverse, shuttling to the opposite extreme. The rendition of clamour makes us increasingly aware of its own spacing, of its existence as and in a certain space. Barthes once imagined the comedy that might ensue if one tried to put the 'novelistic real' into operation. In a similar manoeuvre, here, Joyce tries to imagine a text that would achieve some kind of adequacy to the play of voice. The result is a text that more and more ostentatiously declares itself to be writing. We can neither hear nor fail to hear the voices in this passage from *Ulysses*. We can neither ignore nor fasten exclusively on the practice of writing within it. Writing is both an exterior 'clothing' for voice, and an activity working within and producing voice. Joyce refuses to allow us to decide whether writing or voice 'comes first'. We cannot escape the obligation of thinking both together. In that respect, as in so many others, Joyce remains exemplary for postmodernity.

NOTES

1. Dorrit Cohn's narratological classic *Transparent Minds* offers an interesting example of this position. See Cohn 1978.

2. For Banfield on film, see for instance 'Describing the Unobserved: Events Grouped Around an Empty Centre', Banfield 1987, pp. 265–85.

3. For early criticisms of Banfield, see Cohn 1978; Culler 1978, pp. 607–18; and McHale 1978, pp. 249–87. For later views, see Violi 1986; McHale 1983, pp. 17–45; Yamaguchi 1989, pp. 577–95; and Jahn 1983, pp. 1–20.

4. The phrase is Morson and Emerson's. See Morson and Emerson 1990, p. 233.

5. Morson and Emerson are adamant that the distinction between dialogue and dialectics should be maintained. Holquist specifies Bakhtin's opposition to Hegelian dialectics (p. 73). But Robert Stam wants to close the gap. See Stam 1989, p. 188. The difference is symptomatic of the gap between what Stam calls 'liberal' and 'left' readings of Bakhtin. But what Stam sees as 'liberal' hermeneutics includes two kinds of thought. Whilst the term is clearly appropriate to Booth's or Lodge's accounts of Bakhtin, it will hardly do for Holquist and Morson and Emerson, whose subtler emphases – on 'emergence' and 'eventness' for example – are better termed postmodern.

7. Reservations about the masculinity of the Bakhtinian model can be found elsewhere. See for instance Bauer 1988, pp. 5–6.

8. On speech genres and the distinction between primary and secondary speech genres, see Bakhtin 1986, pp. 60–62.

9. See for instance Eagleton 1988, p. 115.

10. Gloss this in a rather cruder Marxist fashion, and we have Jameson's view: 'the normal form of the dialogical is essentially an *antagonistic* one, and ... the dialogue of class struggle is one in which two opposing discourses fight it out within the general unity of a shared code'. See Jameson 1983, p. 84.

11. Julia Kristeva's account of dialogism makes this very clear, though she intends no criticism. See Kristeva 1980, pp. 64–91, p. 68.

12. See for instance Bakhtin 1981, pp. 175–7, p. 205, pp. 224ff., p. 237. Holquist even suggests that dialogism itself 'is a form of architectonics, the general science of ordering parts into a whole' (Holquist 1990, p. 29).

13. See for instance Docherty 1990, Chapter Six, especially pp. 145–8, 169–70.

14. Quoted and trans. Leon S. Roudiez, 'Introduction', Kristeva 1984, p. 3.

15. Ibid., p. 2.

16. Barthes also refers to a 'fading' of voices. But his conception of the voices in the text is different to mine. See Barthes 1970, p. 49.

17. Fludernik advances this case much further in *Towards a 'Natural' Narratology* (London: Routledge, 1996).
18. See Derrida 1973, pp. 96–7 for a Derridean amplification of this argument.
19. See for instance Lawrence 1981, p. 125. Charles Peake sees the concluding section of the chapter as written in a style of 'slangs and jargons'. See Peake 1977, p. 253. J.S. Atherton refers to the style as 'a literary *equivalent* of drunkenness'. See Atherton 1974, pp. 313–40; p. 334, italics mine.

5

Narrative and the Event

AION AND CHRONOS

Deleuze conceives of time as having two aspects.[1] The first aspect is measurable and relational. It is time as an order of movements and of their units. The second aspect is measureless, incommensurable. It may be thought of as 'the ultimate existence of parts, of different sizes and shapes, which cannot be adapted, which do not develop at the same rhythm' (Deleuze 1973, p. 101). It is what Deleuze calls 'the fundamentally open whole as the immensity of the future and the past' (Deleuze 1986, p. 46). These two aspects of time can be equated with the two kinds of repetition in *Difference and Repetition*:

One is a static repetition, the other is dynamic. . . . One refers back to a single concept, which leaves only an external difference between the ordinary instances of a figure; the other is the repetition of an internal difference which it incorporates in each of its moments, and carries from one distinctive point to another. (Deleuze 1994, p. 20)

The aspects of time are exemplified in the difference between the 'pulsed time' of 'formal and functional' music, and the 'nonpulsed time' of a floating music which has only speeds or 'differences of dynamic' (Deleuze and Guattari 1988, p. 261). They are the two forms of time according to the Stoics, *chronos* and *aion*. *Chronos* measures events and is inseparable from matter. It is the temporal dimension of causation. *Aion* by contrast is the unlimited past and future of incorporeals. It is the dimension of surface effects. It is the time of pure becoming, the pure 'straight line traced by the aleatory point', the continuum of time out of which the present ceaselessly emerges (Deleuze 1990, p. 64). It is independent of matter. As Deleuze tirelessly insists, it is impersonal and pre-individual. It is the *non plus ultra* of time, its pure, empty form, peopled by ghostly effects that never fill it. It is time as produc-tion, as limitless capacity. It is the time of problems, intensities, Deleuze's 'haecceities' (Deleuze and Guattari 1988, p. 261), 'non-subjectified affects' and, most of all, of the event itself.[2]

The difference between *aion* and *chronos* may be crudely summarised as the difference between open and closed concep-tions of time. As such, for Deleuze, its significance is huge, and as much political as it is philosophical and aesthetic. For Deleuze, it is important to grasp the two contradictory views of time wholly and simultaneously. But Western thought in general and contem-porary culture in particular have been responsible for a powerful over-emphasis on and overvaluation of *chronos* as opposed to *aion*. In Heideggerian terms, this is an aspect of the triumph of the technological *Gestell* as confirmation, re-establishment or accom-plishment of metaphysics.[3] Deleuze himself asserts that it is in *aion* rather than *chronos* that our freedom and strength reside, 'in these singularities which are more ourselves than we are, more divine than the gods, as they animate concretely poem and aphorism, permanent revolution and partial action' (Deleuze 1990, p. 72). Today's task is 'to make pre-individual and non-personal singularities speak' (ibid. p. 73). If so, it is hardly a task to which established narratology has been adequate. Narratology has rather served to neutralise singularities as they 'animate' the narrative text. As a supposed science, narratology objectifies and hypostasises the text as measurable whole, inserts and insists upon a distance between text and addressee. It repeatedly closes the text off in an unreal isolation in which the latter belongs only to itself. On the plane of *aion* – in Cage, Boulez, Godard, Sarraute – there is communication through the 'envelope' of forms and subjects. Narratology, on the other hand, has striven to 'keep the different orders intact' (Deleuze and Guattari 1988, p. 272). In doing so, it has left unexamined the metaphysics of form, theme, motif, subject and character that Sarraute – for instance – wished to question (ibid. p. 267).

In particular, narratology has not risked even a speculative venture into differing ways of thinking time. It has remained indifferent to the kinds of question or speculative challenge implicit not only in Deleuzean thought, but in the various aspects of modern and postmodern writing and contemporary theory with which Deleuze has so much in common. The narratological conception of time is always of time as *chronos*. Mieke Bal's *Narratology* may serve as an example. Bal develops an orthodox distinction between what in her terms are fabula and story, 'the sequence of events and the *way in which* these events are presented' (Bal 1985, p. 5). For Bal, events belong only to the world of the fabula. They take place only within certain determinate boundaries. They are not discursive. They are represented or recounted. They are thinkable only as having occurred. In addition, they are describable only in relation to 'actors', by whom they are 'caused or experienced' (ibid. p. 6). Equally, since events involve either a 'doing to' or a 'being done to', agents and reagents are separable from the event and repeatable outside it. They are 'fixed' elements involved in events as 'processes' (ibid. p. 13).[4] Not surprisingly, for Bal, events in a fabula are always 'logically and chronologically related' (ibid. p. 6). The fabula as series is 'constructed according to certain rules' which – after Bremond – we call the '*logic of events*' (ibid. p. 7). It is here precisely that measurable time appears as a necessary constituent of the fabula. Time is inseparable from the logic of the fabula 'and must, consequently, be made describable' (ibid. p. 6). The describability of time on all levels of the narrative text is axiomatic: for Bal, for classic narratology as a whole. Without *chronos*, the very foundations of established narratology are at risk, and with them a psychology, a logic, a theory of the stable subject, and a metaphysics.

The narratologist's assumption of the describability of time also takes place within the common narratological search 'for the universal model for fabula'. The premise is that a homology or structural correspondence exists 'between the fabulas of real narratives and "real" fabulas, between what people do and what actors do in fabulas that have been invented'. Fabulas in general 'can be understood as constructed according to a given 'logic of events' which Bal defines as one experienced by the reader as 'natural and in accordance with the world' (ibid. p. 12). Describable time is intrinsic to this 'logic'. The narratologist thus naturalises measurable time. The structures of *chronos* are the world's. But since it is always measurable, time in narrative can always be segmented or taken apart. The narratological model is always '*structural*: it describes a structure – the relations between phenomena – rather than the phenomena themselves' (ibid. p. 32). It therefore works disjunctively, and invariably involves a geometry or spatialisation of time. In the first instance, there is the 'double linearity' of which Bal writes, the 'two lines' being that of the text or series of sentences, and that of the fabula, or series of events. These lines do not coincide. One of them must be conceived of as somehow 'behind' and asymmetrical with the other. That in itself produces a model of the text as having an initial density or extension in space. Secondly, there is the distinction between the temporal arrangement of the story and the chronology of the fabula. The distinction of course has different aspects: order, rhythm and frequency (ibid. pp. 49–79). But an account of narrative temporality will always be contaminated with spatial metaphor. 'Time units' are spatialised simply in being placed 'in relation to each other' (ibid. p. 58). The notion of *anachrony*, for example, in Genette, Bal and others is haunted by a kind of spatial thought.[5] Take Bal's account of the opening of *The Iliad*:

We indicate the five units presented with A, B, C, D, E in the order in which they are presented in the story. Chronologically, their positions are 4, 5, 3, 2, 1, so that the anachronies can be represented by the formula A4–B5–C3–D2–E1. (Bal 1985, p. 55)

The image is of two horizontal lines connected by transverse lines; or of a space opened up in Bal's use of the word 'covers' (A 'covers' 4, B 'covers' 5, and so on). The narrative text is presented as closed geometric system, as box. Time is neutralised, programmed, reduced to a set of co-ordinates, rid of any disquieting eventuality, of what Deleuze would call its nomadic distributions. The most troubling idea, for Bal, is a narrative time that cannot be spatialised, a time of pure, one-dimensional equivalence, the pure, abstract line that Deleuze opposes to segmentarity.[6] But the spatialisation of time in narratology is perhaps most evident in its preoccupation with the relationship between 'telling time' and 'told time', Müller's '*Erzählzeit*' and '*erzählte Zeit*'. From Percy Lubbock's *The Craft of Fiction* through Müller to Genette, Bal and beyond, narratology has repeatedly returned to this theme.[7] Yet it is inevitably space that enters into the theorist's model with the distinction itself. For, as Bal puts it herself, Müller's terms actually involve the juxtaposition of 'the amount of time covered by the fabula' with '*the amount of space* in the text each event requires: the number of pages, lines or words' (Bal 1985, p. 69, italics mine). Even before the geometric diagram is drawn and the geometric relation between the two 'times' is established, one of the 'times' is already space.

Bal herself objects to 'sterile line-counting', but only because it is likely to be undertaken 'without any relevance to the inter-pretation of the text in question' (ibid.). In other words, it fails to produce the right space, space replete with meaning. Bal's various geometric renditions of narrative time return insistently to ques-tions of meaning. Of Flaubert's reversal of the traditional narrative rhythm of summary and scene, for example, she writes that it 'is naturally very well suited to a fabula that reflects boredom, the emptiness of a person's existence' (ibid. p. 73). Time is segmented, and then organised in spatial terms so that it can be joined together again in a new whole, which is that of coherent sense. If *chronos* is space, space is depth, and its depth is that of the 'narrated universal' as regulated by the rules which control all 'human thought and action' (ibid. p. 19). Indeed, it is the uniform, homogenous, self-evident space of the universal which always acts as a first imperative. Bal clings to it even when geometrisation fails:

It is not always possible to reconstruct the chronological sequence. In many experimental modern novels, we find, for instance, that matters are intention-ally confused, the chronological relations expressly concealed. In such a case, obviously, we are powerless. But what is striking in these cases is that the chronological chaos we note is often still quite meaningful . . . The effect of [Marquez's *One Hundred Years of Solitude*] is to let people, generations, social contexts succeed each other in rapid turmoil in the course of a hundred years which *seem to contain a history of mankind* . . . (ibid. p. 52, italics mine)

If time cannot be given spatial form, then the space of universal meaning must simply be decreed to be there. The becoming of the text must be converted into being, by sheer arbitrary *fiat*, if necessary. Bal's narratology cannot even incidentally admit that narrative or narratives might be engaged in what Deleuze calls 'the production and confrontation of the singular points which are immanent to movement' (Deleuze 1990, p. 61). Narrative must always be understood as referring away to a pre-existent space, rather than as producing or opening up the new (the novel). Narratology turns aside from time as difference, from time as a multiplicity in which the elements ceaselessly vary and alter in relation to others; a time to be thought in terms of fission, for instance, or differences in speed.[8] Deleuze and Guattari suggest that, in certain of his works, Kleist was able to give time a new rhythm, 'an endless succession of catatonic episodes or fainting spells, and flashes and rushes' (Deleuze and Guattari 1988, p. 356). If this or something like it is conceivably the case, then narratology as it has been classically constituted has offered us no possible vocabulary for such 'rhythms'.

NARRATIVE AND *EREIGNIS*: SOME POSTMODERN CRITICS

But might this not be merely a question of the extent to which narratology actually corresponds to something in narrative itself? On this point, at least, narratology might seem to ally itself with postmodern aesthetics. For there is a certain scepticism current in postmodern aesthetics with regard to the adequacy of narrative to the event. The scepticism can be traced at least as far back as Heidegger and his influential valorisation of lyric at the expense of epic.[9] In *Being and Time*, Heidegger privileges poetic discourse as a possible mode of the self-expression of *Dasein*:

In 'poetical' discourse, the communication of the existential possibilities of one's state-of-mind can become an aim in itself, and this amounts to a disclosing of existence. (Heidegger 1990, p. 205)

Poetics and ontology thus participate in a reciprocal disclosure.[10] For the Heidegger of 'The Origin of the Work of Art', the nature of art is 'the truth of beings setting itself to work', not of course in an imitation or depiction of reality, but in the breaching of a new, open place, the 'letting happen' of the truth as event, as something that cannot be 'proved or derived from what went before' (Heidegger 1971, pp. 36, 72, 75). 'Telling a story', on the other hand, is not an appropriate means to understanding 'the problem of Being' at all:

The Being of entities 'is' not itself an entity. If we are to understand the problem of Being, our first philosophical step consists . . . in not 'telling a story' – that is to say, in not defining entities as entities by tracing them back in their origin to some other entities, as if being had the character of some possible entity. (Heidegger 1990, p. 26)

Being must be exhibited in a way of its own that is necessarily different from those of narrative. For narrative discovers entities. It also more or less implicitly claims to be 'derived from what went before'. Poetry can draw us away from the 'tranquillised supposition' of inauthentic Being 'that it possesses everything, or that everything is within its reach' (ibid. p. 223). Narrative by contrast is likely to confirm us in that supposition. The 'first philosophical step' therefore consists in refusing to establish or confirm the homogenising connections of narrative, which can serve only to neutralise the event of Being, Being as *Ereignis*.

Levinas develops a comparable point of view in his essay 'Reality and its Shadow'. He privileges the concept over the image, however, thought over art. Art trades precisely in a caricature of being. It substitutes the image for being, and it does so not less in the difficult or modern or 'pure' than in the classical work of art. For in all art, the represented object is converted into a non-object 'by the simple fact of becoming an image' (Levinas 1989, p. 134). For Levinas, this is particularly true with regard to time. Every artwork is a stoppage of time, as 'eternally Laocoon will be caught in the grip of serpents; the Mona Lisa will smile eternally' (ibid. p. 138). Art denies the mobility and openness of the present, the potential it holds for change and creativity:

A statue realizes the paradox of an instant which endures without a future. Its duration is not really an instant. It does not give itself out here as an infinitesimal element of duration, a flash . . . The imminence of the future lasts before an instant stripped of the essential characteristic of the present, its evanescence. It will never have completed its task as a present, as though reality withdrew from its own reality and left it powerless. (ibid.)

This, art's petrification of the instant in the heart of duration – Niobe's punishment or duration in 'the meanwhile' – has 'something inhuman and monstrous about it'. Thus 'art, essentially disengaged, constitutes, in a world of initiative and responsibility, a dimension of evasion . . . The world to be built is replaced by the essential completion of its shadow' (ibid. pp. 140–2). For Levinas, narrative and the novel constitute a special case of this second-order function, particularly with regard to time. Narrative of its nature encloses beings in fate, not in that it necessarily represents them as crushed by the latter, but because they enter their fate simply in being represented. Narrative neutralises the event, and in that neutralisation lies ethical failure:

That the characters in a book are committed to the infinite repetition of the same acts and the same thoughts is not simply due to the contingent fact of the narrative, which is exterior to those characters. They can be narrated because their being *resembles* itself, doubles itself and immobilizes. Such a fixity is wholly different from that of concepts, which initiates life, offers reality to our powers, to truth, opens a dialectic. By its reflection in a narrative, being has a non-dialectical fixity, stops dialectics and time. (ibid. p. 139)

Narrative turns time into images and 'events' into 'situations' (ibid.). It does not and cannot have 'the quality of the living instant which is open to the salvation of becoming, in which it can end and be surpassed' (ibid. p. 141). The time of narrative does not 'shatter the fixity of images' in any sort of adequation to or luminous appearance as *Ereignis*. It can only reaffirm, indeed apotheosise that very 'fixity' itself (ibid. p. 139).

It is Lyotard above all, however, who has been responsible for articulating the post-Heideggerian critique of narrative as specifically a postmodern critique. Indeed, Lyotard's now famous scepticism with regard to the 'grand narratives' is itself a function of a certain postmodern scepticism about narrative in general.[11] *Discours, Figure* establishes a familiar, Heideggerian opposition in Lyotard's work between rationalisations of space and time and '*la donation première dans son obliquité, dans son ubiquité*' (Lyotard

1985, p. 21). In *Discours, Figure*, the event has an initial alterity. It is an involuntary, unwilled, unattended emergence of the other. This other is not necessarily to be conceived of as occupying a relation of externality. The event can open up in the space of desire. It is thus that, in Lyotard's terms, the irruption of the figural into the discursive is an event in the work of art. In poetry, for example, the figural manifests itself within the discursive as a force that bends language according to 'the vector of desire' (ibid. p. 58). Poetry also imposes discontinuity as a rule of intelligibility (ibid. p. 281). Through rhythm, rhyme and other technical features, through metaphor, too, with its 'enigmatic thickening' of discourse (ibid. p. 288), poetry treats discursive space as plastic space. The sensible aspect of language comes into play in determining meaning, as most obviously in rhyme. As event and desire, the figural, here, constantly disturbs the order of discourse, of language itself. Narrative, on the other hand, is constructed on a founding difference: a dissymmetry between beginning and end, initial and final situations. 'Telling a story' is itself an introduction and elaboration of that dissymmetry, and an ordering of it in terms of succession. Narrative as diachrony does not disturb or transgress the linguistic order, but rather confirms it in its irreversibility.[12] So, too, in its orientation towards an end, its gradual alignment of dissymmetrical features, its final ordering, it pacifies difference, puts it in place within a system, transforms it into opposition (ibid. p. 166). Thus narrative neutralises the event in ceaselessly recuperating the other into the same. The unrepresentable, indiscernible, inarticulable, fleeting life of the body, for instance – desire, inchoate emotion – leaves no trace. Poetry, says Lyotard, is like a world: opaque, obscure, difficult to penetrate (ibid. p. 286). Narrative by contrast is a genre for '*les bons esprits du rangement*' (ibid. p. 135), producing clarity and distinctness, indifferent to figure and event.

So too in *Économie Libidinale*, narrative is described as an art of '*utilités*' rather than '*intensités*'. Rothko's paintings constitute an art of the event. The mobile surface of a Rothko painting is what matters, its texture of subtle shifts, little disparities in colour which are not to be reduced to decidable disjunctions. Emotion sweeps the polymorphous surface (Lyotard 1974, pp. 291–2). The syntheses and disjunctions of narrative discourse, on the other hand, are always connected to the referential function, which narrative privileges over all others (ibid. pp. 289–90). Events are therefore lost in becoming mere attributes within the referential domain as the latter is unified and totalised by narrative. *Économie Libidinale* associates diachrony with accumulation, '*l'histoire capitalisante*' (ibid. p.25). This in turn links narrative to the idea of productive imagination as stockpiling, in which the products are always transformed into monuments of a past activity or means of determining an activity to come. Narrative may be conceived of in terms of an 'upstream' and 'downstream' of production opened up by cumulative, diachronic time.[13] Thus, where the mobile surface of a Rothko painting liberates the event, narrative smothers it in referring it elsewhere, whether 'behind' (into the 'depths' of the referential domain), or backwards and forwards along the diachronic chain.

In *The Differend*, Lyotard rather presents narrative as neutralising the heterogeneity of phrase regimens and genres of discourse as they are in play within the social and commentary on the social. Narrative imposes an end on a differend or differends. That ending 'retroactively organises the recounted events' and thus 'makes sense' (Lyotard 1988a, p. 151). Narrative gives direction to events, places them within a coherent or complete system, decrees a term for them. Diachrony, again, is seen as insisting on the same within the other. 'The recurrence of the before/after' domesticates 'the unleashing of the now' (ibid. p. 152). In not calling its own diachronic structure into question, then, narrative 'swallows up' the event, drives it back 'to the border' (ibid.). As concatenation, order and regime, narrative strips both entities and phrases of their contingency. In denying heterogeneity and the differend, in pacifying the uncertainty and anxiety of linkage, narrative quells 'the marvel of the encounter with the other' and 'the threat of *Ereignis*' (ibid. p. 143). In narrative, gaps do not open up between phrases (or narrative segments). There is none of the surprise of the unforeseeable connection. The 'constitutive discontinuity' of time is thus held at bay (ibid. p. 66). Narrative stands with 'the monotheistic and monopolitical principle' and its 'neutralisation of reality' (ibid. p. 46). Indeed, traditional narrative, at least – certainly when it is the manner in which 'the *Volk* shuts itself up in the *Heim*' – would seem to be close to Lyotard's evil: 'the incessant interdiction of possible phrases, the defiance of the occurrence, the contempt for Being' (ibid. p. 140).

Narrative, then, does not promote the *passibilité* that is open and receptive to the event. Its teleological, progressive formulations would seem intimately to ally it with a modernity committed to a mastery which is the reverse of *passibilité*.[14] Poetry generates occurrences before it knows the rules of generativity (Lyotard 1991, p. 72). It escapes the increasing hegemony of contemporary rationality, the ever-expanding order of knowledge, clarity and appropriation, of techno-scientific predeterminations. It reserves 'the coming of the future in its unexpectedness' (ibid. p. 77). Narrative by contrast raises the threat of the pronouncement of the last word, 'of nothing further happening' (ibid. p. 91). Poetry allies itself with the sublime and the presentation of the unpresentable against that threat. Narrative conspires with 'matter-of-fact positivism' and 'calculated realism' to reinforce it (ibid. p. 105). Narrative thus makes its own contribution to the neutralisation of the present as 'opening onto an uncertain and contingent "afterwards"', and therefore also to a neutralisation of 'the contingency and freedom proper to the human project' (ibid. p. 65, 69). Hence there is a power and an urgency to the postmodern critique of narrative. Within the structure of the *Gestell*, the narrative pacification of difference has a particular political and ethical complexion. If a postmodern (Deleuzean) politics might seize on the indeterminability of the event, and a postmodern (Levinasian) ethics might give priority to immediate responsiveness and constant responsibility, narrative would seem only to provide models running counter to both.

CASES FOR THE DEFENCE: BADIOU, RORTY, KUNDERA

But the Heideggerian valuation of lyric as opposed to epic is surely open to question. The structure of that opposition can be unsettled or blurred, as in Badiou's work. Badiou's larger case is that, since the emergence of set theory, mathematics has become the science of being. It is to Cantor, Gödel and Cohen that we must turn for ontology, rather than – as in Heidegger – Hölderlin, Trakl or Celan. With set theory, Cantor opposed himself to a tradition running from Aristotle through the Scholastics to Descartes and

Spinoza which asserted that no concept of infinite number could be accepted in mathematics. That tradition understood the concerns of mathematics as entirely distinct from the infinite; above all, from God as the absolute Infinite. The Scholastics – and, indeed, for Badiou, Aristotle before them – assumed that there were only finite numbers and precluded any consideration of infinite numbers. The realms of the finite and the infinite were to be kept absolutely apart. For the Scholastics and after them, if number were not confined to the finite, then the Absolute, belonging uniquely to God, might no longer be conceived of as the sole realm of the infinite. But Cantor suggested that there was 'nothing inherently implausible about the existence of the actually infinite *in concreto*' (Dauben 1990, p. 230). He secularised the infinite, conceiving of it as working upon and within the finite. Cantor 'banalises' the infinite in making every situation an infinite one, including our own (Badiou 1992, p. 165). In set theory, the single is always multiple:

The basic idea behind set theoretic analyses of the notion of positive whole numbers is that it is to sets, or collections of things, that numbers are assigned. (Tiles 1989, p. 96)

It is precisely as such that, for Badiou, set theory appears to constitute an ontology. For mathematics now becomes a science of pure multiplicity. As such, it says what is sayable about being (Badiou 1989a, p. 14). And not only that: if, in set theory, the single is always multiple, any multiple is a multiple of multiples. The multiplicity it articulates in a discernible concept is thus itself indiscernible (Badiou 1989b, p. 60). But that means that mathematics has no objects and presents nothing (Badiou 1989a, p. 13). For post-Cantorian mathematics, there is no 'One', in the sense that philosophy has always thought the 'One'. One is just a number. There is only what Badiou calls the 'counts-for-one', as a kind of presentational fiction, something that does not exist in itself, but is always the effect of a structure (ibid. pp. 31, 104). Mathematics registers the radically 'subtractive' (*soustractive*) dimension of being as withdrawn, not just from representation, but from any presentation at all. Thus post-Cantorian mathematics is as close as we can come to the ontological situation. For this situation is the presentation of presentation, the law of presentation now being discovered as limitless dissemination (ibid. p. 43).

Frege, of course, was one of Cantor's fiercest critics, asserting that the multiple can always be encapsulated in a well-made language, that the master of language can always be master of the multiple. But Badiou argues that post-Cantorian theory has refuted Frege. For it has shown that multiplicities can be paradoxical or inconsistent. The axiomatics of set theory knows how to exclude such multiplicities. But natural language is incapable of separating consistency from inconsistency, being from non-being, since it cannot separate itself from the presumption of the 'One'. Natural language can therefore only ever deal in pseudo-presentations. Beyond set theory and mathematical ontology, however, there is always paradox, inconsistency, void and structuration together, being and non-being unthinkable apart. This is the site of chance and the event, which cannot be 'decided on' by knowledge. It supplements the 'multiple situation' (Badiou 1989b, p. 87), and its truth is always indiscernible in advance. It is the site, too, that is proper to philosophy, poetry and politics. Since a concern with 'being as being' can be left to mathematics, philosophy and poetry may focus on what being comprises that is not itself. Poetry maintains *'que l'être inconsiste'* (ibid. p. 52). Thus Badiou seeks to resist Heidegger in 'depoetising' truth and, at the same time, paradoxically, to liberate the poem as the singular operation of truth. For the poem, in Badiou's terms, is the nomination of an event, a supplement or incalculable hazard. That is precisely what poetry becomes in Mallarmé, for instance, where language serves as the trace of an event, the mark of a disappearance which must nonetheless be named. Where Mallarmé is the poet of the event, Rimbaud, on the other hand, is the poet of its undecidability, constantly bearing witness to two universes, the 'ecstatic' and the 'prosaic', and insisting on the undecidability of their relation.

So instead of conceiving of poetry as sustaining or granting a privileged access to being, Badiou sees its primary concern as the event. Unlike Heidegger, too, Badiou does not exclude certain modes of narrative from his conception of the poetic. Thus he sees Beckett, in particular, as a prose writer who has been increasingly concerned with the occurrences of the narrating subject, its supplementation in and by events, its encounters with the instant-aneous surprise of the Other. In *Company*, *Worstward Ho*, *Ill Seen Ill Said*, Beckett's work opens itself up to chance. It surrenders to the breach opened by chance in the 'whole' of being and the self. This breach is the event, and the later Beckett, like Mallarmé, is much concerned with the question – or the problem – of its nomination. Thus Badiou's case against Heidegger actually allows us to think narrative and the event in a different relationship. For Badiou, singularity can be protected within narrative, rather than requiring protection from it. Equally, for Rorty, the protection of singularity is precisely what is endemic to what he sees as the non-philosophical or anti-theoretical cast of narrative. Rorty takes issue with the Heideggerian relegation of narrative to second-rate status. He chooses instead to affirm 'the novelist's taste for narrative, detail, diversity and accident' (Rorty 1991a, p. 73). Rorty thinks that the novel runs counter to the abstraction, essentialism and grandiosity represented in and valued by Hei-degger himself. It does so precisely in its attention and attachment to particularity. It has no fixed or essential form itself, and refuses to believe in the possibility of any final description or to privilege a single vocabulary or point of view over others. It also unweaves the totalising conceptions beloved of theorists, relativises and mocks them through laughter. Narrative in Rorty's book is there-fore an anti-metaphysical genre, a relativistic, ambiguous, toler-ant, curious form of discourse. In the crowded, diverse world of the novel, no single being or Supreme Judge stands for or holds the truth. The novel becomes what Kundera calls 'the imaginary paradise of individuals' (Kundera 1988, p. 159) and Rorty refers to as 'the democratic utopia' (Rorty 1991a, p. 75). Rorty presents the novel as in essence a pluralistic, liberal democratic, equalising form in which everyone can have a say and be heard. This is evident above all in the world of Dickens, with its 'unsubsumable, uncategorizable', idiosyncratic characters and its implicit claim for the individual's right to respect, recognition and under-standing (ibid. p. 78).

Yet to assert that narrative promotes the cause of individuality is not of course to answer the objection that it neutralises singularity. As Bennington has said, the two are not to be conflated (Bennington 1988, p. 9). It is singularity and not individuality that is the radical other of totality. Rorty's argument for the novel as anti-metaphysical genre is actually founded on an unexamined adherence to a familiar metaphysics (of presence, the subject, the unified self and so on). In refusing allegiance to the alleged totalisations of one kind of philosophy, Rorty merely relapses into a kind of thinking that is underpinned by the totalisations of a more established kind. Politically, this amounts to a 'realistic' dismissal of what he refers to as the 'dangerous' philosophers who think ahead to 'radical difference from the past, a dazzlingly unimaginable future' (Rorty 1991b, p. 81), as opposed to the spirit of the 'pluralistic bourgeois democracies' (ibid.). Converted into an aesthetics, such a position involves a refusal to engage with questions of narrative discourse. Rorty never asks whether the absence of the Supreme Judge from a narrated world may not also be amply compensated for in certain aspects of the narration, not least in Dickens. He leaves aside the awkward question of how far representation itself might be seen as the privileging of a certain narrative mode of the novel. He sees Dickens's morality as involving the lesson that we need to notice details rather than to have our 'entire cognitive apparatus restruc-tured' (ibid. p. 80). But the two issues are hardly separable, as the novel itself has shown us again and again. Above all, Rorty sees the novel as saying that there is no escape from time (ibid. p. 77), without inquiring as to whether it might not be a particular conception of 'time' that is in question, a conception whose imprisoning power narrative might seem only to reinforce. In the end, Rorty's case for the novel is practically indistinguishable from the classic liberal defences of thirty or forty years ago, like W.J. Harvey's.[15]

Most remarkably of all, in the name of diversity, tolerance and 'letting be', Rorty not only appropriates but distorts Kundera's distinctively Central European thought in the service of a more commonplace, Western view. Kundera's perspective on the novel is actually much more interesting than Rorty suggests. Like Hrabal's, for example, it is far more Heideggerian than Rorty seems to realise. Kundera takes the novel to be a form of thought and writing that struggles to protect us from 'the forgetting of being' (Kundera 1988, pp. 3, 17). The novel does not produce knowledge, or reproduce it. It discovers and explores the unknown. Any novel that does not – any novel that deals or claims to deal in the already known – must be immoral (ibid. p. 6). A novel must break new ground, must itself be an event. Kafka, for example, does not serve a truth or reality known from the outset, but a truth '*to be discovered* (which is *dazzlement*)'. This is 'the *radical autonomy* of the novel' (ibid. p. 117). So the novel accomplishes a Heideggerian project that Heidegger himself believed to fall within the province of lyric and denied to narrative. For Kundera, each new novel should be understood as a clearing, in the Heideggerian sense. He sees his own novels as engaged in a contemplation of Being as enigma, of Heidegger's *in-der-Welt-sein*. Thus when Kundera says that the novelist's territory is 'the relativity and ambiguity of things human', he means something quite different to what Rorty thinks he means (ibid. p. 13). His interest is in the instability of 'existential categories' (ibid. p. 12) as it is demonstrated, for instance, by Kafka, Broch and Musil. Kundera is particularly responsive to novels that deal in that instability: to the exposition, for example, in Hasek's *The Good Soldier Schweik*, of a force stripped of all rationale, force as event, Heidegger's 'will to will' (Kundera 1988, p. 10); to Kafka's creation of an 'unexpected opening' in the novel, which actualised a possibility that history itself had yet to actualise (ibid. pp. 114–16); to Sterne's poetry of 'the incalculable', 'the other side of causality', the world '*sine ratione*' (ibid. p. 162). Kundera even pitches the novel against the *Gestell* where Rorty seems inclined to establish or reinforce a collusion. For Kundera, the novel resists the Cartesian, post-Cartesian and techno-scientific faith in 'mastery' (ibid. p. 41). It offers truth and reality as event in 'the suddenly kindled light of the never-before said' (ibid. p. 123), rather than the constant repetition of the backward gaze to the pre-existent which unites metaphysics and techno-science with a more traditional, mimetic theory of narrative and the novel.

Kundera's account of the novel would seem to point towards a (perhaps more Foucauldian) history of 'the form' than those we have so far had, a history of the novel as a history of events which would radically disconnect the different instances, rather than seeking to homogenise them, registering the radical singularity of each new form, the history of the novel as a history of 'unexpected openings' on to the new. On the other hand, Kundera does not offer us much ground for a rebuttal of the postmodern critique of narrative in itself as a form or mode of cognition. There is little in Kundera that works against the postmodern allegation that there is an essential closure to narrative. This closure would make of narrative a form within which there can be no writing of the event. For the postmodern critique would see narrative as pushing singularity back towards an originating instance which narrative merely duplicates; as tranquillising difference within diachronic order and its repetitions; as therefore hypostasising or freezing Being into its caricature, occulting the ontico-ontological difference, promoting what Heidegger calls 'the oblivion of the distinction between Being and beings' (Heidegger 1975, p. 50). At the same time, however, Lyotard himself helpfully blurs the Heideggerian distinction between lyric and epic in suggesting that, strictly speaking, there can be no 'writing the event', no encounter with *Ereignis* by means of a text (Lyotard 1974, p. 28). In any text, the event is always registered or reported. There is always a difference and a distance in the writing. Deleuze goes further, arguing that the event is never graspable, that it is only ever available to us as 'has happened' or 'is about to happen', as tale, novella, representation, sign (Deleuze 1990, p. 63). We must therefore think the event in writing as always having an ambiguous aspect, yielding to, enfolded, mediated or muffled by the process of registration. So too with the irruption of the figural into the discursive. Discourse produces, not the event, but its simulacrum. Thus there can thus be no absolute distinction between lyric and narrative. The modes of the simulacrum will be diverse, and will be narrative as well as lyric. In thinking about discourse, we can only use the term 'event' in a 'deconstructed sense', to 'designate something other which resembles it' (Derrida 1991, p. 24).

NARRATIVE BY RENAULT AND TARKOVSKY

So how and in what contexts might it be possible to think of narrative in terms of the event? It is important first of all to distinguish between forms of narrative in which the event is more or less likely to 'appear' and the kinds of narrative temporality evident in those forms. One particular essay of Lyotard's is particularly relevant, here: the 'Petite Économie Libidinale d'un Dispositif Narratif: La Régie Renault Raconte le Meurtre de Pierre Overney', in Des Dispositifs Pulsionnels (Lyotard 1980, pp. 171–213). The essay is substantially concerned with narrative and narratology (especially certain features of Genette's narratology). It also produces a positive valuation of narrative and narrativity from within a position (Lyotard's) that otherwise tends towards scepticism. The 'Overney' essay establishes a contrast that is particularly appropriate to the question of narrative and the event. On the one hand there is the story in which the Renault company tells of the death of the militant Overney outside their factory. This is a narrative that produces – or reproduces – a given social space and, within it, a given social subject. The event is contained and thus lost inside the space this narrative constructs. Overney's death becomes a moment in a process, is subsumed by and understood in terms of *chronos*. This narrative canalises and regulates movement, including movement of and in time. The result is that the event is related to what precedes it and what follows it, or the consequences derived from it. It is put into circulation as part of a narrative economy, made exchangeable with other elements and thus negated. Hence, says Lyotard, a disaffected tone in the narrative which is often the tone of 'classic narrative' itself. The narratee is offered only 'le corps du capital dit productif' where, on principle, intensities are rendered in terms of exchange value. Expressivity shrinks to indifference, since 'la vraie loi est l'équivalence et la vraie valeur l'échange' (ibid. p. 209). Events become currency within the system. This is the normative form of narrative in contemporary, public discourse. The Overney story is underpinned by a naive phenomenology according to which the facts seem to tell themselves. The effect produced is one of objectivity. A banal consecutiveness easily associates time with causality and finality, and the regular, repetitive, economic alternation of 'summary' and 'scene', in Genette's sense, establishes a pattern of expenditure and return on expenditure (ibid. pp. 190–1).[16] There is complete avoidance of 'décalages énormes' – between narrating and narrated time, for example – of the sort whose unsettling power might turn reading into a perilous affair.

On the other hand, Lyotard also discusses narrative as '*errance, ou, pour parler comme Freud, déplaçabilité*' (ibid. p. 174). In works by Rabelais, Sterne, Gogol, Joyce, Proust, Mann and some science fiction writers, narrative produces '*au lieu du corps social-historique . . . une entité monoface à régions hétérogènes parcourues d'intensités aléatoires*' (ibid. p. 175). The discourse in such narratives dismantles forms and formations, including those the reader brings to the text. Here, unlike the Renault narrative, intensities are not attached to an order supposedly underlying them and exerting a kind of dominance over narrative and reader alike. Rather, they are delivered to us '*dans leur singularité d'événements non unifiables*' (ibid.). There is thus no 'dominant instance' to which effects, events, intensities in such narratives can be referred back. Equally, such narratives destroy the Genettian assumption of a common measure or point of reference for the time of the *histoire* and the time of the *récit*, narrating time and narrated time. Proust's *Recherche*, *Tristram Shandy*, *Jacques le Fataliste* all dismantle any such measure, rejoicing instead in multiplying '*des instances temporelles incompossibles*' (Lyotard 1980, pp. 175–6). They do not properly have a temporal 'structure'. In fact, they disallow or refute Bal's kind of narratological spatialisation of time in the interests of the mobile surface. They cannot properly be analysed in terms of the temporal vectors of *chronos*.

The important narrative distinctions as promoted in Lyotard's essay are therefore not between *histoire* and *récit* but between '*intensités événementielles*' and '*réglage unitaire*', and between the degrees of control exerted over the first by the second. Genettian and post-Genettian narratology are quite unable to establish such a distinction. They simply privilege '*réglage unitaire*'. Where Lyotard posits geometric order as a neutralisation of the event in which different narrative texts can more or less acquiesce, classical narratology conceives of geometric order simply as the natural order of narrative. Genette would have no descriptive vocabulary for Philip K. Dick's *Ubik*, for example, where the narrative question is no longer one merely of disruptions of the order of temporal segments, but of the way in which a 'supposed subject' is both carried diegetically through those segments, and constantly disappears within them. Here, says

Lyotard, we must start to think in terms of narrative dieresis and heteroplasty.

So too in Tarkovsky's *Mirror*. Of course, it is possible to reduce *Mirror* to the appearance at least of '*réglage unitaire*', however reductive the latter may look. We can make a coherence out of the film, in particular, perhaps, by producing a 'common measure' for its various and complex times. But this is to represent *Mirror* according to some kind of fantasmal semblance or remnant of *chronos*. If Tarkovsky's film maintains such a 'semblance', it does so only insistently to disrupt it and displace its elements. The film works by constant shifts in time, oscillations between 'presents' and 'pasts', unpredictable variations in speed. There are the abrupt arrests in forward movement, frequent shifts into slow motion, small and inobtrusive (as in the sequence in the printing works) as well as large and dramatic (the extraordinary slowdown in the sequence after the grenade is thrown). Differences in speed may also be disparities between the meaning time has for the figures in the film, and time as the camera constructs it, as when the fire is announced, near the beginning of the film, and the camera then slowly withdraws from the room in which the children have been sitting. Similarly, the past spoken of at any moment by the narrator is not necessarily the past that is appearing on the screen. The temporality of certain specific, narrative relations is thus deliberately left indeterminate, as at the end of the film, where we are uncertain as to whether the two sequences cut together are synchronous or not. These are only a few examples of the film's multiplication of '*instances temporelles incompossibles*'.[17] The temporalisation involved resembles but does not necessarily coincide with the temporality alluded to in the Arseny Tarkovsky poem that is read during the 'Sivash lagoon' sequence ('I'll conjure up which century I like/And enter it and build a home in it . . . what is to come is happening right now'). This is the time 'walked through . . . as through the Ural mountains', rather than the *chronos* 'measured . . . as though surveying land'. The latter is the time played off against the multiplication of temporal instances. It is the time of 'objective', social-historical narrative as alluded to in the sequence that runs from the liberation of Prague in 1945 to the Damansky island affair in 1969;

the time of the printing works in Stalin's Russia ('It's too bad everything's in a rush, nobody has any time'). The film refuses to accept such a 'time'. It does so partly by depriving the viewer of a dominant temporal instance.[18]

But it also both sustains and dissolves the 'supposed subject' of the narrative as Lyotard says *Ubik* does. It thus destabilises the principle of *chronos* as the latter is interdependent with a principle of identity.[19] This is achieved in various ways. The film is traversed by a recurrent narrative aporia. It tells us that it has 'a narrator' (as specified in the credits). Yet the 'narrator's' voice is frequently indeterminate. The confusions of the young Alexei with Ignat sometimes lure us into hearing the voice as the latter's. But equally, the voice can (seemingly) be the director's, or Arseny Tarkovsky's. The film may appear to provide us with a single, homogenous 'focaliser'. But there are also unexpected variations in focalisation or 'blendings' of focaliser. We are given the 'point of view' of the incidental Klanka in the fire sequence, of the veteran of the Spanish Civil War, of the cadet (Asafyev) who throws the hand grenade. The film, then, both establishes and disperses the kind of uniformity of narrative voice and focalisation that underwrites identities within narrative. As a whole, *Mirror* is attributed to what Deleuze would call a 'quasi-cause' (Deleuze 1990, p. 125). Yet it also resists being consistently traced back to the latter as source and origin. This corresponds to the frequent blurrings of actual identity in the film, particularly of Alexei and Ignat, and Natalya and Marya. The shadow of a '*réglage unitaire*' – of identity, too, as '*réglage unitaire*' – is there, in *Mirror*, but only as a surface traversed by intensities '*dans leur singularité d'événements non unifiables*'. From the wind in the grass to the rolling, tumbling lamp to the mark that Ignat watches evaporate from the table, the film obsessively returns to the empty significance of mobilities, conjunctions of forces, confusions between entities, events as encounters as – according to Deleuze – they are in Cézanne. The narrative strategies and narrative pace adopted in *Mirror* give more weight to such mobilities than they do to identities. In Arseny Tarkovsky's words as given in the film, '*at every meeting*, every single moment [is] celebrated like an Epiphany' (italics mine).

NARRATING THE EVENT

But what of the modes of eventuality themselves, in narrative? What modes of narrative simulation of the event are possible? Deleuze points us towards a threefold distinction: between 'representing', narrating and writing the event.[20] Strictly speaking, of course, there can be no representation of the event. The event is an 'extra-être' (Buydens 1990, p. 13). Yet, according to Deleuze, the event can be registered through tale and image, and it is in fact to narrative that he sometimes turns when he wishes to find simulacra of the event.[21] Take for example his account of the battle scenes in the work of Tolstoy, Stendhal and Stephen Crane. Here precisely we encounter the event in its neutrality and impassibility, says Deleuze, its indifference to determinations (of inside and outside, individual and collective, particular and general). Battle as narrated by Crane is larger than individuals. It exceeds victor and vanquished alike. It stands, 'bodiless and impassive, indifferent to the actions and passions that constitute it' (Lecercle 1985, p. 98). Battle is not a single entity, as the protagonist in *The Red Badge of Courage* realises when he finally understands that the whole of the battle is not – as he has assumed – 'directly under his nose' (Crane 1992, p. 33). Part of the battle as event is virtual and can therefore neither be expressed or determined. A battle, thus, is everywhere and yet specifiable nowhere, '[n]ever present but always yet to come and already passed' (Deleuze 1990, p. 100). Like *The Red Badge of Courage* itself, battle is permeated by 'unformed and unstable matters', by 'flows in all directions, by free intensities or nomadic singularities' (Deleuze and Guattari 1988, p. 40). Crane calls this 'the battle-blur' (Crane 1992, p. 58). Battle is an open movement in which there is no privileged position from which the whole can be viewed. The new, the singular and the remarkable are always possible, as the young protagonist in *The Red Badge of Courage* repeatedly discovers with 'a flash of astonishment' (ibid. p. 33). Battle does not belong to the order of *chronos*, as Crane's soldiers expect it to, as a 'drama' they are 'about to witness' (ibid. p. 11). Its time is that of 'strange, squalling upheavals' (ibid. p. 118). It is therefore graspable only by the will of anonymity or indifference, as in the case of Crane's 'youth':

One gray dawn . . . he was kicked in the leg by the tall soldier, and then, before he was entirely awake, he found himself running down a wood road in the midst of men who were panting from the first effects of speed. (ibid. p. 19)

The youth must follow in the wake of events, and constitute and reconstitute himself in their wake, too. Something happens before he construes it as happening to him. He does not come first. It is the 'haecceity' that moves to the fore, individuation '*par composition d'hétérogènes*' emerging in the encounter (a word that frequently appears in Crane's novel); individuation, or, rather, a singularity that is the result of a connection between elements or a relation to non-subjectified affects which come from outside, like the 'subtle suggestion' Crane's young man 'receives' to touch the corpse at the end of Chapter 7. Much of the strangeness of Crane's novel has to do with the extent to which the protagonist, other figures and the narrative itself are considered from the viewpoint of the affections that befall them. Thus for example when 'a certain tall soldier' abruptly 'develops virtues' and goes off resolutely 'to wash a shirt' (ibid. p. 1). Crane's narrative does not follow the customary trajectory from essences to properties, but a less common one from the problematic to the accidental or eventual:

The tall one, red-faced, swallowed another sandwich as if taking poison in despair.
But gradually, as he chewed, his face became again quiet and contented. He could not rage in fierce argument in the presence of such sandwiches. (ibid. p. 23)

Human figures are the prey of affects, as '[a] sort of gust of battle itself can come 'sweeping toward' the 'part of the line' where the youth and his regiment lie, as the battlefield has its 'regions' with their different times or speeds (ibid. p. 84). This is what is involved in Crane's attempt to render what he himself refers to as 'the forceful causes of various superficial qualities' (ibid. p. 96).

Certain narrative texts, then, can be read in terms of representation of the event. They are not to be wholly defined in such terms. Thus a more protracted analysis of *The Red Badge of Courage* would attempt to describe the relation between its 'narrative of events' and its other narratives. Much of the novel for instance, is written in terms of 'masses', 'shadows', waves, heaving tangles, indistinct shapes, 'splashes' of colour and 'blurred and agitated forms' (ibid. p. 26). This impressionism might be set against the youth's more composed 'pictures of glory' (ibid. p. 59), against the pictorial narrative he imagines providing for or encouraging in others (ibid. p. 79). For Deleuze, simulacra of the event are also evident in Proust. *Proust and Signs* is partly about the Proustian modes of representation of the event. One feature of Proustian narrative, for example, is the representation of character as event or multiplicity. Albertine 'is the same and different, in relation to the hero's other loves, but also in relation to herself. There are so many Albertines that we should give a distinct name to each' (Deleuze 1973, p. 66).[22]

But it is not simply a question of Proust's characters having numerous different selves. Proust sees people as '[f]ugitive beings' individuated 'not by subjectivity but by haecceity' (Deleuze and Guattari 1988, p. 268). Furthermore, character in Proust always has a virtual as well as an actual dimension. This emerges particularly forcefully with Charlus and, above all, the 'incredible and inspired aging' to which Proust subjects him. For Proust understands Charlus's aging as 'only the redistribution of his many souls' (Deleuze 1973, p. 18). Proust and Marcel see in Charlus a kind of perpetual exfoliation of self. Even more strikingly, that exfoliation is presented as a kind of 'singularising' out of multiplicity, a movement out along a certain line or 'series' at the expense of different ones. Personality becomes event, as the 'many young girls' that 'lodge within Charlus' may or may not appear, may appear in a kind of 'inward unity' with Charlus the man, and so on (ibid. p. 120).[23] The really important point is that

[t]he least we can say is that Charlus is complicated. But the word must be taken in its full etymological sense. Charlus' genius is to retain all the souls which compose him in the 'complicated' state: this is how it happens that Charlus always has the freshness of a world just created and unceasingly emits primordial signs . . . (ibid. p. 4)

This 'complicated state' out of which Charlus constantly unfolds is analogous to 'time itself', time as original complication which precedes all development, deployment and explication (ibid. pp.

44–5). However, it is certain states in Proust that best correspond
to this original situation. Sleep, for instance:

[t]he sleeper 'holds in a circle around him the thread of hours, the order of
years and worlds': wonderful freedom which ceases only upon awakening,
when he is constrained to choose according to the order of time redeployed.
(ibid. p. 45)

In his accounts of the moment of waking, Proust manifests a
marvellous ability to preserve 'the purity of the encounter or of
chance' (ibid. p. 102). The actual is always implicated with the
virtual or multiple, as given worlds (the Verdurins', the Guer-
mantes') are always shadowed by other worlds they nonetheless
exclude. In the world of the *Recherche*, no throw of the dice
abolishes the chance of its throwing, a cast in which '*[l]es dieux
eux-mêmes sont soumis à l'Ananké, c'est-à-dire au ciel-hasard*'
(Deleuze 1968, p. 257). In *Difference and Repetition*, Deleuze
turns to Péguy for a particularly 'admirable description of the
event':

[he] deployed two lines, one horizontal and another vertical, which repeated
in depth the distinctive points corresponding to the first, and even anticipated
and eternally engendered these distinctive points and their incarnation in the
first. At the intersection of these lines – where a powder fuse forms the link
betwen the Idea and the actual – the 'temporally eternal' is formed ...
(Deleuze 1994, p. 189)

It is precisely to the 'intersection' of the two lines that, in
Deleuzean terms, Proust's art insistently returns, in a ceaseless
play of repetition and difference.

In particular, for Deleuze, there is thus a kind of narration of the
event in the *Recherche*. Proust produces a continual narrative
equivalent of Elstir's beloved patch of yellow in Vermeer's *View of
Delft*, 'planted there as a fragment of still another world' (Deleuze
1973, p. 102). Proust rejects any idea of an organic totality, of
unity as either pre-existent or to be discovered, and fosters a
narrative art of lacunae, breaks, intermittences in which there is
'an extraordinary energy of unmatched parts' (ibid. p. 109).[24] The
contents repeatedly 'dynamite' the container, as the patch of
yellow explodes the homogeneity of Vermeer's painting. Proust
affirms, not any unity supposedly containing the multiple, but the
complication of multiplicity as the whole. Here Proust's sense of

time coincides with Bergson's: time in itself 'signifies that everything is not given, that the Whole is not givable' (ibid. p. 115).
Proust renders the absolute partiality and productivity of time in a
narrative temporality that constantly produces the incommensurable, develops an explicable content that is heterogenous and
fragmented and in excess of its container. As with detail in Kafka
or Vermeer's patch of yellow, elements of narrative throw their
context out of true, and are likewise thrown out of true themselves. The result is a narrative art of variable intervals, distribut-
ing forces of different intensity and superimposing disparate
rhythms, dissolving fixed and homogenous values, constantly
producing narrative as an event from within 'a virtual, qualitative
multiplicity' (Deleuze 1988a, p. 47).

The same description might be applied to Virginia Woolf's
Jacob's Room. Jacob is obviously presented as a multiplicity. The
book is not about a subjectivity or subjectivities but rather about
time as becoming in its operation within and across subjectivities.
Woolf is evidently much less interested in classical modes of
individuation than in singularity or individuation by haecceity.
'Thus if you talk of a beautiful woman you mean only something
flying fast which for a second uses the eyes, lips or cheeks of
Fanny Elmer, for example, to glow through' (Woolf 1976, p. 124).
'Character' is likewise grasped as a complex virtuality out of
which the singular is constantly being actualised, only to 'sever
and become alien' again as a 'phantom of ourselves' (ibid. p. 100).
Jacob's Room repeatedly poises us in a liminal region, as the
virtual and actual are indistinguishable in the various placings of
the sheep's skull at the beginning of the book; as the letter Mrs
Flanders begins to Mr Floyd is not the letter he receives (ibid. pp.
22–3). Woolf repeatedly calls to mind 'the thing' that got 'left out',
like 'the thing [Miss Umphelby] might have said in elucidation of
the text' (ibid. p. 45). Worlds shadow worlds. There are always
oscillations between the determined and the undetermined. Furthermore, this kind of thought is incorporated into the novel as an
extremely subtle narrative practice. Woolf's narrative renounces
any totalising project, any effort to 'see a whole' (ibid. p. 33). 'The
magnificent world – the live, sane, vigorous world ... These
words' can only 'refer to the stretch of wood pavement between
Hammersmith and Holborn in January between two and three in

the morning' (ibid. p. 119). We are constantly being reminded of what is not as much as what is; that Mrs Pascoe's face 'was assuredly not soft, sensual or lecherous', for instance, 'but hard, wise, wholesome rather' (ibid. p. 57). Fragments of other worlds intrude as transient narrative 'focalisations'. The narrative bristles with unpredictable and alien temporal avenues and vistas, not just retrospectively or proleptically, but laterally or conjecturally, as with the projected future of the sheep's skull (ibid. p. 11), the fantastic, brief progress which leaves the reader 'an outcast from civilisation' (ibid. p. 103), and so on. Woolf's narrative constantly brings itself out of multiplicity into singularity, with another determined throw of the dice: 'There are things that can't be said. Let's shake it off. Let's dry ourselves, and take up the first thing that comes handy ... Timmy Durrant's notebook of scientific observations' (ibid. p. 52). Thus the novel emerges out of the world in which we are a 'procession of shadows' into the world where we are nonetheless 'surprised in the window corner by a sudden vision that the young man in the chair is of all things in the world the most real' (ibid. pp. 76–7). This art of the narrative event is one of intermittence (as in the dialogues in the novel, which tend to be disconnected and to point in various different directions. Utterance has all the surprise of an event). The rhythms of the narrative are likewise intermittent, and always liable to be disrupted. They are multiple, too. Only one of them is the storytelling rhythm, a rhythm which is likely to fade and then burst back, as if through something that threatens to be drift or cacophony. Intermittence means variable intervals: the frequent use of dots, for example, often to indicate a kind of narrative 'fadeout'; the hiccups in pace, like the sudden slips into single-sentence paragraphs which are subject themselves to a variable spacing. *Jacob's Room* endlessly evokes, replicates and mimics the 'chasms in the continuity of our ways' (ibid. p. 103). Yet it evokes them *as* chasms in a continuity. As Woolf adds, 'we keep straight on'. In other words, there is a container for the narrative temptation to distraction and lostness, the temptation to give way to 'sudden impulses' (ibid. p. 167), to the ulterior, to the other worlds and other narratives that beckon. There is a chronology. There are also what Deleuze would call 'transversals' that breach the 'envelopes' separating worlds, like the repeated references to

Jacob's distinguished looks. But the chronology is merely one shape amongst others, and the repetitions merely repeat. They do not unify. They are the container that is 'dynamited', as 'the observer is choked with observations' (ibid. p. 73), as *chronos* is assembled only to be torn apart, as 'narrative logic' exists in a set of connectives – 'so', 'for', 'therefore', 'it follows' – which do not *mean* but emerge precisely as a sort of 'lacing together', to adopt Woolf's own metaphor (ibid. p. 103). Narrative form does not exist as a whole or a pattern of which the separate molecules are subordinate parts. It exists so that the event can be narrated.

A third kind of narrative makes possible a certain writing of the event. Deleuze's *The Logic of Sense* is much concerned with paradox as opposed to *doxa*, to sense as good or common sense, with its determinable direction (*sens* (Deleuze 1990, p. 1)). Good sense means choosing one direction and holding on to it. This direction goes from the most to the least differentiated. It puts difference at the beginning and then annuls it. It goes from the singular to the regular, the remarkable to the ordinary, the nomadic to the sedentary. For good sense tells us that its direction is the only one it is possible to follow. But writers like Lewis Carroll question that assertion. Humpty Dumpty, for instance, is an excellent example of the paradoxical operation or 'double direction' which insists that there is no final answer to Alice's question, 'Which way, which way?' (ibid. p. 77). For Carroll, the game of sense has no set and given form. Such rules as it is deemed to have are not in the first instance those of the game at all, but take their models from elsewhere. Carroll exalts the purity of the game outside any such 'rules'. The rules of sense are optional and variable, likely to change with each new move in the game, as Alice continually discovers. Thus the game of sense itself is put forward as a '*nomadic* and non-sedentary distribution' of singularities (ibid. p. 60). Carroll gives us something only apprehended in writing and art: an affirmation and ramification of chance and the *alea* as also 'the reality of thought itself and the unconscious of pure thought' (ibid.). It is in this affirmation of the *alea* that writing and thought 'disturb reality, morality and the economy of the world' (ibid.). Carroll makes us consider good sense as Lyotard says Mallarmé makes us see thought, '*comme combinaison fortuite parmi d'autres possibles'* (Lyotard 1985, p. 70). Carroll thus returns us to the inevitable entanglement that Nietzsche and Freud insisted on of sense with nonsense, to what Deleuze calls the *'distinct-obscur'* (Deleuze 1968, p. 358). Sense is never principle or origin. It is always produced, determined, elicited by the circulation of non-sense and therefore in itself a transient effect. Carroll holds up a parodic mirror-image in which we glimpse the madness and randomness endemic to all thought, glimpse sense as event.

But Deleuze means two things by sense: 'good' sense, and, more largely, sense as 'ideal matter', a complex, incorporeal entity which is 'an acategorical, pre-individual, alogical medium' and includes both good sense and nonsense (Bogue 1989, p. 73). In this larger meaning of the word, absurd and contradictory propositions have sense (as they do in Carroll) and propositions like 'God exists' and 'God does not exist' emerge indifferently. In the endless deferral or infinite regress of sense, I never state the sense of what I am saying. Every proposition can therefore become the object of another proposition denoting its sense (Frege's paradox). Sense is never the double either of the proposition or of the thing or state of affairs. It exists midway between the two. It is an event, *'on the condition that the event is not confused with its spatio-temporal realization in a state of affairs'* (Deleuze 1990, p. 22). There is thus no sense of the event. The event is sense, as the identity of form and void. This is precisely evident in 'nonsense narratives' like Carroll's, where identities shift, relations of causality and temporality are reversed, and the real and the imaginary, the theoretical and the material, the possible and the impossible coexist and interact. In Carroll, everything takes place by means of language. This is a vital element in the difference between Carroll's stories and classical fairy tales, for instance. The Snark, for example, always missing where it is sought, designates what it expresses and expresses what it designates (Deleuze 1968, p. 104). *'Il n'y a qu'un mot qui se dit lui-même et son sens, c'est précisément le mot non-sens'* (ibid. p. 201). In fact, Carroll situates his entire work in 'the flat world of the sense-event' (Deleuze 1990, p. 63). Like the new novel, in Deleuze's account of it, Carroll's work 'remains under the sign of hieroglyphs' (Deleuze

1973, p. 37). It requires that we become Egyptologists, as Proust's world does of the Proustian solitary (ibid. p. 91).

Other narratives, too – particularly modern and postmodern ones – might be thought of as turning us into 'Egyptologists' precisely insofar as they occupy 'the flat world of the sense-event'. The supreme example, here – of the text as hieroglyphic monument, in Foucault's terms, rather than as document – would surely be *Finnegans Wake*. Beckett has written, appropriately enough, of 'the inevitable clarity of the old inarticulation' in *Finnegans Wake*, its 'savage economy of hieroglyphics' (Beckett 1983, p. 28). The 'furious restlessness to the form' of the Wake continually throws up a sense 'which is forever rising to the surface' but to which, nonetheless, the work cannot be reduced. *Finnegans Wake* fully inhabits the realm of the '*distinct-obscur*' as 'an endless verbal germination, maturation, putrefaction, the cyclic dynamism of the intermediate' (Beckett 1983, p. 29). Some of Burroughs's and Arno Schmidt's work might equally seem to generate sense as an effect, a particular formation within a larger complex. So too with much of Beckett's own work. In Beckett's own words, rather than 'binding' the sense-material 'in a spell, item after item' and juggling 'politely with irrefragable values', his work reveals sense as 'the little sparkle hid in ashes, the precious margaret' (ibid. p. 47) in a play of appearance and disappearance or 'punctuation of dehiscence' (ibid. p. 49) which sense itself does not found and to which it does not serve as an end term. Here 'art has nothing to do with clarity, does not dabble in the clear and does not make clear' (ibid. p. 94). The old woman in *Ill Seen Ill Said*, for instance, is only really a 'tenacious trace', emerging under an indefinite number of half-limned aspects as an irregular series of images that blur, fade or dissolve (Beckett 1982, p. 59). *Ill Seen Ill Said* sets certain elements of narrative sense in circulation as one group of possibilities amongst others. Thus for example with this brief 'flashback':

How come a cabin in such a place? Careful. Before replying that in the far past at the time of its building there was clover growing to its very walls. Implying furthermore that it the culprit. And from it as from an evil core that the what is the wrong word the evil spread. (ibid. p. 9)

The 'evil' alluded to here does not 'hang over the text as a whole'. If it connects up with anything, it does so with other isolated elements of a narrative sense which constitute only one particular direction in the text. There are other elements – not necessarily signifying or narrative – which point not only in reverse but in entirely unrelated directions. The text insistently ramifies, falls into pockets of obscurity, lapses into disarray, gathers certain of its elements together whilst others fall apart. Thus with the elements of familiar 'narrative structures': the relationship of old woman to the 'scene', of both to the eye that observes, of the eye to the 'drivelling scribe' (ibid. p. 51). The 'illuminations', the movements towards or into narrativity are only 'figments' which subside again into 'confusion'. Narrative sense is no longer the founding or grounding structure. It is merely one amidst an indeterminate number of textual features. It has no privileged status. Its status, in fact, is the status of the event.

In *The Red Badge of Courage*, *Jacob's Room* and *Ill seen Ill Said*, narrative escapes from narrative. It becomes its own phantom or perversion. It is embroiled in and cannot work free of an anti-narrativity, a resistance which narrative as a whole can never overcome. It thus preserves time as 'a fundamentally open whole'. *Aion* haunts and displaces the residues of *chronos*. It is important to give emphasis to narratives in which this happens. Lyotard's recent concern has been that under capital as 'the principle of reason in human affairs', prescriptions such as 'communicate, save time and money, control the event, increase exchanges, are all likely to extend and reinforce the "great monad"' (Lyotard 1991a, p. 69). The *Gestell* insists on a metaphysical postulate, writes Lyotard, whereby 'every event in the world is to be explained as the effect' of a cause or reason, 'i.e. rationalising the given and neutralising the future' (ibid.). Narrative as *chronos* – narrative as reproduced, consumed and understood within the terms of the *Gestell* – performs a similar function. If Lyotard's anxiety is well-founded, a postmodern theory of narrative might want to break any Bergsonian identification of narrative with closure, control and the *Gestell*, to search out and prize all those points at which any complete identification becomes impossible: to liberate narrative as event, and the event within narrative.

NOTES

1. Cf. Deleuze on 'time as succession of movements, and of their units' and 'time as simultaneism and simultaneity' in Deleuze 1986, p. 46.
2. Cf. Bogue 1989, p. 68.
3. See for instance Martin Heidegger, 'The Age of the World View', in Spanos 1979, pp. 1–15, passim.
4. The emphasis on process is originally Bremond's. See Bremond 1973, passim.
5. See Genette 1980, pp. 35–6.
6. See for example Deleuze and Guattari 1988, pp. 195–200.
7. See Lubbock 1921, passim. See also Müller 1968; and Genette 1980, pp. 33–5. Chatman has recently suggested that the distinction is now axiomatic. The issue has effectively been more or less 'settled'. See Chatman 1990, pp. 3–4.
8. See for example Deleuze and Guattari 1988, p. 381.
9. One important precursor of Heidegger's in this respect would be Bergson. Bergson distrusted the 'story-telling function' as 'creator of gods' and 'inventor of religions', fictitious representations 'which will stand up to the representation of the real and which will succeed, by the intermediary of intelligence itself, in thwarting intellectual work'. See Deleuze 1988, pp. 108–11, 130–1.
10. See Stanley Corngold, 'Sein und Zeit: Implications for Poetics', in Spanos 1979, pp. 99–115, p. 102.
11. For a different view of Lyotard on narrative, see Carroll 1987, p. 160. Bennington, however, is surely right in thinking that Lyotard is not concerned to deny the effects of 'a theatrical-representational type of thinking', but to suggest that it is merely one *dispositif* among others, with no particular privilege. See Bennington 1988, p. 27.
12. The insistence on recalling that narrative is irreducibly diachronic is evident in Lyotard from *Discours, Figure* to *The Inhuman*. As Bill Readings shows, it is here that Lyotard establishes his distance from narratology. See Readings 1991, p. 82.
13. See Bennington 1988, p. 21. Recent 'revisionist' narratology has sometimes returned to the conception of narrative in terms of an 'upstream and downstream', with all its hierarchising and geometrising implications. See Mink 1987, pp. 42–60, pp. 56–7. Karl Kroeber makes much of Mink in his recent *Retelling/Rereading: The Fate of Storytelling in Modern Times*, Kroeber 1990. See in particular pp. 55–6.
14. See Lyotard 1991, p. 59.
15. See Harvey 1965. This is not the only point at which Rorty relies on a classical form of literary criticism to bolster a supposedly postmodern position. See for instance his use of Trilling, Leavis and Kermode in Rorty 1989.
16. See Genette 1980, p. 94 and passim.

17. Tarkovsky himself has emphasised this as a crucial aspect of his aesthetics. See Tarkovsky 1989, pp. 118–20.

18. It also refuses to spatialise time. Tarkovsky has been explicit about his reluctance to conceive of film in spatial terms. See Tarkovsky 1991, p. 92.

19. Mark Le Fanu remarks on the manner in which *Mirror* splits up, unpredictably and without signalling its transitions, between present and past. See Le Fanu 1987, p. 71. But he does not connect the point with the question of identity.

20. Deleuze is particularly appropriate again, here, partly because he has paid attention to narrative more insistently than any other post-structuralist thinker. But there is a Deleuzean as there is a Heideggerian and a Lyotardian scepticism on the subject. His book on Francis Bacon, for instance, associates narrative with figural painting as giving us the sensational rather than the sensation, the horror rather than the cry, representation rather than event. For Deleuze, Bacon's painting has a directness of appeal not commensurable with telling stories. See Deleuze 1981, Vol. 1, p. 9ff. and passim. The emphasis is partly the painter's own. Bacon claimed for instance that he wanted 'to do the thing that Valéry said – to give the sensation without the boredom of the conveyance. And the moment the story enters,' he added, 'the boredom comes upon you'. See Sylvester 1980, p. 63.

21. Jean-Jacques Lecercle has suggested that, for Deleuze, it is *only* the novelist who can give a satisfactory account of the event. See Lecercle p. 98.

22. Compare Samuel Beckett, who writes that Marcel's sense of Albertine's '*pictorial* multiplicity' evolves into a sense of her '*plastic* and moral multiplicity' which is 'the expression of an inward and active variety . . . a turmoil of objective and immanent contradictions over which the subject has no control'. Beckett 1931, p. 13.

23. It is Beckett, again, who writes of Proust's vision of 'the perpetual exfoliation of personality' See Beckett 1931, p. 13.

24. Cf. Beckett on the 'perturbations and dislocations' in the *Recherche*; on its 'grave dissonances and incompatibilities, clashing styles, internecine psychologies and deplorable solutions of continuity'; on Proust's art of '*mésalliance*'. Beckett, 'Proust in Pieces', in Beckett 1983, pp. 63–5.

6

Narrative Laterality

STRATIFICATIONS

In a sense, this book has been about a kind of drawing. The drawing in question largely takes place in minds. But it is also available in graphic form in a host of narratological texts. Narrative texts, however, can only notionally be reduced to diagrams. Imagine a different kind of culture, some way in the future, less programmatic, less immediately post-theological than our own. It would surely be puzzled by our apparent need to discover a diagrammatic order in our narrative texts. Hence the experimental strategies I have adopted here. I have tried to think about narrative according to different dispositions of space to those commonly deployed by narratology and novel theory. I have tried to imagine the possibility of different spatial models for narrative, to theorise new connections between elements of narrative, even to theorise those elements differently. I have attempted to draw some new lines in and across narrative, to find modes of conceptualising it that would break away from the configurations most familiar to us in narrative studies. Fluent form, nomadic distributions, the hymen, heteroplasty, transversals, multiplicities, the excluded third, the *chora*, vectors, lines of force and flight: these are just some of the terms I have borrowed or adapted from critical theory in my attempts to hypothesise a new space for narrative theory. In this respect, I have been much concerned with what Derrida calls textual *laterality*.[1]

Narrative theorists have frequently tended to produce their accounts of narrative texts in terms of what they take to be narrative strata. Such strata are characterised by their supposed

homogeneity and distinctness. There is allegedly a clear definition to the lines which separate the strata off from one another.
The model of the text involved here connotes depth on the one
hand, and stability, solidity and immobility on the other. It turns
the text into a static arrangement of layers. These are deemed to be
fundamental to the text as movements within or connections
between the layers are not. The critic or theorist thus becomes a
geologist, skilled in describing the textual strata. The differences
between the layers will partly have to do with their relative
profundity and penetrability. Yet the stratified model of narrative
actually implies depth less than it does height. Above all, it is a
hierarchical model. It ranks textual elements. It classifies narrative
phenomena according to their status. The boundaries between one
narrative 'rank' and another are almost impossible to cross. It is
only in exceptional circumstances that moves between strata may
take place.[2] The system of narrative strata as described by narratology has the fixity of a Great Chain of Being or a feudal structure of
social relations. Here, again, we find narratology functioning in
terms of a geometry which produces the text as box (or pyramid).
Such a description implicitly asserts that the text is properly
governed and suitably regulated, with its units distributed in
orderly fashion and classified in the appropriate manner.

That narrative texts should so often have been thought of as
arrangements of strata is hardly surprising. The metaphor is at
hand as soon as we begin to conceive of meaning as hidden under
surfaces and authors or narrators as having power over texts. The
need not just to attribute a vertical dimension to narrative texts
but to stratify that dimension seems endemic to traditional
hermeneutics. But narratology has stratified narrative in various
ways. Take recent narratological descriptions of what Rimmon-
Kenan calls the 'narrative communication situation' (Rimmon-
Kenan 1983, p. 86). These stem in the first instance from Wayne
Booth's introduction to novel theory of the concept of the 'implied
author'. In keeping with his robustly moral concerns, Booth
hardly intended the phrase as a technical term at all.[3] But when
Iser produced the concept of the 'implied reader', a new set of
narrative categories appeared to be available. They were systematised by Seymour Chatman. Chatman drew a diagram of the
communication situation in narrative which ran from the real

author to the implied author to the narrator, the narratee, the implied reader and – at the end – the real reader her- or himself (Chatman 1978, p. 151). Chatman's diagram actually presented the relationship between the various participants in the 'situation' as a horizontal one. Yet metaphors of a vertical relation repeatedly occur in narratological discussions of the topic.[4] Indeed, Chatman's construct is horizontal in the way in which it imagines the successive stages of a communication. But it is stratified and hierarchical in its imagination of the relations between the participants. The hierarchy Chatman institutes is actually double. The implied author stands 'above' and controls the narrator. The real author occupies the same position and role in relation to the implied author. The implied reader has a superior vantage-point to the narratee and can scrutinise the narratee from a position of superior knowledge. But the implied reader her- or himself is subject to the superior gaze of the real reader. At all events, communication cannot be conceived of as occurring without those strata being in place.

Chatman's model has not won general acceptance. Rimmon-Kenan, for instance, has proposed the exclusion of the implied author and reader from any description of the communicative situation, and the inclusion of the narrator and narratee as constitutive rather than optional features of it (Rimmon-Kenan 1983, p. 88). Michael Toolan has argued a similar case but suggested that the narratee, at least, remain an optional category (Toolan 1988, p. 77). Ian Reid has recently criticised the concept of the 'implied author' as it is used 'to contain semantic negotiations within the field of a unitary subject' (Reid 1992, p. 102). Whatever the refinements of or disagreements with the hierarchical model, however, its basic structure remains intrinsic to most thought about narrative. There have even been attempts at further elaborations of Chatman's model: Gerald Prince, for example, has argued the need for a 'hierarchy of narratees' (Prince 1982, p. 25). But the most obvious and pervasive example of stratifying thought in narratology is the idea of narrative levels. Genette is most responsible for developing this concept. As he presents it, it actually involves a double geometry: of the hierarchical arrangement and the frame. We might first call the levels themselves to mind again. Genette illustrates with reference to *Manon Lescaut*:

M. de Renoncourt's writing of his fictive *Mémoires* is a (literary) act carried out at a first level, which we will call *extradiegetic*; the events told in those *Mémoires* (including des Grieux's narrating act) are inside this first narrative, so we will describe them as *diegetic*, or *intradiegetic*; the events told in Des Grieux's narrative, a narrative in the second degree, we will call *metadiegetic*. (Genette 1980b, p. 228)[5]

According to Genette, the levels are separated by 'a sort of threshold represented by the narrating itself' (ibid.). On the one hand, the relation between the levels is one of containment: Des Grieux's narrative is '*contained within*' M. de Renoncourt's *Mémoires*. One level frames another: the *Mémoires* 'frame' Des Grieux's narrative 'with a preamble and a conclusion' (ibid.). On the other hand, a given diegetic level is also understood as being '*immediately higher*' than another (ibid.). The very proliferation of metaphors is revealing, here. Certain powerful intellectual imperatives clearly matter more than the appropriateness of one or other system of metaphor. Firstly, there is the compulsion to practice a kind of boxing of narrative, 'hold it in', confine it within a fixed spatial arrangement. Secondly, there is the need to establish a structure of supervision: the boxes or containers are arranged in a downward-looking perspective. This idea is intrinsic to the very notions of narrative 'embedding' and *mise-en-abîme*.[6] The theory of narrative levels is thus an exact embodiment of what Rorty calls 'the metaphysician's metaphor of a vertical view downwards' (Rorty 1991, p. 96). Where Rorty regards that metaphor with ironical distrust, however, narratology simply ignores its metaphoricity. It even seeks to disguise the latter by cloaking it in an aura of scientific authenticity. Finally, there is the importance of purity of composition. It is crucial to the Genettian concept of levels that there be no seepage or osmosis across the threshold. The substance composing each stratum must be unadulterated. There must be no hint of ambivalence or paradox in the definition of a given stratum, no irrational features that might trouble its terms. Equally, there must be no anomalies in any of the strata, nothing mixed or hybrid. In Deleuze's phrase, narratology thus creates a general idea of the 'order or being' of narrative which 'can no longer be thought except in opposition to a nonbeing or disorder in general' (Deleuze 1988, pp. 19, 46–7).

Narratology refuses to think of narrative as heterogenous, a composite or mobile multiplicity.

The concept of narrative levels also involves a set of relations specifically implying domination and subordination. Rimmon-Kenan writes, for instance, of 'a stratification of levels' according to which 'each inner narrative is subordinate to the narrative within which it is embedded' (Rimmon-Kenan 1983, p. 91). This subordination is particularly clear in the functions of metadiegetic or, better, hypodiegetic narrative, as Rimmon-Kenan calls it, in relation to diegetic narrative.[7] In its first, 'actional' function, hypodiegetic narrative maintains or advances the action of the diegetic narrative. In its second, 'explicative' function, the 'hypo-diegetic' level offers an explanation of the diegetic level. Finally, the third function is 'thematic', the relations between hypo-diegetic and diegetic levels being those of analogy (similarity and contrast). Whichever function is in question, however – whatever the logic of the connection between diegesis and hypodiegesis – the structure of the connection remains the same. The hypo-diegetic narrative serves a certain purpose established by the diegetic narrative. We might rechristen them 'master narrative' and 'servant narrative', except for the fact that, at the extradiegetic level, the master narrative is mastered itself. But here again the structure of the relationship between the two levels is the same as that between diegesis and hypodiegesis. For narratology, it is a relationship predicated on certain modes of control or of exerting power. Since the power in question often has to do with the way in which one narrative 'oversees' another, it is partly knowledge as power that is at issue here, too.

The idea of narrative levels is an excellent example of the narratological imaginary as this book has sought to call it in question. It might even be thought of as its apotheosis. The geometry of levels has a comforting clarity and simplicity. With narrative levels, you know where you are. Hence the fact that the concept continues to flourish whilst other aspects of narrato-logical thought are increasingly coming under fire. Indeed, cur-rently, the concept of narrative levels is arguably growing more influential and more widespread as it migrates to other disciplines – sociology, for instance, educational theory and biblical studies.[8] I want to return, here, to Ian Reid's interesting book *Narrative*

Exchanges. Like Brooks, Chambers and others, Reid presents his project as a progression beyond the limitations of established narratology. Like others, too, he identifies the limitations in question as those of structuralism. He is tempted to go 'beyond narratology', but prefers to argue for the need to 'fine-tune' it with exchange theory. It is thus, says Reid, that we will escape 'the dyadic categories of structuralist narratology' and move towards a more acute sense of narrative as interaction. For narrative is undoubtedly interactive: there is nothing 'in' it 'independently of human transactions' (Reid 1992, p. 9). Hence Reid argues for an application of 'frame theory' to narrative which will recognise that 'perceptions of coherence' depend on acts of framing (ibid.). What one makes of narrative is determined by the way in which one 'frames' it. In Reid's sophisticated account of it, however, framing is not a simple matter. It is – precisely – a question of exchange. For the text has already provided various 'elements . . . that solicit particular framings, thus tending to curtail what the text can be made to mean' (ibid. p. 13). Furthermore, other factors counteract the fixity of any 'frame'. Reid calls them substitution and dispossession. The first is the succession of rhetorical features in the text, 'a substitutive shuffle of signifiers' which require attention at the expense of any supposed chain of narrative actions (ibid. p. 14). The second is the constant struggle within the telling situation to possess the meaning of what is told, an effort the text persistently resists. Together, substitution and dispossession disturb what framing would regulate, and constitute the structural specificity of written narrative.

Compared to the static geometry enjoined on us by the narratological description of levels, Reid's is an attractively dynamic model of what happens in the act of reading. The concepts of substitution and dispossession acknowledge a principle of displacement or molecular migration within the narrative text which admits its power to escape all frames and accepts that its sense is never 'finished'. But the concept of the 'frame' itself is surely problematic. Reid distinguishes his use of the term from that current in narratology ('an embedded structure of tales within tales' (ibid. p. 44)). He denies that what he means by frame is analogous to the structure that contains a painting (ibid. p. 15). But his own understanding of a frame – 'a mental schema for

organising information' (ibid. p. 44) – brings its own difficulties
with it. Reid distinguishes four kinds of narrative framing. The
first is circumtextual, and a question of the physical adjuncts to
the narrative, like title, footnotes, epigraph and so forth. The
second is extratextual: the framing information, expectations and
preoccupations that a reader brings to a text. The third is intra-
textual, taking place directly on the page itself. The fourth and last
kind is intertextual, and a matter of the relationship between a
narrative and other texts.

Reid insists that there are no fixed and separate frames. Thus
'the perception of any one framing element may involve an
adjusted perception of others' (ibid. p. 58). But his own 'pragmatic
typology' as outlined above nonetheless insists on a regulated set
of distinctions between an outside and an inside. Each frame has a
set of properties which are excluded from the others. There may
be movement across the dividing lines, but this does not essentially alter the substance peculiar to any given type of frame.
Reid's position with regard to narrative levels is therefore cur-
iously ambivalent. The complexity of his theory allows him to
suggest that there is no 'definitive principle of signification' in *Un
Coeur Simple*, for example, because of the complication of the
exchange of meanings within Flaubert's text (ibid. p. 87), an
exchange which goes on between what Reid is content to call the
levels of Flaubert's narrative. In the end, the exchanges between
levels allow us to question the authority of the narrator, for
instance, and the force with which the latter delivers his 'conde-
scending pronoucements' (ibid.). Thus, according to Reid, the
represented enunciation at the narratorial level can be at least
partly divested of its power. In fact, then, Reid strips the relationship between narrative levels of a structure of power that, as we
have seen, for narratology, is often implicit in narrative. But the
levels themselves remain intact. There may be exchange between
them, but no confusion of one with another. The geometry – and
the terminology – are still in place. Reid principally differs with
Halliday, for instance, because the latter has not availed himself of
a hierarchy of categories provided for us by established narratology. In the end, the trouble with Reid's account of framing is that
it is too seldom self-reflexive, that it asks no questions about
where 'frames' come from, what determines them, whether we

might not cast their terms aside and look for others. Reid's own vocabulary for frames is too often one already on offer in the very narratology of which he is so distrustful.

THEORY AND THE COLLAPSE OF HIERARCHIES

But critical theory, of course, has frequently pitted itself against the kind of geometrical thought that I have just described, and it is there we must look for a radically different model. Foucault's *Discipline and Punish*, for example, partly attempts to render the particular historicity of 'a whole penal, administrative, geographical hierarchy' and its 'exact geometry', thereby exorcising the spectre of both (Foucault 1991, pp. 115, 174). Here if anywhere, in the prison system and the disciplinary society it grows out of and expresses, we have a cultural imaginary to which the thought of levels is indispensable. Indeed, narratological models have tended to construct narrative texts according to the principle of what Foucault calls 'hierarchical observation' as practised within disciplinary society (ibid. p. 171). Foucault refers to the principle in question as 'embedding' (ibid. pp. 171–2), which can hardly fail to remind us of narratology itself. Lyotard, too, has developed a critique of the politics of geometric organisation. In 'Representation, Presentation, Unpresentable', for instance, he suggests that 'optical geometry' – the 'ordering of values and colours' that prevailed in painting for centuries – did much to contribute to a metaphysical and political programme:

Once placed on the perspectivist stage, the various components of [political] communities – narrative, urbanistic, architectural, religious, ethical – were put in order under the eye of the painter, thanks to the *costruzione legittima*. And in turn the eye of the monarch, positioned as indicated by the vanishing-point, receives this universe thus placed in order. (Lyotard 1991a, pp. 119–20)

The geometry of painting lines itself up with 'a Neoplatonically inspired hierarchism', and expresses and confirms that 'hierarchism' as a political principle. But the advent of photography frees painting from its former obligation, letting it become 'a philosophical activity' (ibid. p. 121). With postmodernity, the collapse or at least the interrogation of the old geometry becomes possible.

Derrida and Deleuze, moreover, have begun to hypothesise new modes of spatialisation in aesthetics that are relevant here. Deleuze and Guattari have waged war on the notion of strata, whether defined as the object of literary-critical, philosophical or scientific attention. For strata are always constructions, produced on the basis of a specific choice about how to see matter. Hence Deleuze and Guattari's deployment of metaphors – the rhizome, the 'plane of consistency', transversals, the plateau – that offer images of a very different spatial organisation to that of the geometrical 'box'. These images flatten space, or multiply it, or cut across strata, redistributing their elements.[9] Derrida, too, has sought to obscure the dividing lines that make the thought of strata possible by questioning the distinction between inside and outside. As Derrida deploys it, for instance, the term 'graft' registers an 'essential parasitizing' which opens every stratum 'to its outside' and 'divides the unity of the line [trait] which purports to mark its edges' (Derrida 1987c, p. 7). It is this 'essential parasitizing' that makes Derrida so interested in limits, margins, edges, accessories, supplements, frames themselves, rather than the entities that a different kind of discourse would claim they separated. For part of what Derrida distrusts in Kant and in classical aesthetics, for instance, is the assumption that there can be a rigorous distinction between the intrinsic and the extrinsic, the essential and the incidental. Here again all thought of strata and rigid hierarchies begins to founder. Hence Derrida's critique of the concept of the mise-en-abîme itself as resisting 'the abyss of collapse' and merely reconstituting 'the economy of mimesis' (ibid. pp. 117–18). Indeed, in The Truth in Painting, at least, Derrida plays with the substitution of the term 'stricture' for 'structure'. The stricture runs between or interlaces inside and outside. The thought of it is therefore a rejection of 'the logic of detachment as cut' on which the concept of levels arguably depends (ibid. p. 340).

Like Deleuze and Guattari, then, Derrida seems implicitly to deconstruct the kind of space established by narratology. Not only that: like Deleuze and Guattari again, he begins to conjure up a different space, partly through the strategic deployment of a different aesthetic vocabulary. Serres, too, has been much concerned with the concept of a 'hierarchy of levels' (Serres 1993, p.

118). For Serres, what is at stake in such a concept is what he calls 'the hard logic of boxes' (Serres 1991b, p. 178). This logic establishes relationships that treat the elements in question like Russian stacking dolls. It also ensures that there is always a 'winner' on top (ibid. p. 185). In the 'logic of boxes', the first must always contain the second element, never the other way round. Serres actually gives the *mise-en-abîme* as an example (ibid. p. 187). The 'logic of boxes' therefore 'posits a space which is not deformable', a homogeneous, ireversible, universal space (ibid. p. 178). According to Serres, that space is what remains of God in the sciences and other disciplines. Today, however, we must envision a deformable space. The concept of a 'hierarchy of levels' has always spatialised a given set of power relations. It has turned them into relations of distance and thereby rationalised them, given them a seemingly essential form:

Le rapport de domination, de hauteur, de mépris, de rigueur et de poids s'y réduit au rapport de distance; le rapport de forces s'y transforme en notion de rapport, à la représentation géométrique, à la vue, théorique, au rapport mesurable, rationnel, dicible, au discours. (Serres 1993, p. 125)

The structure of the 'hierarchy of levels' has therefore persisted through and outlasted different modes of social organisation. For it came to inhabit, was even identified with the principle of reason itself. Rational systems themselves seemed necessarily to be hierarchical (ibid. p. 137).[10] Paradoxically, however, the hierarchical principle is now at risk from the sheer burgeoning multiplicity of its applications, the number of diffuse and incommensurable forms of knowledge it underpins:

le buissonnement multiplicatif du savoir, sa croissance (totalisante, souvent, en chaque chaînon du parcours) interdisent, de fait, toute conscience claire de son état synchronique global, à partir d'un point de vue donné. C'est le fameux danger, souligné maintes fois, de Leibniz à Lénine, de revenir à la barbarie sous l'accumulation de l'information consciente, qu'une conscience ne peut dominer ni maîtriser (Serres 1972, p. 39).

The hierarchies of thought can no longer be subsumed into a whole or be arranged hierarchically themselves. This has finally made the hierarchical principle visible in and of itself, as simply a certain mode of construction. There is thus no way of 'ranking' the modes of knowledge:

nulle référence extérieure n'est susceptible de classer les sciences, distinctions pour un ordre hiérarchique, ni partage d'objets pour un découpage en domaines univoques. Toute référence préalable est d'ordre métaphysique . . . (ibid. p. 64)

Knowledge emerges as an open and indefinite space. Its many different 'regions' can no longer be conceived of as autochthonous. Rather, they are constantly subject to a process of 'interference' or 'inter-reference'. A given system is not self-contained. It is laterally related to other systems supposedly entirely outside it. Thus

[l]a théorie dans son ensemble, le monde des objets solides, techniques et vivants, les configurations historiques se trouvent saisis dans les mailles d'un espace fibré multiplement . . . (ibid. p. 133)

Thought can thus no longer involve the apprehension or construction of a hierarchically ordered space. It must rather be a movement or displacement among spaces, a mode of 'errance' or wandering.

Hierarchical systems of thought like that represented in narratology are therefore becoming obsolete (Serres 1977a, p. 39). We can only grow increasingly aware of how far the objects such systems describe are in excess of those systems. Apart from anything else, there is 'no system that functions perfectly, that is to say, without losses, flights, wear and tear, errors, accidents, opacity' (Serres 1982, p. 12). At the same time, however, there is no point in seeking to undo systems, immediately, once and for all. To attempt to do so is only likely to strengthen a given system, which will thrive all the better for an 'opposition' which it can learn to deal with, and subsequently to tolerate. Rather than 'dismantling' a system, says Serres, it is important to 'misconstrue' it (ibid. p. 68). We need to return the disorder the systems exclude back into those systems, to disarrange their symmetries and unsettle their equilibrium, to find ways of dissolving or at least troubling their systematicity. For the 'clear frontiers' that distinguish levels from one another, for instance, Serres seeks to substitute the 'fluid border' or the 'gray band'. Narratology 'erase[s] this band in the name of rigour' (Serres 1991b, pp. 188–9). Serres insists on its importance. We must think *between* systems or the elements arranged within systems, in describing what goes on between them ('[*d*]*e dire ce qui se passe entre eux*' (Serres 1977a, p. 202)).

The category 'between' ('*la catégorie entre*' (ibid.)) is crucial to Serres's thought. It is partly a concept of transaction or exchange. Serres's conception of exchange, however, is different to Reid's. For Reid, exchanges take place only in relation to an order that still remains invariant and hierarchical in itself. For Serres, on the other hand, exchanges are lateral relations between shifting elements that are modified themselves in the exchange. The traditional sciences think of their object as a static ensemble organised around a centre (ibid. p. 12). In that respect, narratology is still a traditional science. For postmodernity, on the other hand, according to Serres, the 'static ensemble' disappears. The object of knowledge explodes into multiplicity. It cannot be thought outside the 'distribution' of its elements and their multiple relations within that distribution (ibid. p. 32). One of Serres's major figures for such relations is the parasite. Serres calls the parasite 'the essence of all relation' (Serres 1982, p. 79). A large part of Serres's endeavour has been to counter the 'work of purification' that he sees as having preoccupied philosophy since Kant, in challenging the very idea of 'pure forms' (Serres 1992, p. 215). The thought of the parasite is a form of strategic resistance to the 'work of purification'. For the parasite is a reversible or ambivalent, 'impure' figure. It is the noise or the static in a system, an interference from another system or a crossing between systems. It resists the notion of levels because it refuses to grant them the 'purity of composition' with which, as we saw earlier, a system like narratology endows them. For no system or element in a system is without its parasite. The parasite pulls the element away from itself, makes it more (or less) than itself, compromises its identity, troubles its self-sufficiency. As a figure, the parasite announces the irreducible hybridity of – and therefore a certain equality of relation within – all thought, science and discourse. As it destroys all purity, so the parasite necessarily denies the possibility of that vertical dimension without which the concept of levels cannot survive. In effect, the work of the parasite means the collapse of all hierarchies.

NARRATIVE LATERALS FROM ROBBE-GRILLET TO FIELDING

Postmodern writers have repeatedly shared Serres's distrust of the 'logic of boxes'. Christa Wolf, for example, has written of the tension between 'the incredibly tangled mesh' of what she seeks to translate into narrative, and narrative itself. 'To speak about superimposed layers', writes Wolf, '"narrative levels" – means shifting into inexact nomenclature and falsifying the real process [of narration]' (Wolf 1988, p. 272). In *S/Z*, Barthes even questions the usefulness of seeing the classic realist text in terms of a 'rhetorical hierarchy'.[11] In *Le Plaisir du Texte*, he suggests that the reader does not experience a text in terms of supposed 'levels', either. For in reading, categories are suspended, modes of exclusion abolished. The boundaries on which classifications depend are blurred (Barthes 1973, p. 9). Neither Wolf nor Barthes provides us with a different model, however. Hence we return to Serres. For spatialisation in terms of levels, Serres substitutes the multiple spaces that I discussed in my introduction. Within those spaces, there is always the parasite. There are always circulations, fluxes and flows, connections and 'crossroads', confluences and intersections, 'knottings' and 'interlacings' (*entrelacs*), etc. Serres offers us the text as a composite of multiple spaces traversed by lateral connections. It is in such terms, for example, that he describes '*l'éblouissant montage de Sarrasine, complexe multiple de réunions associées, parallèles comme des reflets ou croisées comme des chimères*' (Serres 1987, p. 86).

Such a conception of the narrative text is easily and appropriately applied to much postmodern fiction. Like many of Robbe-Grillet's texts, for example, *The Voyeur* seems precisely to resist all categorisation in terms of levels. Right from the start, Robbe-Grillet refuses to produce the initial horizontal line which founds any arrangement of levels. The narrative fails to 'get going'. It eddies 'pointlessly' around the docking ship, for example, delays at length over the descriptions of the structure of the pier and the jetty, the 'amplitude and rhythm' of the rising and falling of the sea, the movements of the seaweed, the 'ball of blue paper', etc. (Robbe-Grillet 1965b, pp. 8–10). Forward propulsions of the narrative peter out into incidental notation. Robbe-Grillet also immediately establishes repetition as a narrative principle (e.g. the recurrent, identical gulls in more or less identical positions). Le Voyeur begins with a deliberate production of redundancy or excess, consciously repudiating a narrative economy. As a result, the spaces of the narrative start to proliferate. Initially, the narrative produces the 'story' of Mathias drawing the gull, as a child (ibid. pp. 10–13). There is no logic to the inclusion of the story, here, no narrative 'motivation' of it. There is no 'realistic' or 'thematic' connection between the story and the surrounding context. The narrative does not even provide any clear sign that Mathias is recollecting the scene. Rather the reverse: the phrase that opens the sequence ('He had often heard the story before' (ibid. p. 10)) suggests that Mathias is not producing the story but having it produced for him. Yet the narrative context clearly makes this idea a ludicrous one. In any case, the phrase will recur again and again throughout The Voyeur. That recurrence in itself deprives the formula of any precise meaning or value with regard to an ascertainable narrative logic. Nor is there any determinate relation between the sequence involving the drawing and its context in terms of either time or the logic of cause and effect or narrative levels. The story simply appears in the text as something else that the narrative declares it can do. Effectively, the narrative generates a second, non-assimilable narrative space. Yet story and context are not devoid of all relation. Such relation as emerges, however, is a question of cross-referral, the repetition with variations of certain elements in both (gull, string, etc.). Story and context, therefore, are not to be thought of as being on different levels. Rather, narrative starts to manifest itself as a succession of multiple spaces with lateral connections between them. In Deleuzean terms, the 'rhizome' displaces the box.

The spaces in Le Voyeur then start to proliferate rapidly. We shuttle backwards and forwards between Mathias on the ship and the 'drawing' scene (ibid. pp. 13–15), between various stages of Mathias's disembarkation and 'earlier' embarkation (ibid. pp. 15–25), fragments of seemingly unrelated narrative (the bedroom scene (ibid. pp. 19–20)) and various incompatible accounts of what happens to Mathias once he gets ashore (ibid. pp. 25–32). Certain elements in the narrative can of course be read as prolepses and analepses, here. But the very multiplicity of those elements insistently poses problems, as does the principle of difference within repetition that simultaneously both links and decisively separates given sets of elements. There is no single past or future that the narrative refers to. In both cases, a range of different possibilities rapidly makes itself available. Thus a movement in narrative time actually becomes a movement in space, a lateral shift, rather than a narrative movement forwards or backwards. Equally, there is no static grid which will allow us categorically to separate extradiegesis, diegesis and hypodiegesis. The space of the text cannot possibly be conceived in anything like Euclidean terms, here. Intermittently, at least, this is the case throughout *Le Voyeur*. Take the passage detailing the encounter of the giant man and the girl immediately after Mathias has read his newspaper article (ibid. pp. 62–3). Is this a fantasy of Mathias's, or does it have some connection with the newspaper cutting? What relation does it bear to earlier, briefer fragments of the same sequence or similar sequences? The figures in the scene are recycled versions of figures in the earlier 'real life' sequence in the café '*À l'Espérance*'. Why, then, are 'certain differences of detail' nonetheless 'noticeable', to quote the novel itself (ibid. p. 103)? To answer these questions would be to start sorting the narrative out, construing it in the terms of a systematic geometry, getting our bearings. But Robbe-Grillet's narrative refuses to allow the reader 'to situate' its 'elements' with any 'assurance' at all (ibid. p. 130). Hence it is impossible to know how to attribute the phrase which begins the sequence I have just discussed: 'He is on the first floor, standing in the narrow vestibule . . .' (ibid. p. 62). Is Mathias serving as a Jamesian 'reflector'? Is the narrator confining himself to Mathias's fantasy world? Is there a more authoritative narrator present who actually provides information that is at least valid for his own small narrative fragment? What, then, is his relation to other narrators in the text? Should we assume that there is a single or at least a dominant narrator in the book thus far who is present in this sequence, too? If yes, does this sequence have the same validity and narrative status as others preceding it?

All these are questions involving narrative level. *Le Voyeur* makes them all irrelevant. The last phrase I quoted from Robbe-Grillet's text is a narrative equivalent of Serres's 'fluid border' or 'grey band'. It refuses to define the nature or extent of the relation between two narrative segments, to indicate how they should be ordered or rendered commensurable. It gives no hint of a scheme to which such relations might be reduced. The narrative is rather like those 'traces of foam' it describes as left by the sea and 'ceaselessly effaced and revived in ever-fresh designs' (ibid. p. 71). Like all of Robbe-Grillet's work, of course, the book is rich in metaphors for its own procedures. The reader's experience of the text might seem increasingly to mirror Mathias's experiences as 'the narrative goes on'. But the reverse is really the case. There is no single narrative 'going on', and it is Mathias's 'experiences' that increasingly resemble the reader's experience of the narrative. Arguably, at the representational level, at least some of Robbe-Grillet's texts are partly engaged in producing metaphors for the reader's complex experience of the text. This experience involves what Serres calls '*errance*'. Reading becomes a lateral movement from one space to another, contiguous space. But the second space is never entirely distinct from the first. There is always 'inter-reference', always the 'gray band' between space and space. In Robbe-Grillet, narrative no longer produces or duplicates or hierarchically arranges the supposedly homogeneous space of the world. It does not produce the world at all. In producing a multiplicity of possible spaces, it rather produces the virtual spaces of thought itself.

In part. In part, *The Voyeur* also seems to retreat from the very multiplicity of the spaces it produces. For *The Voyeur* does not entirely abandon the novelistic. The opening sequence as I have just analysed it is considerably more complex than much of the rest of the novel. The initial narrative is a *parcours* among multiple spaces. But much that follows is at least partly reducible to a familiar kind of novelistic clarity. Take the section which runs from Mathias's arrival in the town centre (ibid. p. 33) to the point at which he sits down on the rocks near the old town wall (ibid. pp. 59–60). It is possible, here, to make out something like a linear sequence of events. The same is true of the long section that runs from the start of Mathias's ride back to the harbour (ibid. p. 129) to his missing the ship (ibid. p. 137) to his return into town, arrangements for a room, return to the cliffs, interviews with the Mareks, with Julian Marek, etc., almost right up to the end (ibid. pp. 143–206). In this section of the book, Robbe-Grillet arguably even produces a plot involving Mathias's desperate attempts to cover up his crime. Thus certain parts of *The Voyeur* appear to resolve the indeterminacies which others create. Far from being simply 'a seamless series of dislocations' (ibid. p. 46), the text might appear to lure the reader into radically unorthodox expectations and then frustrate *them*. This would suggest that there are at least two narrative levels. On one, a dominant narrator tells a story. On another, that story is obscured. But the possibility of 'levels' only emerges after the dominance of a different set of narrative possibilities has been established. The 'logic of boxes' is there in *The Voyeur*. But it manifests itself only in residual form, as a phantom possibility among others within a world subjected to a principle of lateral connection. Insofar as the 'logic of boxes' seems apparent, like the logic of narrative linearity, it is ironised from the start. For it obviously simplifies a prior complexity. The 'logic of boxes' is consciously presented as producing determinacy out of an initial indeterminacy. It is made available in the text only as something the reader may want to rest on for support, like a banister for the old and infirm. Robbe-Grillet even provides a parodic version of that kind of logic when he recapitulates 'the story so far' near the beginning of the third section of the book (ibid. p. 77). *The Voyeur* does not entirely 'cancel out' hierarchical space. But it makes it available only as one among various spaces that the reader is required to traverse or hold in mind. Hierarchical space is always situated in relation to a multiple or conditional space.

Both the modes of spatialising narrative that I have just described may be appropriate in some respect to all narrative texts. What is crucially at issue is the relation between the two, and this will differ widely from, say, *The Voyeur* to *Project for a Revolution in New York* to a text that is usually taken as a classic example of narrative levels, like the *Arabian Nights*. To conceive of any narrative solely in terms of levels is surely to ignore the possibility of reading it in terms of a different space. The reader may repress this latter, or it may be repressed within the text. But conditional space is arguably intrinsic to all narratives. Thus a text like *The Voyeur* is probably more representative of narrative than we have allowed ourselves to imagine. Finally, we might turn to two classic works of English fiction that seem to invite construction in terms of levels, and ask what happens if we seek to apprehend them according to a different thought of space. *Vanity Fair* would seem to occupy a firmly delimited, hierarchical space, with extradiegetic, diegetic and hypodiegetic levels all clearly demarcated. The presence of an extradiegetic narrator is a marked feature of the novel, for example. Equally, the extra-diegetic level of the text is very specifically distinguished from the diegetic, not least in terms of time (the 1840s as opposed to the time of the Napoleonic Wars). Hypodiegetic narration may not be as common or as important in *Vanity Fair* as it is, say, in *Don Quixote*. But there are nonetheless some obvious examples (Becky's letters to Amelia, and so on).

If we look at the text a little more closely, however, we will find that the three 'levels' in question are merely notional, at least insofar as their constituent elements have no real unity. There is no homogeneity or consistency to any given narrative level in *Vanity Fair*. One obvious example would be the extradiegetic narrator's self-contradictions. More than narratorial subjectivity is at stake, here:

[Amelia] fell to thinking over the passed week, and the life beyond it. Already to be looking sadly and vaguely back: always to be pining for something which, when obtained, brought doubt and sadness rather than pleasure; here was the lot of our poor little creature, and harmless lost wanderer in the great struggling crowds of Vanity Fair. . . . And so she sat for a while indulging in her usual mood of selfish brooding . . . (Thackeray 1978, p. 311)

The sudden shift in tone at the end, here, is not just a shift in 'attitude' but a shift in distance. It disturbs the apparent steadi-ness of the downward-looking, extradiegetic gaze. The narrator appears to move close to the diegetic level of the text, only to move away from it, again. In other words, the distance between extradiegesis and diegesis is a variable one. This is true in other ways, too. In *Vanity Fair*, the gap between diegesis and extra-diegesis alternately opens and closes as the narrator chooses a more or less expressive mode of narration, as he refers to Jos

Sedley by name, for example, or in other terms: 'the head under the neckcloth', for instance, at the beginning of Chapter Three (ibid. p. 55). The relationship between extradiegetic and diegetic levels likewise shifts markedly according to whether the narrator is acting as puppeteer and 'Manager of the Performance' (ibid. p. 34) or as chronicler. For the two roles suggest quite distinct and even incompatible narratorial positions relative to the diegesis. In one of these roles, the narrator is master of all he surveys. In another, he is not, and the diegesis is likely to elude him and his clutches and defy certainty, as when he confesses himself uncertain as to Rawdon Crawley's motives (ibid. p. 304). Here again the narrator's distance from the diegesis is a variable one. It is impossible for us to think of him as occupying a single 'level' of the text.

In some ways, however, the hypodiegetic is the most revealing and intriguing 'narrative level' in *Vanity Fair*. For in Thackeray's novel, hypodiegesis is a complex and multifarious phenomenon. On the one hand, it exists in large, clear, distinct sections of the book, like the letters I mentioned earlier. But it can also emerge in a single phrase or sentence, only to disappear again:

[Rawdon] vowed, with a great oath, that there was no woman in Europe who could talk over a creditor as [Becky] could. *Almost immediately after their marriage, her practice had begun* . . . (ibid. p. 265, italics mine)

The last phrase in this passage is surely hypodiegetic, the fragment of a story within a story that disappears again, almost at once. Hypodiegeses can be series of multiple fragments. They may be presented in the form of either summary or scene; directly narrated by characters, in speech or in writing; rendered in indirect speech (as above); or reported by the narrator:

Then, having a particular end in view, this dexterous Captain proceeded to describe Mrs Major O'Dowd packing her own and her Major's wardrobe, and how his best epaulettes had been stowed into a tea canister . . . (ibid. p. 295)

In this passage, an extradiegetic narrator diegetically relates a hypodiegetic narrative. The passage surely belongs to all three narrative levels at once. In *Vanity Fair*, dialogue often incorporates more or less minute elements of hypodiegesis. So does reported thought:

Turning over one after another, and musing over these memorials, [Mr Osborne] passed many hours ... What pride he had in his boy! He was the handsomest child ever seen. Everybody said he was like a nobleman's son. *A royal princess had remarked him, and kissed him, and asked his name in Kew Gardens.* (ibid. p. 280, italics mine)

It may be that the two sentences preceding the italicised one should count as hypodiegesis, too. They surely count as such if we understand more than mere bald storytelling as involved in hypodiegesis, which is what we assume with diegetic narrative. In fact, there is an uncertainty as to demarcation, here. In general, that uncertainty insistently troubles any attempt to isolate the hypodiegetic elements in *Vanity Fair*. If a character tells a story about another character, that is clearly hypodiegesis. So, too, if a character recounts a few of another character's recent doings. But what if A merely gives an account of B's character? After all, he or she is doing no more than a narrator will do in diegetic narration. What if A simply remarks that s/he has recently met B? And so on. A great deal of the dialogue and reported speech in *Vanity Fair* and in many other novels begins to look as though it must logically be described as hypodiegesis. But, equally, the concept of hypodiegesis itself begins to give way under the strain. There is simply too much for it to encompass.

The three narrative levels in *Vanity Fair*, then, might actually be thought of as variable *modes* of narrative communication. Their relation to each other does not take the rigid form of a hierarchical structure. Rather, they constantly break in upon and 'interfere' with each other, to return to Serres's terminology. There are no clear limits to one of these modes as opposed to another. The 'level' of a given narrative utterance will often be indeterminate. The distinction between the diegetic and hypodiegetic modes, for example, will often be only a 'gray band'. A given narrative mode may exert a kind of lateral pull on a narrative sequence that is otherwise progressing in a different mode. Diegesis may briefly cede to hypodiegesis, as in the case of Rawdon's vow. The extradiegetic narrator may make himself briefly (and often playfully) felt in a hypodiegetic narrative, as when Becky describes the rain beginning to fall at a place called Leakington (ibid. p. 110), or when Poe describes George Osborne's dalliance with a woman called Mrs Highflyer (ibid. p. 315). Extradiegesis may yield to diegesis by various indeterminate degrees, as in the gradual movement into diegetic narrative at the beginning of Chapter 28. In *Vanity Fair*, there is a constant interplay of the three narrative modes. Thackeray's novel therefore prompts us to conceive of narrative 'levels' as more like interwoven strands, with a range of differing and heterogenous narrative positions distributed along them. Of course, the weaving takes place around a single narrative line. In that respect, of course, it is not the kind of multiple weave we find in Robbe-Grillet. *Vanity Fair* is not *The Voyeur*. But the space in question in *Vanity Fair* is nonetheless not the stratified space denoted in the concept of narrative levels. The novel rather exists as a constant play of and between varied narrative instances, as a flux and flow of mobile elements which should not be forced into determinate moulds.

Joseph Andrews provides a rather different example. Fielding's novel is much concerned with hierarchies, of course, of both the social and the moral kind. In keeping with that concern, the novel itself appears to be rigidly stratified. The hypodiegetic narratives, for example, are cleanly and precisely distinguished from the diegesis. *Joseph Andrews* has a very pronounced extradiegetic narrator. He not only serves as commentator or vehicle for 'sentiments' and as self-reflexive narrative agency, but is also 'endowed with a subjectivity'. He is clearly set apart, then, from the narrative he relates. Yet at the same time, he cannot be wholly set apart from it. Extradiegetic space continues to haunt or be confounded with diegetic space. The diegetic level of the narrative reveals itself as determined by or in some kind of relation to the extradiegetic level. One obvious example of this would be Fielding's use of flagrant coincidence:

'Now, believe me [said Mr. Adams], no Christian ought so to set his heart on any person or thing in this world, but that, whenever it shall be required or taken from him in any manner by Divine Providence, he may be able, peaceably, quietly, and contentedly, to resign it.' At which words one came hastily in, and acquainted Mr Adams that his youngest son was drowned. He stood silent for a moment, and soon began to stamp about the room and deplore his loss with the bitterest agony. (Fielding 1961, p. 265)

There is a sense in which we cannot simply read this passage on a diegetic level. It cannot but draw our attention to another space behind the diegetic, the extradiegetic space of the narrator's 'purpose'. It is that space that makes the diegetic arrangement what it is. We must read the passage with a simultaneous consciousness of both spaces, and the fact that they are laterally connected or 'inter-refer'. But the interdependence of diegesis and extradiegesis in *Joseph Andrews* can be posited in more sophisticated ways. Here is a different kind of example:

No sooner was young Andrews arrived at London than he began to scrape an acquaintance with his party-coloured brethren . . . His hair was cut after the newest fashion, and became his chief care: he went abroad with it all the morning in papers, and drest it out in the afternoon. *They could not, however, teach him to game, swear, drink, nor any other genteel vice that the town abounded with* . . . (ibid. p. 20, italics mine).

Is that last sentence diegetic or extradiegetic? Presumably the former; and yet it is a notation of what did not happen, of a non-event. As such, it bears the traces of an extradiegetic situation in which an array of possibilities must be presumed to exist before the diegesis cuts its path through them. In *Joseph Andrews*, Fielding repeatedly refers to the possible or probable, or the hypothetical, to 'ifs' and 'mights'. When the fluctuations in Lady Booby's responses to Joseph give Mrs Slipslop ideas, for instance, Fielding tells us that '[t]his wavering in her mistress's temper probably put something into the waiting-gentlewoman's head' (ibid. p. 29). This is arch, of course. We imagine we know what we are supposed to think. But the sentence nonetheless suggests the extradiegetic possibility of nothing having been in Mrs Slipslop's mind at all. The same is true when we are told of the traveller who is 'perhaps a *little* moved' by Joseph's dreadful condition (ibid. p. 43); when Adams is described as eating either rabbit or fowl ('I never could with any tolerable certainty discover which', says the narrator (ibid. p. 56)); when the narrator professes uncertainty about characters' motives; and so on. Again and again, we become aware of a kind of virtual space co-existing with the 'actual space' of the diegesis, to the point where actual and virtual are close to being indistinguishable. This virtual, extradiegetic space is deemed to be the reader's, as well, since Fielding recognises the fact that readers will skip chapters if they so wish (ibid. p. 74). Interestingly, too, when we look at the hypodiegetic narratives in

Joseph Andrews, we discover the same basic feature in them. It is as though Fielding has translated an element of indeterminacy from hypodiegetic narrative, where we would expect it, to diegetic narrative, where we would not. Extradiegetic space and its possibilities, then, intrude on diegetic space and its 'actuality', calling their determinacy in question. It would of course be absurd to try to read *Joseph Andrews* as *The Voyeur* in eighteenth-century guise. But it is nonetheless the case that the conditional space of *The Voyeur* is already present in *Joseph Andrews* and a host of other more traditional narratives. Hierarchical and conditional space must be thought together, in *Joseph Andrews*, as indeed they surely must throughout the history of narrative.

Finally, though, my accounts of *Vanity Fair* and *Joseph Andrews* may not seem to advance us very far beyond the conception of narrative levels present in – say – Reid's book. But I am not sure that a radical advance beyond Reid's kind of thinking is immediately possible. As we saw earlier, according to Serres, for the present, there is no decisive break with a system like narratology that does not risk the possibility of actually confirming its structures. My difference with Reid has to do with his reluctance to 'misconstrue' an established set of narratological categories, in the sense in which Serres writes of 'misconstruction'. What Reid means by 'exchange' and what I mean by 'laterality' are not the same thing. For Reid, insofar as it concerns levels, exchange takes place between self-identical entities. They remain themselves through and after an exchange. My suggestion would be that the entities in question were illusory in the first place. In other words, narrative levels do not exist as blocks of homogeneous 'narrative substance.' Rather, from the start, they are always in hybridised or composite relations with each other. Those relations subject the levels themselves to constant modification. Narrative, then, does not require us to stratify it. Rather, it is itself a form of resistance to our stratifying procedures. It ceaselessly denies or obscures the clear distinctions that it fleetingly appears to encourage. It allows hierarchical structures to emerge only as phantom shapes which can never prove adequate to the phenomena they seek to formulate. It is precisely for that reason that the anti-novel as practised by the likes of Robbe-Grillet has seemed to some to constitute an expression of the very spirit of narrative itself.[12]

Notes

1. For the concept of 'laterality', see Derrida 1981a, pp. 249–54.
2. See Genette on what he calls metalepsis in Genette 1980, pp. 234–7.
3. Booth explicitly denies an interest in 'narrative technique' in what for him is the narrow sense of the word. See Booth 1987, p. 74.
4. See for example Rimmon-Kenan 1983, pp. 87–8.
5. Genette first proposed his terms in *Figures of Literary Discourse (Figures II)*.
6. On 'embedding', see Prince 1988, p. 25. On *mise-en-abîme*, see Rimmon-Kenan 1983, p. 93.
7. On the confusion caused by the prefix 'meta-' in 'metadiegetic', see Rimmon-Kenan 1983, p. 140, fn. 7. In practical terms, Rimmon-Kenan is surely right to prefer Bal's term 'hypodiegetic'.
8. See for instance Riessman 1993; Powell 1993, p. 27; and Cortazzi 1993, pp. 67–74.
9. See for instance Deleuze and Guattari 1988, pp. 6–7, 21, 49, 69, 134, 158.
10. Cf. Serres 1977a, p. 25.
11. Barthes 1970. See for instance p. 96.
12. See for example Shklovsky on *Tristram Shandy* as 'the most typical novel in world literature', Shklovsky 1965, p. 57. See also Deleuze and Guattari on Beckett's *Molloy* as 'the beginning of the genre of the novel', Deleuze and Guattari 1988, p. 174.

7

Narrative and Monstrosity

THEORY AND MONSTROSITY

In the end, there is a sense in which narratology has only ever had two categories to work with. We might loosely term them the anthropological and the textual, though they have different aspects: the represented and the linguistic, the human and the material, world and structure, even signified and signifier and content and form. Whichever doublet we choose, the structure of the thought involved is always the same: we are either within a narrated, 'human world', immersed in its depth, or outside it, in a world of expressive means that is at once complementary and subordinate to the 'narrated world', and instrumental to its creation and maintenance. On the one hand, the human, on the other, the non-human: but the relationship between the two is never simply a question of either/or. The first term always has priority. In the very structure of such thought, our accounts of narrative ceaselessly confirm their own anthropocentric premises. Yet they are premises that some novelists, at least, particularly modern and postmodern ones from Musil and Woolf to Calvino and Robbe-Grillet, have actually sought to resist. Contemporary theory has frequently resisted them, too, or suggested that ours is an age in which they are collapsing. Serres, for example, has given us an account of this:

Du coup, le monde perdit son statut muet d'ensemble objectif des objets passifs de l'appropriation . . . Nous devînmes, du même coup, des objets parmi d'autres, et ceux-ci des sujets, ni plus ni moins que nous . . . Une rééquilibra-tion historique advient dans notre rapport au monde, une justice requise, dès l'aurore de notre histoire, par Anaximandre. Se ferme l'immense parenthèse de trois millénaires où les objets souffrirent de leur séparation d'avec les sujets-hommes dont le narcissisme les fit se croire d'une espèce différente, étrangère, divine, mécontente, exceptionelle, niante et méchante. (Serres 1993, pp. 102–4)

So, too, Donna Haraway has recently argued that one of the constitutive features of postmodernity is precisely the sense that there is no longer any ground 'for ontologically opposing the organic, the technical, and the textual' (Haraway 1991, p. 212). There is thus a case for experimenting with terms that will 'cut across' the commonplace anthropological structure, or gesture towards a site outside that structure, even if, in the end, it is only a phantom site. Theory has actually been putting such terms into circulation and one of them is monstrosity.

The theorists' concern with 'monstrosity' has not to my knowledge been articulated as such. Monsters in the commonplace sense loom large in theory, and so do those who have written about them: Aldrovandi in Foucault, Considérans and Buffon in Derrida's 'Force and Signification', Geoffroy Saint-Hilaire in Deleuze and Guattari's A Thousand Plateaus.[1] But such references are indices of something larger: for postmodernity, the idea of the monstrous involves a disruption of the supposed orders of nature. The monstrous is Derrida's 'species of the non-species' (Derrida 1978, p. 293), a 'transversal communication' across what Deleuze and Guattari refer to as the 'strata' (Deleuze and Guattari 1988, p. 49 and passim). Monstrosity transgresses the metaphysics underlying symbolic boundaries, the boundaries that determine all those categories and classifications that separate kinds of being off from one another. Most obviously, monstrosity repudiates what Rorty has called the 'natural cut' (Rorty 1989, p. 192): the 'bad old metaphysical notion that the universe is made up of two kinds of things', human and non-human (Rorty 1980, p. 351). In Heideggerian terms, the idea of the monstrous entails a refusal of the assumption that 'the essence of Being and the Being of being would be completely the making of the human conception' ('ein Gemächte des menschlichen Vorstellens' (Heidegger 1974, p. 63)).

The postmodern concern with monstrosity goes back to Nietzsche. For Nietzsche, of course, the Socratic choice and valuation of reason and the repudiation of Dionysian irrationalism themselves create a realm of the monstrous. Socrates himself was a self-designated foe to the *monstrum in animo* (Nietzsche 1987b, p. 33). After Socrates, anything that is radically ulterior to Socratic rationalism can only take place under the sign of the monstrous: Zarathustra (a 'Dionysian ogre' (Nietzsche 1986, p. 102)); Nietzsche's own doctrine of the infinity of interpretations (a 'monster of an unknown world' (Nietzsche 1974b, p. 336)). But monstrosity in Nietzsche should not simply be equated with Dionysianism. More largely, it is the shocking form of the new before the latter is incorporated within the human. It is also the entirely forgotten, unknown or future thought, what a given age or civilisation can only define as beyond it, as likely to threaten its very being. The monstrous has an aesthetic aspect, too. It is exemplified in the Dionysianism of German music, for example, or in the art of a Delacroix or a Wagner, both 'born enemies of logic and straight lines, constantly hankering after the strange, the exotic, the monstrous, the crooked, the self-contradictory' (Nietzsche 1974a, p. 170). In aesthetic terms, the monstrous is what lies beyond any definition of the beautiful whatsoever, and may 'secretly rouse the imagination' more than all the forms encompassed in such definitions (Nietzsche 1987a, p. 240).

It is Foucault above all who develops the Nietzschean conception of monstrosity. The Foucauldian concept of it is possibly best summed up in 'The Order of Discourse': 'there are monsters on the prowl, whose form changes with the history of knowledge' (Foucault 1981, p. 60). For Foucault, the monstrous is that which is exiled by the normative judgments within a given *episteme*. Each discipline 'recognises true and false propositions', writes Foucault, but 'pushes a whole teratology of knowledge back beyond its margins' (ibid.). The monstrous is the Other conceived of in a double that is taken for a single form. It is 'denatured', 'unnatural', 'vomited' by nature. But it is also a kind of treachery to social norms (Foucault 1991a, pp. 78, 90–1). In other words, monstrosity is epistemic illegitimacy understood as outrage in or against nature. It is what Foucault calls the 'unthought', everything that falls outside man's self-representation at any given point in knowledge. Monstrosity, then, is that savage exteriority of which Foucault writes as the very context of a truth organised and sustained by certain institutionalised, discursive rules. The organising power of discursive practices holds monstrosity at bay, wards it off as dismaying or inadmissible threat. Monstrosity, in fact – and not error – is what most menaces the will to truth, because it is radically heterogenous to and cannot be accommodated by that will. Not surprisingly, thus, Foucault associates monstrosity with writers like Nietzsche, Artaud and Bataille. For they try to tear away the mask 'true discourse' uses to disguise its will to truth, and are therefore defined as 'mad' by the guardians of truth.

For Foucault, then, monstrosity is the otherness that undermines any concept of man as unitary, knowable being. The monstrous in this sense is only a given space that is repeatedly filled, a category that is actually empty. Foucault repeatedly demonstrates that the forms of the monstrous are actually reversible as epistemic shifts take place. Thus those who so horribly execute the 'monster' Damiens are themselves considered 'monsters' by a later age (ibid. p. 57). If the monsters on the prowl constantly change their form, then the forms of knowledge are themselves continually revealing themselves to be monstrous. Foucauldian genealogy repeatedly unmasks what Foucault calls the 'exorbitant singularity' of forms of knowledge, their status as chance events. The idea of the monstrous only ever exists in relation, like the idea of madness (Foucault 1991b, p. xiii). But if this is the case, then the category of the human can only be an empty one, too. In the absence of epistemic constants, the human and the monstrous are always likely to exchange masks. Thus Foucault makes the human indistinguishable from the monstrous.[2] Indeed, he makes the idea of the monstrous *comprise* the idea of the human. For the idea of the monstrous contains in itself a sense of the contingency of any given definition of the human – the fact that it is not an ontological given, but an epistemological construct – as that definition itself does not.

In Foucault, too, there is an aesthetic dimension to the idea of monstrosity. The 'quality of monstrosity' – 'the stark impossibility of thinking *that*' – is what attracts Foucault to the 'passage in Borges', for instance, on which he reflects in the preface to *The Order of Things* (Foucault 1970, pp. xv–xvi). In modern literature – Joyce, Artaud, Roussel, Beckett – Foucault finds a kind of monstrous 'counter-discourse' where classical values, such as taste, pleasure, naturalness, truth are wilfully eschewed in favour of the ugly, the scandalous, and the impossible. For Foucault, art becomes a kind of privileged locus in which a gesture towards the monstrous is possible. For art can offer challenges, not only to the established orders of discourse, but to the very principle that underlies the fact of such 'orders'. If only fleetingly, art can at least seem to give life to the 'starkly impossible' thought. But Deleuze's aesthetic of the monstrous is still more ample than Foucault's. In the first instance, it is Deleuze who performs the relevant abstraction, not least, in his work on Foucault himself, where the human is seen as a *pli*, a fold in a substrate, a conjunction of forces and circumstances which are always composing and recomposing with others (Deleuze 1988b, pp. 114–24). As all forms are mere *pliages* in the aformal, so man is an interiorisation of an outside (ibid. p. 96). Hence what we know as the interminable hermeneutics of the self, for instance.[3] Subjectivity is a more or less transitory production, an accident that has happened to a pre-formal, pre-individual substrate. For Deleuze, there is no essential limit to the *découpages* by which we might seek to determine what is human. Hence there are other modes of individuation – other crystallisations of the outside – which produce neither man nor the subject. This is very much what Deleuze and Guattari mean by the well-known concept of the rhizome: '*des concrescences transversales, des agencements inédits . . . opérants par capture et saisissant des animaux, de la terre et du temps*' (Buydens 1990, p. 34). Such modes of individuation are thinkable as hybrids, blends, grafts. The 'strata' are never distinct, as systems of classification would like to make them. The boundaries between the species are always shifting and porous. Degrees of development are not at uniform speeds, and development is not a question of increasing perfection, but of differential relations and coefficients. There are no rules for discrimination, for separating the proper off from the improper. Inside the depths of bodies, there are only mixtures and fearful combinations (Deleuze 1990, p. 130). There is always what Leibniz called 'fluxion', pure becoming itself; for, according to Deleuze, becoming is best conceived of, not as the production of identities nor as a process of metamorphosis, but as a practice of alliance or contagion. In Deleuze, therefore, the idea of monstrosity is the very image of what he calls multiplicity. Language and logic furnish man with the illusion that he is superior to and apart from the rhizomic nature of forms. But it is only an illusion, the result of our own systems of overcoding. In Deleuze, thus, as in Foucault, we are closer to a kind of truth in the idea of the monstrous than we are in a given conception of the human. In 'The Age of the World View', Heidegger writes that it is a feature of the modern age that, in it, man becomes the existent in which all that exists is supposedly grounded in the character of its existence and its truth. Man appears to be the centre to which the existent as such is related (Heidegger 1979, p. 9). In this respect, Deleuze both resists and looks beyond modernity. Postmodernity precisely involves the thought of the monstrous. 'The thought of the outside', writes Deleuze – an outside in which the human is merely a fold – 'is a thought of resistance', since 'the outside is always an opening on to a future' (Deleuze 1988b, p. 89). The collapse of the human into the monstrous is thus profoundly political. The idea of the monstrous – the refusal to remain wedded to an image of the human as final and all-encompassing description – is an affirmation of the possibility of the new, of our no longer being the same. Monstrosity thus participates in or is an effective metaphor for what Foucault called 'the critical ontology of ourselves', involving 'a critique ... of the limits that are imposed on us and an experiment with the possibility of going beyond them' (Foucault 1991c, p. 50).

In Deleuzean aesthetics, the monstrous has nothing to do with the representable. Deleuze insists that the outside is not representable nor even thinkable in itself. It is what Heidegger calls the 'incalculable', a space withdrawn from representation, something it is denied to us to know (Heidegger 1979, p. 13). Art can nonetheless deal in the monstrous, precisely as part of a 'critical ontology of ourselves'. Deleuze sees *Moby Dick*, for example, as a masterpiece of becoming. He thinks of Kafka and Lawrence, too, as able to 'tie' their writing to 'real and unheard-of becomings', as creators of great anomalies or border forms (Deleuze and Guattari 1988, p. 243). Virginia Woolf's *The Waves* presents its characters as multiplicities, rhizomes, grafts, crossing over into each other (ibid. p. 252). Kleist and Hölderlin deal in becomings, too, in a dissolution of forms and persons in which 'an inhumanity is immediately experienced in the body [or the person] as such' (ibid. pp. 268, 272). Deleuze specifically opposes Kleist and Hölderlin, here, to Hegel, Goethe and classical aesthetics. A slightly different example is provided by Klee, who feels that visual material must now capture non-visible forces; or Varèse, who puts the sound process in contact with other elements beyond sound matter. Similarly, Deleuze writes of Francis Bacon's waiting figures as never actually waiting to act. Their waiting is just contortion. They appear as prey to forces that are germinating in and working on their own flesh (Deleuze 1981, Vol. 1, p. 29 and passim). The result is a monstrous deformation of the figure, or what Bacon himself called 'deep injury to the image' (Sylvester 1980, p. 41). Or, in the philosopher's more Bergsonian terms, Bacon also opens up our own duration to recognise and affirm the existence of other durations, above or below our own (Deleuze 1988a, pp. 31–2). Most strikingly of all, perhaps, Deleuze and Guattari suggest that, from Quixote on, the novel has always been defined by the adventures of characters who are stricken by folly or forgetting, who have lost a part of their substance, 'who no longer know their name, what they are looking for, or what they are doing, amnesiacs, ataxics, catatonics' (Deleuze and Guattari 1988, p. 173). They are mixtures, in fact, and, in their own way, equivalents of Saint-Hilaire's 'human monsters'. Thus Beckett's *Molloy* becomes, not a work exemplifying the final degeneration of the tradition, but the very paradigm of the novel as form (ibid. p. 174).

For Deleuze, then, postmodern art – or art viewed with a 'postmodern twist' – accomplishes a particular, Nietzschean project, in putting thought in immediate relation to an outside and its forces. Nonetheless, it is surely Derrida who elaborates an idea of monstrosity that is most closely connected to a particular understanding of contemporary culture. In Derrida, the idea of the monstrous is linked to and partly interchangeable with that of the unnameable. In *Of Grammatology*, for instance, it is the 'Unnameable' that glimmers through the 'crevice' that deconstruction opens up in our present 'closure', the closure of 'the age of the sign' (Derrida 1976, p. 14). In *Speech and Phenomena*, we begin to descend towards the unnameable – 'across the inherited concepts'

– in the act of deconstruction (Derrida 1973, p. 77). In *Positions*, the unnameable is a 'certain exterior' which allows us to dream that we might conceive of what the history of philosophy 'has been able to dissimulate or forbid'; something 'that *could not be presented* in the history of philosophy, and which, moreover, is *nowhere present*' (Derrida 1987b, pp. 6–7). In 'Structure, Sign and Play in the Discourse of the Human Sciences', the unnameable 'proclaims' itself in and beyond the question broached by the presently irreducible difference between the two interpretations of interpretation. In '*Différance*', the unnameable is the *diapherein* itself, beyond the Greco-Western *logos* and the history of Being, that cannot itself be properly designated, not even as *différance* (Derrida 1982, pp. 25–6). The unnameable is the possibility – only uncertainly adumbrated, since our age of the sign may 'never end' (Derrida 1976, p. 14) – of thinking otherwise.

Or rather, it is the guise in which that possibility must presently appear. At the end of 'Structure, Sign and Play', Derrida calls it the 'form of monstrosity' (Derrida 1978, p. 293). In Derrida's thought of the interim or threshold, we remain prisoners of certain modes of representation or, as he puts it in *Of Spirit*, certain dogmatisms (e.g. *subjectum*, *hypokemeinon*, 'subject, soul, consciousness, spirit, person' (Derrida 1991, pp. 16, 92)). Yet we are also drawn 'towards the more matutinal dawn of what is not yet born' (Heidegger's *das Ungeborene* (ibid. p. 91)). For the present, then, '[m]etaphysics always returns', as 'the double which can never be separated from the single' (ibid. p. 40). Or, as Derrida puts it when thinking of Levinas, 'we are obliged to think in opposition to the truisms which we believed – which we still cannot not believe – to be the very ether of our thought and language' (Derrida 1978, p. 95). It is out of this kind of doubleness that the monstrous emerges. The conditions of our thought remain those of the theological era and are determined by the essentialism and the metaphysics of the latter even after its foundations have been eroded. The form of the monstrous is the token of an ungainly paradox, an illogicality, even an absurdity, an inescapable and insoluble contradiction (as in the coexistence of the two interpretations of interpretation). The monstrous, according to Derrida, is the figure of our threshold.

An important part of what Derrida thus provides us with – more important, perhaps, in the end, than deconstruction, so easily assimilated to a familiar, technocratic conception of literary criticism[4] – is a distinctively postmodern aesthetics which is in large measure an aesthetics of the monstrous. This is arguably particularly evident in the extent to which Derrida has conveyed a sense of a monstrous dimension to the work of various modern or postmodern artists: Mallarmé, Artaud, Joyce, Valéry, Sollers, Adami and so on. In *Dissemination*, for example, Derrida writes of Mallarmé's work:

[It] *gets caught in*, but thereby disorganizes, the whole ontological machine. It dislocates all oppositions. It carries them off, impresses upon them a certain play that propagates itself through all the text's moving parts, constantly shifting them, setting them out of phase, more or less regularly, through unequal displacements, abrupt slowdowns or bursts of speed, strategic effects of insistence or ellipsis, but always inexorably. (Derrida 1981a, p. 236)

Mallarmé works from an ambivalent position that leaves him both inside and outside 'the ontological machine', 'caught in' but also disrupting its operations. Monstrosity in Mallarmé's poetry – in modern art, in postmodern aesthetics – is precisely the embodiment, the figure of that ambivalence. It emerges out of the 'inexorable dislocation' of presently inescapable terms and structures. It is the hybrid image of our current crisis.[5]

RECEPTION THEORY AND THE ANTHROPOLOGICAL DYAD

In Foucault, Deleuze and Derrida, then, the concept of monstrosity refers us to a new dimension in aesthetics. It works to undermine anthropocentrism. It takes us beyond the classical structure which opposes spirit to matter, the human to the inert, (anthropocentric) content to (linguistic or textual) form. It suggests that we might consider reading at least some of our literary texts in terms of an insoluble doubleness in which the idea of the human is actually inseparable from what it seeks to exclude. As such, the concept of monstrosity challenges various aspects of contemporary literary theory and criticism, not least narratology, and the structuralism out of which, in large measure, narratology emerged. But the concept might also be thought of as confirming and extending a process that actually begins with structuralist narratology. For what narratology achieved was not merely a decisive shift in the study of narrative in the direction of a new formalism. In its French version, at least, and in the work of the best narratologists – above all, in Barthes's work – structuralist narratology was powerfully opposed to the humanism which dominated the study of narrative before the advent of structuralism. For structuralist narratology described and analysed narrative systems as determining and producing the forms of 'the human,' rather than reflecting or expressing them. It saw 'the human' in narrative as caught up in a network of signs which actually construct it in terms of the relations and differences internal to the signifying network itself. The human became an effect of the system, rather than the reverse. Structuralist narratology thus at least 'up-ended' a traditional hierarchy. In that respect, it functioned, in a manner that is now easily forgotten, as a critical project. The trouble was that, even at its most critical, narratology could only ever substitute the linguistic for the anthropological premise, textual for represented, human space. It subverted anthropocentrism only by fleeing to its opposite. It thus lent support to the very structure of thinking that, ostensibly, it set out to question. But then, as Wallace Martin points out, structuralism itself had never really escaped anthropology:

Structuralist critics conceived the study of literature as a subdivision of the 'sciences of man' (what we would call the humanities and social sciences), and they used the most scientific of humanistic disciplines – linguistics – as the model or paradigm for the development of theories that would link literature, anthropology and sociology together. (Martin 1986, p. 23)

Even as it privileged communicative system over human agent or content, in fact, structuralist narratology reconfirmed the terms of a human depth, and converted its subject back into them, precisely by working with 'models or paradigms' supposedly endowed with the generality of 'the human' itself. As Christopher Norris was to say at the high point of the deconstructive critique of structuralist methodology, the attempt seemed ultimately to be 'to ground critical theory in an all-but-transcendental philosophy of mind' (Norris 1991, p. 15). Norris was specifically thinking of the work of Jonathan Culler. He saw Culler and Culler's kind of narratological structuralism as at the conservative end of the structuralist spectrum. Like others, Norris thought of Culler as the most striking example of the tendency 'in structuralist thought to tame and domesticate its own best insights' (ibid. p. 2). In particular, he saw Culler as 'evasive' about whether or not the 'structures' he discussed were 'unchangeably vested in the human mind' (ibid. p. 3). With hindsight, however, we can see that that ambiguity was endemic to structuralism itself and the narratology that stemmed from it. Structuralism de-humanised narrative only to re-humanise it as global phenomenon, with individual narratives open to study 'as unique realisations' of a 'general system' which might ultimately be identified with that of the human mind itself.[6]

In its established forms, narratology in the eighties remained afflicted by the double-bind I have just outlined. That very fact allowed a revisionist narratology to use the same double-bind for more frankly orthodox ends. Reception theory, too, has been caught up in the same dualism, if in rather different ways. In some of its aspects, reception theory has been quite precisely concerned to question 'a concept of classical art' deemed incapable 'of serving as a general foundation for an aesthetics of reception beyond the period of its origination, namely, that of humanism' (Jauss 1982, p. 31). Reception theory refused to construct the narrative text in the terms of traditional and structuralist narratology, as a stable, knowable object, entirely transparent to the human subject. Rather, reception theory argued that the work cannot be separated from the particular act of reading to which it gives rise, and does not exist independently of what the individual occasion makes of it (Iser 1974, p. 279). There are no 'facts' of the narrative text, according to Iser, except as we determine them for ourselves. Or, as Jauss would have it, the 'character' of the narrative text is necessarily dialogical:

A literary work is not an object that stands by itself and that offers the same view to each reader in each period. It is not a monument that monologically reveals its own timeless essence. It is much more like an orchestration that strikes ever new resonances among its readers and that frees the text from the material of the words and brings it to a contemporary existence: 'words that must, at the same time that they speak to him, create an interlocutor capable of understanding them'. (Jauss 1982, p. 21)[7]

For both Iser and Jauss, if the text has a given 'structure', it also has a virtual dimension which is only realised or 'concretised' in the individual act of reading. As Jauss says, in such a conception of the text, not only does 'the aesthetics of mimesis' lose 'its obligatory character', but so does 'the substantialist metaphysics . . . that founded it' (ibid. p. 31). And along with those losses goes another: reception theory dismantles the established, dyadic structure whereby the text is seen as material vehicle for a fixed and given human content. It might therefore seem to offer a more radical challenge than structuralism to narratological anthropocentrism.

Yet reception theory, in fact, has always remained profoundly tied to anthropology. For if reception theory dispenses with the anthropological dyad on one level, it does so only to reintroduce it on another, most often in its account of text/reader relations. This is evident enough in Ross Chambers's *Story and Situation* and *Room for Maneuver. Story and Situation* appears to offer a radical challenge to the terms of the anthropological dyad, but ultimately lapses back into them. Chambers both draws on and seeks to progress beyond a structuralism perceived as insufficient because its 'grammars' and 'rhetorics' fail to recognise how far meaning is contextual. But for Chambers, 'context' is not historical, not the author's nor the reader's. Context actually has a textual character. Chambers argues that narrative is always a transactional phenomenon, that it mediates exchanges. He thus attempts to conduct 'relatively formal [or structural] and entirely text-based studies of the apparatus – the discursive *dispositifs* – by which . . . texts designate themselves as contractual phenomena' (Chambers 1984, p. 9). In other words, he is concerned with the 'textual indices' which allow texts to identify their own 'narrative situation' (ibid. p. 10). He thus appears radically to disrupt and confuse the terms of an established opposition between inside and outside, text and 'human world'.

The critique of metaphysics implied in such a position, however, is intertwined in Chambers with another conception of the text which does not escape metaphysics at all. Chambers may

recognise the force of the structuralist and poststructuralist critique of humanist assumptions, and be critical of a narratology
that he sees as deeply rooted in a metaphysics of the human
subject. But as he himself admits, he also implicitly refers us to 'a
common-sense world in which speakers produce discourse for
hearers, as opposed to speakers and hearers being produced by
their shared discourse' (ibid. p. 21). He acknowledges that it is
only 'a long humanistic tradition' which 'predisposes us to think
of "man" as the producer of discourse and of discourse as a kind
of malleable tool available to us for whatever purpose we may
wish to bend it' (ibid.). He knows that the human is 'an *effet du
sens*, that is, a product of the symbolic order as much as the
symbolic order is a product of the human' (ibid.). But he cannot
relinquish a conception of narrative as 'one of the principal ways
by which human beings *relate*' (ibid. p. 219). Not surprisingly, he
also thinks of the significance of his project as ultimately anthropological, in that it 'suggests yet another way in which the study
of literature escapes the specialization and the technical definitions we impose on it and shades into a study of human beings'
(ibid. p. 222). In fact, then, Chambers ducks out of structuralism's
complicity with humanism only to duck back into it with a
vengeance, by virtue of the familiar, dualistic structure of anthropocentric thought. Most notably of all, he repudiates the anthropological dyad in the form of a relationship between a text and its
outside, but reintroduces it on the inside of the text itself, as a
textual phenomenon. Indeed, he reintroduces it anthropomorph-
ically: effectively, by humanising or personifying the text itself.
Chambers produces a metaphysics of the narrative relationship as
an erotic one in which authority and seduction are always the
keys and 'all narratives are necessarily seductive', even if as
'complex and varied' in their tactics 'as . . . the erotic seductions
of everyday life' (ibid. pp. 217–18). Thus, if the text is 'a
performative, discursive act' (ibid. p. 54), it is also unruly in its
seductiveness, and the reader must pacify it in translating the
'disordered subject' of the writing into the ordered object of the
reading activity – not, however, by an effort of the intellect, but
via the agency of his or her 'Rousseauesque *coeur*' (ibid. p. 30). In
the figure of this sentimental, erotic dalliance, any critique of the
metaphysics of the human subject seems very far away. Rather,

that metaphysics has actually spread – as it never does in structuralist narratology – in a manner that even further distances and diminishes the textuality of the text.

Chambers has recently extended and developed this model in *Room for Maneuver*, but in a manner that only serves further to confirm the anthropocentric logic of his project. He continues to think of the text in terms of authority (or power, as he now calls it) and seduction. In the later book, however, the reader is no longer thought of as taming the text, but rather as finding his or her desire changed in reading it. This process makes reading an oppositional practice:

reading ... brings about change because ... it produces the text as the seductive occasion for a deflection of desire, a *clinamen* resulting from what is on the reader's part an act of self-recognition, involving the emergence of a desire repressed by the codes of control. The text thus mediates a shift in the forms of desire mediated by the structures of power. (Chambers 1991, p. 235)

The structures of power are not set in abeyance, of course. But the text works seductively, above all, through irony, to shift desire from certain repressive attachments. At the same time, however, it makes of reading a discipline whose *raison d'être* must axiomatically be the production of power. Thus the changes it makes possible are always generated within a system of power even as they work against it. Chambers's case has apparently taken on an attractively deconstructive slant. But he nonetheless persists in endowing the text in its materiality with human presence, and treats reception as a relationship between beings. Chambers is as much given to anthropomorphism in *Room for Maneuver* as in *Story and Situation*. Narrative, for instance, is both ' "Court Poet" at the behest of the mighty', and enabled by that very fact to act as 'an oppositional "wild child" ' (ibid. p. 4). It is not surprising, then, to find Chambers misreading Foucault, for example, as insisting not on 'the thought of the unthought' but on the simple inexistence of any exteriority: '*il n'y a pas de hors-pouvoir*', there is no outside of power (ibid. p. xiv). In other words, what Chambers cannot think is monstrosity.

It is in Iser's development, however, that we can most clearly see the movement 'from reader response to literary anthropology', to quote the subtitle of one of his more recent books (Iser 1989). For the Iser of *The Implied Reader*, on the one hand, there was the reader, on the other, the text. But it was the work that really mattered, and it inhabited what Iser presented as effectively a new and different space to those created by a more traditional criticism, a zone between text and world which was not to be identified either with the reality of the text or with the individual disposition of the reader. It was therefore a space that might have seemed to resist or elude the structure of the anthropological dyad. This was the space of 'concretisation' itself. In this respect, however, Iser was following his mentor Ingarden. Where he differed from Ingarden, in specifically developing a theory of *narrative* reception, was in allowing the anthropological dyad a certain purchase all over again. Ingarden had suggested that no 'object' in the work was ever determinate in itself, that it was the reader who did the determining. Iser agreed that any concretisation at all must ultimately be a subjective production. But this did not mean that the reader could derive any significance whatsoever from a given text. For all the importance of ideas of 'indeterminacy' in Iser's theory, he never conceived of either indeterminacy or play as intrinsic to the very being of a given narrative text. He rather argued that the text also structured the reader's response (Iser 1974, p. 44). Hence, whilst stressing the 'inexhaustibility' of the text (ibid. p. 280), Iser also theorised it as constraining the reader into certain inevitable decisions. They were decisions that produced a coherence. For the reader was understood as engaged in a process of continual *gestalt* formation enjoined on her or him by the text. For Ingarden, the text is an infinite number of 'spots of indeterminacy' (Ingarden 1973). For Iser, indeterminacies or blanks are vacancies *in the narrative system* of a given text, spaces or boundaries (for instance) between textual segments or perspectives. They are 'gaps' in a structure that is nonetheless still there. The text is not purely and simply open to construction, *but itself constructs the terms in which it is thus open*. In Iser, thus, the space in which concretisation takes place does not so much replace the two terms of the anthropological dyad as stand midway between them. The terms themselves are weakened as a result, without the structure underlying them being thereby dissolved. This remains the case when Iser goes on to subtilise his model, positing a two-way relationship between text and reader in which the text challenges the concretisations the reader produces and forces him or her to modify them. For all the insistence that the text corrects and refines our *gestalten*, the assumption remains, not only that *gestalten* are always what narrative texts will produce, but that texts themselves are identifiable, determinate, exterior entities that have designs on the reader. Indeed, the model of communication employed here vitally depends on the premise that reader and text do not coincide.

So what Iser (in *Prospecting*) calls 'the old intrinsic-extrinsic dichotomy' insistently reappears in his own work (Iser 1989, p. vii). In *Prospecting*, however, he in actually explicitly concerned to do away with it. Iser argues that the reader's imagination – or what he now begins to call 'the imaginary' – 'cannot possibly be regarded as a separate and self-contained *materia prima*' (Iser 1989, p. 275). It is a function and never a substance, not to be marked off 'in contradistinction to reality'. It is conditioned 'by what it is supposed to transcend' (ibid.). In fact, it is inseparable from what Iser now terms 'the fictive', the medium by which it (the imagination) assumes 'a tangible *gestalt*' (ibid. p. 276). Correspondingly, Iser decentres the text, describing it as 'nothing but a collection of positions which it presents in a variety of relationships without ever formulating the focal point at which they converge' (ibid. p. 16). But he 'formulates' that 'focal point' himself as the reader, conceived – for all the text's challenges to his or her concretisations – as a whole subject. Indeed, Iser now suggests that there is a fundamental and apparently unchanging coherence to the reader which is what makes it possible for him or her to 'build up the pattern of the text' (ibid. p. 17). *Prospecting* thus falls back on the very metaphysics of the reader as subject that it also seeks to move beyond. Indeed, it is required to do so: for, in *Prospecting*, Iser announces that he is concerned to turn his theory precisely in the direction of a 'literary anthropology'. This latter is designed to ascertain 'what literature may tell us about our anthropological makeup' (ibid. p. vii), and open up 'insights' into 'the working of the human mind' (ibid. p. 6). The heuristics of literary anthropology are not simple. Narrative texts may help us to learn more about 'the anthropological makeup of humankind' (ibid. p. 269). But there would appear to be no anthropological

constants, save the need for the fictive itself. If, then, the 'mirroring relation' established by narrative texts whereby they reflect
readers back to themselves 'enables us to concentrate our atten-
tions on the nature of our human resources', literary anthropology
will not subject those resources 'to any premature definition', but
simply explore them in all their 'multifarious forms' (ibid. p. 278).
At the same time, however, it will undertake no less grandiose a
project than a diagnosis of the 'human condition' (ibid. p. 279),
along with a description of 'the nature of the human faculties'
(ibid. p. 280).

In a sense, for Iser in *Prospecting*, the 'process of self-reflection'
triggered off by narrative texts seems to hold out two alternating
prospects: a baffling wilderness of multiple views in which the
anthropological dyad threatens to dissolve, and a vision of
essences in which it is majestically sustained. So, too, in the
recent *The Fictive and the Imaginary*, even as he seeks further to
break down the dividing line between 'intrinsic' and 'extrinsic',
Iser repeatedly resorts to it. If literature is still being conceived of
as a 'mirror', here, it is now as a mirror of 'human plasticity' itself,
one which invalidates all anthropological axioms (Iser 1993, p.
xi). The fictive and the imaginary 'cannot be determined trans-
cendentally', Iser says (ibid. p. xiv). They are not to be thought of
in terms of essences at all. They are thus not essentially distinct,
and literature *is* their 'paradigmatic interplay' (ibid.). Hence a new
insistence on what Iser calls 'boundary-crossing' as a feature of
reception: the extent to which, in simultaneously disrupting and
doubling the referential domain, the fictive 'makes inroads' into
the 'existing versions of the world' that are those of the context-
bound imaginary. Unlike the mind of the *gestalt*-forming reader of
Prospecting, the imaginary of the latest book is only ever a
featureless potential, never self-activating, always awaiting the
fictive to bring it into play (ibid. pp. xvi–xvii). It 'can never be
defined as a "whole" ' (ibid. p. 223), but only perceived in the
forms it is compelled to take on by the spaces of play opened up
for it by the fictive. Yet, at the same time, human beings apparently share an 'urge . . . to become present to themselves', an urge
which is 'inveterate', even if it can never issue 'into a definitive
shape' (ibid. p. xi). It is this urge that literature indicates. Of
course, we 'can never be fully present to ourselves' (ibid. p. 236).

But our 'continual self-unfolding . . . through a constant alternation of composing and decomposing fabricated worlds' is precisely what is both brought about and illuminated as the fictive
mobilises the imaginary. It is enactment, then, in the terms of *The
Fictive and the Imaginary* – concretisation out of the possibilities
of the fictive – that may itself be considered the 'transcendental
condition' (ibid.). But it is precisely in enactment, as literature,
above all, makes it perceptible, that we grasp ourselves, and grasp
ourselves as something other than the world beyond us, including
the narrative text that made a particular enactment possible. Thus
Iser is not only substantially concerned to bring into focus 'the
anthropological equipment of human beings' (ibid. p. xi). He is
also still intent on closing down the most troublesome doubts
about whether that equipment can finally be separated at all from
the world with which it seeks to grapple.

In the end, Iser is betrayed by what Vattimo sees as classical
grandiosity. For all the more adventurous aspects of his theory of
narrative, he remains attached to the 'grandiose nature' of concepts inherited 'from the aesthetics developed within the metaphysical tradition', in Vattimo's phrase (Vattimo 1988, p. 60). But
as Vattimo suggests, a gulf yawns ever wider between that
'grandiose conceptual language' and contemporary aesthetic
experience. Part of what limits Iser's theoretical position might be
expressed as a lack of what, in 'The Origin of the Work of Art',
Heidegger calls the idea of the work as a *Herstellung* (production)
of the earth, as well as an *Aufstellung* (exhibition) of a world
(Heidegger 1971, pp. 15–89).[8] For Heidegger, says Vattimo, 'the
earth is the dimension which in the work connects the world as a
system of discrete and unfolded meanings to its "other", the
physis', to the processes of birth, growth and death (Vattimo 1988,
p. 63). 'The earth' is what *temporalises* the work, depriving it of
what traditional aesthetics deemed to be its 'necessarily eternal
form' and its supposed connection, 'at a deeper level', with 'Being
as permanence, grandeur, force' (ibid.). The work is tied to the
earth, and therefore always subject to change, transformation,
decay, decline, death. The idea of the monstrous suggests that we
might see more art as Deleuze sees Bacon, as *Aufstellung* constantly traversed by *physis* or becoming, placed in relation to an
exteriority, in a coupling of 'human' and 'inhuman'. But the sense

of the work of art as *Herstellung* and *Aufstellung* together that is captured in the idea of monstrosity is denied in the hypostasising thought of structuralism and reception theory alike, and the anthropological dualism intrinsic to both.

'Virtual Realism', Cyberfeminism

How would it be possible to conceive of narrative in terms of monstrosity? In the first instance, monstrosity has been looming large in postmodern narrative. From Grass's *The Tin Drum* to William Gibson's *Neuromancer* to Süskind's monstrous assault on Enlightenment values in *Perfume*; from *Predator* and *Nightmare on Elm Street* to Ridley Scott's *Alien* and David Cronenberg's and John Carpenter's films; from David Lynch's *Eraserhead* and *The Elephant Man* to techno-fabulism (*Terminator, Terminator II*) to contemporary Japanese cyberpunk film (*Tetsuo, Tetsuo II: Body Hammer*) and science fiction animation or film *manga* (*Akira, Appleseed*); the monstrous has recurred more and more frequently as a sign of our times and a foreboding of the future. Most conspicuously of all, perhaps, it has recently left its mark on computer-generated and virtual reality narratives. Right from the start – from Ivan Sutherland's announcement of 'the ultimate display' – virtual reality has been associated with the power of reinventing physicality (Sutherland 1965, pp. 506–8). Virtual reality is an elastic reality, in which physical being can be monstrously stretched. It offers a world with no apparent final determinations in which new combinations are made possible. It thus offers the possibility of experimentation with forms beyond material and biological constraints. Virtual reality appears to produce a kind of literalisation of anti-essentialist thought at precisely those limits where the latter is commonly most powerfully challenged. As Háyward and Wollen put it, 'digital technologies' are starting to 'spawn hybrid forms of protean capabilities' (Hayward and Wollen 1993, p. 4). Virtual reality 'represents a kind of extension and re-mapping of the body, a de-naturing of its organic, holistic nature and a reconstruction of it . . . as digital cyborg' (ibid. p. 170). It offers the possibility of creating forms from a different or a purely imaginary evolutionary time-frame. Narratives by 'virtual realists', relying as they do on narration by stochastic process, are therefore often very much involved in the production of monstrosity.

Moreover, as Hayward and Wollen point out, 'virtual reality, an audio-visual-haptic medium *par excellence*, is not so much a closed text as a responsive environment in which sensors react to movement and gesture by changing the sounds and images within the programme' (ibid. p. 6). As 'virtual realists' repeatedly emphasise, in virtual reality, there is no clear boundary between the matter controlled by the computer and the material of the observer. For the virtual realists, in fact, this is precisely 'what cyberspace is about', because 'their technology offers the possibility of a union between users and their virtual doppelgängers – a true state of human-machine "symbiosis"' (Woolley 1993, p. 149). Body and computer and thus narrative and its interacting creator/receiver are collapsed into each other. There are monstrous leakages between the human and non-human. We catch a glimpse of what is indeed a Deleuzean 'border form', a postmodern post-identity and post-self created in art in which the anthropological dyad is surpassed and rendered obsolete, and the structures of difference are escaped. Equally, narratives of the kind found in computer-generated work like Robert Meek's *Proteus* or Karl Sims's *Liquid Selves* are not to be brought back to the anthropomorphic tale. Rather, they defy the terms of that tale. They might even be thought of as gesturing towards an as yet unnameable world in which those terms will be redundant.

But many of the most significant contemporary narrative uses of monstrosity are in recent feminist writing, especially feminist science fiction. There has been a correspondingly powerful theorisation of the monstrous, too, in the work of cyberfeminists like Sadie Plant and, above all, Donna Haraway.[9] For Haraway, some of the most crucial ideological struggles are currently taking place around the question of the reinvention of nature. It is in this context and according to what Haraway calls a postmodernist, non-naturalist mode of thought that a 'cyborg feminism' offers important possible strategies. It insists on the redemption of

odd boundary creatures – simians, cyborgs and women – all of which have had a destabilizing place in the great Western evolutionary, technological and biological narratives. These boundary creatures are, literally, *monsters*, a word that shares more than its root with the word, to *demonstrate*. Monsters signify. (Haraway 1991, p. 2)

But not only that:

Monsters have always defined the limits of community in Western imaginations. The Centaurs and the Amazons of ancient Greece established the limits of the centred polis of the Greek male human by their disruption of marriage and boundary pollutions of the warrior with animality and woman. Unseparated twins and hermaphrodites were the confused material in early modern France who grounded discourse on the natural and supernatural, medical and legal, portents and diseases – all crucial to establishing modern identity. The evolutionary and behavioural sciences of monkeys and apes have marked the multiple boundaries of late twentieth-century industrial identities. Cyborg monsters in feminist science fiction define quite different political possibilities and limits from those proposed by the mundane fiction of Man and Woman. (ibid. p. 180)

For Haraway, the thought of the monstrous reflects the current destabilisation of 'the symbolic privilege of the hierarchised, localized, organic body' and its replacement by a sense of the body as 'a highly mobile field of strategic differences' (ibid. p. 211). The idea of monstrosity is a means to coming 'to linguistic terms with the non-representability, historical contingency, artefactuality, and yet spontaneity, necessity, fragility and stunning profusions of "nature" ' (ibid.). Monstrosity can therefore help us reconfigure the kind of persons we might be or become. On one level, the image of the monstrous is testimony to the very fabric of postmodern life, in which we are all becoming chimeras, 'theorized and fabricated hybrids of machine and organism' (ibid. p. 150). On the political-epistemological terrain of postmodernism, moreover, the boundaries, not only of Rorty's 'natural cut' or of the 'technological determination' separating natural and artificial, but also between the physical and the non-physical themselves are now equally dissolving. For Haraway, an infinite variety of new interfaces now appears on the horizon. A progressive politics must thus necessarily be partly microelectronic and biotechnological. But it must also be linked to questions of the transgression of boundaries and the potency of fusions. It is possibly thus that we can begin to learn 'how not to be Man, the embodiment of the Western logos' (ibid. p. 173).

It is exactly here, too, that cyborg authors subvert some of the principal myths of Western culture and question the structure and modes of reproduction of Western identity. Anne McCaffrey's *The Ship Who Sang*, for instance, explores the consciousness of a cyborg hybrid of girl's brain and complex machinery. Joanna Russ's *The Female Man* is the story of four versions of one genotype, all of whom meet. James Tiptree Jr tells tales of reproduction based on non-mammalian technologies. In Octavia Butler's *Clay's Ark*, an extra-terrestrial disease changes human beings at the level of their most basic selves. In general, as Mária Brewer says, Butler repeatedly invents 'an alternate fictional world in which the other (gender, race, species) is no longer subordinated to the same' (Brewer 1987, p. 45). The result is 'an ontology based on mutation, metamorphosis and the diaspora' (Haraway 1991, p. 226). So, too, as Jenny Wolmark says, Gwyneth Jones's science fiction 'undermines the essentialism of the binary division between human and alien, self and other' (Wolmark 1993, p. 51). Pat Cadigan's fiction explores the human-machine interface, the ambiguous relation of what *Synners* refers to as 'the synthesizing human and the synthesized human' (Cadigan 1991, p. 386). And novelists like Marge Piercy and Elisabeth Vonarburg use the figure of the cyborg to examine the unstable boundaries between the real and the simulated, the human and the cyber-netic. What is so important in all such writing, according to Haraway, is that 'difference is theorized *biologically* as situational, not intrinsic, at every level from gene to foraging pattern, thereby fundamentally changing the biological politics of the body' (Har-away 1991, p. 200). The point, then, is not the emergence of a new 'truth' of the body in the image of monstrosity, but the latter's power as a critical repudiation of all assumption of essence. For Haraway, the cyberfeminists and feminist writers of science fiction narrative, this is especially the case with regard to the assumption of an essence of gender. But their arguments also turn back everywhere against the assumptions of fixity that are intrin-sic to the anthropological dyad.

The concept of monstrosity, then, offers a vitally important entry into various practices evident in contemporary narrative. But what of the place and significance of monstrosity in older narrative traditions? From Menippean satire to *Gargantua and*

Pantagruel and *Gulliver's Travels*, to *Frankenstein, Dracula*, the Gothic and Poe, to *The Temptation of St Anthony* and *The Island of Doctor Moreau* to Pynchon and Burroughs, monstrous forms have stalked through our fiction. Yet monstrosity in our narratives has been repeatedly humanised, given human shape and human purpose, made instrumental to human ends. In fact, its very prominence radically questions the assumed centrality to the traditions of Western narrative of a known, familiar, recognisable humanity, with features deemed to be constant. To isolate and emphasise monstrosity in narrative might mean tracing, foregrounding, opening up the fissures between the many, various and contradictory understandings of 'the human' in the Western narrative tradition. It would constitute a refusal too readily to conflate all our multifarious narrative 'worlds' and reduce them to our own terms. The result would necessarily be a Foucauldian exchange between or blurring of the distinct categories of the monstrous and the human. Narrative has repeatedly measured men and women in new and monstrous terms. Dostoevsky, for instance, offers us worlds of an extraordinary and quite unassimilable monstrosity, whose power and indeed 'truth' lies, not in their communication of some essence of 'the human', but in their unforeseeable, unrepeatable and radical contingency. From Defoe's 'souls just emerging from the animal kingdom', as Joyce referred to them (Joyce 1964, Vol. 1, no. 1, p. 23), to Richardson's demented, incredible letter-writers, to Balzac's and Dickens's volcanically energised grotesques, to Gogol's hyperbolically vacuous non-entities, the classical novel has insistently plunged into the realm of the monstrous in all its 'exorbitant singularity', to use Foucault's words, again. It remains for a postmodern criticism free of disablingly grandiose, humanist presuppositions to bring that monstrosity to light.

AESTHETICS OF MONSTROSITY: BECKETT'S *TRILOGY*

But such a criticism might be even more concerned with an aesthetics of monstrosity. If art can gesture towards the 'starkly impossible', Foucauldian thought of a monstrous exteriority which is also a 'critical ontology of ourselves', how does narrative do so? If we strip away the assumptions that confine our perceptions of our narratives to the plane of the feasible, the 'humanly plausible', the logically consistent, what emerges in the wake of such an activity? How might we theorise at least some received narratives as compound forms or 'rhizomes' which confuse rather than confirm the terms of the anthropological dyad? One response would be to theorise creatively around the issue of 'bad' form and its relation to a critique of representationalism. Lyotard, for instance, has suggested that one of his crucial concerns has always been to preserve 'the unharmonizable' (Lyotard 1991, p. 4). Hence his early attack on Dufrenne's aesthetics of reconciliation, harmony and good form (Lyotard 1985, pp. 291–5). The unrepresentable – exteriority – will leave its traces in art precisely in the shape of the unharmonised: in unfinished or unformed or 'bad' forms, as the *deformation* of form. This for Lyotard is the world of the major avant-garde, Klee's *Zwischenwelt* or *Nebenwelt*. It shows us 'the invisibility in the visual' (Lyotard 1991a, p. 126), the non-discursive in the discursive, and so on. It shows them to us precisely through what Lyotard calls *'la découverte et la culture de la force critique (ironique) de la déformation'* (Lyotard 1985, p. 225). As far as narrative is concerned, we might think in terms of what Lyotard calls anamorphosis (ibid. p. 70): the production in narrative discourse of the monstrous through the distorting force of something entirely outside the discursive order itself. Classical narratology, however, has had no terms for such a practice, or been able only to consider it in terms which negate it from the outset. One function of a postmodern theory of narrative would thus be to register such elements of monstrous deformation in narrative and to explore their implications. My example will be Beckett's *Trilogy*.

Beckett himself was partly engaged in developing an aesthetic of monstrosity.[10] His reading of Proust, for example, offers a radically abstract Proust whose sense of the complex extent and reaches of time within human being is so powerful that it overwhelms his sense of human existence as bodies, of the human dimension in space. Hence Beckett's interest in a passage in the *Recherche* where Marcel declares his willingness to privilege time over space, 'even at the risk of giving' men 'the appearance of monstrous beings' (Beckett 1931, p. 2). For Beckett, that is partly the inevitable consequence of the Proustian break with habit. A monstrous heterogeneity is what begins to loom on the far side of the petrified structures of classical and everyday cognition. Thus, according to Proust, '[a] being scattered in space and time is no longer a woman but a series of events on which we can throw no light' (ibid. p. 41). This is one version of what Derrida calls the 'neutralisation of every metaphysical and speculative thesis as concerns the unity of the anthropos' (Derrida 1982, p. 115). Hence too Beckett's insistence on both the multiplicity of time in Proust, and its deforming power. Multiplicity, indeed, is in large measure the key to Proustian monstrosity, as far as Beckett is concerned: the immanent multiplicity, for example, that turns Albertine from 'a human banality into a many-headed goddess' (Beckett 1931, p. 34). This is not to be understood simply as a multiplicity of selves. The problem has partly to do with the multiplicity of the object of desire, as when, for Marcel, 'Albertine and the sea together' form a monstrous 'amalgam of human and marine' (ibid. pp. 33–4). In Beckett's version of him, the Proust so immensely contemptuous of realism sets out to replace it with an art of what Beckett calls 'fabulous creatures' (ibid. p. 61), in which there is constant assimilation, exchange, Deleuze's 'practice of alliance or contagion', of subject and object by each other (ibid. pp. 20, 37), of experience by 'elements' that are logically unrelated to it (ibid. p. 55) and so on. Proust's is an art – as the *Disjecta* essay claims – of *mésalliance*, a weird blend of incongruous elements, of 'cathexes not only multivalent but interchangeable' (Beckett 1983, p. 92). It resembles Geer van Velde's art, too, with its '*équilibres qu'un rien doit rompre, qui se rompent et se reforment à mesure qu'on regarde*' (ibid. p. 128). Here precisely, says Beckett, is an art given over to the outside, in which time prevents us from seeing the things in which alone, nonetheless, it can be apprehended; an art in which the invisibility of the object is turned into an object itself (ibid. p. 130). Here and in Bram van Velde we have Lyotard's unfinished, unformed or 'bad' forms – '*irraisonné*', '*ingénue*', '*non-combiné*', '*mal-léché*' (ibid. p. 127). The van Veldes offer what Beckett himself calls '*une peinture à déformation*' (ibid. p. 121). It draws the human up into its process, rather than being dominated by the human. It refuses to be burdened and blackened by what Beckett ironically calls '*la seule vie qui compte, celle des bipèdes sans plumes*' (ibid. p. 119).

Beckett also invented monstrosities in his prose works, as in the case of *Watt*, for instance, and Watt's 'funambulistic stagger' in particular (Beckett 1963, pp. 28–9). He refuses the terms of the 'natural cut'. It is as though he were not merely relativising the dimensions of the human, but working into his representations of the human that surrounding context of the inhuman which an anthropocentric and humanistic ontology excludes or annihilates. Indeed, 'the whole fabric comes unstitched, it goes *ungebund*'. Beckett engineers a 'slump in the human solid', 'discerns the principle of disintegration in even the most complacent solidities, and activates it to their explosion' (Beckett 1983, pp. 45, 86). But Beckett is also much concerned to produce texts that are themselves discursive monstrosities, with incommensurable elements, for example, or strange and alien growths. In Beckett's work, as in Proust's, there is a monstrous departure from a Balzacian 'sweet reasonableness' in the 'narrative trajectory' of the work: a departure evident in the 'perturbations and dislocations' of the text, its 'grave dissonances and incompatibilities, clashing styles', 'deplorable solutions in continuity', 'discord and dissension', awkward doublenesses, 'indeterminates' and 'inconsequences' (ibid. pp. 63–4). If Proust's is an art of *mésalliance*, so too is the younger Beckett's, with its bizarre combinations, for example, of erudite meticulousness and slack indifference; knowledge and ignorance; haste and slowness; the grandiose, lyrical, base and comic; incongrous perspectives, incongruous narrative logics, and so on. This discourse is characterised precisely by the 'errancy' Derrida associates with monstrosity in *The Truth in Painting* (Derrida 1987, pp. 108–9), the kind of 'hyperbole' that Derrida describes as 'a project of exceeding every finite and determined totality' and pointing towards 'the unforeseeable "resistant to all categories" ' (Derrida 1978, pp. 60, 95). In Beckett, then we find that play that Derrida sees as propagating itself 'through all the text's moving parts' in Mallarmé, and disorganising the 'ontological machine'.

The discursive 'play' in question in the *Trilogy* can be described in the terms of the Foucauldian, Deleuzean or Derridean conceptions of the monstrous. To theorise *Molloy* in Foucauldian terms, for example, is to become aware of the extent to which it deals in a monstrosity of the body. For if the monstrous is set beyond the borders of a given *episteme*, in Foucault's later work, it is thus also what is unacceptable within the horizons of a particular 'anatomo-' or 'bio-politics' or 'regimen'.[11] For the later Foucault, of course, the codification of the body takes place according to a given 'epistemologico-juridical formation' which is assumed to be 'the very principle . . . of the knowledge of man' (Foucault 1991, p. 23), a 'knowledge and . . . mastery' which 'constitute what might be called a political technology of the body' (ibid. p. 26). This latter is the product of a given 'apparatus of knowledge' (ibid. p. 126) or 'regime of discourses' (Foucault 1990a, p. 27) which knows what it means when it designates a particular individual as 'a kind of biological danger to others' (ibid. p. 138). Such an apparatus of knowledge will have its 'anatomico-metaphysical register' according to which bodies are 'manipulated' and 'trained', 'shaped and maintained', but which also 'traces the limit that will define difference in relation to all other differences, the external frontier of the abnormal' (Foucault 1992, p. 163; Foucault 1991a, pp. 136, 183). On the far side of the world of the acceptable or manageable body as determined by a given *techne tou biou*, however, there is necessarily also a realm of physical monstrosity to which belongs the inadmissibility, even the horror or disaster of the aberrant body. This zone is the bodily equivalent – even the bodily representation – of epistemic illegitimacy.

Molloy offers a clear example of a postmodern form of narrative that has sought to resist the conception of the body produced by a modern or contemporary 'anatomo-politics'. In the first instance, *Molloy* is concerned with cripples or the process of becoming crippled, and finds value in both. But if the cripple is marginalised by a given 'anatomo-politics', he or she is nonetheless defined by and apprehensible in its terms. More important, here, is the extent to which Beckett's treatment of physical damage and deterioration is hyperbolic or 'unreal'. Both Molloy and Moran deteriorate, for instance, with a comically unnatural speed. An element of excess is everywhere in the treatment of the body. Moran and Molloy always seem likely to develop monstrous features or dimensions, as though their bodies are the products of 'a failed act of birth', to use Leslie Hill's terms (Hill 1990, p. 119). Molloy frequently stresses the 'extraordinary' enormity of his body, his 'great big Adam's apple', for instance (Beckett 1979, pp. 45, 23). At various different moments, he informs us that he can produce 315 farts in nineteen hours (ibid. p. 29); that he appears to have more than the usual number of testicles, which dangle 'at mid-thigh at the end of a meagre cord' (ibid. p. 34); that his knees are 'enormous' (ibid. p. 57); and that he has bristled with boils ever since he was a brat (ibid. p. 75). Indeed, he is partly or intermittently imaginable as a monster, so when Moran finally does imagine him in frankly monstrous terms – 'massive and hulking, to the point of misshapenness', 'his whole body a vociferation', etc. (ibid. p. 104) – the passage seems less like an outrageously ironic misrepresentation of Molloy than an elabora-tion of a certain nonsensical or monstrous 'implausibility' that has been that of Molloy's body from the start. Part of Moran's story would seem to have to do with losing the comfortable security of a precisely defined and circumscribed body and starting to conceive of his own physicality as much more akin to Molloy's in its monstrous possibilities. Indeed, Moran, towards the end, bent double, advancing with roars 'of triumph and distress' (ibid. p. 153), clearly resembles his own earlier fantasy of a monstrous Molloy.

But *Molloy* also takes us further than mere resistance to a specific 'anatomo-politics'. If it is 'haunted and possessed by chimeras' (ibid. p. 105), that is because it strains at 'the limits of the calculable' body itself as that body is known to '*homo mensura*' (ibid. pp. 105, 59). By implication, *Molloy* resists the stable structure of any given 'anatomo-politics' at all, in setting before us the 'image' of a non-unifiable or non-composable body in which there is always the possibility of a certain rebellious monstrosity. In *Molloy* as elsewhere in the *Trilogy*, there is an implicit refusal of a conception of the flesh as reducible to or expressible in terms of any 'technology' whatsoever. For the presentation of the body in *Molloy* is also caught up in and affected by the aporetic nature of Beckett's narrative discourse. In *Molloy*, the body is afflicted with indeterminacy. Molloy gets to his knees, for example (or almost says he does) when he has already told us that it is physically impossible for him (ibid. p. 28). When he wakes up in Lousse's house, he tells us that he tries door and window and switches on the light before he remembers that he ought to be using his crutches (ibid. p. 36). And so on. This, one might argue, is partly Beckett's drastic way of communicating what he calls the 'instability' of that 'fugitive thing, still living flesh' (ibid. p. 12). But physical indeterminacy in *Molloy* also has another, more radical aspect. For Molloy plays with the idea that he may possibly be dead already, that he has 'ceased to live' (ibid. p. 25). In effect, he suggests that he exists in and speaks from some liminal zone or hinterland, a kind of *Zwischenwelt* of the body. For Molloy, there are degrees of being dead. One may or may not be dead 'enough to bury', for instance (ibid. p. 9). There is no vocabulary or set of categories adequate to this zone:

My life, my life, now I speak of it as something over, now as of a joke which still goes on, and it is neither, for at the same time it is over and it goes on, and is there any tense for that? (ibid. p. 35)

This strange, equivocal place exists beyond the terms of that 'anthropology' which Molloy ironically praises for 'its inexhaustible faculty of negation, its relentless definition of man . . . in terms of what he is not' (ibid. p. 38). In contradistinction to all 'technologies of the flesh', it opens up a sense of the lack of all finality to discourses about the body. It exposes the unitary body to traversal by its excluded other; in a way, since, according to Molloy, 'the resources of nature are infinite apparently' (ibid. p. 42), to traversal by history. It is precisely in the figure of monstrosity that this traversal is accomplished.

The same is true of *Malone Dies*. But we may illuminate a different side of the question, here, by bringing Deleuzean terms of reference into play. In the first instance, even more than Molloy, Malone is likely to strike us as literally monstrous, as what Deleuze calls an 'anomaly' or 'border form'. He describes himself, variously, as having a monstrous head (Beckett 1979, p. 169), as of indeterminate age (ibid. p. 170), as neither washing nor getting dirty, feeling neither hot nor cold (ibid.), living in a hole (ibid. p. 179), a creature with his head almost the wrong way round (ibid. p. 182), possibly dead (ibid. p. 201), not yet born (ibid. p. 207), an 'old foetus' (ibid.), a body with feet that are 'leagues away' (ibid. p. 215), with 'extremities' so far receded that if he shat, the turds 'would fall out in Australia' (ibid.), a body that 'makes no sound' (ibid. p. 247), a 'swelling' figure who fears he will 'burst' (ibid. p.

259). It is a brave woman or man who will try to sustain strict anthropological closure in the face of that catalogue. In Deleuzean terms, Malone is a conjunction of possibilities or becomings which threaten at any moment to overflow their containing form. It is therefore hardly surprising that Malone should joke so freely and inventively about the 'natural cut', as after his 'visit':

> It was so long since I had seen a biped of this description that I had my eyes out on stalks, as the saying is, for fear of not being able to credit them. I said to myself, One of these days they'll start grazing the trees. (ibid. p. 249)

On occasions, indeed, Malone turns out to be hardly able to recognise the human race any more ('And the face they have! I had forgotten' (ibid.)). Again, the categories of the monstrous and the human constantly threaten to merge. It is hard for Malone to sustain any sense of strict distinction between interior and exterior in general, between self and world, human and inhuman. We are in the world of Deleuzean becoming, where exterior and interior are relative, and exist only through exchanges (Deleuze and Guattari 1988, p. 49), though Malone's versions of the process tend to be rather sourer than Deleuze's. ('The noises of nature, of mankind and even my own, were all jumbled together in one and the same unbridled gibberish' (Beckett 1979, p. 190).) Hence those extraordinary moments when distinctions between the animate and inanimate break down, as when what Malone calls 'the multitude' of 'faintly stirring, faintly struggling things' is made to include 'lodges' and 'gates' as well as people and children (ibid. p. 255). At times, Malone's world is merely and indiscriminately 'a sweat of things', as he puts it (ibid. p. 255). He even experiences himself in terms of an indeterminacy that is altogether more radical and absurd than its equivalent in *Molloy*. Apparently, there are times when he turns 'liquid', for example, and becomes 'like mud', and others when he 'would be lost in the eye of a needle', he is 'so hard and contracted' (Beckett 1979, p. 206). Malone is given up to a world in which, in the depths of bodies, everything is monstrous mixture, and there are no appropriate modes of discrimination.

Malone might therefore be partly understood as an instance of a new and distinctively postmodern conception of subjectivity in which there is an immanent double that is always other, always a not-self, an interiorisation of an outside, a *pli*. Hence Malone's sense of himself as a 'turmoil' in which thought struggles on (ibid. p. 171). Hence, too, what Malone calls 'the business of Malone . . . and the other' (ibid. p. 204). Malone refers repeatedly to 'the other'. It is partly Beckett himself. But it is also the other as becoming, as what Deleuze calls *'grouillement moléculaire'* and Malone the 'innumerable babble' (Beckett 1979, p. 252). Malone himself is set before us, in Deleuze's terms, as an unpredictable accident in a pre-formal and pre-individual substrate. Hence his existence as monstrous forms and compositions. He is always in production, never an essence. Effectively, Beckett forsakes organic representation for a sense of what works through and within the organic. Bergson called it the *élan vital*. Beckett's own version of it would be closer to Malone's 'chaotic conflux of oozings and torrents' (ibid. p. 255). But the reference to different speeds is important, here, since, according to Deleuze, the thought of differences in speed must be inherent in any attempt to conceptualise the multiplicity of the *élan vital*. For Bergson and Deleuze, the *élan vital* constantly changes direction, meeting new obstacles, developing new impulses, creating new and monstrous compositions. Beckett arguably translates that kind of conception of multiplicity into the narrative and aesthetic practice of *Malone Dies*. If, as Deleuze suggests, writing itself constantly involves monstrous becomings and unnatural participations (Deleuze and Guattari 1988, p. 240), then *Malone Dies* might be thought of as exemplifying this in its very narrative unevenness, its unpredictable shifts and variations, its fluctuations in narrative pace, its bizarre changes in narrative mode and register. A sort of narrative multiplicity or waxing and waning is evident everywhere. The narrative itself keeps on developing curious and peculiar growths, like a monster's body. This necessarily makes for incompleteness, breakdown, amnesia, disconnection, constant lapses into 'shapelessness' (Beckett 1979, p. 166). Form repeatedly cedes, gives way to what it can no longer encompass, what must therefore continually deform and threaten to break through it. As in Bacon, according to Deleuze, there is always an imminent prospect of an *'insurrection des molécules'*. The work has the quality of *'une pierre un millième de seconde avant qu'elle ne se désagrège'* (Beckett 1983, p. 128). Like Deleuze and Bacon, Beckett seems to point towards a form of art which itself captures the deforming pressure of force on form. The result in *Malone Dies* is *narration à déformation*, narrative anamorphosis.

But *The Unnameable* constitutes perhaps the most striking example of Beckett's concern with monstrosity. We might turn to Derridean aesthetics, here, all the more effectively for Derrida's own equation of 'the unnameable' with monstrosity. Beckett's Unnameable is self-evidently not to be thought of as a properly human entity. Insofar as it can be said to have a determinate existence it is more as monster than human being – a 'monster' with a carapace, for instance, whom 'they' couldn't manage to bring to life (Beckett 1979, p. 298). The forms in which it imagines itself are more monstrous than human, or monstrous versions of the human. It is, among other things, a being whose 'two retinae' may be 'facing each other' (ibid. p. 276); 'a cylinder, a small cylinder'; 'an egg, a medium egg'; 'a big talking ball' ('but do I roll', it asks, 'in the manner of a true ball?' (ibid. p. 280)); a being of whom 'only the trunk remains (in sorry trim) . . . surmounted by the head . . . [s]tuck like a sheaf of flowers in a deep jar' (ibid. p. 300); a being who has 'lost all my members, with the exception of the one-time virile' (ibid. p. 300); a 'one-armed, one-legged wayfarer' (ibid. p. 303) and so on. It conjectures that it might not have been born at all ('the slut has yet to menstruate capable of whelping me'); and that it may after all be just a sperm ('no, the testis has yet to descend that would want any truck with me' (ibid. p. 349)).

The Unnameable clearly constitutes a peculiarly radical Beckettian refusal to subject the writing of the text to anthropological closure. Such impressions of a familiar humanity as it might seem to convey are recognisable as an incidental offspin of language itself. The monstrosity, again, is also discursive. The Unnameable's discourse is thick with bizarre exfoliations, the 'unequal displacements' Derrida finds in Mallarmé's work. Its multitudinous parts form no coherent whole. It has no purportedly central or essential elements. Instead, it repeatedly self-destructs in manifold 'yesses and noes', as a series of what the Unnameable itself calls 'supposes' that are outlandish, self-contradictory, incongruous one with another. There are the curious incidental flourishes. Thus, for instance, with, of all things, realistic detail, as when a voice suddenly turns out to be in the Rue Brancion, or 'Mahood' tells us about rubbing himself with Elliman's Embrocation. Equally, there are all the refusals to perform the conventional discursive tasks: the reluctance, as a voice puts it, simply 'to manifest' (Beckett 1979, p. 271); the delight in narrative collapse ('I don't mind failing, it's a pleasure', (ibid. p. 284)); the stark indifference to the hermeneutic and proairetic dimensions of narrative; the haughty contempt for discursive drama.

The Unnameable, then, is a discursive monstrosity that would appear to have as its 'source' some sort of unnameable quantity which cannot 'manifest' itself at all save under a sort of set of secondary aspects, a series of monstrous appearances. The Unnameable resists full humanisation, struggles against being claimed for, as and by the human. That is partly the meaning of its monstrousness. 'Getting humanised' is equated with 'losing' (ibid. p. 331). 'They' have lectured the Unnameable on man, it tells us, 'before they even began trying to assimilate me to him!' (ibid. p. 297). 'The things they have told me!', it moans:

About men, the light of day. I refused to believe them . . . They also taught me to count, even to reason. Some of this rubbish has come in handy on occasions, I don't deny it . . . I use it still, to scratch my arse with. (ibid. pp. 272–3)

It 'always liked not knowing', but they 'said it wasn't right' (ibid. p. 283). 'They' have insisted on rationality, proficiency, knowledge, identity. Accordingly, they have sought to infect the Unnameable with their thought ('all their balls about being and existing', (ibid. p. 320)) so that 'in no time I'd be a network of fistulae, bubbling with the blessed pus of reason' (ibid. p. 325). They have attempted to fill the Unnameable with their speech, their voice. The Unnameable itself has been determined to defy them. It has after all what it calls its 'inaptitude to assume any identity' (ibid. p. 303) as a weapon, its seemingly inexhaustible capacity for muddle and disintegration, its sheer stupidity: 'my inability to absorb, my genius for forgetting, are more than they reckoned with. Dear incomprehension, it's thanks to you I'll be myself, in the end' (ibid. p. 298).

As the Unnameable resists 'them', so too *The Unnameable* as monstrous discourse works as a form of resistance to humanising codes and conventions. Hence its weirdly paradoxical quality: as a finished work that refuses to become one; as representation that aspires to non-representation; as discourse whose desire for an end to speech is precisely what enables it to continue. *The Unnameable* gleefully rejects 'the spirit of method' (ibid. p. 278), revels in its own powerlessness, vaunts its own failures, refuses to add up or make sense. It is seemingly indifferent to questions of accuracy, even clarity, definition. It is even apparently indifferent to its own mode of address. Again and again, *The Unnameable* refuses to do the necessary, to compose itself into a properly human document. In this respect, it develops a subtle, ironical critique of that 'determinate anthropology' of our times in which, according to Derrida, the 'play' of 'functions (sensibility, imagination, understanding, reason)' is 'finalized under the name of man occupying a privileged place in nature' (Derrida 1987c, p. 105). The *Trilogy* rebukes the process whereby man calls himself man 'only by drawing limits excluding his other from the play of supplementarity', the other for example of 'animality, primitivism, childhood, madness, divinity' (Derrida 1976, p. 244). It calls in question those classical and metaphysical 'determinations of the proper in man' (Derrida 1982, p. 124) as they are still with us today. The *Trilogy* bears comparison with Artaud's enterprise in Derrida's account of it: it evades representation (and its negation in doubling of the represented); and it does so the better to gesture towards the non-representable origin of representation.[12] In Beckett as in Artaud and Derrida, it is 'the security of the near' – 'that is, the co-belonging and co-propriety of the name of man and the name of Being' – that begins to tremble; as, according to Derrida, it is 'trembling today'.

But only trembling. For the critique of a 'determinate anthropology' in both Derrida and the *Trilogy* is actually ironical, ambivalent. It works both from inside and outside the 'determinations', is 'caught in' but also 'disorganises' the 'ontological machine'. If the limits excluding the other from the play of supplementarity are made to waver in *The Unnameable*, they are also not cancelled out. As Mahood's voice is always 'mingled with mine' (Beckett 1979, p. 283), as the Unnameable is repeatedly both ventriloquist and doll, so its monstrosity is only perceptible as such insofar as it includes a human residue. It sometimes seems to the Unnameable that it is 'tottering under the attributes peculiar

270   TOWARDS A POSTMODERN THEORY OF NARRATIVE

to the lords of creation', after all (ibid. p. 289); that it is 'not far short of a man', or 'sufficiently a man to have hopes one day of being one' (ibid. p. 289). Correspondingly, however, if the 'rubbish' the humanisers have taught it is useful only 'on occasions which would never have arisen if they had left me in peace' (ibid. p. 273), that peace is nonetheless unavailable now. Between the Unnameable 'and the right to silence, the living rest, stretches the same old lesson, the one I once knew by heart and would not say' (ibid. p. 280). This is the wryly resigned version of a paradox[13] that Beckett expresses more aggressively in his letter of 1937 to Axel Kaun:

As we cannot eliminate language all at once, we should at least leave nothing undone that might contribute to its falling into disrepute. To bore one hole after another in it, until what lurks behind it – be it something or nothing – begins to seep through; I cannot imagine a higher goal for a writer today. (Beckett 1983, p. 17)

Either way, the point is that 'for the time being we must be satisfied with little' (ibid.). Beckett's 'time being' is Derrida's sense of our threshold. In both Derrida and the *Trilogy* as a whole, monstrosity is a token of the alterity that is beginning to make itself felt behind the familiar configurations of our thought, and to exert a distorting pressure upon their contours. Seen from a different angle, it is presentation 'under erasure [*sous rature*]' (Derrida 1976, p. 60). This is obviously an appropriate way of seeing *The Unnameable*. It is also partly appropriate to Heidegger, particularly in some of Derrida's accounts of him. One clear example of the connection would be Heidegger's practice of letting certain words stand in his texts under 'lines of erasure' ('*kreuzweise Durchstreichung*', Derrida 1991, p. 52). The practice indicates the insufficiency of the word along with the fact that we are presently constrained to use it, and is a major instance of Heideggerian avoidance, *Vermeidung*, 'saying without saying, writing without writing, using words without using them' (ibid. p. 2). The words *sous rature* take on a 'deconstructed sense', designating 'something other' which nonetheless 'resembles' the original sense and is not its opposite (ibid. p. 24). In other words, the sense of the word is monstrously but not unrecognisably deformed. Something similar takes place in the *Trilogy*. The Unnameable is by no means the opposite of a familiar conception of humanity. Rather, the degree of its divergence from that conception is undecidable. There is play in the relation between the two. Monstrosity in the *Trilogy* is the human in a 'deconstructed sense', designating 'something other' which it nonetheless resembles. The *Trilogy* offers the human *sous rature*, a kind of second-order humanity which is therefore also a kind of monstrosity.

Such a transmutation of the human is necessarily political. The Beckett of the *Trilogy* is engaged in creating a kind of Nietzschean monster between form and the formless.[14] The *Trilogy* is arguably that 'new art' of which Nietzsche dreamt (Nietzsche 1987a, p. 236), in which time-honoured categories – sense and nonsense, truth and error, appearance and reality, the human and the non-human – are no longer found in simple opposition. Deleuze has written of power as connected to the desire to see, the insistent demand for clarity. For Beckett, it is precisely in art that that demand can be resisted. If power denies or represses the obscure and the unassimilable, Beckett's art redeems them. In that respect, his art is what he claimed art has always been, 'pure interrogation, rhetorical question less the rhetoric' (Beckett 1983, p. 91). So, too, to begin to think of narrative in terms of monstrosity, to turn aside from the clarity with which narratology conceives of its objects, is precisely to resist an expression of power. Equally, if power renders chimerical all critique of a certain determinate set of representations of the body, the idea of monstrosity insists on sustaining that critique. If power needs to be protected from intrusions from an outside, which will always threaten to unmask its contingency, the thought of narrative monstrosity is an aspect of Foucault's 'critical ontology of ourselves'. Finally, if power increasingly determines interiority and individuality and seeks to attach all singularity to known and recognised identities, the thought of monstrosity is a liberating thought. It affirms the right to difference and variation, the possibility of becoming other. It reminds us that, as Nietzsche tells us, reality is always endowed with 'the luxuriance of a prodigal play and change of forms' (Lyotard 1991a, p. 46). After all, 'man is the animal *whose nature has not yet been fixed*' (Nietzsche 1974, p. 69).

Hence, finally, the political inadequacy of reception theory, too. Iser sees literature as 'making conceivable the extraordinary plasticity of human beings who, precisely because they do not seem to have a determinable nature, can expand into an almost unlimited range of culture-bound patternings' (Iser 1993, p. xviii). Yet, for Iser, these patternings are also homogenous. On one level, their homogeneity is ensured by the idea of the *gestalt*, on another, by the continual resort to the reassuring thought of certain basic constants: 'the urge of human beings to become present to themselves', 'the human need for fictions', and so forth (ibid. p. xiv). Iser cannot see the reception of narrative as drawing the reader forwards towards the new, into strange, unfamiliar and monstrous compounds. He is rather inclined to a view of it as pushing the reader backwards into a particular perception of what is already known. It may be a reflective or a critical perception. But it is nonetheless concentrated on the already given. It is not even required to 'abandon' the 'natural attitudes', since, whilst they are 'bracketed off' in reading, they are also kept 'as a kind of background or testing ground' (ibid. p. 229). Because Iser's thought remains caught in the structure of the anthropological dyad – even when apparently progressing beyond it – it cannot envisage the possibility of the reader of narrative being traversed by or drawn towards an outside, as Nietzsche saw Sterne as conferring something of his own 'suppleness' of form upon his reader (Nietzsche 1987a, p. 239). The appropriate contrast to Iser, here, might be Foucault's effort 'to free thought from what it silently thinks, and so enable it to think differently' (Foucault 1992, p. 9). What interested Foucault was a philosophy which not only brought a 'critical work' to bear on itself, but also explored 'what might be changed, in its own thought, through the practice of a knowledge that is foreign to it' (ibid.). It is precisely that practice of a foreign within a familiar knowledge that is enjoined by the thought of narrative monstrosity. The thought of narrative monstrosity also implies a reader involved – like Foucault's 'knower' – in 'straying afield of himself'. He or she would be endowed, not with the 'curiosity' that merely 'seeks to assimilate' (or even reflect back on) 'what it is proper for one to know', but with that curiosity 'which enables one to get free of oneself' (ibid.

p. 8). It was precisely that kind of reader Nietzsche wanted: 'a monster of courage and curiosity . . . something supple, cunning, cautious, a born adventurer and discoverer' (Nietzsche 1987b, p. 73). It is in the idea of monstrosity that we may start to grasp how far certain narratives ask us to become creatures of this kind.

NOTES

1. See Foucault 1970, pp. 17–45, passim; Derrida 1978, p. 20; and Deleuze and Guattari 1988, p. 45ff.

2. However, it would also seem that, for Foucault, it is partly specifically our time that has collapsed the distinction between the two. See Foucault 1991, p. 13.

3. Mireille Buydens argues that Deleuze sees subjectivity as always involved in an interminable hermeneutics of self. See Buydens 1990, p. 34.

4. Derrida himself has minimised the importance of the word 'deconstruction': 'I had the impression that it was a word among many others, a secondary word in the text which would fade or which in any case would assume a non-dominant place in a system'. See Derrida 1985, p. 86.

5. Not surprisingly, Derrida's own writing has increasingly seemed to take on a monstrous dimension, notably in that bizarre and extraordinary hybrid, The Post Card.

6. The phrases quoted here are from another classic of established narratology, Slomith Rimmon-Kenan's Narrative Fiction: Contemporary Poetics, Rimmon-Kenan 1983, p. 4.

7. Jauss is quoting from Gaetan Picon, Introduction à une Esthétique de la Littérature (Paris, 1953).

8. My argument here derives from one aspect of Vattimo's account of Heidegger's essay. See Vattimo 1988, pp. 61–4.

9. For an earlier example in feminist thought not connected with cyberfeminism, see Wittig 1973, passim.

10. Beckett had a pronounced interest in literal monstrosity. See Leisure, 'Murphy, or the Beginning of an Aesthetic of Monstrosity', in Morot-Sir, Harper and McMillan III 1976, pp. 189–201.

11. For an understanding of what Foucault means by 'anatomo-politics' and 'bio-politics', see Foucault 1990a, p. 139. On the idea of the 'regimen' in Ancient Greek culture, see the discussion of enkrateia in Foucault 1992, pp. 63–77, though the term 'regimen' itself is not used here; and the chapter on dietetics, pp. 115–39. On 'regimens' in Roman culture, see Foucault 1990b, pp. 39–68.

12. See Derrida 1978, pp. 232–50, especially p. 234.
13. For a different view of the paradox, see Thiher 1983, pp. 80–90, 86.
15. For an account of such a 'monster', see Nietzsche's account of *Tristram Shandy*, Nietzsche 1987a, pp. 238–9.

Appendix

INTERACTIVE FICTION, SPACE, EVENT

Neither interactive fiction nor current accounts of it can simply be reduced to an establishment or confirmation of geometrical models. Greg Costikyan, for example, has recently argued that interactive fictions are not stories and are inherently non-linear (Costikyan 1994, p. 23). Some distinctions are worth making: the much-praised and highly rated recent LucasArts adventures, for instance (*Day of the Tentacle*, *Secret of Monkey Island 2*, *Indiana Jones and the Fate of Atlantis*) are less linear than the cruder Sierra games like the *Space Quest* adventures. Nonetheless, whilst there may be a linear default path through such IF – a clear, sequential plot – that plot is not the essence of the narrative in question. Rather, it is simply one among myriad possibilities, a Platonic ideal of the narrative line which is never that of the actual narrative as it emerges under the user's control. Narrative or the experience of narrative – for with IF, the two become inseparable – involve a species of what Serres calls *errance* and what the producers of IF call *browsing* in narrative environments, exploring different avenues leading in different directions, encountering frustrations and blocks to forward progress. As Costikyan suggests, then, the concepts appropriate to traditional narrative are finally inappropriate to interactive fiction, because the narrative line has vanished, disintegrated, become merely one of a number of operable logics. But if the narrative line has gone, then so, too, has the geometry of narrative space beloved of narrative theory. For the narrative line is the foundation of that geometry.

So models other than the standard geometrical ones are required for interactive fiction. For all their intermittent resorts to geometrics, the programmers and theorists of IF have themselves been producing some very different models. David Graves writes of 'decision trees', for instance (Graves 1991, pp. 10–12). Phil Goetz introduces the concept of the 'maze of links' (Goetz 1994, p. 100). Goetz draws parallels between IF and Cortázar's *Hopscotch* or IF and Borges's work, particularly 'The Garden of Forking Paths'. Costikyan suggests a parallel with Cage, where 'the designer provides the theme, the players the music' (Costikyan 1994, p. 24). In *Hamlet on the Holodeck, or Towards an Aesthetics of Cyberspace*, Janet H. Murray writes of a model that is 'part of the postmodern mythos', the labyrinth.[1] Yet none of these models quite comes to terms with one particular feature of IF. IF makes the user choose from among a set of radiating possibilities as readers of novels cannot. The shadow of the excluded possibility becomes part of the narrative itself. In interactive narrative, the possible always shadows the actual, as a kind of virtual space. This is perhaps most startlingly evident in recent adventures from Revolution Software, like *Lure of the Temptress* and *Beneath a Steel Sky*. Revolution Software have developed an innovative system called Virtual Theatre in which all characters and objects continue to move about the game whether they are on-screen or not, turning up after the initial encounter in modified forms and different locations. It is even possible to watch characters carrying on their actions in 'other worlds'. The user 'peeps in' through observation windows on what the present narrative situation is excluding. IF therefore effectively de-realizes narrative, in containing within itself and making us aware of a range of narrative alternatives which might equally have become the narrative itself. Narrative can no longer be imagined as constrained by certain steely determinations, however much the possibilities are arranged by the programmers. Rather, the user must experience narrative itself as the simplification it always was and must be; which is also to experience the *eventuality* of narrative, narrative as emergence.

The geometric model asserts that narrative space is uniform, homogenous, single and universally valid. The creators of IF, by

contrast, delight in creating multiple and (often radically) heterogenous spaces. In the first instance, this is true at the simplest of
levels, in the creation of multiple worlds. In *Ultima Underworld 2*,
for instance, the user moves between eight separate worlds. The
multiple spaces may be designated as time-zones, as in the case of
the three separate 'worlds' in *Day of the Tentacle*. In Coktel
Vision's *Inca, or Lost in Time*, the narrative can be shifted between
present-day Brittany, a Caribbean island in 1840, and AD 2092.
Equally, there are the 'recreational' spaces that are incidental to
the main narrative business, as in certain Japanese *anime*, or
Cobra Mission, where it is possible to take time off from irksome
puzzle-solving and spy through a telescope on a group of scantily-
clad girls. One variant on this kind of incidental space would be
the game within the game, as, in *Day of the Tentacle*, it is possible
to play LucasArts's original game, *Maniac Mansion*, instead of
playing *Day of the Tentacle* itself. Yet another version of heterogenous space would be the anachronistic *mélange*: the mediaeval
wizard's mud hut, complete with fridge, in *Simon the Sorcerer*, or
the troubadour in *Legend* who sings Annie Lennox songs whenever the enemy annoys him. In IF, in fact, any specific space is
also a heterogenous space, a space of actualisation out of potentials, of a multiplicity of possible constructions. The single
character in *Shadowcaster* is able to go through a range of
transformations, each of his shapes having a different set of
powers and limitations, a different perspective on its surroundings, a different sense of the dimensions and angles of the space
observed. The experts call this 'morphing'. It is symptomatic of
something written much more largely into IF: in *Ultima Underworld*, the user's actions at one stage of the narrative will determine what he or she encounters at another stage. In *Dungeon
Hack*, the mazes and their contents are randomly generated at
each new stage. In *Dark Seed*, not only are there two worlds, but
any action the user performs in one has repercussions in the other,
even though the latter is off-screen. Actuality impacts upon a
virtuality and thus upon what will later become narrative actuality itself. Multiple space is also a conditional or modifiable space.
Most strikingly of all, perhaps, in *Indiana Jones and the Fate of
Atlantis*, there are three possible routes through the narrative
material: the Fist Path, where Indiana Jones must fight; the Wits

Path, on which he must think; and the Team Path, on which he joins forces with Sophia. Each path modifies the narrative situations accordingly. There is thus no fixed or single narrative space in this adventure. There is only a set of potentials which can be activated in different ways, and where each activation is an event.

NOTE

1. Janet H. Murray, *Hamlet on the Holodeck, or Towards an Aesthetics of Cyberspace* (forthcoming).

Bibliography

Atherton, J.S. (1974) 'The oxen of the sun', in C. Hart and D. Hayman (eds), *James Joyce's 'Ulysses': Critical Essays*, University of California Press, pp. 313–40.

Auerbach, E. (1973) *Mimesis: The Representation of Reality in Western Literature* (trans. W.R. Trask), Princeton University Press.

Austen, J. (1953) *Northanger Abbey*, London: Collins.

Bachelard, G. (1987) *The Psychoanalysis of Fire* (trans. A.C.M. Ross, with intro. by N. Frye), London: Quartet.

Badiou, A. (1975) *Théorie de la Contradiction*, Paris: François Maspero.

Badiou, A. (1982) *Théorie du Sujet*, Paris: Éditions du Seuil.

Badiou, A. (1989a) *L'Être et L'Événement*, Paris: Éditions du Seuil.

Badiou, A. (1989b) *Manifeste pour la Philosophie*, Paris: Éditions du Seuil.

Badiou, A. (1990) *Le Nombre et les Nombres*, Paris: Éditions du Seuil.

Badiou, A. (1992) *Conditions*, Paris: Éditions du Seuil.

Bakhtin, M. (1981) *The Dialogic Imagination: Four Essays* (ed. M. Holquist, trans. C. Emerson and M. Holquist), University of Texas Press.

Bakhtin, M. (1984) *Problems of Dostoevsky's Poetics* (ed. and trans. C. Emerson with intro. by W. Booth), Manchester University Press.

Bakhtin, M. (1986) *Speech Genres and Other Late Essays* (ed. C. Emerson and M. Holquist, trans. V.W. McGee), University of Texas Press.

Bakhtin, M. (1990) *Art and Answerability: Early Philosophical Essays* (ed. M. Holquist and V. Liapunov, trans. and with notes by V. Liapunov and supplement trans. by K. Brostrom), University of Texas Press.

Bal, M. (1985) *Narratology: Introduction to the Theory of Narrative* (trans. C. van Boheemen), University of Toronto Press.

Bal, M. (1992) 'Narratology and the rhetoric of trashing', *Comparative Literature*, 44:3 (Summer), pp. 293–306.

Banfield, A. (1982) *Unspeakable Sentences: Narration and Representation in the Language of Fiction*, London: Routledge and Kegan Paul.

Banfield, A. (1987) 'Describing the unobserved: events grouped around an empty centre', in N. Fabb, D. Attridge, A. Durant and C. McCabe (eds), *The*

Linguistics of Writing: Arguments between Language and Literature, New York: Methuen, pp. 265–85.

Barthes, R. (1970) *S/Z*, Paris: Éditions du Seuil.

Barthes, R. (1973) *Le Plaisir du Texte*, Paris: Éditions du Seuil.

Barthes, R. (1985) 'Introduction to the structural analysis of narratives', in *Image – Music – Text* (trans. S. Heath), London: Fontana, pp. 79–124.

Baudrillard, J. (1975) *The Mirror of Production* (trans. M. Poster), St Louis: Telos Press.

Baudrillard, J. (1990) *Selected Writings* (ed. and intro. M. Poster), Oxford: Blackwell.

Bauer, D.M. (1988) *Feminist Dialogics: A Theory of Failed Community*, State University of New York Press.

Bazin, A. (1967) *What is Cinema?* (2 vols, essays selected and trans. H. Gray), University of California Press.

Beckett, S. (1931) *Proust*, London: Chatto and Windus.

Beckett, S. (1963) *Watt*, London: Calder.

Beckett, S. (1979) *The Beckett Trilogy*, London: Pan.

Beckett, S. (1982) *Ill Seen Ill Said*, London: Calder.

Beckett, S. (1983) *Disjecta: Miscellaneous Writings and a Dramatic Fragment* (ed. and with foreword by R. Cohn), London: Calder.

Bennington, G. (1988) *Lyotard: Writing the Event*, Manchester University Press.

Berben-Masi, J. (ed.) (1992) *Narrative in Nice, Style*, 26:3 (Fall).

Bhabha, H. (1988) 'The commitment to theory', *New Formations*, 5 (Summer), pp. 5–23.

Blanchard, M. (1992) 'His master's voice', in Kropf and Palmer, pp. 61–78.

Bogue, R. (1989) *Deleuze and Guattari*, London: Routledge.

Booth, W. (1961/1987) *The Rhetoric of Fiction*, 2nd edn, Harmondsworth: Penguin.

Bordwell, D. (1985) *Narrative in the Fiction Film*, University of Wisconsin Press.

Bordwell, D. and K. Thompson (1990) *Film Art: An Introduction*, 3rd edn, New York: McGraw-Hill.

Braidotti, R. (1991) *Patterns of Dissonance: A Study of Women in Contemporary Philosophy*, Oxford: Polity.

Braidotti, R. (1994) *Nomadic Subjects: Embodiment and Sexual Difference in Contemporary Theory*, Columbia University Press.

Bremond, C. (1973) *Logique du Récit*, Paris: Seuil.

Brewer, M.M. (1987) 'Surviving fictions: gender and difference in postmodern and postnuclear narrative', *Discourse*, 9, pp. 37–52.

Brooke-Rose, C. (1981) *A Rhetoric of the Unreal: Studies in Narrative and Structure, Especially of the Fantastic*, Cambridge University Press.

Brooks, P. (1984) *Reading for the Plot: Design and Intention in Narrative*, New York: Vintage.

Brooks, P. (1994) *Psychoanalysis and Storytelling*, Oxford: Blackwell.

Brunette, P. and D. Wills (1989) *Screen/Play: Derrida and Film Theory*, Princeton University Press.

Burgin, V. (1991) 'Realizing the reverie', *Digital Dialogues, Ten-8*, 2:2, pp. 1–11.

Burke, K. (1954) *Permanence and Change: An Anatomy of Purpose*, Indianapolis: Bobbs-Merrill.

Buydens, M. (1990) *Sahara: L'Esthétique de Gilles Deleuze*, Paris: J. Vrin.

Cadigan, P. (1991) *Synners*, New York: Bantam.

Carroll, D. (1987) *Paraesthetics: Foucault, Lyotard, Derrida*, New York and London: Methuen.

de Chalonge, F. (1992) 'Une quête de l'origine? Identité et parcours spatial dans *Le Vice-Consul* de Marguerite Duras', *Littérature*, 88 (December), pp. 33–43.

de Chalonge, F. (1993) 'Énonciation narrative et spatialité: à propos du "Cycle Indien" de Marguerite Duras', *Poétique*, 95 (September), pp. 325–46.

Chambers, R. (1984) *Story and Situation: Narrative Seduction and the Power of Fiction*, University of Minnesota Press.

Chambers, R. (1991) *Room for Maneuver: Reading Oppositional Narrative*, University of Chicago Press.

Chatman, S. (1978) *Story and Discourse*, Cornell University Press.

Chatman, S. (1990) *Coming to Terms: The Rhetoric of Narrative in Fiction and Film*, Cornell University Press.

Claudel, P. (1941) *Art Poétique*, Paris: Mercure de France.

Clayton, A.J. (1989) *Nathalie Sarraute ou le Tremblement de l'Écriture*, Paris: Lettres Modernes.

Cohn, D. (1978) *Transparent Minds: Narrative Modes for Presenting Consciousness in Fiction*, Princeton University Press.

Connor, S. (1990) *Postmodernist Culture: An Introduction to Theories of the Contemporary*, Oxford: Blackwell.

Connor, S. (1992) *Theory and Cultural Value*, Oxford: Blackwell.

Cornell, D. (1991) *Beyond Accommodation: Ethical Feminism, Deconstruction and the Law*, London: Routledge.

Cornell, D. (1992) *The Philosophy of the Limit*, London: Routledge.

Cornell, D. (1993) *Transformations, Recollective Imagination and Sexual Difference*, London: Routledge.

Corngold, S. (1979) '*Sein und Zeit*: implications for poetics', in Spanos, pp. 99–115.

Cornis-Pope, M. (1992) *Hermeneutic Desire and Critical Rewriting: Narrative Interpretation in the Wake of Poststructuralism*, London: Macmillan.

Cortazzi, M. (1993) *Narrative Analysis*, London, Falmer Press.

Coste, D. (1989) *Narrative as Communication* (with foreword by W. Godzich), University of Minnesota Press.

282   TOWARDS A POSTMODERN THEORY OF NARRATIVE

Costikyan, G. (1994) 'I have no words and I must design', *Interactive Fantasy*, 1:2 (December), pp. 22–39.

Crane, S. (1992) *The Red Badge of Courage*, with intro. by M. Bradbury, London: Dent.

Crawford, C. (1990) 'Nietzsche's physiology of ideological criticism', in Koelb, pp. 161–86.

Critchley, S. (1992) *The Ethics of Deconstruction: Derrida and Levinas*, Oxford: Blackwell.

Culler, J. (1975) *Structuralist Poetics*, London: Routledge and Kegan Paul.

Culler, J. (1978) 'On trope and persuasion', *New Literary History*, 9:3, pp. 607–18.

Culler, J. (1981) *The Pursuit of Signs: Semiotics, Deconstruction, Literature*, London: Routledge and Kegan Paul.

Cumberland, R. (1795) *Henry*, London: Charles Dilly.

Cunningham, V. (1994) *In the Reading Gaol: Postmodernity, Texts and History*, Oxford: Blackwell.

Dauben, J.W. (1990) *George Cantor: His Mathematics and Philosophy of the Infinite*, Princeton University Press.

Deleuze, G. (1968) *Différence et Répétition*, Paris: Presses Universitaires de France.

Deleuze, G. (1973) *Proust and Signs* (trans. R. Howard), London: Allen Lane.

Deleuze, G. (1977) 'Nomad thought', in D.B. Allison (ed.), *The New Nietzsche*, MIT Press, pp. 142–9.

Deleuze, G. (1981) *Francis Bacon: Logique de la Sensation* (2 vols), Paris: Éditions de la Différence.

Deleuze, G. (1983) *Nietzsche and Philosophy* (trans. H. Tomlinson), London: Athlone.

Deleuze, G. (1986) *Cinema 1: The Movement-Image* (trans. H. Tomlinson and B. Habberjam), London: Athlone.

Deleuze, G. (1988a) *Bergsonism* (trans. H. Tomlinson and B. Habberjam), New York: Zone Books.

Deleuze, G. (1988b) *Foucault* (trans. and ed. S. Hand), London: Athlone.

Deleuze, G. (1989) *Cinema 2: The Time-Image* (trans. H. Tomlinson and R. Galeta), London: Athlone.

Deleuze, G. (1990) *The Logic of Sense* (ed. C.V. Boundas, trans. M. Lester with C. Stivale), London: Athlone.

Deleuze, G. (1991) *Empiricism and Subjectivity: An Essay on Hume's Theory of Human Nature* (trans. with intro. by C.V. Boundas), Columbia University Press.

Deleuze, G. (1994) *Difference and Repetition* (trans. P. Patton), London: Athlone.

Deleuze, G. and F. Guattari (1988) *A Thousand Plateaus: Capitalism and Schizophrenia* (trans. with a foreword by B. Massumi), London: Athlone.

Deleuze, G. and C. Parnet (1987) *Dialogues* (trans. H. Tomlinson and B. Habberjam), London: Athlone.

Derrida, J. (1973) *Speech and Phenomena and Other Essays on Husserl's Theory of Signs* (trans. with intro. by D.B. Allison, with a preface by N. Garver), Northwestern University Press.

Derrida, J. (1976) *Of Grammatology* (trans. with preface by G.C. Spivak), Johns Hopkins University Press.

Derrida, J. (1978) *Writing and Difference* (trans. with intro. and additional notes by A. Bass), London: Routledge.

Derrida, J. (1979) *Spurs: Nietzsche's Styles* (trans. B. Harlow), University of Chicago Press.

Derrida, J. (1981a) *Dissemination* (trans. with intro. and additional notes by B. Johnson), London: Athlone.

Derrida, J. (1981b) *Positions* (trans. and annotated by A. Bass), London: Athlone.

Derrida, J. (1982) *Margins of Philosophy* (trans. with additional notes by A. Bass), Brighton: Harvester.

Derrida, J. (1985) *The Ear of the Other: Otobiography, Transference, Translation* (ed. C.V. McDonald, trans. P. Kamuf and A. Ronell), New York: Schocken Books.

Derrida, J. (1987a) *The Archaeology of the Frivolous: Reading Condillac* (trans. with intro. by J.P. Leavey Jr), University of Nebraska Press.

Derrida, J. (1987b) *The Post-Card: From Socrates to Freud and Beyond* (trans. A. Bass), University of Chicago Press.

Derrida, J. (1987c) *The Truth in Painting* (trans. G. Bennington and I. Macleod), Chicago University Press.

Derrida, J. (1991) *Of Spirit: Heidegger and the Question* (trans. G. Bennington and R. Bowlby), University of Chicago Press.

Docherty, T. (1983) *Reading (Absent) Character: Towards a Theory of Characterization in Fiction* Oxford: Clarendon.

Docherty, T. (1996) *After Theory*, Edinburgh University Press.

Duckworth, A. (1971) *The Improvement of the Estate: A Study of Jane Austen's Novels*, Johns Hopkins University Press.

Eagleton, T. (1983) *Literary Theory: An Introduction*, Oxford: Blackwell.

Eagleton, T. (1988) *Against the Grain: Essays 1975–85*, London: Verso.

Eagleton, T. (1990) *The Significance of Theory*, Oxford: Blackwell.

Eco, U. (1979) *The Role of the Reader: Explorations in the Semiotics of Texts*, Indiana University Press.

Empson, W. (1984) '*Ulysses*: Joyce's intentions', in *Using Biography*, London: Chatto and Windus, pp. 203–16.

Fehn, A., I. Hoesterey and M. Tatar (eds) (1992) *Neverending Stories: Towards a Critical Narratology*, Princeton University Press.

Feyerabend, P. (1987) *Farewell to Reason*, London: Verso.

Fielding, H. (March 1752) review of Charlotte Lennox, *The Female Quixote*, *The Covent Garden Journal*.

Fielding, H. (1961) *Joseph Andrews* (ed. with intro. and notes by M.C. Battestin), Boston: Houghton Mifflin.

Fludernik, M. (1993) *The Fictions of Language and the Languages of Fiction: The Linguistic Representation of Speech and Consciousness*, London: Routledge.

Fludernik, M. (1996) *Towards a 'Natural' Narratology*, London: Routledge.

Foucault, M. (1970) *The Order of Things: An Archaeology of the Human Sciences* (trans. from the French), London: Tavistock.

Foucault, M. (1981) 'The order of discourse', in R. Young (ed.), *Untying the Text: A Poststructuralist Reader*, London: Routledge and Kegan Paul, pp. 48–76.

Foucault, M. (1987) *Death and the Labyrinth: The World of Raymond Roussel* (trans. C. Ruas, with intro. by J. Ashbery), London: Athlone.

Foucault, M. (1990a) *The History of Sexuality*, Vol. 1, *Introduction* (trans. R. Hurley), Harmondsworth, Penguin.

Foucault, M. (1990b) *The History of Sexuality*, Vol. 3, *The Care of Self* (trans. R. Hurley), Harmondsworth, Penguin.

Foucault, M. (1991a) *Discipline and Punish: The Birth of the Prison* (trans. A. Sheridan), Harmondsworth: Penguin.

Foucault, M. (1991b) *Madness and Civilization: A History of Insanity in the Age of Reason* (trans. R. Howard), London: Tavistock.

Foucault, M. (1991c) *The Archaeology of Knowledge* (trans. A. Sheridan), London: Routledge.

Foucault, M. (1991d) 'What is enlightenment?' (trans. C. Porter), in P. Rabinow (ed.), *The Foucault Reader*, Harmondsworth: Penguin, pp. 32–50.

Foucault, M. (1992) *The History of Sexuality*, Vol. 2: *The Use of Pleasure* (trans. R. Hurley), Harmondsworth: Penguin.

Fowler, R. (1977) *Linguistics and the Novel*, London: Methuen.

Freud, S. (1953–74) *Beyond the Pleasure Principle*, in *The Standard Edition of the Complete Psychological Works* (ed. J. Strachey), London: Hogarth Press, Vol. 18, pp. 1–64.

Genette, G. (1980a) *Figures of Literary Discourse* (trans. A. Sheridan, intro. by M.-R. Logan), Oxford: Blackwell.

Genette, G. (1980b) *Narrative Discourse* (trans. J.E. Lewin, with foreword by J. Culler), Oxford: Blackwell.

Genette, G. (1982) *Palimpsestes: La Littérature au Second Degré*, Paris: Éditions du Seuil.

Genette, G. (1988) *Narrative Discourse Revisited* (trans. J.E. Lewin), Cornell University Press.

Gibson, A. (1990) *Reading Narrative Discourse: Studies in the Novel from Cervantes to Beckett*, London: Macmillan.

Gibson, A. (1996) 'Interactive fiction and narrative space', in W. Chernaik, M. Deegan and A. Gibson (eds), *Beyond the Book: Theory, Culture and the Politics of Cyberspace*, Oxford: Oxford Humanities Publications, pp. 79–92.

Girard, R. (1965) *Deceit, Desire and the Novel*, Johns Hopkins University Press.

Goetz, P. (1994) 'Interactive fiction and computers', *Inter*Action*, 1:1 (September), pp. 98–117.

Goldmann, L. (1975) *Towards a Sociology of the Novel* (trans. A. Sheridan), London: Tavistock.

Graff, G. (1981) 'Literature as assertions', in Konigsberg, pp. 36–59.

Graves, D. (1987) 'Second generation adventure games', in *Journal of Computer Game Design*, 1:2 (August), pp. 4–7.

Graves, D. (1988) 'Bringing characters to life', in *Journal of Computer Game Design*, 2:2 (December), pp. 10–11.

Graves, D. (1991) 'Plot automation', in *Journal of Computer Game Design*, 5:1 (October), pp. 10–12.

Green, H. (1978) *Living*, London: Picador.

Greimas, A.J. (1966) *Sémantique Structurale: Recherche de Méthode*, Paris: Larousse.

Greimas, A.J. (1970) *Du Sens*, Paris: Éditions du Seuil.

Greimas, A.J. (1971) 'Narrative Grammar: Units and Levels', *Modern Language Notes*, 86:6 (December), pp. 793–806.

Greimas, A.J. (1983) *Structural Semantics: An Attempt at a Method* (trans. D. McDowell, R. Schleifer and A. Velie, intro. by R. Schleifer), University of Nebraska Press.

Hamon, P. (1992) 'Narratology: status and outlook', in Berben-Masi, pp. 363–7.

Haraway, D.J. (1991) *Simians, Cyborgs and Women: The Reinvention of Nature*, London: Free Association Books.

Hardt, M. (1993) *Gilles Deleuze: An Apprenticeship in Philosophy*, UCL Press.

Harvey, W.J. (1965) *Character and the Novel*, London: Chatto and Windus.

Hassan, I. (1982) *The Dismemberment of Orpheus: Towards a Postmodern Literature*, Oxford University Press.

Havas, R.E. (1992) 'Who is Heidegger's Nietzsche? (on the very idea of the present age)', in H. Dreyfus and H. Hall (eds), *Heidegger: A Critical Reader*, Oxford: Blackwell, pp. 231–46.

Hayles, K. (1990) *Chaos Bound: Orderly Disorder in Contemporary Literature and Science*, Cornell University Press.

Hayward, P. and T. Wollen (eds) (1993) *Future Visions: New Technologies of the Screen*, London: BFI Publications.

Heath, S. (1972) *The Nouveau Roman: A Study in the Practice of Writing*, London: Elek.

Heath, S. (1981) *Questions of Cinema*, London: Macmillan.
Heidegger, M. (1971) *Poetry, Language, Thought* (trans. with intro. by A. Hofstadter), London: Harper and Row.
Heidegger, M. (1979) 'The age of the world view' (trans. M. Grene), in Spanos, pp. 1–15.
Heidegger, M. (1974) *The Question of Being* (trans. with intro. by W. Kluback and J.T. Wilde), London: Vision Press.
Heidegger, M. (1975) *Early Greek Thinking* (trans. D.F. Krell and F. Capuzzi), New York: Harper and Row.
Heidegger, M. (1990) *Being and Time* (trans. J. Macquarrie and E. Robinson), Oxford: Blackwell.
Heidegger, M. (1991) *Nietzsche* (2 vols) (trans. D.F. Krell), New York: HarperCollins.
Hill, L. (1990) *Beckett's Fiction: In Different Words*, Cambridge University Press.
Hite, M. (1989) *The Other Side of the Story: Structures and Strategies of Contemporary Feminist Narrative*, Cornell University Press.
Holquist, M. (1990) *Dialogism: Bakhtin and his World*, London: Routledge.
Hume, K. (1984) *Fantasy and Mimesis: Responses to Reality in Western Literature*, London: Methuen.
Hutcheon, L. (1984) *Narcissistic Narrative: The Metafictional Paradox*, New York and London: Methuen.
Hutcheon, L. (1988) *A Poetics of Postmodernism: History, Theory, Fiction*, New York: Routledge.
Ingarden, R. (1973) *The Cognition of the Literary Work of Art* (trans. R.A. Crowley and K.R. Olson), Northwestern University Press.
Irigaray, L. (1985) *This Sex Which Is Not One* (trans. C. Porter with C. Burke), Cornell University Press.
Irigaray, L. (1993) *Je, Tu, Nous: Toward a Culture of Difference* (trans. A. Martin), London and New York: Routledge.
Iser, W. (1974) *The Implied Reader: Patterns of Communication in Prose Fiction from Bunyan to Beckett*, Johns Hopkins University Press.
Iser, W. (1989) *Prospecting: From Reader Response to Literary Anthropology*, Johns Hopkins University Press.
Iser, W. (1993) *The Fictive and the Imaginary*, Johns Hopkins University Press.
Jahn, M. (1983) 'Narration as non-communication: on Banfield's unspeakable sentences', *Kölner Anglistische Papiere*, Vol. 23, pp. 1–20.
James, H. (1934) *The Art of the Novel* (with intro. by R.P. Blackmur), London: Scribner's.
James, H. (1936) *The Novels and Tales*, Vol. 11, New York: Scribner's.
James, H. (1948) *The Art of Fiction* (with intro. by M. Roberts), Oxford University Press.

James, H. (1957) *The House of Fiction* (ed. with intro. by L. Edel), London: Rupert Hart-Davis.

James, H. (1984) *Literary Criticism Volume Two: French Writers, Other European Writers and The Prefaces to the New York Edition*, New York: Library of America.

Jameson, F. (1983) *The Political Unconscious: Narrative as a Socially Symbolic Act*, London: Methuen.

Jameson, F. (1991) *Postmodernism, or the Cultural Logic of Late Capitalism*, London: Verso.

Jardine, A. (1985) *Gynesis: Configurations of Women and Modernity*, Cornell University Press.

Jauss, H.R. (1982) *Toward an Aesthetic of Reception* (trans. T. Bahti, with intro. by P. de Man), Brighton: Harvester.

Jefferson, A. (1980) *The Nouveau Roman and the Poetics of Fiction*, Cambridge University Press.

Jones, E. (1953) *The Life and Work of Sigmund Freud*, New York: Basic Books.

Joyce, J. (1957) *Letters*, Vol. I (ed. S. Gilbert), London: Faber and Faber.

Joyce, J. (1964) 'Daniel Defoe' (ed. and trans. J. Prescott), *Buffalo Studies*, 1:1 (December), pp. 3–27.

Joyce, J. (1984, 1986) *Ulysses* (ed. H.W. Gabler et al.), New York and London: Garland Publishing.

Kenner, H. (1980) *Ulysses* London: Allen and Unwin.

Kerouac, J. (1972) *On the Road*, Harmondsworth, Penguin.

Koelb, C. (ed.) (1990) *Nietzsche as Postmodernist: Essays Pro and Contra*, State University of New York Press.

Konigsberg, I. (ed.) (1981) *American Literature in the Poststructuralist Age*, University of Michigan Press.

Kristeva, J. (1969) *Sēmiōtikē: Recherches pour une Sémanalyse*, Paris: Éditions du Seuil.

Kristeva, J. (1975) 'La fonction prédicative et le sujet parlant', in J. Kristeva, J.-C. Milner and N. Ruwet (eds), *Langue, Discours, Société*, Paris: Éditions du Seuil, pp. 229–59.

Kristeva, J. (1980) *Desire in Language: A Semiotic Approach to Literature and Art* (ed. L.S. Roudiez, trans. T. Gora, A. Jardine and L.S. Roudiez), Oxford: Blackwell.

Kristeva, J. (1982) *Powers of Horror: An Essay on Abjection* (trans. L.S. Roudiez), Columbia University Press.

Kristeva, J. (1984) *Revolution in Poetic Language* (trans. M. Waller, with intro. by L.S. Roudiez), Columbia University Press.

Kristeva, J. (1988) *Étrangers à Nous-Mêmes*, Paris: Fayard.

Kristeva, J. (1991) *Strangers to Ourselves* (trans. L.S. Roudiez), London: Harvester Wheatsheaf.

Kroeber, K. (1990) *Retelling/Rereading: The Fate of Storytelling in Modern Times*, Rutgers University Press.

Kropf, C.R. and R.B. Palmer (eds) (1992) *After Genette: Current Directions in Narrative Analysis and Theory, Studies in the Literary Imagination*, 25:1 (Spring).

Kundera, M. (1988) *The Art of the Novel*, London: Faber and Faber.

Lanser, S.S. (1991) 'Towards a feminist narratology', in R.R. Warhol and D. Price Herndl (eds), *Feminisms: An Anthology of Literary Theory and Criticism*, Rutgers University Press, pp. 610–29.

Lanser, S.S. (1992) *Fictions of Authority: Women Writers and the Narrative Voice*, Cornell University Press.

Laurel, B. (1986) 'Towards the design of a computer-based interactive fantasy system', Ph.D. dissertation, Ohio State University.

de Lauretis, T. (1984) *Alice Doesn't: Feminism, Semiotics, Cinema*, London: Macmillan.

de Lauretis, T. (1989) *Technologies of Gender: Essays on Theory, Film and Fiction*, London: Macmillan.

Lawrence, D.H. (1967) *Selected Literary Criticism* (ed. A. Beal), London: Heinemann.

Lawrence, D.H. (1970) *Women in Love*, Harmondsworth: Penguin.

Lawrence, K. (1981) *The Odyssey of Style in 'Ulysses'*, Princeton University Press.

Lecercle, J.-J. (1985) *Philosophy Through the Looking-Glass: Language, Non-sense, Desire*, London: Hutchinson.

le Dœuff, M. (1988) 'Women and philosophy' (trans. D. Pope), in T. Moi (ed.), *French Feminist Thought: A Reader*, Oxford: Blackwell, pp. 181–209.

le Dœuff, M. (1989a) *L'Étude et le Rouet: des Femmes, de la Philosophie, etc.*, Paris: Éditions du Seuil.

le Dœuff, M. (1989b) *The Philosophical Imaginary* (trans. C. Gordon), London: Athlone.

Le Fanu, M. (1987) *The Cinema of Andrei Tarkovsky*, London: BFI Publications.

Leisure, M. (1976) '*Murphy*, or the beginning of an aesthetic of monstrosity', in E. Morot-Sir, H. Harper and D. McMillan III (eds), *Samuel Beckett: The Art of Rhetoric*, Chapel Hill, North Carolina Studies in the Romance Languages and Literatures, Symposium 5, pp. 189–201.

Levin, R. (1979) *New Readings vs. Old Plays*, University of Chicago Press.

Levinas, E. (1985) *Ethics and Infinity: Conversations with Philippe Nemo* (trans. R. A. Cohen), Duquesne University Press.

Levinas, E. (1989) *The Levinas Reader* (ed. S. Hand), Oxford: Blackwell.

Lévi-Strauss, C. (1977) 'The structural study of myth', in *Structural Anthropology*, Vol. 1 (trans. C. Jacobson and B. Grundfest), Harmondsworth: Penguin, pp. 202–28.

Livingston, P. (1991) *Literature and Rationality: Ideas of Agency in Theory and Fiction*, Cambridge University Press.

Lovell, T. (1980) *Pictures of Reality: Aesthetics, Politics and Pleasure*, London: BFI Publications.

Lowry, M. (1981) *Under the Volcano*, Harmondsworth: Penguin.

Lubbock, P. (1921) *The Craft of Fiction*, London: Duckworth.

Lukács, G. (1964) *Studies in European Realism* (with intro. by A. Kazin), New York: Grosset and Dunlap.

Lukács, G. (1978) *The Theory of the Novel* (trans. A. Bostock), London: Merlin.

Lukács, G. (1979) *The Meaning of Contemporary Realism* (trans. J. and N. Maunder), London: Merlin.

Lyotard, J.-F. (1974) *Économie Libidinale*, Paris: Éditions de Minuit.

Lyotard, J.-F. (1980) *Des Dispositifs Pulsionnels*, Paris: Christian Bourgois.

Lyotard, J.-F. (1985) *Discours, Figure*, Paris: Klincksieck.

Lyotard, J.-F. (1988a) *The Differend* (trans. G. van den Abbeele), Manchester University Press.

Lyotard, J.-F. (1988b) *L'Inhumain: Causeries sur le Temps*, Paris: Éditions Galilée.

Lyotard, J.-F. (1988c) *Peregrinations: Law, Form, Event*, Columbia University Press.

Lyotard, J.-F. (1991a) *The Inhuman: Reflections on Time* (trans. G. Bennington and R. Bowlby), Oxford: Polity.

Lyotard, J.-F. (1991b) *The Lyotard Reader* (ed. A. Benjamin), Oxford: Blackwell.

Martin, W. (1986) *Recent Theories of Narrative*, Cornell University Press.

McCabe, C. (1980) *Godard, Images, Sounds, Politics*, London: BFI Publications.

McHale, B. (1978) 'Free indirect discourse: a survey of recent accounts', in *Poetics and Theory of Literature*, 3:2, pp. 249–87.

McHale, B. (1983) 'Unspeakable sentences, unnatural acts: linguistics and poetics revisited', in *Poetics and Theory of Literature*, 4:1, pp. 17–45.

McHale, B. (1987) *Postmodernist Fiction*, London: Methuen.

McLure, R. (1987) *Sarraute: Le Planétarium*, London: Grant and Cutler.

Miller, J.E. Jr (ed.) (1972) *Theory of Fiction: Henry James*, University of Nebraska Press.

Miller, J.H. (ed.) (1971) *Aspects of Narrative*, Columbia University Press.

Miller, J.H. (1982) *Fiction and Repetition*, Oxford: Blackwell.

Miller, J.H. (1992) *Ariadne's Thread: Story Lines*, Yale University Press.

Mink, L.O. (1987) 'History and fiction as modes of comprehension', in B. Fay, E.O. Golub and R.T. Vann (eds), *Historical Understanding*, Cornell University Press, pp. 42–60.

Morgan, S. (1980) *In the Meantime: Character and Perception in the Novels of Jane Austen*, University of Chicago Press.

Morson, G.S. and C. Emerson (1990) *Mikhail Bakhtin: Creation of a Prosaics*, Stanford University Press.

Müller, G. (1968) 'Erzählzeit und erzählte Zeit', in *Morphologische Poetik*, Tübingen.

Murray, J.H. (forthcoming) *Hamlet on the Holodeck, or Towards an Aesthetics of Cyberspace.*

Nash, C. (1990) *Narrative in Culture: The Use of Storytelling in the Sciences, Philosophy and Literature*, London: Routledge.

Nietzsche, F. (1968) *The Will to Power* (ed. W. Kaufmann, trans. W. Kaufmann and R.J. Hollingdale), London: Weidenfeld and Nicolson.

Nietzsche, F. (1974a) *Beyond Good and Evil* (trans. and with intro. and commentary by R.J. Hollingdale), Harmondsworth: Penguin.

Nietzsche, F. (1974b) *The Gay Science* (trans. and with commentary by W. Kaufmann), New York: Vintage.

Nietzsche, F. (1986) *Ecce Homo: How One Becomes What One Is* (trans. and with intro. and notes by R.J. Hollingdale), Harmondsworth: Penguin.

Nietzsche, F. (1987a) *Human, All Too Human: A Book for Free Spirits* (trans. R.J. Hollingdale, with intro. by E. Heller), Cambridge University Press.

Nietzsche, F. (1987b) *Twilight of the Idols* (trans. and with intro. by R.J. Hollingdale), Harmondsworth: Penguin.

Norris, C. (1991a) *Deconstruction: Theory and Practice* (revised edn), London: Routledge.

Norris, C. (1991b) 'Mimesis and politics', *Prose Studies*, 14:1 (May), pp. 97–107.

Norris, C. (1992a) *The Truth about Postmodernism*, Oxford: Blackwell.

Norris, C. (1992b) *Uncritical Theory: Postmodernism, Intellectuals and the Gulf War*, London: Lawrence and Wishart.

Nuttall, A.D. (1983) *A New Mimesis: Shakespeare and the Representation of Reality*, London: Methuen.

Oppel, F. (1993) ' "Speaking of immemorial waters": Irigaray with Nietzsche', in Patton, pp. 88–109.

Papineau, D. (1987) *Reality and Representation*, Oxford: Blackwell.

Parrinder, P. (1984) *James Joyce*, Cambridge University Press.

Patton P. (ed.) (1993) *Nietzsche, Feminism and Political Theory*, London: Routledge.

Pavel, T.G. (1986) *Fictional Worlds*, Harvard University Press.

Peake, C. (1977) *James Joyce: The Citizen and the Artist*, London: Edward Arnold.

Phelan, J. (1989a) *Reading People, Reading Plots: Character, Progression and the Interpretation of Narrative*, University of Chicago Press.

Phelan, J. (ed.) (1989b) *Reading Narrative: Form, Ethics, Ideology*, Ohio State University Press.

Powell, M.A. (1993) *What is Narrative Criticism?: A New Approach to the Bible*, London: Society for Promoting Christian Knowledge.

Prince, G. (1973) *A Grammar of Stories*, The Hague: Mouton.

Prince, G. (1982) *Narratology: The Form and Functioning of Narrative*, Berlin: Mouton.

Prince, G. (1988) *A Dictionary of Narratology*, Aldershot: Scolar Press.

Propp, V. (1968) *Morphology of the Folk Tale* (trans. L. Scott), University of Texas Press.

Putnam, H. (1987) *The Many Faces of Realism*, La Salle: Open Court.

Quine, W.V. (1969) *Ontological Relativity and Other Essays*, Columbia University Press.

Ray, W. (1990) *Story and History: Narrative Authority and Social Identity in the Eighteenth-Century French and English Novel*, Oxford: Blackwell.

Read, F. (ed.) (1967) *Pound/Joyce: The Letters of Ezra Pound to James Joyce, with Pound's Essays on Joyce*, New York: New Directions.

Readings, B. (1991) *Introducing Lyotard: Art and Politics*. London: Routledge.

Reid, I. (1992) *Narrative Exchanges*, London: Routledge.

Rhys, J. (1993) *Wide Sargasso Sea*, Harmondsworth: Penguin.

Richard, J.-P. (1961) *L'Univers Imaginaire de Mallarmé*, Paris: Éditions du Seuil.

Riessman, C.K. (1993) *Narrative Analysis*, London: Sage Publications.

Rimmon-Kenan, S. (1983) *Narrative Fiction: Contemporary Poetics*, London: Methuen.

Robbe-Grillet, A. (1965a) *Snapshots and Towards a New Novel* (trans. B. Wright), London: Calder and Boyars.

Robbe-Grillet, A. (1965b) *The Voyeur* (trans. R. Howard), London: Calder.

Rorty, R. (1980) *Philosophy and the Mirror of Nature*, Oxford: Blackwell.

Rorty, R. (1989) *Contingency, Irony and Solidarity*, Cambridge University Press.

Rorty, R. (1991a) *Objectivism, Relativism and Truth: Philosophical Papers*, Vol. 1, Cambridge University Press.

Rorty, R. (1991b) *Essays on Heidegger and Others: Philosophical Papers*, Vol. 2, Cambridge University Press.

Rosset, C. (1976) *Le Réel et Son Double*, Paris: Gallimard.

Rosset, C. (1977) *Le Réel: Traité de L'Idiotie*, Paris: Éditions de Minuit.

Rosset, C. (1979) *L'Objet Singulier*, Paris: Éditions de Minuit.

Rosset, C. (1982) *Le Philosophe et les Sortilèges*, Paris: Éditions de Minuit.

Rosset, C. (1988) *Le Principe de Cruauté*, Paris: Éditions de Minuit.

Rosset, C. (1991) *La Philosophie Tragique*, Presses Universitaires de France.

Rushdie, S. (1990) *In Good Faith*, London: Granta Publications.

Ryan, M.-L. (1991) *Possible Worlds, Artificial Intelligence and Narrative Theory*, Indiana University Press.

Ryan, M.-L. (1992) 'The modes of narrativity and their visual metaphors', in Berben-Masi, pp. 368–87.

Sarraute, N. (1956) *L'Ère du Soupçon*, Paris: Gallimard.

Sarraute, N. (1958) *Portrait of a Man Unknown* (trans. M. Jolas), London: Calder.

Sarraute, N. (1961) 'New movements in French literature', *The Listener* (9 March), pp. 428–9.

Sarraute, N. (1963) *Tropisms and the Age of Suspicion* (trans. M. Jolas), London: Calder.

Sarraute, N. (1965) *The Planetarium* (trans. M. Jolas), London: Calder.

Sarraute, N. (1986) *Paul Valéry ou l'Enfant de l'Éléphant et Flaubert le Précurseur*, Paris: Gallimard.

Scholes, R. (1974) *Structuralism in Literature*, Yale University Press.

Scholes, R. (1982) *Semiotics and Interpretation*, Yale University Press.

Scholes, R. (1985) *Textual Power*, Yale University Press.

Serres, M. (1969) *Hermès I: La Communication*, Paris: Éditions de Minuit.

Serres, M. (1972) *Hermès II: L'Interférence*, Paris: Éditions de Minuit.

Serres, M. (1974a) *Hermès III: La Traduction*, Paris: Éditions de Minuit.

Serres, M. (1974b) *Jouvences sur Jules Verne*, Paris: Éditions de Minuit.

Serres, M. (1975) *Feux et Signaux de Brume: Zola*, Paris: Grasset.

Serres, M. (1977a) *Hermès IV: La Distribution*, Paris: Éditions de Minuit.

Serres, M. (1977b) *La Naissance de la Physique dans le Texte de Lucrèce: Fleuves et Turbulences*, Paris: Éditions de Minuit.

Serres, M. (1980) *Hermès V: Le Passage du Nord-Ouest*, Paris: Éditions de Minuit.

Serres, M. (1982) *The Parasite* (trans. L.R. Schehr), Johns Hopkins University Press.

Serres, M. (1987) *L'Hermaphrodite: Sarrasine Sculpteur*, Paris: Flammarion.

Serres, M. (1991a) *Le Tiers-Instruit*, Paris: Éditions François Bourin.

Serres, M. (1991b) *Rome: The Book of Foundations* (trans. F. McCarren), Stanford University Press.

Serres, M. (1992) *Éclaircissements: Entretiens avec Bruno Latour*, Paris: Éditions François Bourin.

Serres, M. (1993) *Les Origines de la Géometrie*, Paris: Flammarion.

Shiach, M. (1991) *Hélène Cixous: A Politics of Writing*, London: Routledge.

Shklovsky, V. (1965) 'Sterne's *Tristram Shandy*: stylistic commentary', in L.T. Lemon and M.J. Reis (eds and trans.), *Russian Formalist Criticism: Four Essays*, University of Nebraska Press, pp. 46–72.

Showalter, E. (1978) *A Literature of their Own: British Women Novelists from Brontë to Lessing*, London: Virago.

Sims, R.L. (1992) 'From fictional to factual narrative: contemporary critical heteroglossia: Gabriel García Márquez's journalism and bigeneric writing', in Kropf and Palmer, pp. 21–60.

Spanos W.V. (ed.) (1979) *Martin Heidegger and the Question of Literature: Towards a Postmodern Literary Hermeneutics*, Indiana University Press.

Stam, R. (1989) *Subversive Pleasures: Bakhtin, Cultural Criticism and Film*, Johns Hopkins University Press.

Stanzel, F.K. (1984) *A Theory of Narrative* (trans. C. Goedsche, with preface by P. Hernadi), Cambridge University Press.

Stevenson, R.L. (1979) *Dr Jekyll and Mr Hyde and Other Stories*, Harmondsworth: Penguin.

Sutherland, I. (1965) 'The ultimate display', *Proceedings of the International Federation of Information Processing Congress*, pp. 506–8.

Sylvester, D. (1980) *Interviews with Francis Bacon*, London: Thames and Hudson.

Tallis, R. (1988) *In Defence of Realism*, London: Edward Arnold.

Tambling, J. (1990) 'Power and the silent majorities', in A. Abbas (ed.), *The Provocation of Jean Baudrillard*, Hong Kong: Twilight Books, pp. 11–28.

Tarkovsky, A. (1989) *Sculpting in Time: Reflections on the Cinema* (trans. K. Hunter-Blair), London: Faber.

Tarkovsky, A. (1991) *Time Within Time: The Diaries 1970–1986* (trans. K. Hunter-Blair), Calcutta: Seagull.

Thackeray, W. (1978) *Vanity Fair*, Harmondsworth: Penguin.

Thiher, A. (1983) 'Wittgenstein, Heidegger, *The Unnameable* and some thoughts on the status of voice in fiction', in M. Beja, S.E. Gontarski and P. Astier (eds), *Samuel Beckett: Humanistic Perspectives*, Ohio State University Press, pp. 80–90.

Tiles, M. (1989) *The Philosophy of Set Theory: An Introduction to Cantor's Paradise*, Oxford: Blackwell.

Todorov, T. (1969) *Grammaire du Décaméron*, Paris: Mouton.

Toolan, M. (1988) *Narrative: A Critical Linguistic Introduction*, London: Routledge.

Trigg, R. (1989) *Reality at Risk: A Defence of Realism in Philosophy and the Sciences*, London: Harvester Wheatsheaf.

Vasseleu, C. (1993) 'Not drowning, sailing: women and the artist's craft in Nietzsche', in Patton, pp. 71–87.

Vattimo, G. (1988) *The End of Modernity* (trans. with intro. by J.R. Snyder), Oxford: Polity.

Vattimo, G. (1992) *The Transparent Society* (trans. D. Webb), Polity: Oxford.

Vattimo, G. (1993) *The Adventure of Difference: Philosophy after Nietzsche and Heidegger* (trans. C. Blamires with the assistance of T. Harrison), Oxford: Polity.

Violi, P. (1986) 'Unspeakable sentences and speakable texts', *Semiotica*, 60:3–4, pp. 361–78.

Virilio, P. (1986) *Speed and Politics* (trans. M. Polizzotti), New York: Semiotext(e).

Virilio, P. (1991a) *The Aesthetics of Disappearance* (trans. P. Beitchman), New York: Semiotext(e).

Virilio, P. (1991b) *The Lost Dimension* (trans. D. Moshenberg), New York: Semiotext(e).

Warhol, R. (1989) *Gendered Interventions: Narrative Discourse in the Victorian Novel*, Rutgers University Press.

Wittig, M. (1973) *The Lesbian Body* (trans. D. LeVay), New York: Avon.

Wolf, C. (1988) *A Model Childhood* (trans. U. Molinaro and H. Rappolt), London: Virago.

Wolf, C. (1991) *Cassandra: A Novel and Four Essays* (trans. J. van Heurck), London: Virago.

Wolmark, J. (1993) *Aliens and Others: Science Fiction, Feminism and Postmodernism*, London: Harvester Wheatsheaf.

Woolf, V. (1976) *Jacob's Room*, London: Panther.

Woolley, B. (1993) *Virtual Worlds: A Journey in Hype and Hyperreality*, Harmondsworth: Penguin.

Yamaguchi, H. (1989) 'On "Unspeakable Sentences": a pragmatic review', *Journal of Pragmatics*, 13:4, pp. 577–95.

Index

295

imaginary, 1–5, 19
inauguration, 87–102
Indiana Jones and the Temple of Doom, 138
Ingarden, Roman, 250
intensities, 52–4, 58, 59, 60, 129, 161, 187–8, 196–7, 199, 200, 204
interactive fiction, 10–12, 275–8
Irigaray, Luce, 106, 126, 142n, 158
Iser, Wolfgang, 4, 246–7, 249–53, 272

James, Henry, 6–7, 52–5, 81–2
'In the Cage', 52–5
Prefaces, 6–7
What Maisie Knew, 149
Jameson, Frederic, 71, 177n
Jardine, Alice, 121, 123, 124
Jarmusch, Jim, 131
Down by Law, 131–2
Jauss, Hans Robert, 246–7
Jones, Gwyneth, 257
Joyce, James, 47, 77, 101, 150, 161, 162, 172–6, 197, 239, 244, 258
Finnegans Wake, 47, 208
A Portrait of the Artist as a Young Man, 151
Ulysses, 62, 150, 172–6

Kafka, Franz, 52, 77, 194, 204, 241
Kant, Emmanuel, 13, 90, 112, 155, 223
Karina, Anna, 95–6
Kenner, Hugh, 151, 174–5
Kermode, Frank, 67n, 210n
Kerouac, Jack, 100–3
On the Road, 100–3
Klee, Paul, 242, 259
Kleist, Heinrich von, 184, 241–2
Kristeva, Julia, 127–8, 159–63, 168, 169, 177n
Kroeber, Karl, 7, 210n
Kubrick, Stanley, 132
Full Metal Jacket, 132–3
Kuhn, Thomas, 84
Kundera, Milan, 192–5

Lanser, Susan, 121, 123, 157–8, 163
laterality, 117, 212, 220–34
Lautréamont, Comte de, 161, 162
Maldoror, 161
Lawrence, D.H., 52, 55–8, 65, 241
'Morality and the Novel', 55
Women in Love, 55–8, 65

Lecercle, Jean–Jacques, 200, 211n
le Dœuff, Michèle, 2–3, 19, 30n, 127, 130, 158–9, 166
Le Fanu, Mark, 211n
Lefebvre, Henri, 71
Leibniz, G.W., 3, 116, 240
Lennox, Annie, 277
Lennox, Charlotte, 7
The Female Quixote, 7
Levinas, Emmanuel, 87, 185–6, 189, 243
Lévi-Strauss, Claude, 76, 107–8, 122
lines of flight, 54, 212
lines of force, 52–5, 57–8, 212
Livingston, Paisley, 8
Lodge, David, 67n, 177n
logic of boxes, 110, 114, 181–4, 212–13, 215, 221, 244, 228
Lovell, Terry, 103n
Lowry, Malcolm, 93, 97–100
Under the Volcano, 97–100
Lubbock, Percy, 6, 183
LucasArts, 275, 277
Lucretius, 15
De Rerum Natura, 15–16
Lukács, Georg, 77–8, 82, 154
Lynch, David, 254
The Elephant Man, 254
Eraserhead, 254
Lyotard, Jean-François, 9, 23, 28–30, 59–66, 78, 87, 113, 125, 153, 156, 186–9, 195–9, 209, 210n, 219, 259, 260

McCabe, Colin, 104n
McCaffrey, Anne, 257
The Ship Who Sang, 257
Mach, Ernst, 92
McHale, Brian, 70
McLure, Roger, 128–9
Mallarmé, Stéphane, 47, 61, 116–17, 191, 244, 261, 267
Mimique, 170
Malraux, André, 145
Mandelbrot, Benoit, 9
manga, 254
Mann, Thomas, 77, 145, 197
Márquez, Gabriel García, 183
One Hundred Years of Solitude, 183
Martin, Wallace, 245
Meek, Robert, 255
Proteus, 254
Mekas, Jonas, 9